Communications in Computer and Information Science 1852

Rationale
The CCIS series is devoted to the publication of proceedings of computer science conferences. Its aim is to efficiently disseminate original research results in informatics in printed and electronic form. While the focus is on publication of peer-reviewed full papers presenting mature work, inclusion of reviewed short papers reporting on work in progress is welcome, too. Besides globally relevant meetings with internationally representative program committees guaranteeing a strict peer-reviewing and paper selection process, conferences run by societies or of high regional or national relevance are also considered for publication.

Topics
The topical scope of CCIS spans the entire spectrum of informatics ranging from foundational topics in the theory of computing to information and communications science and technology and a broad variety of interdisciplinary application fields.

Information for Volume Editors and Authors
Publication in CCIS is free of charge. No royalties are paid, however, we offer registered conference participants temporary free access to the online version of the conference proceedings on SpringerLink (http://link.springer.com) by means of an http referrer from the conference website and/or a number of complimentary printed copies, as specified in the official acceptance email of the event.

CCIS proceedings can be published in time for distribution at conferences or as post-proceedings, and delivered in the form of printed books and/or electronically as USBs and/or e-content licenses for accessing proceedings at SpringerLink. Furthermore, CCIS proceedings are included in the CCIS electronic book series hosted in the SpringerLink digital library at http://link.springer.com/bookseries/7899. Conferences publishing in CCIS are allowed to use Online Conference Service (OCS) for managing the whole proceedings lifecycle (from submission and reviewing to preparing for publication) free of charge.

Publication process
The language of publication is exclusively English. Authors publishing in CCIS have to sign the Springer CCIS copyright transfer form, however, they are free to use their material published in CCIS for substantially changed, more elaborate subsequent publications elsewhere. For the preparation of the camera-ready papers/files, authors have to strictly adhere to the Springer CCIS Authors' Instructions and are strongly encouraged to use the CCIS LaTeX style files or templates.

Abstracting/Indexing
CCIS is abstracted/indexed in DBLP, Google Scholar, EI-Compendex, Mathematical Reviews, SCImago, Scopus. CCIS volumes are also submitted for the inclusion in ISI Proceedings.

How to start
To start the evaluation of your proposal for inclusion in the CCIS series, please send an e-mail to ccis@springer.com.

Habiba Drias · Farouk Yalaoui · Allel Hadjali
Editors

Artificial Intelligence Doctoral Symposium

5th Doctoral Symposium, AID 2022
Algiers, Algeria, September 18–19, 2022
Revised Selected Papers

Springer

Editors
Habiba Drias
University of Sciences and Technology
Houari Boumediene
Algiers, Algeria

Farouk Yalaoui
University of Technology of Troyes
Troyes, France

Allel Hadjali
Laboratory of Computer Science
and Automatic Control for Systems
Poitiers, France

ISSN 1865-0929 ISSN 1865-0937 (electronic)
Communications in Computer and Information Science
ISBN 978-981-99-4483-5 ISBN 978-981-99-4484-2 (eBook)
https://doi.org/10.1007/978-981-99-4484-2

This Springer imprint is published by the registered company Springer Nature Singapore Pte Ltd.
The registered company address is: 152 Beach Road, #21-01/04 Gateway East, Singapore 189721, Singapore

Preface

This volume contains the papers from the 5th Artificial Intelligence Doctoral Symposium (AID 2022), held in Algiers during September 18–19, 2022. The objective of AID 2022 was to offer doctoral students a meeting place to discuss the advances and challenges of artificial intelligence (A.I.). The symposium provided an opportunity for them to exhibit their work and meet eminent invited researchers on up-to-date topics in A.I. The themes addressed during the scientific event revolved mainly around the latest developments in artificial intelligence and their applications. They included the fields of data mining, machine learning, deep learning, metaheuristics, swarm intelligence, computer vision and robotics, data science, computational intelligence, text mining, natural language processing, industrial applications, analysis of images and A.I. applications, on which most of the articles are focused.

The event was organized by the Artificial Intelligence Research Laboratory (LRIA) of the Department of Artificial Intelligence and Data Science (IASD) of the University of Science and Technology Houari Boumediene (USTHB). It inaugurated the post-COVID-19 period and attempted to reconnect with the scientific events that the laboratory has been organizing for a long time. The symposium series is already well established after four successful editions in the same domain.

38 submissions were received following the call for papers. Each article was double-blind reviewed by at least three members of the program's international committee and external reviewers. Only 22 top-rated papers were selected for oral presentation and publication in this volume, as they all reflect Springer's publication policy. The accepted and presented papers deal with novel research and innovative applications and stimulated fruitful debates and knowledge acquisition. We hope the future readers find these contributions useful and inspiring.

The proceedings editors would like to thank all the contributors who made the symposium successful: the organizing group, the program committee chairs, the scientific committee, the external reviewers, the keynote speakers, the authors for submitting their work, the participants for their discussions and for the rich debates they aroused during the sessions, and our sponsors who helped in terms of logistics. Our special thanks go to Springer for publishing the proceedings of AID 2022.

Habiba Drias
Farouk Yalaoui
Allel Hadjali

Organization

General Chair

Habiba Drias	USTHB Algiers, Algeria

Program Chairs

Lyes Abada	USTHB Algiers, Algeria
Yassine Drias	Algiers University, Algeria
Ilyes Khennak	USTHB Algiers, Algeria

Local Organizing Committee

Mohamed Ait-Mehdi	Algiers University, Algeria
Lydia Sonia Bendimerad	USTHB Algiers, Algeria
Naila Aziza Houacine	USTHB Algiers, Algeria
Selma Kaliali	USTHB Algiers, Algeria
Naoual Mebtouche	USTHB Algiers, Algeria

Webmaster

Lyes Abada	USTHB Algiers, Algeria

Steering Committee

Saliha Aouat	USTHB Algiers, Algeria
Hamid Azzoune	USTHB Algiers, Algeria
Dalila Boughaci	USTHB Algiers, Algeria
Habiba Drias	USTHB Algiers, Algeria
Samir Kechid	USTHB Algiers, Algeria
Feryel Souami	University of Algiers, Algeria

Keynote Speakers

Houari Sahraoui	University of Montreal, Canada
Farouk Yalaoui	University of Technology of Troyes, France
Allel Hadjali	ENSMA Poitiers, France

International Program Committee

Lyes Abada	USTHB Algiers, Algeria
Nouara Achour	USTHB Algiers, Algeria
Yasmine Alaouchiche	University of Technology of Troyes, France
Saliha Aouat	USTHB Algiers, Algeria
Hamid Azzoune	USTHB Algiers, Algeria
Hajer Baazaoui	CY Cergy Paris University, France
Sadjia Baba-ali	USTHB Algiers, Algeria
Nadia Baha-Touzène	USTHB Algiers, Algeria
Salem Benferhat	University of Artois, France
Sadok Benyahia	Tallinn University of Technology, Estonia
Lamia Berkani	USTHB Algiers, Algeria
Dalila Boughaci	USTHB Algiers, Algeria
Souleymane Chaib	ESI Sidi Bel Abbès, Algeria
Lokmane Chebouba	University of Constantine, Algeria
Djamila Dahmani	USTHB Algiers, Algeria
Yassine Drias	University of Algiers, Algeria
Abdelatif El Afia	University Mohammed V in Rabat – ENSIAS, Morocco
Maria Gini	University of Minnesota, USA
Fatima Guedjati	University of Reims Champagne-Ardenne, France
Nicolas Gutowski	University of Angers, France
Allel Hadjali	ENSMA Poitiers, France
Drifa Hadjidj	University of Boumerdes, Algeria
Kamel-Eddine Heraguemi	University of M'sila, Algeria
Walid-Khaled Hidouci	ESI Algiers, Algeria
Célia Hireche	University of Blida, Algeria
Saida Ishak-Boushaki	University of Boumerdes, Algeria
Nadjet Kamel	University of Sétif 1, Algeria
Saroj Kaushik	Indian Institute of Technology Delhi, India
Samir Kechid	USTHB Algiers, Algeria
Meriem Khelifa	USTHB Algiers, Algeria
Faiza Khellaf	USTHB Algiers, Algeria
Ilyes Khennak	USTHB Algiers, Algeria

Nacéra Laiche	USTHB Algiers, Algeria
Slimane Larabi	USTHB Algiers, Algeria
Mimoun Malki	ESI Sidi-bel-Abbes, Algeria
Imane Messaoudi	USTHB Algiers, Algeria
Hadjer Moulai	USTHB Algiers, Algeria
Messaouda Nekkaa	University of Boumerdes, Algeria
Nhan Quy Nguyen	University of Technology of Troyes, France
Mourad Oussalah	University of Oulu, Finland
Abdellah Rezoug	University of Boumerdes, Algeria
Houari Sahraoui	University of Montreal, Canada
Lakhdar Sais	University of Artois, France
Amina Serir	USTHB Algiers, Algeria
Zahia Tamen	USTHB Algiers, Algeria
Sunita Tiwari	Indian Institute of Technology Delhi, India
Giuseppe Vizzari	Milano-Bicocca University, Italy
Farouk Yalaoui	University of Technology of Troyes, France

Invited Speakers

On Intelligent Combinatorial Decision Making

Allel Hadj-Ali

ENSMA-Poitiers, France

Abstract. Short Description: In many real-life applications (e.g., groups recommendation, investments selection, detection of fire/crime-most dangerous places, expert teams selection, etc.), users do not only require analyzing individual objects but also groups of objects to make decisions. Skyline paradigm is one of the most popular and useful approach for multi-criteria data analysis and decision-making. It aims at identifying a set of skyline points that are not dominated in Pareto sense by any other point in a dataset. In the recent two decades, the skyline definition has been extended with different variants and the skyline computation problem for finding the skyline of a given dataset has been studied extensively. One important problem that has been surprisingly neglected to the large extent is the need to find groups of points that are not dominated by others as many real-world applications may require the selection of a group of points. In this talk, we focus on extending the skyline model to the combinatorial context to deal with group skyline set, i.e., groups that are not dominated by any other group in a given dataset. We present the recent developments on group skyline both from the semantic and computational sides. We also tackle explicitly the important issue related to controlling the size of group skyline. Some open challenges on the topic are discussed as well.

Biography

Allel Hadjali is Full Professor in Computer Science at the National Engineering School for Mechanics and Aerotechnics (ISAE-ENSMA), Poitiers, France. He is a member of the Data & Model Engineering research team of the Laboratory of Computer Science and Automatic Control for Systems (LIAS/ISEA-ENSMA). His main area of research falls within Data Science field, and more specifically, the research topics related to Data Exploitation & Analysis (sensor data, semantic data, incomplete data), Knowledge Extraction and Recommendation. His current research interests include Soft Computing and Computational Intelligence in Databases (Cooperative/Intelligent Databases, Data fusion/integration, Data quality, Data Uncertainty, Data Privacy and Trust), Machine Learning-based Recommendation, Approximate/Uncertain Reasoning with applications to Artificial Intelligence and Information Systems. His recent works were published in well-known journals (e.g., Applied Soft Computing, Knowledge and Information Systems, Fuzzy Sets and Systems, International Journal of Intelligent Systems, Journal of Intelligent Information Systems and Annals of Mathematics and Artificial Intelligence). He also published several papers in International Conferences (ESWC, ICTAI, Fuzz-IEEE, DEXA, FQAS, SUM, ISMIS, IPMU, CoopIS, IFSA, ACM SAC, ICWS, SCC, ER, VLDB and EDBT (demo papers)). He co-organized several special sessions on "Advances in Soft Computing Applied to Databases and Information Systems" in conjunction with EUSFLAT (2009 and 2011) Conference, "Advances in Bipolarity in Databases" in conjunction with EUSFLAT (2013), "Advances in Data Management in the Context of Incomplete Databases" in conjunction with IFSA (2015) Conference, "Uncertainty in Cloud Computing" in conjunction with DEXA (2017). He co-organized also several special issues in well-known journals, among them, "Flexible Queries in Information Systems" in Journal of Intelligent Information Systems (2009), "On Advances in Soft Computing Applied to Databases and Information Systems" in Fuzzy Sets and Systems Journal (2011), "Post LFA 2015 Conference" in Fuzzy Sets and Systems Journal (2017), "Uncertain Cloud" in International Journal of Approximate Reasoning (2019). The complete list of his publications is available in http://www.lias-lab.fr/members/allelhadjali.

Decision-Making Support of Industries in the World of Data and Transitions

Farouk Yalaoui

University of Troyes, France

Abstract. In the era of steady and rapid transitions of technology and society interconnectivity, industries are in an environment of continuing transformations. This profound and constant process of transformation is multifaceted: the production and the manufacturing process, the product creation, the market emerging, the client's interaction and data management. This work focuses on the two fields of industries which are textile and healthcare. A review will be done on recent trends of the technologies transition, coupling with the transition in client's consumption behaviors. The different visions and strategies in governmental levels around the worlds will be also stated. Facing the imminent changes, one can highlight the impact on the large and complex flow of information's. We propose in this work three large approach which impact decision from strategical level to operational level. The work tends to pave the understanding on the impact of data to global vision to real-time decision. Second, we propose three approaches for industry of the future. The first one is the novel Network of Supply Systems (NSS) where the classic supply chain become supply system that considers of the non-linear elements. The NSS takes the interconnectivities as evidence to provide a new point of view of the position of each industry in a larger and connected network of value chains. The second one the Process – Product – Market (PPM) approach where the three elements are active and takes part in the decision in the circular way. The third approach is on the data strategy where we identify the value and the diversity of data. With the three mentioned approaches, we come up with the real time decision in an environment that we have a complete information, a partial information, or no information. That leads to the fields of online and semionline scheduling. We introduce the notation of valuable and valueless information in production, that could be helpful in the case of identifying non-adding value activities in the value chains. In addition, to support the PPM approach, we present in this work our recent research on the smart pricing problem. We close the work with a roadmap to Industries in the world of Data and Transitions.

Biography

Professor Farouk Yalaoui is currently a full Professor at Troyes University of Technology (UTT), France, where he is the Senior Vice President for Research of UTT. He is also scientific director of Industrial Chair "Connected Innovation" of UTT since 201 https://chaire-connected-innovation.fr/ and https://www.faroukyalaoui.com/https://orcid.org/0000-0001-7360-2932. He is the former director of LOSI Lab. (Logistiques et Optimisation des systèmes Industriels) of UTT and former director of Services and Industries of The future of Troyes Institute (ISIFT). He obtained his Engineering degree in Industrial Engineering from the Polytechnics School of Algiers (Algeria) in 1995, his master's degree in Industrial System Engineering from Polytechnics Institute of Lorraine (Nancy, France) in 1997, his Ph.D. degree in Production Management from the Troyes University of Technology (UTT) in 2000 and followed by a Habilitation à diriger les recherches (Dr. Hab) from Compiegne University of Technology (UTC) in 2006. His research topic focuses on the scheduling problems, system design, operations research, modeling, analysis and optimization of logistic and production systems, reliability and maintenance optimization and on optimization problems in general. He supervised or co-supervised 28 Ph.D thesis and more than 82 projects since 2001. He is founder and partner of OPTA LP SAS company since 2013 http://www.opta-lp.com/fr/.

He is author or co-author of a pattern and more than 500 contributions, publications or communications with 1 patent; 3 books (Ellipses, Hermes-Lavoisier, Willey and Sons), 6 edited books (Springer), 16 book chapters and 95 papers in journals such as IIE Transactions, European Journal of Operational research, International Journal of Production Economics, IEEE Transactions on Reliability, Reliability Engineering and System Safety, Computer & Operations research, Journal of Intelligent Manufacturing. He also published more than 310 papers in conference proceedings. He had presented 51 invited speeches (seminaries or conferences plenary sessions). He was invited by different universities (11) more than 20 times. He is member of editor board of the book series "Automation and Control - Industrial Engineering", ISTE Wiley, London, since 2014. He served or serves as editor to 20 International journal Boards: Engineering Applications of Artificial Intelligence (EAAI, Elsevier, IF. 6,212, 2022), The Scientific World Journal as part of the journal's Operations Research subject area (TSWJ), International journal of Supply and Operations Management (IJSOM), British Journal of Mathematics &computer Science (BJMCS), Journal of Risk Analysis and Crises Response (JRACR), Journal., American Journal of Operations Research (AJOR), Industrial Engineering and Management (IEM), Advances in Computer Science and Engineering (ACSE), Modeling and Simulation in Engineering (MSE), Advances in Artificial Intelligence (AAI), International Journal of Applied Logistics (IJAL). He served as guest editor for Journal special issue (Journal of Multiple Valued Logic and Soft Computing, Journal of Intelligent Manufacturing). He is reviewer for more than 36 international journals.

He is founder and member of steering committee of IWOLIA (since 2010) SHEIC (since 2019) and member IESM-MOSIM Steering Committee, since 2019, Membre IFAC/MIM Steering Committee, since 2021. He is advisory Committees/Organizing Committees members of 36 conferences. He is also member of several international conference committees (about 154 conferences) as (INCOM 2021, IFAC WC 2020,

IEEE ICALT'2019, INCOM 2018, ICINCO 2017, ACIIDS 2017, IEEE SSCI 2016, MIM 2016, INCOM 2015, IESM 2015, MIC'2015, SSEMO-WCCI 2014, IEEE-CIPLS 2014, FLINS'14, IEEE-CIPLS 2013, CIIA'2013, EMO 13, MIM 2013, CoDIT 2013, ICSENT'2012, IEEM 2012), member more than 25 organization committees of conferences and general Chair of IFAC MIM 2016. He organized and or Chair more than 115 tracks or sessions in conference.

He is Vice Chair of IFAC (International federation of Automation and Control) TC group 5.2. He is Chair of a Working Group on multiobjective optimization. He is member of IFAC TC group 5.1. He is member of French Universities National Council (CNU) field Automation, Control, Industrial Engineering (section 61). http://losi.utt.fr/fr/membres/yalaoui.html. He is member and expert for French ANR agency, and for different agency such French AERES Agency, Natural Sciences and Engineering Research Council of Canada (NSERC), Algerian PNR program. He is member of Algerian Academy of Science and Technology (AAST) since 2015. He obtained of Annual Award 20117 of the IFAC French National Member Organization (NMO).

Learning Software Artefacts from Examples Using Genetic Programming

Houari Sahraoui

Department of Computer Science and Operations Research,
University of Montréal Canada

Abstract. Over the past decades, the software engineering research community has made significant advances in automating software development and maintenance tasks. This was achieved thanks to the accumulation of knowledge produced by many clusters of researchers working on general-purpose artefacts such as automatic generation of test data, refactoring, program repair or feature location. However, automating domain-specific tasks did not benefit from the same critical masses of researchers. This is particularly the case of manipulating models described with domain-specific languages or domain-specific code libraries (APIs) usage. In this presentation, we discuss the use of genetic programming to transform data or examples of a specific domain into knowledge to automate the development and maintenance tasks of that domain.

Biography

Houari Sahraoui is a professor at the software engineering lab GEODES of the department of computer science and operations research, Université de Montréal. He holds a Computer Engineering Diploma from the INI, the National Institute of computer science (1990), Algiers, and a Ph.D. in Computer Science from Pierre & Marie Curie University - LIP6 (1995), with a specialization in AI. His research interests include automated software engineering (SE) and the application of AI techniques to SE. He has published around 200 papers in conferences, workshops, books, and journals. He has served as a program committee member in several IEEE and ACM conferences, as a member of the editorial boards of four journals, and as an organization member of many conferences and workshops. He was the general chair and program chair of many conferences such as IEEE/ACM International Conference on Automated Software Engineering (ASE), ACM/IEEE International Conference on Model Driven Engineering Languages and Systems (MODELS), and IEEE Working Conference on Software Visualization (VISSOFT).

Contents

Data Mining

Metaheuristics and Swarm Intelligence

Computer Vision

NLP and Text Mining

Data Mining

A Firefly Algorithm for Energy Efficient Clustering in Wireless Sensor Networks

Mohamed Sahraoui[1,2](✉) and Abd Elmalik Taleb-Ahmed[1,2]

[1] LIAM laboratory Mohamed Boudief University of M'sila, M'sila, Algeria
taleb@uphf.fr
mohamed.sahraoui@univ-msila.dz
[2] IEMN DOAE Laboratory Hauts de France Polytechnic University of Valenciennes, Valenciennes, France

Abstract. The fundamental metric token by clustering algorithms in Wireless Sensor Networks (WSN) is energy enhancement to maximize network lifetime. One of the crucial issues is network coverage in order to use all of the network's resources, which increases the lifetime of the network. Moreover, load balancing techniques play an essential role in improving network lifetime due to their efficient way of distributing the load between nodes. The goal of this work is to assemble these two approaches in clustered WSN in order to improve resources utilization and increase network lifetime. Thus, we present a new clustering algorithm named Firefly optimization based Adaptive Clustering for Energy Efficiency (FACEE) which uses a novel clustering based firefly optimization algorithm for coverage improvement and load balancing. The simulation results indicate that our proposed algorithm can significantly improve the network lifetime as well as the delivery rate.

Keywords: WSN · Firefly · Clustering · Optimization · Coverage · Load balancing

1 Introduction

In order to sense and monitor certain events in the environment, such as temperature, sound, and pressure, numerous sensors are placed across the concerned area to form a wireless sensor network (WSN). Then, the gathered information is transmitted via the network to the sink node which is typically more potent than the other nodes. To this end, The BS allows for the analysis and transmission of information via the internet [1]. Every sensor node is a low-power, single-antenna device with a half-duplex radio that should operate for a very long time as much as possible. In the absence of an energy-efficient method, a node's battery would quickly run out. Furthermore, the energy consumed in communication is more significant than the energy consumed in computations [2].

Over the last decade, extensive research has been done on clustering, one of the most effective power-saving techniques. The use of clustering allows for

H. Drias et al. (Eds.): AID 2022, CCIS 1852, pp. 3–14, 2023.
https://doi.org/10.1007/978-981-99-4484-2_1

energy-efficient communication between sensor nodes, which are organized into various clusters. The node in charge of each cluster is called the Cluster Head (CH). The goal of clustering is to reduce the number of nodes or CHs that may communicate with other clusters and shorten the distance that data must travel. Additionally, clustering stops redundant information from being transmitted utilizing data aggregation [3]. Although clustering is energy efficient, it is difficult to exploit routing information to achieve clustering process with proper load balancing. As a result, the issue becomes NP-hard, and is made considerably more difficult in wide WSNs because the weight of overhead has to be shared by all the nodes. Hence, an appropriate clustering strategy has become to be crucial for extending the WSN's lifetime.

Consequently, many optimization algorithms have been used to propose different clustering solutions such as in [9–16]. The use of Firefly optimization Algorithms (FAs) can be either independently such as in [14–16] or hybridized with another optimization algorithm such as in [12,13].

However, the absence of a good clustering strategy that focuses on optimal coverage and load balance aspects between the nodes can lead to the disjointing of a certain number of nodes and overloading of some clusters compared to the others. Thus, the network lifetime can be decreased by the loss of the disjointing nodes and the fast death of the overloaded cluster members which can occur due to the increased level of both collisions and communication overhead. To overcome this limitation, we have proposed the Firefly optimization based Adaptive Clustering for Energy Efficiency (FACEE) Algorithm to improve coverage and balance the load between the cluster heads in the network. The purpose is to improve the network lifetime and the delivery rate which ultimately makes the entire network reliable and live more time.

The remainder of this paper is structured as follows: In Sect. 2, a summary of related work is provided. In Sect. 3, we present our algorithm FACEE. In Sect. 4, the simulation experiment findings and discussions of those results are provided. In Sect. 5, we conclude this work with further extension proposals.

2 Related Works

Clustering methods have been widely used in wireless sensor networks to provide efficient routing algorithms. Some of them don't take into account the load balance aspect. The most popular algorithms for WSNs is the Low Energy Adaptive Clustering Hierarchy (LEACH) protocol introduced by the authors of [4]. According to LEACH, an ideal number of cluster heads is estimated to be 5% of the total nodes. Also, the CH list change randomly from a round to another in order to balance the energy consumption of nodes. The node makes this determination by selecting at random a value between 0 and 1. If the number is below a predetermined threshold, the node n becomes a CH for the current round. This protocol has seen several enhancement giving rise to new versions of hierarchical routing protocols. The literature contains numerous proposals for improved versions of LEACH, such as the LEACH-C presented in [5] by the same authors of LEACH. Hence, the energy level is included in the cluster selection process in LEACH-C made by the BS, which leads to an improvement in the network lifetime. In [6], an other improved version of LEACH is suggested to guarantee scalability and speed up broadcasting by adding static and dynamic periods utilized for broadcast messages, however the finding results reveal increased energy usage.

Some other works have focused on load balancing issue such as the load-balanced clustering protocol for WSNs (LBCP) proposed in [7]. It is a compromise between three models: an energy-aware cluster head selection model (EACH) for optimal cluster head selection, which performs clustering based on distances and residual energy, giving clusters the ability to choose their CHs with the least amount of intra-cluster distance, and a delay and energy-aware routing model (DEAR) for optimal inter-cluster communication, which is used to provide the best routes to the BS and calculates the amount of energy used. Furthermore, In order to perform load-balanced clustering according to the amount of energy consumed by given CH nodes, which can be reduced by supporting fewer cluster members, equal traffic for energy-efficient clustering (EQTEEC) is applied. Based on routing overhead, EQTEEC is performed to redistribute cluster members among CHs. Even though this protocol resolves the load balance problem, it suffers from the huge communication overhead needed to route the necessary information to the sink in order to execute the three models. In [8], the authors have proposed a hybrid unequal clustering algorithm for load balancing which focuses on partitioning the network into number of layers and cluster of various groups. The number of neighboring nodes, energy available, available data in the node and the distance to the sink are parameters considered to select the nodes as CHs. Clustering is formed with unequal number of nodes with an equal load to balance the data in the network in such a way that the nodes which are present within a threshold distance will become a part of cluster.

Since the clustering process with adequate load balancing is an NP-hard problem, many optimization algorithms have been used to propose different clustering solutions such as Ant-Colony Optimization (ACO) in [9], Particle Swarm Optimization (PSO) in [10,11] and Firefly optimization Algorithms (FAs) which are detailed in this section due to their relevance to our proposed algorithm. Hence, FA based algorithms can be categorized into two types: independent FAs and FAs hybrid with an other optimization algorithm such as the hybridization with the ACO algorithm in [12], where the authors developed the Butterfly Optimization Algorithm (BOA) and ACO based energy efficient cluster based routing scheme for WSNs. Using the BOA, a number of factors are taken into account for choosing optimal CH, including node degree and centrality, distance to the sink node, distance to neighbors, and node residual energy. The ACO is used to determine the best route between the CH and the sink node while taking into account a number of factors, including distance, residual energy and node degree. An other hybridization between FA and fuzzy logic approach is made in [13], where the authors suggested a three-phase multi-phase routing system, consisting of clustering the network nodes, figuring out the paths between CHs and maintaining the paths. The nodes are clustered using the firefly technique, then the proper primary path and backup path using fuzzy logic is determined. Hence, CHs use backup paths in the event that the primary paths fail while still transmitting data packets to the sink node.

Although the hybridization of the FA can achieve good results in terms of latency and delivery rate, it requires more data control exchanges resulting in more collisions and overhead communication costs.

As mentioned before, some other works are based on the independent FAs. In [14], routing using firefly algorithm in wireless sensor networks is used. To convey aggregated data, a spanning tree is used in the routing process. Thus, each node in the network reports its energy consumption, and based on various including throughput, packet lost rate, distance between nodes and residual energy, each node compares the obtained values to find the best attracted rout. The network lifetime has been increased in [15] by using an enhanced firefly algorithm. The clusters are formed with based on the firefly algorithm, which is also utilized to choose the cluster head. Two critical aspects in the CH selection are token in the proposed function: first is the energy dissipation of the communication between cluster members and the CH, and second, the energy required for data aggregation and transmission to the sink. Furthermore, the technique includes a step that substitutes a pseudo-random solution produced inside the search space for the worst solution from the population. In [16], an approach called EM-FIREFLY is proposed in order to increase the power of WSN by gathering common data based on efficient clustering. In this method, the network is divided into hexagon which is divided into equal zones. For each zone a fixed sink is assigned to rely data to the BS. Thus, the firefly algorithm replaces the light intensity with the remaining energy of the node, making attraction inversely proportional to distance and directly correlated with energy. Using the four criteria of residual energy, noise rate, number of hops, and distance, the most optimal node is selected as a CH based on the fitness function to transfers the data packets of its cluster to the dependent sink.

It is observed that the main focus of all the previous works is the energy balancing issue with giving less consideration to the coverage aspect even though it plays an important role in reliability guarantees as it increases the use of the network resources, and thus improves the network lifetime and delivery rate. Consequently, our proposed FA takes into account the coverage aspect in addition of the energy balancing one.

3 Firefly Optimization Based Adaptive Clustering for Energy Efficiency (FACEE)

3.1 Network Model

We define a WSN as a set G of N nodes. We denote the i_{th}sensor by n_i and the corresponding sensor node set SN = n1, n2,,, nN. The network's nodes are dispersed across a square region, with M denoting the length of each side.

We suppose that:

- Every node also knows the BS coordinate value in addition to its own.
- BS is situated in a predetermined location, either within or outside the sensor field.
- Nodes in the network are pseudo-static.
- The energy of the BS is unlimited.
- Battery power restrictions apply to all sensor nodes. They have a limited communication range too.

3.2 Firefly Optimization Alghorithm

Firefly algorithm (FA) was introduced in 2008 which is inspired by the behavior and flashing patterns of fireflies in nature [17]. FA belongs to swarm-based meta-heuristics and replicates the way that fireflies communicate by flashing their lights. Since all fireflies are assumed to be unisex, any firefly can be attracted to any other firefly, and a firefly's attractiveness is directly proportionate to its brightness, which depends on the objective function. Hence, a firefly will be drawn to a firefly that is more visible and the brightness diminishes with distance according to the inverse square law as in 1.

$$I \prec \frac{1}{r^2} \tag{1}$$

The light intensity with a light absorption coefficient λ at a distance of r from the source can be described as in 2.

$$I = I_0 \exp^{-\gamma r^2} \tag{2}$$

where I_0 represents the source's light intensity. The brightness can also be expressed as in 3.

$$\beta(r) = \beta_0 \exp^{-\gamma r^2} \tag{3}$$

The algorithm assigns a light intensity to fireflies, which are randomly produced feasible solutions, based on how well they perform in the objective function. The brightness of the firefly will be calculated using this intensity. For minimization issues, the solution with the lowest functional value will receive the most light. Each firefly will thereafter follow fireflies that have better light intensity. A firefly that shines the brightest will conduct a local search by randomly walking around its neighborhood. However, for two fireflies i and j, firefly i will migrate in the direction of firefly j using the updating method in 4, if firefly j is brighter than firefly i.

$$X_i = X_i + \beta_0 \exp^{-\gamma r(i,j)^2} (X_j - X_i) + \alpha(rand - 1/2) \tag{4}$$

where rand is the random number drawn from either a uniform distribution or a Gaussian distribution, and *alpha* is the randomization parameter.

The flow diagram of the firefly algorithm is shown in Fig 1.

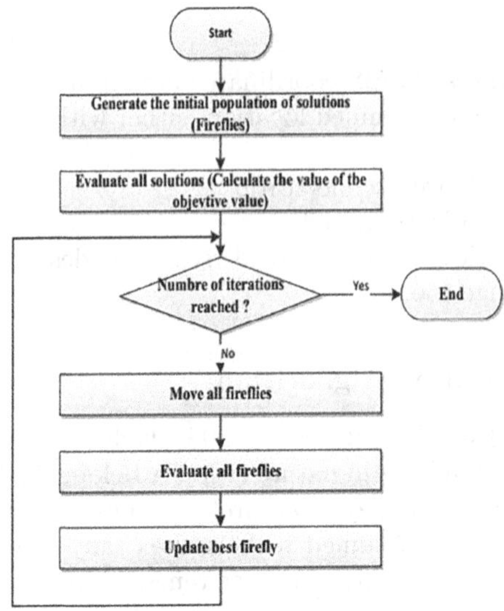

Fig. 1. The firefly algorithm's flowchart.

3.3 FACEE Proposed Algorithm

FACEE approach utilizes adaptive clustering scheme in such a way that if the number of clusters changes over time and the nodes' membership changes, a clustering system is referred as adaptive. For absorbing data transmission overload in FACEE, nodes with a specific high condition (Ich) can serve as the CH. All nodes should alternately take turns serving as CH in order to prevent early mortality from high energy consumption. Hence various considerations must be taken into account when choosing a CH candidate. Node-weight, residual energy, node-to-node distance and distance from the BS are taken into account in FACEE. Consequently, we define the following equations:

$$IW_{ij} = 1 - \frac{W_i}{W_j} \quad \forall i, j \tag{5}$$

where, W_i and W_j are node-weight of nodes i and j respectively. The node-weight of node n represents the length of its the cluster members and it defined by 6 as follow:.

$$W_n = |CL_n| \tag{6}$$

where CL_n represents the cluster headed by the node n which includes the node n to initialize the length of the CL_n list by 1. Note that each node have two lists: cluster list (CL) for the cluster members and parent list (PR) for the temporary elected CHs.

$$ID_{ij} = \begin{cases} 1 - \frac{D_{Bs,i}}{D_{Bs,j}} & \text{if} \, i \neq j \\ 1 - \frac{D_{Bs,i}}{D_{Max}} & \text{otherwise} \end{cases} \tag{7}$$

The Cartesian distances between the node i and the sink (s) and the node neighbor j and the sink are denoted as $D_{Bs,i}$ and $D_{Bs,j}$ respectively. D_{Max} is the maximum distance between all the nodes and the BS, and it is equal to M that represents the length of the side. The Eq. 8 calculates the Cartesian distance between nodes (i and j).

$$D_{i,j} = \sqrt{(x_i - x_j)^2 + (y_i - y_j)^2} \tag{8}$$

where, (x_i,y_i) and (x_j,y_j) are the coordinate values of the node i and j respectively.

$$IE_{ij} = \begin{cases} \frac{Er_i}{Er_j} & \text{if } i \neq j \\ Er_i & \text{otherwise} \end{cases} \tag{9}$$

where Er_i and Er_j are the residual energy of the nodes i and j respectively. According to 10, the residual energy of the node n Er_n is determined as follows:

$$Er_n = \frac{E_{Rm}(n)}{E_{Init}(n)} \tag{10}$$

$E_{Rm}(n)$ and $E_{Init}(n)$ are the remaining and initial energies of the node n.

Finally, the different node compete to be a Ch by the maximization of the sum of the Eqs. 7, 5 and 9 according to the Eq. 11.

$$Ich_i = Max \sum_{j=1}^{W_i} \lambda 1 IE_{i,j} + \lambda 2 ID_{i,j} + \lambda 3 IW_{i,j} \tag{11}$$

where $\lambda 1, \lambda 2$ and $\lambda 3$ are parameters that control the importance of the metrics in such a way that $\lambda 1 + \lambda 2 + \lambda 3 = 1$.

In order to get a suitable cluster distribution (unresolved problem with several protocols), FACEE algorithm uses threshold distance for each firefly in such a way that the nodes belonging to this distance compete to select the best CH, however the other nodes (far from this distance) have an other choice to select an other CH. By this way, our proposed method can ensure the coverage and thus the reliability of all the network.

Algorithm

The application and adaptation of the FACEE algorithm to address coverage and load balancing in clustered WSN are described in this section. FACEE algorithm is presented in Algorithm 1.

In fact, there are 4 phases involved in running the FACEE algorithm:

- Step 1: in first step, all the nodes are taken as population with initialization of the different parameters (line1 to 4).

Algorithm 1: FACEE

1. Generate initial population of solutions ni, (i = 1, 2, 3, . . . , N);
2. Light intensity Ii is defined by Ich_i
3. Define Threshold(Δ), $\lambda 1$, $\lambda 2$ and $\lambda 3$
4. Define number of iterations Nit
5. **while** t < Nit **do**
6.   **for** i = 1 to N **do**
7.   **for** j = 1 to N **do**
8.   **if** ($Ich_j < Ich_i$) and ($D_{i,j}<$ Threshold(Δ)) **then**
9.   Move solution j towards solution i (Add j to CL_i)
10.   Update parent list of the node i ($PR_i(j)$)
11.   Update parent list of the node j ($PR_j(i, Pch_i)$)
12.   **end if**
13.   **end for**
14.   **end for**
15. **end wile**
16. **for** j = 1 to SN **do**
17.   **if** $PR_j \neq \varnothing$ **then**
18.   Select the best i as CH
19.   **else**
20.   Select j as CH
21.   **end if**
22. **end while**

- Step 2: In the second stage, The Eq. 11 is used to determine the attractiveness of each artificial firefly i in comparison to another firefly j. Hence the Eq. 3 is defined by 12 as follows:

$$\beta_i = Pch_i \tag{12}$$

  In our work, we took into account the idea that a firefly's attraction is solely dependent on the amount of light it emits through its objective function. Therefore, the distance between the fireflies does not have the only effect on how attractive they are.
- Step 3: The algorithm explores the search space in this step to produce new solutions. Therefore, Adding the moved fireflies to the destination firefly's cluster list and updating the parent lists of both the moved and the destination fireflies in such a way that the moved firefly updates the parent only if it has the largest β_i, but the destination firefly deletes the moved one from its parent list if it exists, are how new solutions are generated by moving fireflies that are at a certain threshold distance away from better solutions (from 8 to 12).
- Step 4: Any meta-heuristic's effectiveness is achieved by fusing the exploration and exploitation behaviors that are used to find the optimal solution. According to our method, the exploitation is carried out by using a local search around the best solution (solution with the highest light intensity). The local search consists on selecting other CH at a time. This process is

repeated until the number of iterations is reached, then optimal CHs will be selected (from 17 to 21).

4 Simulation and Results

The simulation results of our algorithm FACEE in comparison to the protocols LEACH-C and EM-FIREFLY [16] are presented in this section. In addition to our FACEE algorithm, we have implemented EM-FIREFLY due to the lack of its source code. The simulation is performed in MATLAB and the collection of outputs after specific number of rounds considered by 1000. The same simulation parameters are used for the different protocols. These simulation parameters are shown in Table 1.

Table 1. Simulation parameters.

Parameters	Values
Number of nodes	100
Area	150 m * 150 m
Radio range	20 m
Initial energy	0.5 j
Sink location	In the middle
Data packet size	4000 bit
Control packet size	500 bit

In order to give priority to the energy parameter in our protocol FACEE, we have fixed the parameters that control the importance of the metrics presented by $\lambda1, \lambda2$ and $\lambda3$ by 0.5, 0.3 and 0.2 respectively. Also the threshold(Δ) is fixed by 20 m (the same as radio range).

The execution of the different protocols is presented in Figs. 2(a),2(b) and 2(c) in which it is demonstrated the well coverage of the protocol FACEE (Fig. 2(c)) taking in account the whole network and more precisely the dense eras by specifying more CHs, the case that is not exist in EM-FIREFLY nor in LEACH-C.

For this comparison, Fig. 3(a) shows for the network lifetime that is considered here by the number of dead nodes via the different number of rounds for each protocol. We found that our protocol can ensure more life time for the network due to the adaptive clustering with best coverage and balance strategies which are used, unlike the fixed sinks used by EM-FIREFLY in different sides of the hexagonal to collect data that quickly makes them die.

In Figs. 3(b), 3(c) and 3(d), the delivery packets to the sink per round in the different protocols is presented. Throughout these figures, it is shown that our protocol succeeds in routing more packets to the sink due to its well strategy of coverage as well as the one of energy conservation.

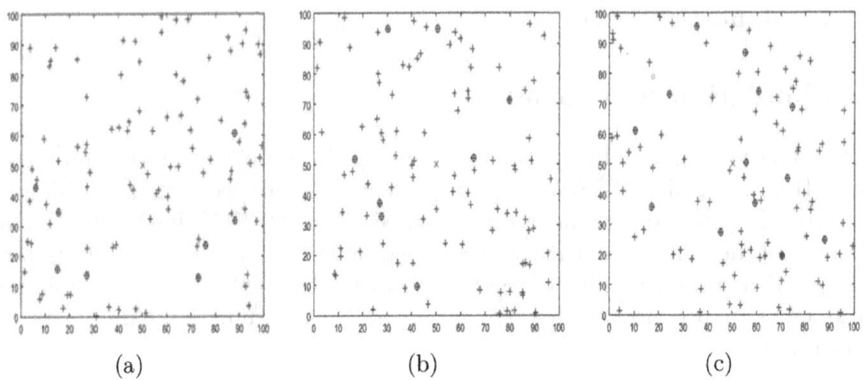

Fig. 2. (a) LEACH-C Coverage, (b) EM-FIREFLY Coverage and (c) FACEE Coverage

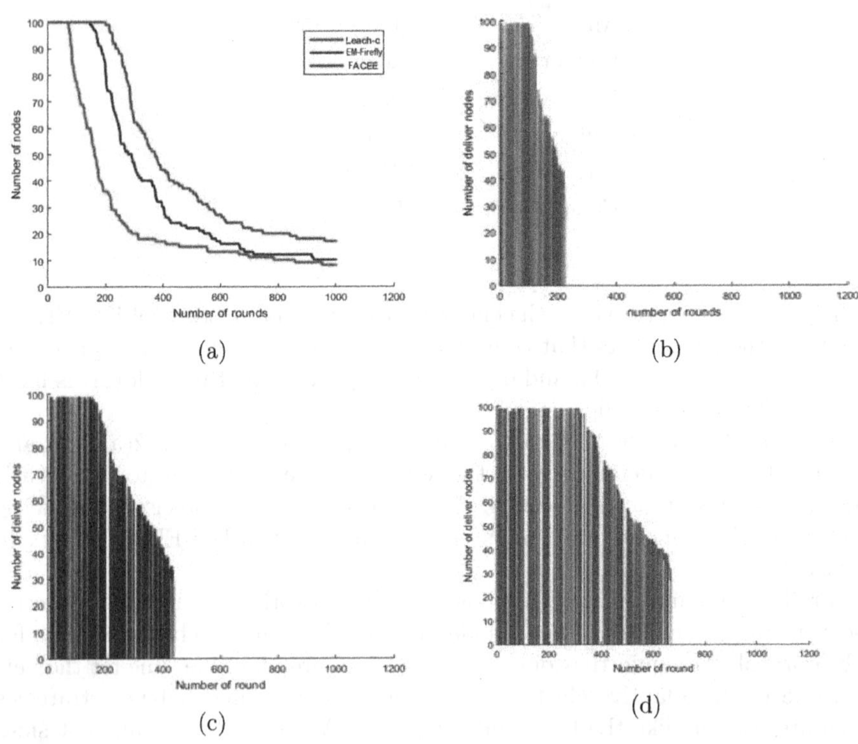

Fig. 3. (a) Network lifetime for the three protocols: LEACH-C, EM-FIREFLY, FACEE, (b) Delivery packets in LEAH-C, (c) Delivery packets in EM-FIREFLY and (d) Delivery packets in FACEE.

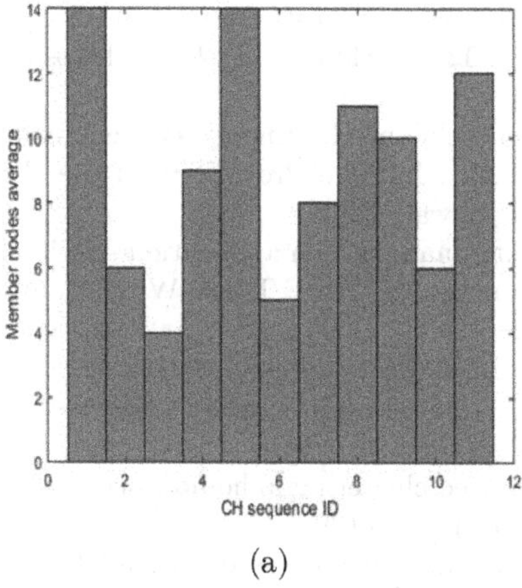

(a)

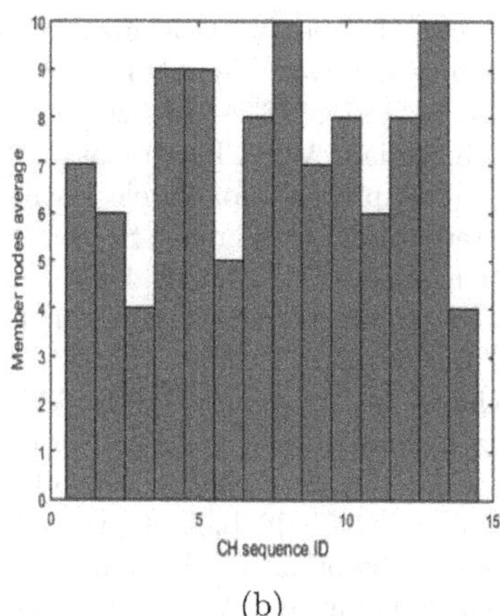

(b)

Fig. 4. (a) The average of CHs load in EM-FIREFLYP and (b) The average of CHs load in FACEE.

Figures 4(a) and 4(b) show the average of CHs load through the execution in different rounds by the two protocols EM-FIREFLY and FACEE. It must be noted that our protocol succeeds more than the protocol EM-FIREFLY in load balance between CHs. This is proved by the fact of exploiting more number of CHs then EM-FIREFLY in addition of the butter dividing of nodes between CHs more than EM-FIREFLY.

5 Conclusion

In this paper, we propose a novel scheme for coverage improvement with energy balancing in clustered wireless sensor networks based Firefly optimization algorithm. The main challenge of such work is the improvement of the network lifetime. For this reason, a special consideration is given to the coverage process that is less considered in the previous works. In addition, a load balance mechanism is added in order to achieve the maximum of the network lifetime improvement. Through simulations and experiments, we demonstrate that our protocol FACEE significantly reduces the energy consumption and improves the network lifetime with good amounts of packet delivery. As a future work, it seems more suitable to design a decentralized version of our technique and compared it with the present work.

References

1. Karaki, J.N., Kamal, A.E.: Routing techniques in WSN: a survey. In: IEEE Wirel. Commun. (2004)
2. Ridha, S., Minet, P.: Multichannel assignment protocols in wireless sensor networks: a comprehensive survey. Pervasive Mob. Comput. **16**, 2–21 (2015)

3. Zhang, H., Wu, Y.: Optimization and application of clustering algorithm in community discovery. Wirel. Pers. Commun. **102**(4), 2443–2454 (2018). https://doi.org/10.1007/s11277-018-5264-x
4. Heinzelman, W., Chandrakasan, A., Balakrishnan, H.: Energy efficient communication protocol for wireless sensor networks. In: The Proceeding of the Hawaii International Conference System Sciences, Hawaii (2000)
5. Heinzelman, W., Chandrakasan, A., Balakrishnan, H.: An application-specific protocol architecture for wireless micro sensor networks. IEEE Trans. Wirel. Commun. **1**(4), 660–670 (2002)
6. Khiati, M., Djenouri, D.: Bod-leach: broadcasting over duty-cycled radio using leach clustering for delay/power efficient dissimulation in wireless sensor networks. J. Commun. Syst. **28**(2), 296–308 (2015)
7. Souissi, M., Meddeb, A.: Optimal load balanced clustering in homogeneous wireless sensor networks. Int. J. Commun. Syst. **30**(7), 1–15 (2017)
8. Shashikumar, R., Anupama, A.D., Nak, B.M.: Cluster based on load balancing for environmental monitoring in wireless sensor network. Int. J. Comput. Trends Technol. (IJCTT) **54**(2), 97–104 (2017)
9. Ghosh, N., Banerjee, I., Sherratt, R.S.: On-demand fuzzy clustering and ant-colony optimisation based mobile data collection in wireless sensor network. Wirel. Networks **25**(4), 1829–1845 (2019)
10. Sahoo, B.M., Pandey, H.M., Amgoth, T.: GAPSO-H: a hybrid approach towards optimizing the cluster based routing in wireless sensor network. Swarm Evol. Comput. **60**, 100772 (2021)
11. Song, Y., Liu, Z., He, X.: Hybrid PSO and evolutionary game theory protocol for clustering and routing in wireless sensor network. J. Sens. **2020** (2020)
12. Maheshwari, P., Sharma, A.K., Verma, K.: Energy efficient cluster based routing protocol for WSN using butterfly optimization algorithm and ant colony optimization. Ad Hoc Networks **110**, 102317 (2021)
13. Shahbaz, A. N., Barati, H., Barati, A.: Multipath routing through the firefly algorithm and fuzzy logic in wireless sensor networks. Peer-to-Peer Network. Appl. 1–18 (2020)
14. Hossein, K., Ali, G.: Cluster-based routing scheme for wireless sensor network using PSO and Fire. African J. Comput. ICT **8**(4), 27–32 (2015)
15. Manshahia, M.S.: A firefly based energy efficient routing in wireless sensor networks. Afr. J. Comput. ICT **8**(4), 27–32 (2015)
16. Miodrag, Z., Nebojsa, B., Eva, T., Ivana, S., Timea, B., Milan, T.: Wireless sensor networks life time optimization based on the improved firefly algorithm. In: 2020 International Wireless Communications and Mobile Computing (IWCMC), Limassol, Cyprus (2020)
17. Tilahun, S.L., Ngnotchouye, J.M.T., Hamadneh, N.N.: Continuous versions of firefly algorithm: a review. Artif. Intell. Rev. **51**(3), 445–492 (2019)

Big Data Analytics in Weather Forecasting Using Gradient Boosting Classifiers Algorithm

Kamel Maaloul[1(✉)] and Brahim Lejdel[2]

[1] LIAP Laboratory, El-Oued University, El-Oued, Algeria
maaloul-kamel@univ-eloued.dz
[2] Computer Science Department, University of El-Oued, El-Oued, Algeria

Abstract. The process of predicting the weather, which is essential and fundamental to people's daily lives, evaluates the change that the atmosphere is currently undergoing. Analyzing large amounts of data to find hidden patterns and important information that could lead to better results is known as big data analytics. The meteorological institute shares the current obsession with big data shared by many parts of society. As a result, big data analytics will improve weather forecasting outcomes and help forecasters make more precise weather predictions. Several big data approaches and technologies have been proposed to organize and evaluate the vast volume of weather data from various resources in order to accomplish this goal and provide helpful solutions. A smart city is a project that uses computers to process vast amounts of data gathered from sensors, cameras, and other devices in order to manage resources, provide services, and address problems that arise in daily life, such as the weather. Forecasting the weather is a crucial process in daily life because it assesses changes in the atmosphere's current state. In this study, a model for forecasting the weather based on machine learning is proposed. It is then put into practice using 5 classifier algorithms: the Random Forest classifier, the Decision Tree Algorithm, the Gaussian Naive Bayes model, the Gradient Boosting Classifier, and Artificial Neural Networks. A publicly accessible dataset was used to train these classification systems. Gradient Boosting Classifier algorithm, which had a plus 98% projected accuracy, won when the model's performance was evaluated.

Keywords: Weather forecasting · Big data · Machine Learning · Smart city · Gradient Boosting Classifier

1 Introduction

The first weather predictions were made in the nineteenth century. Weather forecasting is defined as the process of analyzing atmospheric data, such as temperature, radiation, air pressure, wind speed, wind direction, humidity, and rainfall. There must be a large amount of data generated or collected in order to anticipate the weather. These data are also not well arranged. As a result, using weather data to predict the weather is a difficult task because it has too many variable variables [1].

H. Drias et al. (Eds.): AID 2022, CCIS 1852, pp. 15–26, 2023.
https://doi.org/10.1007/978-981-99-4484-2_2

By fusing probabilistic forecasts, for instance of snow, with data from the ground, smart cities may benefit from weather forecasting and choose where to place their snowplows. Given their known performance and available margin for demand response reasons, the smart city may also estimate the energy load of their own buildings by monitoring high local temperatures and humidity. Additionally, predicting the likelihood of traffic accidents by location and correlating precise fog forecasting to accident data. This will make it easier to set up variable speed limit signs and glare-reducing smart roadway lighting [2].

Before suggesting an algorithm, we need consider the unique characteristics of weather forecasting, including continuity, data intensity, and multidimensional and chaotic behaviors. Originally a labor-intensive human effort, weather forecasting has evolved into a computational process, necessitating high-tech machinery. Numerous variables can affect how accurate forecasts are. Some of these crucial variables are season, geographic location, data input accuracy, weather classifications, lead time, and validity time [3].

Machine learning, a branch of data science, fundamentally manipulates data in a statistical manner. Machine learning, on the other hand, is more resilient to disruptions and doesn't require a full understanding of the fundamental principles underlying the atmosphere. In order to forecast the weather, machine learning may be a useful alternative to physical models [4].

Big data is a term for massive, disorganized, and heterogeneous digital data. Big data processing cannot be accomplished simply or effectively using traditional data management techniques. We need look for a high-performance platform and a practical big data mining technique to obtain useful information in order to analyze this kind of data effectively. Huge data analytics is a big data search operation that aims to reveal hidden patterns, undiscovered relationships, and other relevant information to help people make better decisions. Big data has the potential to improve decision-making in the area of weather forecasting [5].

In theory, AI and machine learning will make it possible for human forecasters to work more productively, devoting less time to producing routine forecasts and more to explaining the implications and impacts of those forecasts to the general public, or, in the case of private forecasters, to their clients. We think the best way to accomplish these objectives and increase confidence in computer-generated weather forecasts is through rigorous collaboration between scientists, forecasters, and forecast users [6].

Following is the organization of the remaining portions of the essay: Sect. 2 provides details of a similar study on weather forecasting that utilized several machine learning algorithms and methods. In Sect. 3, it is explained how to use the data and the methods to develop the artificial intelligence approach. In Sect. 4, which is titled "Evaluation and Results," it is explained how the approach's outcome was assessed. At the end, it includes conclusions and suggestions for further work.

2 Related Work

Since the modern world depends on data, smart cities heavily rely on artificial intelligence. Researchers have used a variety of metrological traits, features, and data produced from diverse sources to successfully apply a number of algorithms and models to forecast meteorological conditions. This section clarifies big data as the primary subject while talking about weather forecasting. Finally, the variables that affect the accuracy of weather forecasts are discussed.

FENTE et al. [7] collected a number of meteorological parameters from the National Climate Data Center using long-term memory (LSTM) technology. Several different combinations were used to train the neural network. Weather variables like temperature, precipitation, wind speed, pressure, dew point visibility, and humidity were used to train the neural network used in LSTM weather forecasting. After utilizing these parameters to train the LSTM, the weather for the upcoming days is predicted.

Prior to discussing big data, Sahasrabuddhe and Jamsandekar [8] first discussed weather forecasting, covering fundamental procedures and several techniques. After that, they provided an overview of several publications and explained various data structures utilized in big data and weather forecasting.

The implications of weather forecasting on the agriculture/food sector, tourism industry, sports industry, construction business, transportation business, disaster management industry, and energy industry were explored by Jain and Jain [9]. Following that, they discussed the technical difficulties associated with weather forecasting, such as processing massive amounts of data, having access to historical data, overcoming technological obstacles, having access to prediction models, complexity, expensive maintenance, and cost overruns.

In the context of agriculture, Rao [10] introduced the subject of big data and climate change and big data technologies in agriculture, big data for climate-smart agriculture, and an implementation roadmap for big data for climate-smart agriculture in India. The work did not provide a comprehensive assessment of the literature because there were no sections devoted to the research methods, taxonomy, or commentary.

For short-range prediction, Murugan et al. [11] recommended combining a hybrid C5.0 decision tree method with k-means clustering algorithm in order to improve forecasting effectiveness and accuracy. Similar datasets were grouped together using the k-means clustering technique. Using mean absolute error and root mean square error, the model's prediction accuracy was 90.18%.

The attributes, technology, and analytics of big data were introduced by Mittal and Sangwan [12]. Following that, they gave a review of the literature from 11 papers and discussed difficulties in applying traditional data mining techniques to large datasets. The Bayesian model, the MR-KNN and k-means method on the MapReduce platform, the MapReduce and linear regression approach, and the KNN classification algorithm were all contrasted with one another. They also displayed the results in terms of the data set, the techniques, the parameters, and the outcomes of the experiments. The summary and subsequent work were subsequently created. However, none of the strategies we looked at discussed research technique or taxonomy.

MOOSAVI et al. [13] introduced a novel use of machine learning approaches to interpret, forecast, and reduce uncertainty in the WRF model while predicting precipitation as a result of the interplay of numerous physical processes contained in the model. They used probabilistic methodologies to investigate the relationships between the configuration of the physical processes used in the simulation and the observed model's prediction errors. These linkages are then used to resolve two important problems regarding model faults and the identification of physical processes.

3 Proposed Architecture

This section provides an outline for a thorough analysis of the research on big data analytical techniques for weather forecasting. As seen in picture 1, there are four layers that help us describe design architecture:

- **Data Acquisition Layer:** The input layer works on data gathering procedures; it gathers information from many sources that are managed by public and governmental entities.
- **Cloud Layer:** Large datasets are kept in the cloud by the cloud layer. All large datasets are stored in this layer and are processed in distributed parallel fashion.
- **Data Processing Layer:** Large quantities of financial and economic records are provided and used by the data layer, which uses distributed parallel computing.
- **User Layer:** The user layer serves as the user's interface for accessing large datasets and controls query management for analysis and report generation.

Our design architecture aims to produce accurate and efficient weather forecasts. To do this, we will carefully analyze the incoming data, identify the chosen features, and process the data. The processing performance of our suggested design depends on the following metrics (Fig. 1).

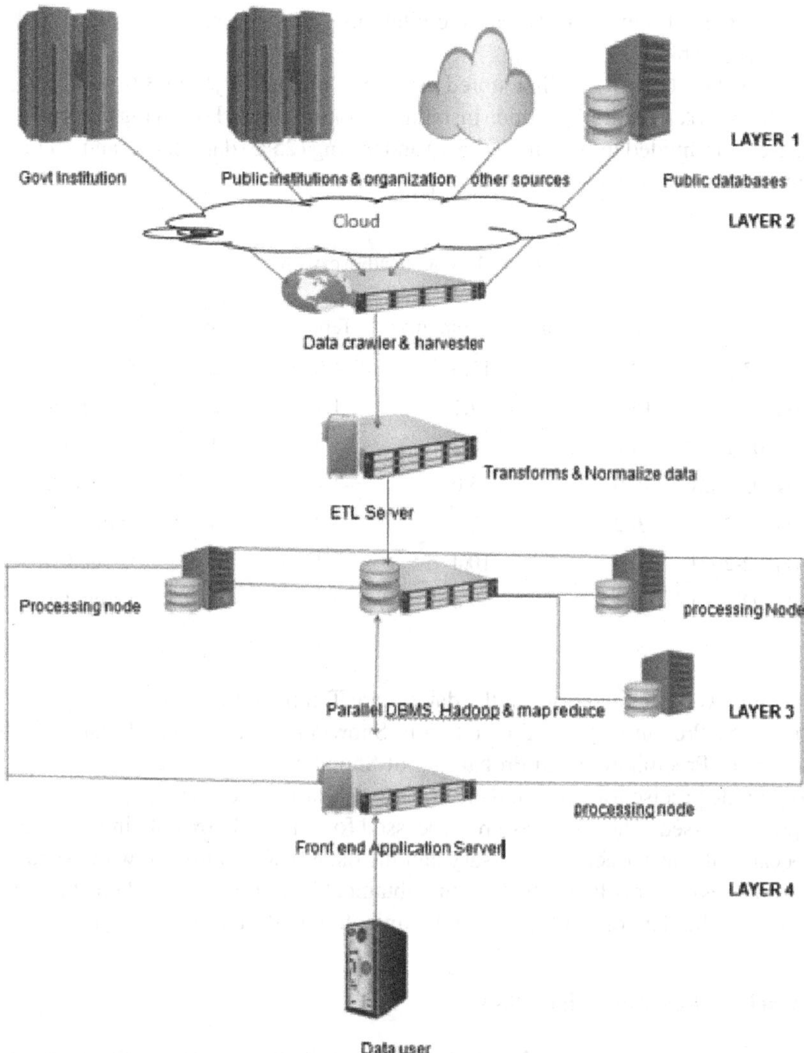

Fig. 1. Proposed architecture [14]

4 Methodology

4.1 Dataset

This section includes a description of the dataset, its acquisition and pre-processing, as well as an analysis of the algorithm used, as well as the proposed model for weather forecasting using machine learning.

The dataset used for this analysis was obtained from an online data repository company; the data was for the town of Algeria from 11 February 2021 to 31 December 2021; it was licensed under CC BY-NC-SA 4.0; the file format was a comma separated file (CSV); the columns were Date, Precipitations, Temp_max, Temp_min, Wind, and Weather (See Table 1).

The weather dataset was first stored as a CSV file, and Python 3.6 was utilized in Jupyter Notebook with the Anaconda installation for this work. Following preprocessing, the dataset was divided into training (75%) and testing (25%) datasets at random in order to train the algorithms and evaluate their performances.

Table 1. data head overview

N	Date	Precipitations	Temp_max	Temp_min	Wind	Weather
0	01–02-2021	0.0	12.5	4.0	2.4	Cloud Cover
1	02–02-2021	15.1	7.1	1.1	3.3	Precipitation
2	03–02-2021	14.8	8.2	1.3	1.8	Pressure
3	04–02-2021	0.0	5.0	−1.4	2.8	Solar Radiation
4	05–02-2021	0.2	12.1	3.8	4.4	Wind
5	06–02-2021	0.5	10.4	5.1	3.0	Cloud Cover
6	07–02-2021	1.1	9.8	4.2	2.4	Precipitation

The nine weather categories in the dataset are Temperature

Humidity, Pressure, Wind, Precipitation, Snowfall, Cloud Cover, Solar Radiation, Probability of Precipitation and Probability of Snowfall.

To provide precise forecasts and ensure great algorithm performance, the data needs to be pre-processed. The data was pre-processed for this study by deleting the date column because it was judged unnecessary and the dataset was complete with no null values. Pre-processing involves transforming obtained data into a comprehensible format, eliminating redundant or null values, and eliminating undesired features [15].

4.2 Machine Learning Algorithms

Choosing the right learning The technique is difficult to use because the problem and the facts at hand are so crucial. Given the chaotic nature of atmospheric dynamics and the nonlinear nature of the fundamental phenomena that govern weather, we believe that the methodologies of these algorithms are ideally suited to capture related characteristics [16].

Our dataset has input and output labels, a supervised learning algorithm will be best for the problem. Supervised learning can be segregated further based on the type of output and if the data is sequential. Multiple parameters are needed to train the model [17], so we chose the Decision Tree Algorithm that works well in this direction. Random Forest was also used because it deals with classification and regression problems in ML, and it was implemented using classifier algorithms, including the Gaussian Naive Bayes model, the Gradient Boosting Classifier, and Artificial Neural Networks.

- **Random Forest Classifier**
  A random forest classifier, as its name implies, consists of an ensemble of multiple interconnected decision trees. The class that receives the most votes determines the class our model will predict from each individual tree in the random forest. The Random forest classifier produces a set of decision trees based on a subset of training data that is randomly selected. It basically consists of a group of decision trees that are assembled from a subset of the training set that is randomly selected, and the final prediction is made using those decision trees [18].
- **Decision Tree**
  Let's rapidly explore decision trees since they serve as the model's building block for the random forest. Fortunately, they are not too difficult to understand. At some point in their lives, whether consciously or unconsciously, the majority of people have probably used a decision tree. The Decision Trees method is a subset of supervised machine learning, where input is repeatedly divided by a certain parameter and represented by a tree structure. The majority of the time, classification and regression problems use this machine learning technique [19].
- **Gaussian Naive Bayes**
  A number of categorization applications can use the Naive Bayes method of probabilistic machine learning. For applications like document categorization, spam filtering, prediction, and other things, naive bayes is commonly employed. This method was built on the discoveries of Thomas Bayes, hence its name [17]. The Naive Bayes classifier has the following benefits: It can handle both continuous and discrete data, is clear and easy to build, requires little training data, is rapid, and can be used in real-time [20].
- **Gradient Boosting Classifier**
  A weak hypothesis or learning method can be strengthened by a succession of minor modifications, a process known as gradient boosting. The theoretical underpinning of this kind of hypothesis boosting is the idea of Probability Approximately Correct Learning. With the aid of the AdaBoosting algorithm and weighted minimization, gradient boosting classifiers update the weighted inputs and the classifiers. Reduce the loss, or the difference between the actual class value of the training example and the projected class value, is the objective of Gradient Boosting classifiers. Although it is not required to understand how the classifier's loss is decreased, it works similarly to gradient descent in a neural network [21].

In a regularized (L1 and L2) objective function, or in other words, the regression tree functions, gradient boosting classifiers minimize a convex loss function (based on the difference between the predicted and target outputs) and a penalty term for model complexity. The training procedure is carried out iteratively by adding new trees that forecast the residuals or errors of prior trees, which are then combined with earlier trees to give the final prediction. The method is known as "gradient boosting" because it uses a gradient descent algorithm to minimize loss when introducing new models [22].

- **Artificial Neural Networks:**
  The basis of an ANN is a group of interconnected units or nodes called artificial neurons, which mimic actual brain neurons in some ways. Each link has the capacity to communicate with nearby neurons, just like synapses do in the human brain. After

interpreting signals that are delivered to it, an artificial neuron can communicate with neurons that are attached to it. Each neuron's output is determined by some kind of non-linear function of the total of its inputs, and the "signal" at a connection is a real integer. Edges are the ties between things. As learning progresses, edges and neurons' weight frequently shift [23].

An artificial neural network is best represented as a weighted directed graph, in which the nodes are the artificial neurons. The connection between a neuron's inputs and outputs is represented by the directed edges with weights. Pattern input for the artificial neural network and vector input for the picture originate from outside sources, respectively [24].

5 Results and Discussion

5.1 Results

In our research, we used machine learning metrics for accuracy, precision, and recall to assess model performance. Five algorithms were used in this experiment with the aim of improving location prediction:

- **Accuracy = (TN + TP)/(TP + TN + FP + FN)**

where TP= True positive, TN= True Negative, FP= False positive and FN = false negative.

- **Precision = TP/(TP + FP)**

  where TP= True positive, FP= False Positive.

- **Recall = TP/(TP + FN)**

  where TP= True positive, FN= False Negative.

- **F1-score = 2*(Recall * Precision)/(Recall + Precision)**

Table 1 displays the detection rate for each model based on the testing dataset. (Table 2):

Table 2. Displays Performance comparison of Model prediction.

Model Name	Accuracy	Precision	Recall	F1-score
Random Forest C	93.73%	90.00%	89.77%	2.85
Decision Tree	79.35%	72.42%	70.01%	1.98
Gaussian Naïve Bayes	89.51%	87.39%	85.85%	2.59
Gradient Boosting C	98.12%	97.15%	97.00%	3.4
ANN	85.94%	84.66%	83.96%	2.41

Figure 2 depicts the count of activities for the training data set for additional clarity and analysis of the findings.

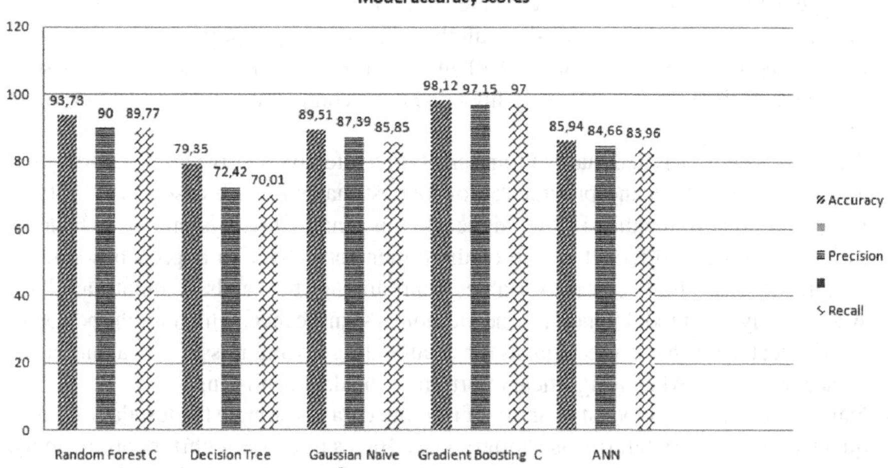

Fig. 2. Model accuracy scores of Weather Forecasting using Algorithms

5.2 Discussion

- The Gradient Boosting classifiers algorithm is the best for others, as seen in Table 2 and Fig. 2 above. Results from the Gradient Boosting classification technique are favorable. It benefits from being the easiest of the five machine learning algorithms evaluated to understand and apply. We achieved a prediction accuracy of greater than 98% for weather forecasting. This algorithm works well. It does effectively with small, big, intricate, and data with subgroups. However, it struggles with sparse data and can also have difficulties with data that is widely dispersed. On those kinds of data problems, it typically performs better than the majority of supervised learning algorithms [25].
- The results were positive for the Gradient Boosting classifiers algorithm because the gradient boosting model adheres to ensemble learning, handling and interpreting the data is simpler. It is more accurate than many other algorithms, and accurate results can be obtained using cutting-edge techniques like bagging, random forest, and decision trees. Additionally, one of the best algorithms for processing bigger datasets and computing with weak learners at least loss is this one. This technique is effective at handling category data as well as numerical datasets. A robust technique for machine learning that can quickly detect over fitting training datasets is the gradient boosting algorithm [26].
- The results are less accurate for Artificial Neural Networks algorithm because the input data set is unbalanced, this may cause the neural network to learn patterns that are not representative of the real world. This may eventually lead to a less accurate model [27].
- Compared to other methods, decision trees require less labor to pre-process the data. Additionally, the decision tree does not require data uniformity. The results are weaker and less precise, though, because a small change in the data could cause a significant

change in the decision tree's structure, leading to instability. A decision tree's computation can occasionally be more difficult than that of other algorithms. They typically have a tree in them. The choice lengthens the model training process. The cost of training a decision tree is relatively high due to its complexity and time commitment [28].

- The results demonstrated that random forests can effectively solve both classification and regression issues and provide reasonable estimates in each case. The ability of Random Forest to handle sizable, higher-dimensional datasets is one of its benefits that most appeals to me. It is one of the dimension reduction approaches since it may identify the most crucial variables from among thousands of input variables. Additionally, the model generates the variable's significance, which might be a very helpful feature. It has a mechanism for accurately guessing missing data and keeps its accuracy even when a significant portion of the data is missing [29].
- Naive Bayes needs a modest quantity of training data to estimate the test data. Consequently, the training duration is shorter. Naive Bayes is also straightforward to apply. Naive Bayes implicitly assumes that all of the attributes are independent of one another. In practice, obtaining a group of predictors that are completely independent is nearly never attainable [30].

6 Conclusion

In this study, we used Big Data Analytics in Weather Forecasting and machine learning algorithms to assess and compare the performance of five different predictors. We come to the conclusion that the five algorithms performed weather forecasting fairly accurately. Numerous weather situations, including mist, fog, rain, snow, and sun, are predicted by this study. A model was also provided. This project's objectives were to create a weather forecasting model, assess its effectiveness, and review pertinent literature. The Gradient Boosting Classifier model was found to be the most accurate of the used algorithms; the output of the model provided exact prediction and useful guidance for meteorologists in their operational forecasting activities.

There is still a lot of work to be done before the model can be used to forecast weather in real-time and give meteorologists helpful guidance for their operational weather forecasting. Various methods can be used to further build the model as needed.

References

1. Kumari, S., Muthulakshmi, P.: A wide scale survey on weather prediction using machine learning techniques. J. Inf. Knowl. Manag. 2250093 (2022). https://doi.org/10.1142/S0219649222500939
2. Mehrpour, F.: Prediction of Bridge Fires Characteristics Using Machine Learning, Text, Carleton University, 2022. Consulté le: 26 novembre 2022. [En ligne]. Disponible sur: https://curve.carleton.ca/7e4a23e9-ddf5-4836-9224-e14a71769434
3. Ren, X., et al.: Deep learning-based weather prediction: a survey. Big Data Res. **23**, 100178 (2021). https://doi.org/10.1016/j.bdr.2020.100178
4. Maaloul, K., Brahim, L.: Comparative analysis of machine learning for predicting air quality in smart cities. WSEAS Trans. Comput. **21**, 248–256 (2022). https://doi.org/10.37394/23205.2022.21.30

5. Ngiam, K.Y., Khor, I.W.: Big data and machine learning algorithms for health-care delivery. Lancet Oncol. **20**(5), e262–e273 (2019). https://doi.org/10.1016/S1470-2045(19)30149-4
6. Munoko, I., Brown-Liburd, H.L., Vasarhelyi, M.: The ethical implications of using artificial intelligence in auditing. J. Bus. Ethics **167**(2), 209–234 (2020). https://doi.org/10.1007/s10551-019-04407-1
7. Shivaprasad, T.K., Shetty, J.: Sentiment analysis of product reviews: a review. In: 2017 International Conference on Inventive Communication and Computational Technologies (ICICCT), pp. 298–301 (2017). https://doi.org/10.1109/ICICCT.2017.7975207
8. Sahasrabuddhe, D.V., Jamsandekar, P.: Data structure for representation of big data of weather forecasting: a review. Int. J. **3**(6), 10 (2015)
9. Jain, H., Jain, R.: Big data in weather forecasting: applications and challenges. In: 2017 International Conference on Big Data Analytics and Computational Intelligence (ICBDAC), pp. 138–142 (2017). https://doi.org/10.1109/ICBDACI.2017.8070824
10. Rao, N.H.: Big data and climate smart agriculture - review of current status and implications for agricultural research and innovation in India. Rochester, NY, (2017). https://doi.org/10.2139/ssrn.2979349
11. Murugan Bhagavathi, S., et al.: Retracted: Weather forecasting and prediction using hybrid C5.0 machine learning algorithm. Int. J. Commun. Syst. **34**(10), e4805 (2021). https://doi.org/10.1002/dac.4805
12. Mittal, S., Sangwan, O.P.: Big data analytics using data mining techniques: a survey. In: Luhach, A.K., Singh, D., Hsiung, P.-A., Hawari, K.B.G., Lingras, P., Singh, P.K. (eds.) ICAICR 2018. CCIS, vol. 955, pp. 264–273. Springer, Singapore (2019). https://doi.org/10.1007/978-981-13-3140-4_24
13. Moosavi, A., Rao, V., Sandu, A.: Machine learning based algorithms for uncertainty quantification in numerical weather prediction models. J. Comput. Sci. **50**, 101295 (2021). https://doi.org/10.1016/j.jocs.2020.101295
14. Alam, M., Amjad, M.: Weather forecasting using parallel and distributed analytics approaches on big data clouds. J. Stat. Manag. Syst. **22**(4), 791–799 (2019). https://doi.org/10.1080/09720510.2019.1609559
15. Shehadeh, A., Alshboul, O., Al Mamlook, R.E., Hamedat, O.: Machine learning models for predicting the residual value of heavy construction equipment: an evaluation of modified decision tree, LightGBM, and XGBoost regression. Autom. Constr. **129**, 103827 (2021). https://doi.org/10.1016/j.autcon.2021.103827
16. Mukhin, D., Hannachi, A., Braun, T., Marwan, N.: Revealing recurrent regimes of mid-latitude atmospheric variability using novel machine learning method. Chaos Interdiscip. J. Nonlinear Sci. **32**(11), 113105 (2022). https://doi.org/10.1063/5.0109889
17. Sarker, I.H.: Machine learning: algorithms, real-world applications and research directions. SN Comput. Sci. **2**(3), 1–21 (2021). https://doi.org/10.1007/s42979-021-00592-x
18. Kamalov, F., Moussa, S., Avante Reyes, J.: KDE-based ensemble learning for imbalanced data. Electronics **11**(17), 17 (2022). https://doi.org/10.3390/electronics11172703
19. Boonnam, N., Udomchaipitak, T., Puttinaovarat, S., Chaichana, T., Boonjing, V., Muangprathub, J.: Coral reef bleaching under climate change: prediction modeling and machine learning. Sustainability **14**(10), 10 (2022). https://doi.org/10.3390/su14106161
20. Ampomah, E.K., Nyame, G., Qin, Z., Addo, P.C., Gyamfi, E.O., Gyan, M.: Stock market prediction with Gaussian Naïve Bayes machine learning algorithm. Informatica **45**(2), 2 (2021). https://doi.org/10.31449/inf.v45i2.3407
21. Qinghe, Z., Wen, X., Boyan, H., Jong, W., Junlong, F.: Optimised extreme gradient boosting model for short term electric load demand forecasting of regional grid system. Sci. Rep. **12**(1), 1 (2022). https://doi.org/10.1038/s41598-022-22024-3

22. Sibindi, R., Mwangi, R.W., Waititu, A.G.: A boosting ensemble learning based hybrid light gradient boosting machine and extreme gradient boosting model for predicting house prices. Eng. Rep. **5**(4), e12599 (2023). https://doi.org/10.1002/eng2.12599
23. Jayakumar, C.H., Mogili, R.P., Mansa, V.E., Devi, G.S.: Using the artificial neural networks to predict the solubility effects of theophylline drug in hydrotropic solutions (2021). https://doi.org/10.31838/ijpr/2021.13.02.344
24. Wang, F., et al.: Dynamic spatio-temporal correlation and hierarchical directed graph structure based ultra-short-term wind farm cluster power forecasting method. Appl. Energy. **323**, 119579 (2022). https://doi.org/10.1016/j.apenergy.2022.119579
25. Maaloul, K., Abdelhamid, N.M., Lejdel, B.: Machine learning based indoor localization using wi-fi and smartphone in a shopping malls. In: Artificial Intelligence and Its Applications, Cham, p. 1–10 (2022). https://doi.org/10.1007/978-3-030-96311-8_1
26. Madhavi, M., Nethravathi, D.: Gradient boosted decision tree (GBDT) and grey wolf optimization (Gwo) based intrusion detection model, (16), 15 (2022)
27. Sambasivam, G., Opiyo, G.D.: A predictive machine learning application in agriculture: Cassava disease detection and classification with imbalanced dataset using convolutional neural network. Egypt. Inform. J. **22**(1), 27–34 (2021). https://doi.org/10.1016/j.eij.2020.02.007
28. Lipinski, P., Brzychczy, E., Zimroz, R.: Decision tree-based classification for planetary gearboxes' condition monitoring with the use of vibration data in multidimensional symptom space. Sensors **20**(21), 21 (2020). https://doi.org/10.3390/s20215979
29. Kanervo, A.: Random Forests an Application to Tumour Classification, p. 51
30. Maaloul, K.,Brahim, L., Abdelhamid, N.M.: Real-time human activity recognition from smart phone using linear support vector machines. Telkomnika (Telecommun. Comput. Electr. Control), **21**(3), 574–583 (2023). https://doi.org/10.12928/telkomnika.v21i3.24100

A Predictive Model of the Effect of Austerity Policies on Road Safety: A Case Study of Algeria

Billal Soulmana(✉) and Salim Boukebbab

Laboratory of Transport Engineering and Environment, Department of Transport Engineering, Frères Mentouri University, Constantine, Algeria
{soulmana.bilal,boukebbabs}@umc.edu.dz

Abstract. Our objective is to study the effect of economic austerity policies on the number of road accidents through predictive models. Therefore, we selected the traffic accident data in Algeria country for the period between 2004–2018 for each month, where we divided data into two parts before and after the austerity policy year 2014. Accordingly we used ARIMA model, linear regression and forecast difference of two years as methods of analysis. As results we found that Algeria's prediction model is ARIMA (2, 1, 3) before and after the application of austerity economic policies. However, traffic accidents have greatly decreased following the implementation of austerity policies. Furthermore, this study proved that economic policies could be a factor contributing to the reduction of traffic accidents.

Keywords: Austerity · ARIMA · Accidents

1 Introduction

The percentage of accidents and deaths on our roads is one of the world's most serious issues today. Every year, the number of deaths from road accidents is estimated at 1.35 million people, and among 20 to 50 million people are injured, cost more than 3% of gross domestic product [1]. The recent report found that, if immediate action is not taken, road traffic accidents could become the 7th leading cause of death by 2030 [2].

In Algeria, a large number of persons are killed in traffic accidents consistently. As per the CNPSR (The National Centre for Road Safety and Prevention). 42,846 Road traffic collision was registered in 2013. Causing 4540 deaths and 69,582 injured unfortunate casualties. The current total incident cost is assessed at more than 1 billion U.S $ every year [3].

Over 93% of the world's mortalities on the roads happen in low- and middle-revenue countries, although these countries have around 60% of the world's vehicles [1]. In Algeria, this number emerges to 11.7 traffic deaths per 100.000 populations in 2013, while HIC (high-income countries) indicate a proportion less than 0.6, there is a similar difference when comparing the number of crash-correlated deaths per vehicle. However, deaths in high income countries (HICs) are less than one death every 100,000 automobiles. Although this frequency is 9.24 for Algeria [4]. Therefore, Algeria's performance in road safety is poor compared to other high-income countries.

H. Drias et al. (Eds.): AID 2022, CCIS 1852, pp. 27–40, 2023.
https://doi.org/10.1007/978-981-99-4484-2_3

In this framework, the reasons of road accidents are multifactorial and involve interaction between the various pre-crash elements that contain vehicles, human and road environment [5]. However, some studies proved that there is relationship between traffic accident and others factors, such as the implementation of novel public policy strategy and the economic and social situations of the country [6, 7], public authorities could interpose through executing certain regulations and countermeasures to limit the associated adverse effects.

A methodological point of view, other studies model the liaison between road safety performance and the economic context using quadratic relationship estimation [8–15]. In addition, other studies utilize the hypothesis of cycles or AR-MA type models (autoregressive moving Average) to examine momentary effects between economic policy and the development of the road safety [16–18]. Using an ARIMA model, Wagenaar (1984), found an inverse and significant connection between the joblessness rate and the number of road crashes in the US [18]. García Ferrer et al. (2007), suggest an analysis of economic phases to study the short-range causality between road safety and industry activity. The authors presented that the number of accident and road accident victims shared a common sequence with Spain's industrial production index for the period 1975–2005 [16]. The scientific literature proved also a positive relation between economic growth and certain road safety factors [13, 16, 18]. Economic growth is connected with more road injuries. While economic retreat improves the road safety condition [4].

Furthermore, few studies are existing about the influence of public policy on traffic safety, and information is quite limited particularly on road safety modeling in Algeria. The aim of this paper is to examine the impact of the austerity economic policy on the traffic accidents that Algeria has applied after 2014 with using the ARIMA model and linear regression.

2 Method

2.1 Data Sources

The CNPSR (The National Centre for Road Safety and Prevention) is the government agency in Algeria, with the legal obligations to manage road safety, among the different roles of CNPSR are giving immediate attention and care to the casualties of accidents, doing intensive examination on the immediate contributing variables to road accident and submitting their reports. They collect incident data through immediate assessment of accident, environmental conditions, vehicle, and cross-interviews of collision victims (passengers, drivers or walkers) and the onlookers. For this study, a combined monthly dataset of slight, serious and fatal accidents was used in the analysis. Only statistics from 2004 to 2018 were used. Figure 1 shows annual data and Fig. 2 explains the time series of monthly aggregate data of accidents.

In order to compare the impact of austerity economic policies on the toll of traffic accidents, we had to divide the data into two parts, before and after 2014, where we used predictive models ARIMA in R software.

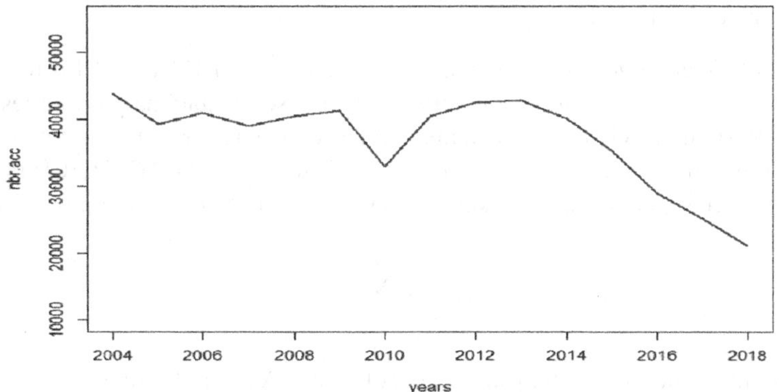

Fig. 1. Annual traffic accident data *NCPRS.*

2.2 Data Analysis Methods

The Autoregressive Integrated Moving Average or ARIMA Model. ARIMA prediction method includes a two-step time series mainly. (1). First step is examining the series. (2) Develop an appropriate model that can predict the data presented in the data set.

Box and Jenkins (1976) recommended the ARIMA (p. d. q) model for cooperation between autoregressive (q = AR) function and moving average (p = MA) models, also, expressly incorporates differencing in the plan of the model appropriate for single-variable time-series analysis. The autoregressive (AR) model explains a time-series where the present perception relies upon its previous values, while MA model is utilized to explain a time-series as a linear function of present and past irregular errors [19], the general function of ARIMA is provided as;

$$\nabla^{d} y_{t} = \frac{\theta(B)}{\varphi(B)} \varepsilon_{t} \quad (1)$$

y_t tis a series of monthly number of incidents response, t is the trend of time, ε_tis the irregular error at a time period t, B is the lag operator, ∇ signifies the integrated procedures (where $\nabla y_t = y_t - y_{t-1}$), d is the index of non-seasonal difference necessary to realize time-series stationarity, and the supplementary factors in the model is determined as follows;

$$\theta(B) = (1 - \theta_1 B - \theta_2 B^2 - \ldots - \theta_q B^q) \quad (2)$$

$$\varphi(B) = (1 - \varphi B - \varphi_2 B^2 - \ldots - \varphi_q B^q) \quad (3)$$

Terms $\varphi_1 . \varphi_2 . \ldots . \varphi_p$ are the autoregressive (AR) factors $\theta_1 . \theta_2 . \ldots . \theta_q$ are the moving average (MA) factors, p is the arrangement of autoregressive side and q is the arrangement of the moving average side. An important and comprehensive statistical model ARIMA (p. d. q) for time-series modeling and forecasting is developed following Box-Jenkins approach [19]. To choose the best model, Box and Jenkins (1976) suggested a three-step iterative process of model:

(1). *Model identification.* The first point in introduce an ARIMA model is to check if the time-series is stationary or otherwise. A time-series stationary is a series whose statistical characteristics for example variance, average or autocorrelation are all fixed over time. Stationarity was tested using the graph of ACF, PACF functions and the ADF (Augmented Dickey Fuller) test, that is given as in Eq. (4) [20].

$$\mathrm{y_t} = \alpha + \rho \mathrm{y_{t-i}} + \sum_{\mathrm{i=1}}^{\mathrm{k}} \varphi_{\mathrm{i}} \Delta \mathrm{y_{t-i}} + \beta \mathrm{t} + \varepsilon_{\mathrm{t}} \quad (4)$$

y_t signifies the response variable (number of collisions) Δy_{t-i} is the time lagged variation in the response variable, ε_t is the random error parameter, t is the time trend. In the ADF (Augmented Dickey-Fuller) check, if t the calculated p-value is bigger than the significance alpha value 0.05, one cannot refuse the null hypothesis that confirmed the existence of a unit root for the series, means the data is not-stationary, and it could be made stationary generally using the differencing method, after that define the orders of the AR (autoregressive) and MA (moving average) with drawing plot of the ACF (Autocorrelation Function) and PACF (Partial autocorrelation Function).

(2). *Model parameter estimation Akaike information criterion (AIC).* The maxi-mum likelihood value was used to evaluate the parameters of the characteristic model and the t-values were used to verify if the model created is measurably significant or not. For this research, many ARIMA models were observed and the lowest Akaike information criterion (AIC) was used to determine the best model from the significant models that generated using ARIMA. The AIC is stated as in Eq. (5) [21].

$$\mathrm{AIC} = -2. \ln(\mathrm{l}) + 2.\mathrm{K} \quad (5)$$

Term L is the likelihood value, and k is estimated factors number.

(3) *Model diagnostic checking.* The compatibility of the model, taking into account the characteristics of the residuals, was examined utilizing the residuals PACF and ACF, and the Ljung Box indicators $(Q^*).Q^*$ is found from the Eq. (6) [22].

$$\mathrm{Q}^* = \mathrm{n(n+2)} \sum\nolimits_{\mathrm{m=1}}^{\mathrm{r}} \mathrm{r_j^2 n/{-m}} \quad (6)$$

where r_j is residual autocorrelation at lag m, n = residuals number, P = time lags number in the test. If the P-value related with the Q^* indicator is less than alpha (p < α), the model is not suitable. The model could be changed or replaced until an acceptable model is found [23].

3 Results

3.1 Before Austerity Economic Policies

For the analysis and forecasting, we used R software. The data is uploaded to the program and Fig. 2 shows the time-series graph of total reported car collision. Through observing the patterns, we can discover that data plot has additive seasonality.

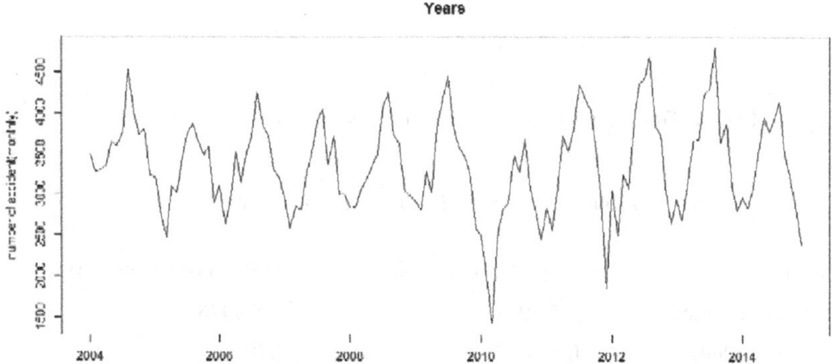

Fig. 2. Time-series graph for monthly traffic accident data NCPRS (2004–2014).

Figure 3 Shows the illustration ACF (autocorrelation function) of the transformed data, which clearly notes that the series is not stationary because several lags are outside the confidence interval. The ADF (Augmented Dickey-Fuller) test shown in Table 1, affirmed that the series is non-stationary ($p = 0.4143$). This means that at least the first difference of data is necessary to make it stationary.

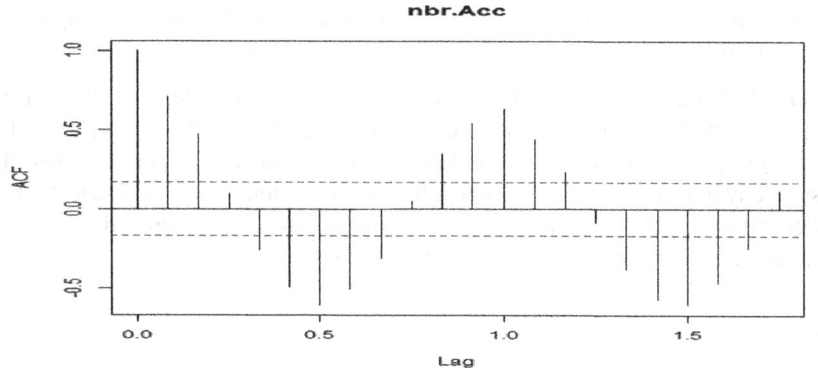

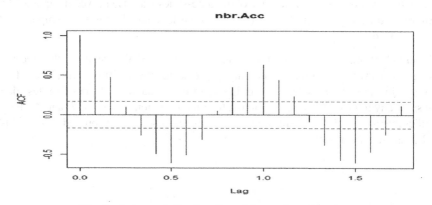

Fig. 3. Autocorrelation function of the number of crashes

Figure 4 indicates the time-series graph of first non seasonal difference of accident data, that the trend was deleted from the data after only the first differencing. Figure 5

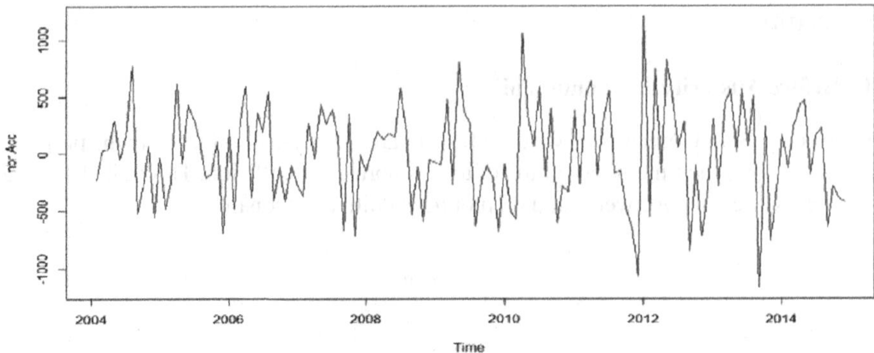

Fig. 4. Time-series graph of the first difference of the accidents data.

Table 1. The ADF Test for accident number.

Parameter	Original Time Series	Differenced Time Series
Tau (Observed value)	−2.3901	−5.9976
p-value (one-tailed)	0.4143	0.01
Alpha	0.05	0.05
Lag order	10	10

shows the graph of ACF (autocorrelation function) of the first difference of the accident time-series. It can be perceived that the plot of the ACF decays when compared with the first ACF Fig. 3. Also shows the PACF (partial autocorrelation function) which indicate the occurrence of autoregressive component in the series that means d = 1. The stationarity of the first difference of the time-series was also proved using the ADF (Augmented Dickey-Fuller) Table 1 (p = < .01) is less than the significant alpha level. That means d = 1.

Model Selection. Figure 5 and the lowest AIC value 1878.69 reported that the best model is ARIMA (2.1.3) for the monthly traffic accident data 2004–2014. There-fore, this specific model was select for further analysis. In addition, Ljung Box test does not show any indication for getting non-zero autocorrelation (p = 0.3437) and ADF test verifies that for (p = 0.01) the residuals are stationary. These results proved that ARIMA (2.1.3) is the final model (Fig. 6).

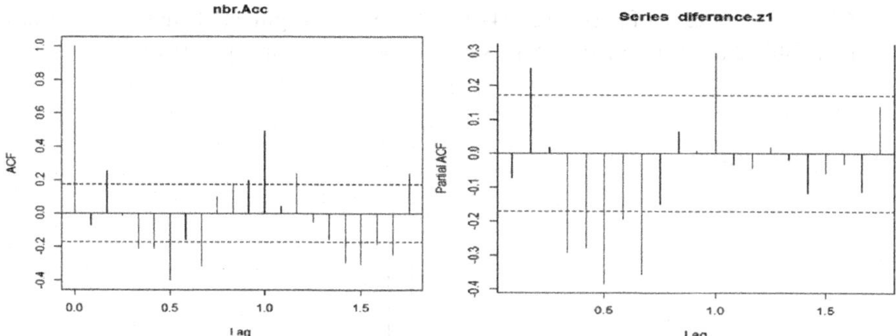

Fig. 5. ACF and PACF of the first difference of the number of accidents.

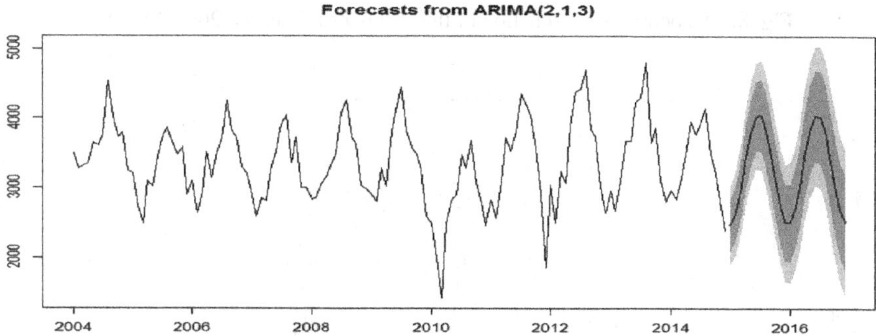

Fig. 6. Forecast graph for monthly traffic accident data ARIMA (2.1.3).

3.2 After Austerity Economic Policies

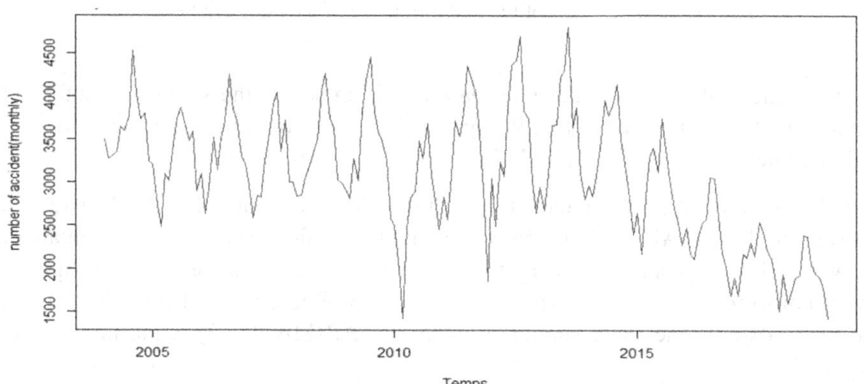

Fig. 7. Time series plot for monthly traffic accident data NCPRS (2004–2018).

ACF shows in Fig. 8 of period (2004–2018) and The Augmented Dickey-Fuller test shown in Table 2 are confirmed that the series is non-stationary (p = 0.9715).

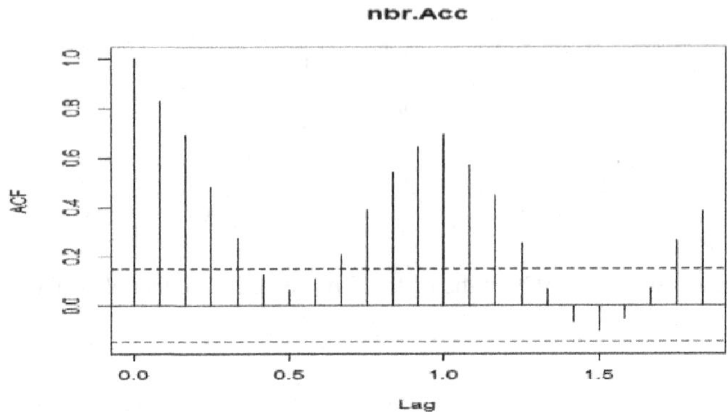

Fig. 8. Autocorrelation function of the number of Crashes (2004–2018).

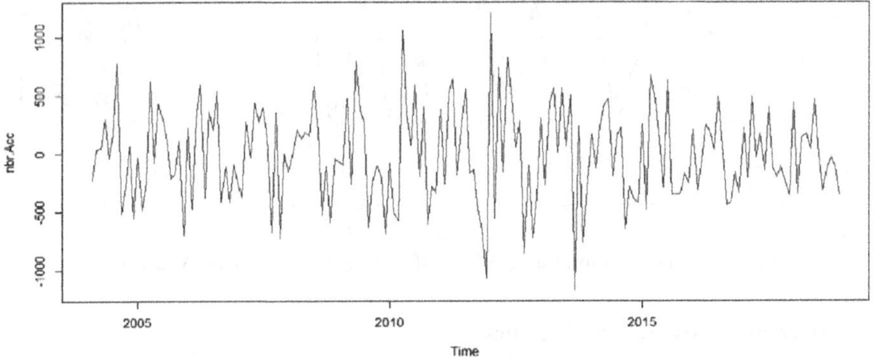

Fig. 9. Time series plots of the first difference of the number of crashes.

We found that the first-order non-seasonal difference of the series was sufficient to make the time series stable Fig. 9, Fig. 10. That also confirmed by the Augmented Dickey-Fuller test (p = < .01) Table 2.

Model Selection. Also, for data between 2004–2018, we found that ARIMA (2.1.3) reported the lowest AIC 2547.63 for the Monthly Traffic Accident. The residuals of ARIMA (2.1.3) were analyzed using Ljung Box test which does not show any sign for having non-zero autocorrelation (p = 0.8181), and ADF test attests that for (p = 0.01). The residuals are practically stationary; therefore ARIMA (2.1.3) is the final model (Fig. 11).

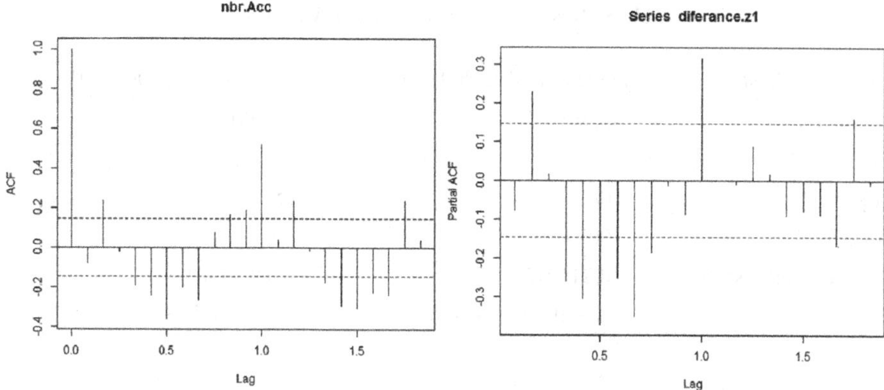

Fig. 10. ACF and PACF of the first difference of the number of crashes (2004–2018).

Table 2. The Augmented Dickey-Fuller test of the number of crashes.

Parameter	Original Time Series	Differenced Time Series
Tau (Observed value)	−0.66941	−7.8135
p-value (one-tailed)	0.9715	0.01
Alpha	0.05	0.05
Lag order	10	10

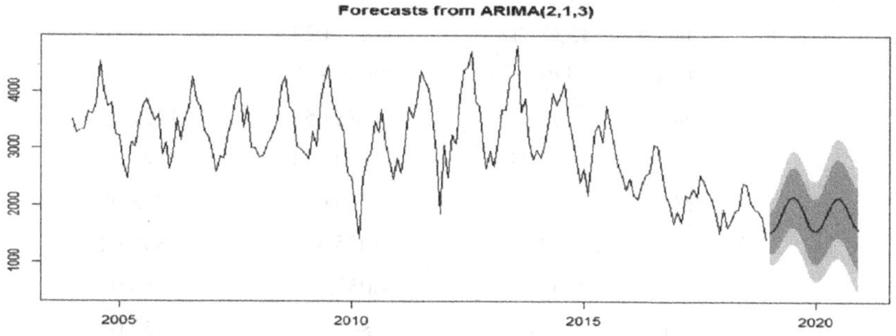

Fig. 11. Forecast graph for monthly traffic crashes data.

3.3 Correlation Test

Using Pearson's product-moment correlation function called "Cor.Test" in R, we found:

Table 3. Result of correlation test of two period

Correlation Test	Forecast of data 2004–2018	Forecast of data 2004–2014
t-statistics	−3.6457	−0.12007
Df	13	9
Alpha	0.05	0.05
p-value	0.002961	0.9071
sample estimates: Cor	−0.7110137	−0.03999004
Formula	y = −1099.7x + 45699	y = −34.645x + 40515

The results in Table 3 indicate that the linear regression before and after 2014 is unequal as we argued that the slope of the regression is significantly negative only before 2014 Fig. 2. In addition, from Table 2, we noticed that the difference between the two periods is very large and it indicates that the period after 2014 is significantly decreasing of ARIMA (2.1.3)

Table 4. Monthly comparisons of forecast accident before and after 2014.

		Forecast of data 2004–2018	Forecast of data 2004–2014	difference forecast
Model ARIMA		(2.1.3)	(2.1.3)	
AIC		1878.69	2547.63	
Forecast of the first year	Jan	1532.918	2473.024	940.106
	Feb	1579.9	2644.835	1064.935
	Mar	1701.387	2988.657	1287.27
	Apr	1863.273	3409.044	1545.771
	May	2020.658	3789.63	1768.972
	Jun	2130.294	4025.336	1895.042
	Jul	2162.468	4051.385	1888.917
	Aug	2109.052	3861.099	1752.047
	Oct	1985.529	3507.609	1522.08
	Sep	1826.527	3088.992	1262.465
	Nov	1676.106	2721.116	1045.01
	Dec	1575.561	2505.512	929.951
sum		22163.673	39066.239	16902.566

(*continued*)

Table 4. (*continued*)

		Forecast of data 2004–2018	Forecast of data 2004–2014	difference forecast
Forecast of second year	Jan	1552.084	2501.385	949.301
	Feb	1611.417	2709.349	1097.932
	Mar	1736.472	3071.405	1334.933
	Apr	1892.243	3487.114	1594.871
	May	2035.601	3841.457	1805.856
	Jun	2127.23	4036.664	1909.434
	Jul	2142.408	4019.183	1876.775
	Aug	2077.669	3794.375	1716.706
	Sep	1951.562	3424.882	1473.32
	Oct	1799.341	3013.175	1213.834
	Nov	1663.117	2673.137	1010.02
	Dec	1580.209	2498.562	918.353
sum		22169.353	39070.688	16901.335

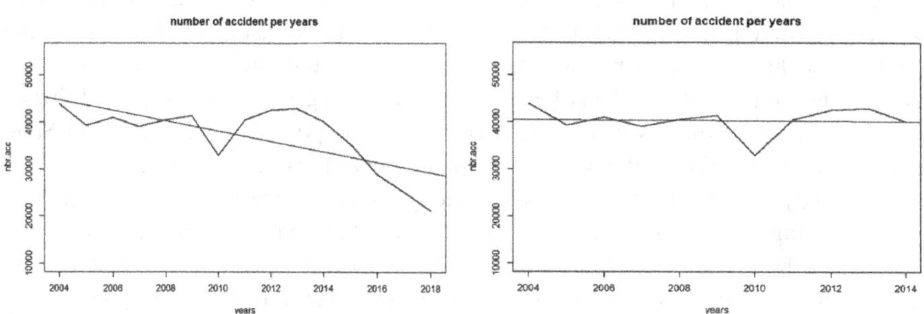

Fig. 12. Represent of linear regression of two periods

4 Discussion

The goal of improving road safety is surely to have almost unanimous support. Most likely, it is possible to stop death and injury on the roads, we must do it. Nevertheless, how strict action should we chose? society requires transport. The choices of excluding it or set a speed limit near zero are discounted. If the com-munity is believed to need an efficient transportation system that is as safe as possible that is as secure as possible, the policy is set in the domain of exchanging conflicting goals and making concessions between them [24]. The significant mission that the government face is the necessity to place the country on a path where the economic policy growth is in line with better conditions for road safety.

Furthermore, always economic policies have a significant impact on the behavior of societies. Bougueroua and Carinis 2016, proved that the economic growth of a country can be linked with a declination of road safety performance so that it can involve a greater number of fatalities and injuries. For the specific instance of Algeria, it also implies that this country has not already achieved the edge at which road accident could decline with a greater economic improvement [4]. Moreover, since 2014, the state of Algeria has implemented austerity policies due to its low oil revenues, such as stopping the import of cars, raising the price of gasoline, building cars locally and doubling their price.

In this study, we examined the effect of these austerity policies on roads safety considering the data of traffic accidents as the main factor, we used ARIMA model before and after years of austerity policies 2014 and regression linear simple to better understanding the difference between two periods.

We analyzed the total number of traffic accidents in Algerian Fig. 1, Figure 7. All of these subset's data show non-stationary behavior which was confirmed using ACF and ADF test Fig. 3, Figure 8, Table 1, Table 2. Then this subset data became stationary after one differencing Fig. 4, Figure 8. We used Box- Jenkins, and regression linear simple on the data, and the implications of these results show that road accident is decreasing Fig. 12, Table 4. The ARIMA model with the smallest AIC was chosen as the best model. Moreover, Ljung Box statistics were also used to evaluate the quality of the model ARIMA (2. 1.3) emerged as the best model for Algerian traffic accident data.

In addition, the results clearly indicate that there are great paradoxes before and after year 2014 although the prediction model has not changed ARIMA (2.1.3) Table 3, to the fact that there is a significant difference in the number of accidents Table 4. As the results show that, the number of accidents was fixed around the average before 2014, but then the number of accidents has become decreasing with time in period 2014–2018 Fig. 12, this indicates that the austerity economic policies of the Algerian State contributed significantly to the decrease in the number of traffic accidents.

This study adds to the road safety knowledge package and presents a forecasting approach using many human, environmental and vehicle factors. The results of this study would be helpful to all partners, road users, road designers, road builders, law enforcement, organizations and policymakers in that they are in a better position to control a variety of factors that affect road safety. It would be valuable in creating economic policies that can avert and diminish the number of accidents.

One limitation of this study is that only the accumulated monthly census data from one country (Algeria) was used in analysis and forecast, generalizing the prediction made with the approach to the whole world is not advisable.

The future research goals in this field should compare the forecast performances among other developed modeling systems, for example, artificial neural network. Additionally, it would be helpful to include covering the study to all other developing countries; examining the influence of other road accident con-tributing indications such as use of smart phone while driving, influence of sleepiness and factors of demographic

5 Conclusion

Our results indicate that the austerity economic policies implemented by the Algerian government have greatly reduced the number of traffic accidents. This reduction is clearly evident in the period before and after 2014, as we observe a shift in the trend of the number of accidents from being stable every year to a significant decrease. Where the general model that represents the accident number is ARIMA (2, 1, 3).

References

1. WHO: Global status report on road safety 2018. World Health Organization (2018)
2. WHO: Global Status Report on Road Safety 2015. World Health Organization (2015)
3. NCPRS: Analytical Study on Road Accidents in Algeria. National Center of Prevention and Road Safety (NCPRS), Algiers. National Center of Prevention and Road Safety (NCPRS) (2014)
4. Bougueroua, M., Carnis, L.: Economic development, mobility and traffic accidents in Algeria. Accid. Anal. Prev. **92**, 168–174 (2016). https://doi.org/10.1016/j.aap.2016.03.016
5. Haddon, W., Jr.: Advances in the epidemiology of injuries as a basis for public policy. Pub. Health Rep. **95**, 411 (1980)
6. Goniewicz, K., Goniewicz, M., Pawłowski, W., Fiedor, P.: Road accident rates: strategies and programmes for improving road traffic safety. Eur. J. Trauma Emerg. Surg. **42**(4), 433–438 (2015). https://doi.org/10.1007/s00068-015-0544-6
7. Haque, M.O., Haque, T.H.: Evaluating the effects of the road safety system approach in Brunei. Transp. Res. Part Policy Pract. **118**, 594–607 (2018)
8. Bishai, D., Quresh, A., James, P., Ghaffar, A.: National road casualties and economic development. Health Econ. **15**, 65–81 (2006)
9. Brüde, U., Elvik, R.: The turning point in the number of traffic fatalities: two hypotheses about changes in underlying trends. Accid. Anal. Prev. **74**, 60–68 (2015)
10. Iwata, K.: The relationship between traffic accidents and economic growth in China. Econ. Bull. **30**, 3306–3314 (2010)
11. Kopits, E., Cropper, M.: Traffic fatalities and economic growth. Accid. Anal. Prev. **37**, 169–178 (2005). https://doi.org/10.1016/j.aap.2004.04.006
12. Law, T.H., Noland, R.B., Evans, A.W.: The sources of the Kuznets relationship between road fatalities and economic growth. J. Transp. Geogr. **19**, 355–365 (2011)
13. Antoniou, C., Yannis, G.: State-space based analysis and forecasting of macroscopic road safety trends in Greece. Accid. Anal. Prev. **60**, 268–276 (2013)
14. Bliss, J.P., Acton, S.A.: Alarm mistrust in automobiles: how collision alarm reliability affects driving. Appl. Ergon. **34**, 499–509 (2003)
15. Eusofe, Z., Evdorides, H.: Assessment of road safety management at institutional level in Malaysia: a case study. IATSS Res. **41**, 172–181 (2017)
16. García-ferrer, A., Juan, A.D., Poncela, P.: The relationship between road traffic accidents and real economic activity in Spain: common cycles and health issues. Health Econ. **16**, 603–626 (2007). https://doi.org/10.1002/hec.1186
17. Van Den Bossche, F., Wets, G., Brijs, T.: A regression model with ARIMA errors to investigate the frequency and severity of road traffic accidents (2004)
18. Wagenaar, A.C.: Effects of macroeconomic conditions on the incidence of motor vehicle accidents. Accid. Anal. Prev. **16**, 191–205 (1984)
19. Box, G.E., Jenkins, G.M.: Time series analysis: Forecasting and control San Francisco. Calif Holden-Day (1976)

20. Dickey, D.A., Fuller, W.A.: Likelihood ratio statistics for autoregressive time series with a unit root. Econometrica **49**, 1057–1072 (1981). https://doi.org/10.2307/1912517
21. Akaike, H.: Maximum likelihood identification of Gaussian autoregressive moving average models. Biometrika **60**, 255–265 (1973)
22. Ljung, G.M., Box, G.E.P.: On a measure of lack of fit in time series models. Biometrika **65**, 297–303 (1978). https://doi.org/10.1093/biomet/65.2.297
23. Ihueze, C.C., Onwurah, U.O.: Road traffic accidents prediction modelling: an analysis of Anambra State. Nigeria. Accid. Anal. Prev. **112**, 21–29 (2018)
24. Elvik, R.: How to trade safety against cost, time and other impacts of road safety measures. Accid. Anal. Prev. **127**, 150–155 (2019)

Metaheuristics and Swarm Intelligence

A Survey on Using Evolutionary Approaches-Based High-Utility Itemsets Mining

Abderrahim Boukhalat[1,2(✉)], KamelEddine Heraguemi[1], Mouhamed Benouis[1], Samir Akhrouf[1], and Brahim Bouderah[1]

[1] University of M'Sila, M'Sila, Algeria
{Abderrahim.Boukhalat,KamelEddine.Heraguemi,Mouhamed.Benouis, Samir.Akhrouf,BrahimBouderah}@univ-msila.dz
[2] LIM Laboratory, University of Souk Ahras, Souk Ahras, Algeria

Abstract. Frequently item-sets mining, also known as FIM, is a data mining technique used to extract useful knowledge from datasets. FIM is plagued by a number of issues, including high storage charges, a huge time and memory consumption. Classical FIM algorithms suffer with the great number of generated itemsets which contains useless items. And presupposes that all itemsets have the same importance. To deal with these limitations, high-utility itemsets (HUI) is proposed, which are as subset of FIM with the consideration of Utility or profit measure. In the last decade, evolutionary approaches become a trend to solve HUIs mining problem (EA). This paper explores the use of evolutionary techniques in HUIs mining. Moreover, we present an evolutionary techniques-based HUIs mining classification including single objective, multi-objective and Hybrid optimization techniques. This article provides a comparative examination of methodologies and discusses theoretical features of a wide variety of algorithms that are inspired by nature.

Keywords: HUIs mining · Bio-inspired algorithms · Evolutionary approaches

1 Introduction

The volume of data is always increasing day after day, where they can obtain information in commercial transactions, scientific reports, images and so forth. As a result, we want a solution to regains the content of clear data and quickly generating results, perspectives, or statistical summaries for wise decision. The result of mining is grouped in general into association rules, classification, clustering, and high-utility itemsets, Frequent item set mining (FIM) has been studied for more than 25 years, it depends on the native approach that is not a very good approach, for example scan a data base with some algorithm to count the frequency of each possible item set giving by the user A minimal support threshold when its level of confidence is greater than the user-defined lowest level of confidence Agrawal and Srikant (1994) [1, 2] employed the Apriori approach to mine association rules (ARs), which takes a very long time to retrieve frequently itemsets. Evolutionary computing (EC) methods have been adopted to mining ARs that

H. Drias et al. (Eds.): AID 2022, CCIS 1852, pp. 43–57, 2023.
https://doi.org/10.1007/978-981-99-4484-2_4

meet the limits of need in terms of runtime and a large number of potential itemsets. In day-to-day life user are interested to sell the itemset which gives more profit. FIM find the large amount of frequent itemset but it does not consider the quantity and number of items purchased. It also loses the useful information of profit gaining itemset having less selling frequency. Hence, frequent itemset mining cannot satisfy the demand of user who wants to search the profit gaining itemset. The high utility itemset mining (HUIM) strategy has been presented as a solution to circumvent these restrictions. This helps to optimize the company plan by taking into account both the amount of earnings and the total quantity of things bought. In HUIM there is no need to set threshold value. If the amount of a frequent itemsets is higher or equal for k, then that set is considered to have high utility; else, the is thought to have a lower utility. For example, the high utility items in basket analysis problem means make lot of money, it could be time in another domain. Another example if we have caviar and an expansive product are the high utility item set that gives a high profit, but people don't buy it so often. With high utility itemsets mining we can find the patterns that generate high profit that may be are not so frequent. Any item is considered high-utility if its utility exceeds the minimal threshold based mostly on user's profitability or price decisions. Chan et al. [3] initially suggested HUIs using several methods. Utilizing two values, Yao et al. [10] discover all HUIs. Internal utility is item quantity, while outward utility represents item revenue. Liu et al. [11] introduced a two-phase transactional weighted utility (TWU) concept using TWDCP to mine HUIs. Guo-Cheng Lan and Tseng [4] utilize pruning with index-projection for identify HUIs.Tseng et al. suggested UP-Growth with UP tree for detect HUIs. In 2012, Liu and Qu [5] proposed a list-based HUI-Miner without candidate generation. To address the issue of spending more computation time to find an item from big data set in traditional HUIs mining algorithms, this problem can be solved by evolutionary computation which decrease the mining process time such as genetic algorithms which provide the optimum solution for NP-hard and nonlinear issues.

Recent articles only covered a tiny portion of an evolutionary techniques for HUI methods; nonetheless, various new research have already been released in recent times. As a result, one of our goals was to construct, from various articles that we had gathered, an exhaustive assessment of the developing work on algorithms applied to the HUI process. The following are some of the ways in which our study is different from other state-of-the-art research focus on FIM: In the first place, we will discuss HUI mining strategies that are based on evolutionary optimization taxonomies. Second, a current theoretical and in-depth study of methodologies that have been considered to be state-of-the-art. Thirdly, the article presents a comparison of the characteristics and features of the many state-of-the-art methods that are now accessible. The following are some of the most important contributions made by this article:

1. This paper provides a description of the many ways of mining HUIs using evolutionary strategies.
2. A HUI mining classification that is based on evolutionary methods is presented in this research since the year of 2016.

3. This study also classifies HUI processing into Swarm intelligence-based approaches, GA-based approaches, Multi-Objective, and Hybrid methods.

The remainder of the paper is structured in the following manner: Background of high utility itemsets (HUIs) mining, definitions, attributes, and a review of Techniques based on evolutionary computation for of high-utility itemsets are included in Sect. 3 of this paper. Discussion about HUI's multiple mining techniques can be found in Sect. 4. And finally, a conclusion and some recommendations for future work.

2 Background of High Utility Itemsets (HUIs) Mining

This section offers preliminary information, terminology, and general ideas about the extraction of utility itemsets. Defines the issue solutions associated with HUI processing as well. Let $I = \{I_1, I_2, \ldots, I_M\}$ be just a collection of items that is finite. Then, set $X \subseteq I$ is a set of items, and an itemset with k items is a k-itemset. Suppose $D = \{T1, T2, \ldots, TN\}$ is a transaction database. Each transaction $Ti \in D$, with unique identifier tid, is a subset of I. As illustrated in Table 1, the quantitative dataset D will be utilized as a working example. Table 2 displays the income amount or outward usefulness of each item [6].

Definition 1. "The Utility of an Item": The product of the frequency and revenue of an item in a transaction can be described as the utility of that item in that transaction. In other words, U(Ii) = F (Ii, Tid) P(Ii) [6]. *Example*: utility for item 'g' in transaction T2 is $2 \times 8 = 16$, and for item'd' in T4 is $3 \times 1 = 3$.

Definition 2. "The utility of the set S": For example, the utility of item-sets d and f in transaction T4 is equal to $31 + 26$, which equals 57 [6].

Table 1. Transactional Dataset D

Tid	Transaction	TU
T_1	(c:3), (e:2), (h:5)	31
T_2	(a:1), (c:3), (e:2), (g:2)	37
T_3	(a:2), (d:2), (h:2)	18
T_4	(a:1), (b:2), (d:3), (e:2), (f:2)	28
T_5	(b:1), (c:3), (d:2), (e:2), (h:1)	23
T_6	(b:1), (e:2), (f:3), (g:2)	40

Table 2. Income of each Items

a	b	c	d	e	f	g	h
5	2	4	1	2	6	8	3

Definition 3. "Transaction Utility": A transaction's utility is stated as the total of all its elements' utility values is known as TU (T_{id}). For example, TU(T3) equals U(a) + U(d) + U(h) i.e. TU(T3) = 18 for transaction T3 [6].

Definition 4. "Transaction Weighted Utility (TWU)" [6]: The transaction weighted utility, or TWU, is the total of the transaction values for all the transactions that include the itemset S. For illustration, TWU (d, h) = 18 + 23 = 41

Definition 5. "Utility of the database": The total of all the transaction utilities is the measure used to define the utility of the collection. For example, U(D) = TU(T1) + TU(T2) + TU(T3) + TU(T4) + TU(T5) + TU(T6) = 177 [6].

Property: "TWU Pruning": If such TWU of a data items S is lower than the minimum utility, then none of the itemset's supersets are considered to be HUIs. Transaction Weighted Utility is used by HUIM methods in order to fulfill the requirements of the anti-monotonic feature.

Definition 6. "High utility Itemset (HUI)": An itemset X in a dataset D is considered to be a high-utility item (HUI) if and only if its utility is greater than or equal to the minimum utility count [6], which is calculated as follows:

$$\mathrm{HU\,I} \leftarrow \{X|U(X) \geq TD \times \delta\}$$

For example, the utility of itemsets {b} and {a,b} is, respectively as U({b}) = 8 and U({a,b}) = 9. Therefore, {b} is a HUI since U({b}) = 8 ≥ 4

3 Techniques Based on Evolutionary Computation for of High-Utility Item Sets

In order to use the complete HUIM techniques to detect HUIs inside a huge search area, the output has to be in the exponentially problem. To find a solution to this problem The use of computational has been suggested as a method for finding the best solution, which is based on the natural evolutionary process. In order to solve the NP-hard problem, evolutionary computing, which is modeled after the process of biological evolution, was developed. In the field of privacy-preserving data mining, a great number of techniques have been presented [7–10] to conceal sensitive data itemsets. PPUM is an extension of PPDM that allows for the usage of utilities and the modification of item quantities. Multiple solution methods are used in order to conceal the sensitive data contained inside the PPUM. The use of genetic algorithms as a movable approach to disguise sensitive HUIs was common for a while. The Genetic Algorithm (GA) is still a heuristic approach that utilizes natural behavior to tackle nonlinear and NP-hard problems. GAs may offer improvement in a variety of areas, including robotics, architecture, and optimization models. Particle Swarm Optimization (PSO) [11] is inspired by the social flock of organisms, and every particle has its own unique set of speeds that define it. PSO takes into account two values best and global best in order to determine which particle in the neighborhood is the best. It provides faster optimal solutions as Ga approaches if we have a low number of populations. PSO is used in many field-like routings problems, clustering, and other domains. The multi-Objectif optimization (MOE) is address optimization issues [12].and have various applications in clustering, classification, association rules, pattern recommendation. MOE is utilized and proposed in neural network and portfolio optimization [13, 14].Ant colony optimizer, also known as ACO, is an exceptionally effective method for finding nearly optimum solutions. This method is used in situations in which the ant community chooses similar pathways, which then opens the door to other potential options. The method known as dolphin sound waves (DE) is a technique in which the method for finding feed by dolphins is using an echolocation mechanism and the evaluation measures the distance of foods.

3.1 Techniques Based on Genetic Algorithm Evolution

HUIM Approach Based on the Improved Genetic Algorithm (HUIM-IGA): The fact that typical High Usefulness Itemset Mining (HUIM) methods do not take into account the possibility that the utility of sets may change over the course of time is a significant shortcoming of these algorithms. Therefore, conventional HUIM algorithms are unable to discover itemsets who may not have a high utility while taking into consideration the whole dataset, but that do have a high value during certain time periods. This issue is brought about as a consequence of the optimization problem. In order to discover the best solutions, numerous different EC-based strategies have been developed. In order to efficiently mine HUIs, Zhang et al. [15] recommended using a HUIM technique that was based on an enhanced evolutionary algorithm (HUIM-IGA). The authors outlined four primary strategies: (1) A strategy for maintaining population variety is provided in order to broaden the search area and lower the number of undiscovered HUIs. Because of this purpose, the HUIMIGA DM S (HUIM-IGA without the population diversity maintenance strategy) has been designed. Both methods were shown to have equal early-stage resolution times, although HU IMAGA was found to be faster. HUP-IGADM Scan mine HUIs significantly more slowly than HUGA, which is why it is recommended. The proposed technique outperforms three other algorithms that are not EC-based: IHUP, UP-Hist Growth and UP-Growth. It also beats the most recent iteration of the EC-based HUIM techniques, which are considered to be state-of-the-art. Bio-HUIF-PSO, Bio-HUIF-GA.

HUI Mining Using Genetic Algorithm (GAHUIM): To effectively mine HUIs, a number of GA-based algorithms are presented. There are still many opportunities to massively increase memory consumption and speed up the mining process. Javangula [16] proposed a method which he referred to as GAHUIM (HUI mining using genetic methods). HUIs mining problem necessitated the employment of a non-binary variation of the evolutionary computation in the proposed solution since it put certain limits on the process. Both the crossover and selecting procedures, which are part of the genetic method, have been improved so that they can work more efficiently in the mining problem. HUIM issue, fitness selection serves two purposes, which are as follows: (1) the HUISelect option, and (2) the MatSelect option. HU ISelect is responsible for copying chromosomes that represent HUIs to the output, whereas MatSelect is in charge of selecting chromosomes that have high chances of mating. The formation of children requires the combination of two chromosomes. During the phase known as "breeding," the chromosomes from the major part of the candidate solution are extracted one at a time and the children are used in the process. Starting from a small sample of the population, the algorithm searches through the data to locate appropriate collections of things. The results of the experiments show that it outperforms existing algorithms in terms of operational speed and memory requirement.

3.2 Swarm Intelligence-Based Algorithms

High-Utility Itemsets Mining by Ant Colony System (HUIM-ACS): PSO and genetic programming (GA) do not provide a useful solution as ACOs do. They can provide as few nonsensical responses as possible. When using a well-defined ACO approach, the end outcome is always satisfactory. An ant colony system is given as HUIs mining by an ant colony system. It is impossible to ensure that the answer given by an EC technique will be the global optimal solution in general. Complete optimal solutions into route graphs, on either hand, are created using the HUIM-ACS approach. In the absence of a candidate edge from the starting point, it ensures that all HUIs are retrieved. Furthermore, HUIM-ACS doesn't really calculate it in order to prevent repeating the same feasible answer and wasting computer resources. Wu et al. [17] go on to elaborate on this study in some detail. Following studies of the natural quest for food carried out by wild colonies, we developed the larger-than-life Ant System (ACS). In the proposed HUIM-ACS technique, the TWU model is used to build an ant routing network to uncover 1-HTWUIs. The route graph is then reduced in size by deleting components that are no longer required. A route graph is constructed before any ants begin their missions. Each node in the graph represents a group of things that may be classified as HUI or not by the user. Using heuristics, ants are guided to HUIs quickly. The ant population is effectively regulated by it. HUIM-ACS only calculated an item's TWU the first time an ant arrived at the appropriate node. The following three eventualities are possible when it comes to the TWU of the items: First, there is no TWU information for the matched commodities. Secondly, the process stores all TWUs related to the items in question. TWUs for the paired items exist to varying degrees throughout the procedure. HUPEumu-GRAM, HUIM-BPSO and EFIM are evolutionary and nonrevolutionary methods, respectively, that perform better in terms of runtime, number of identified HUIs, and fast convergence from huge datasets than the suggested approach. There is a verification method that can be used to verify whether all of the HUIs in the data have been discovered by ACS operators using the suggested approach. Nevertheless, the best global solutions may be found by using an effective tree structure to map the whole solution space.

HUIM Based on Artificial Bee Colony (HUIM-ABC): An artificial bee colony-based approach dubbed HUIM was developed by Song and Huang (2018) in order to more effectively mine HUIs (HUIM-ABC). For the proposed method, an artificial bee colony (ABC) based on the foraging patterns of bees was used as a starting point. The ABC method has three distinguishing traits. Decentralization of authority and self-management. To the best of our knowledge, this is the first time the ABC method has been used to mine HUIs. The suggested HUIM-ABC method consists of the following three stages:

Consider the ABC approach's perspective on the matter. Bitmap patterns are used to represent the information and save search space. Each of the three bee kinds in the ABC algorithm has a specific role to play. The number of bees in use is proportional to the quantity of nectar sources. Each worker bee builds on the prior answer in order to come up with something new. Observers are informed of the quality of the answer once all of the bees have finished their search. Each bee selects a nectar source based on the fitness value calculated from the bees deployed. Scout bees constantly search for nectar sources, utilizing the direct nectar source generation (DNSG) strategy in order to manufacture more HUIs. To decrease the search area, direct utility computation and bit-wise operations are employed. The experimental experiments demonstrated that the proposed HUIM-ABC approach outperforms the methods HUPEu-GRAM, HUPE-BPSOsig, and HUPE-BPSO.

Boolean-Based Modified Grey Wolf Optimization (BGWO): The standard grey wolf optimizer (GWO) was updated by Pazhaniraja and Kumar [18] into a Boolean-based BGWO method for mining HUIs from big datasets. A bio-inspired, customized optimization is proposed to solve the HUIM issue. It's been tweaked to work with Boolean operators to overcome HUIM problems. This is one of the most recent and widely used methods for solving the HUIM: the grey wolf optimization approach. Because of its ease of use in searching over the solution space with fewer parameters and high accuracy, the grey wolf optimization was chosen over other evolutionary computations already in use (Wang and Li 2019). Modifying continuous GWO to use non-standard Boolean operators, which clearly defines each GWO operator, requires the use of Boolean operators. The Grey Wolf optimization has been upgraded to solve HUI issues with the binary representation of solution space. In order to preserve the uniqueness of the search method, the GWO flow has been preserved while the operators have been modified to accommodate Boolean values. Boundary checks ensure that all searches are carried out inside the GWO's boundaries, unlike traditional GWO. HUPEUMU-GARM, HUPEUMU-BPSO, UP-Growth, Bio-HUIF GA, Bio-HUIF PSO, and Bio-HUIF BA are compared with the proposed technique utilizing performance metrics including convergence, runtime, and the number of HUIs that have been detected in comparison to other algorithms. Experimental evaluation shows that the proposed model is relevant when comparing results from different approaches currently in use.

Meta-Heuristic Algorithm Based on Dolphin Echolocation Optimization (HUIM-DEO): A meta-heuristic approach that works based on the genetic algorithm and the Dolphin echolocation optimizer was suggested by Pazhaniraja and Sountharrajan [19]. This algorithm was created for use in HUI mining (DEO). The purpose of these evolutionary computing (EC) approaches on the DEO is to compare well to the methods that are based on the GA in terms of the number of parameters that must be specified. Since the traditional DEO process has been identified to address this ongoing difficulty, an effective strategy that is built on the DEO approach and is called the high-utility itemset mining-DEO was proposed. The proposed DEO that is being created will find that 1-HTWUIs are the dolphin echoes search frequency that is founded on the concept that is often referred to as the TWU, and this may result in a reduction in the combinational complexity of the evaluation process. The proposed method may be broken down into two steps that are as follows: (1) During the first phase, it finds all of the search space that is even remotely possible. (2) The next stage investigates potential improvements to the situation. It has been determined, using the TWU model and the HUIM-DEO suggestion, that 1-HTWUIs are the appropriate search size for dolphin echoes. The DEO method that was presented is effective and has superior performance to the state-of-the-art approaches such as greedy search, GA, HUPEUMU-GARM, BIO-HUIF-GA, and HUIM-BPSO.

Ant Colony Approach for High Utility Infrequent Itemsets Mining (ACHUIIM): Identification of item sets whose frequency of appearance goes to below the established cut-off point is known as "infrequent itemset mining". Rare though they may be, these sets of items may bring in a significant amount of profit. Because of this, there is a need to keep an eye on such uncommon, profitable things from a business standpoint. That's why the term "high utility infrequent itemset mining "has been coined. Rare objects are now the focus of increased study by researchers. The anti-ant colony algorithm ACHUIIM [20] is expected to be developed in 2020 to identify HUIIs. On four real-world datasets, the proposed method was tested on four distinct ant populations and varying minimal utility and threshold ratios. According to this algorithm, the following is how it works: There are two steps involved in determining the initial utility value and TWU for each item: The ant traversal mechanism necessitates a change to these parameters. As the ant colony expands, a single route is used by all ants at the same time, regardless of size. TWU's downward closure attribute is employed in a further pruning strategy to reduce the search space by alphabetical order of values. In the experimental findings, a comparison of the suggested method's efficiency on the chess and food datasets is made. All real-time datasets are able to run the suggested approach faster than the current high utility rare item technique.

High-Utility Itemset Mining for Artificial Fish Swarm (HUIM-AF): Heuristic methods such as the artificial fish swarm methodology have a broad variety of uses. Artificial fish keep just a record of their current l0ocation. Similar to the HUI mining issue, the results aren't usually concentrated in a few severe regions. According to Song et al. [21], a HUIM method that follows the AFSA paradigm and explicitly models the issue with AFs having three different behaviors is proposed. Fish engage in swarming behavior to defend themselves from predators while avoiding overburdened areas. A fish's predilection towards a particular area where food is plentiful is known as "predation." Follow is a kind of behavior in which a fish finds a food source as well as other fish pursue it. A position vector depicts the AF's current location. The 1-HTWUIs in PV's vector representation are arranged in decreasing order. According to the experiment findings, the suggested HUIMAF method is faster and finds more HUIs than the existing top state-of-the-art algorithms, HUPEU MU-GARM and HUIM-BPSOsig.

Improved Binary Particle Swarm Optimization for High Utility Itemsets Mining (HUIM IBPSO): An evolutionary computing (EC)-based approach to HUIM has recently been proposed, with promising results in the mining of HUIs. There have been several approaches to uncovering HUIs, such as the EC-based methods, but they tend to only expose certain HUIs in a short period of time, or to uncover all of the HUIs takes time. In 2022, Wei Fang et al. [22] developed an improved HUIM-IBPSO (improved binary particle swarm optimization for HUIM) using new adjustment approaches to tackle these limitations. In order to keep the same HUIs throughout the evolution phase, a technique is provided in HUIM-IBPSO to alter the particle movement. HUIM-IBPSO uses a local exploration strategy to better use HUIs that are often used and to enhance search capabilities. HUIM-IBPSO employs a population restart strategy meant to prevent premature convergence before the discovery of any HUIs. For effective HUI mining, HUIM-IBPSO provides particle modification and fitness value hashing techniques. Researchers found that the HUIM-IBPSO approach beat not only current EC-based techniques but also three specific HUIM algorithms in terms of defining HUIs, convergence speed, and time required to mine the necessary HUIs. The proposed approach outperformed all three of these EC-based methods.

3.3 Multi-objective Computational Methods

Multi-objective Technique Based on Closed Itemset Properties (CP-MOEA): When Cao et al. [23] proposed a closed itemset property-based multi-objective technique (CP-MOEA) in 2019, they compared it to the design utilized in NSGA-II to mine FHUIs. Individuals are represented using binary encoding according to the proposed method. For each single itemset, the bit is either set to 1 or 0 depending on whether the item appears. USC and USA are two update strategies that are designed to increase the mining process's efficiency by using closed and estimation itemsets, respectively. The experimental findings on six actual datasets indicated that the proposed method CPMOEA is more successful than the state-of-the-art multi-objective optimization algorithms FHUI-MOEA. These findings were obtained by comparing the two algorithms. On the benchmark datasets, it has been found that CP-MOEA works better than its variants USA and USC, both of which use just one updating technique. The benchmark datasets are used to evaluate the performance of machine learning algorithms.

Multi-objective Optimization Evolutionary Algorithm to Resolve the Exhaustive Sparsity MOPs (SparseEA): Over the past two decades, members of the evolutionary computing community have carried out a significant amount of research on a broad variety of multi-objective optimization issues (MOPs). The vast majority of currently available evolutionary computation, on the other hand, struggles when confronted with MOPs whose Pareto efficient optimum solutions are sparse, and this is especially true when the percentage of decision variables is increased. Large-scale sparse MOPs are used for a variety of applications, including selecting features, which seeks to find a small segment of candidate attributes from a huge number of selected features, and stepping mainly of neural networks with sparse links in order to minimize fitting problems. Both of these applications seek to find a small set of attributes from among a large number of candidate features. 2019 saw the introduction of sparseEA by Tian et al. [24],which is a multi-objective optimization evolutionary algorithm (MOEA) for resolving comprehensive sparsity MOPs. The structure that NSGA-II was based on was used to construct the suggested method. In order to enhance the practicality of the SparseEA, the four sparse MOPs that are listed below have been included: (2) Pattern recognition (3) the identification of critical nodes neural network training. The feature selection helps to improve classification performance while simultaneously reducing the total number of features. It is a multi-objective process that has been shown to be useful by a number of

MOEAs. The proposed strategy outperforms seven previous methods in resolving sparse MOPs, according to results from the testing process and four application scenarios. In terms of hypervolume, test cases, fast convergence, diversity, complexity, and errors for sparseMOPs, NSGA-II, SPEA2, SMS-EMOA, and EAGMOEA/D are the leading techniques. The suggested sparseEA methods exceed these strategies.

Multi-objective Evolutionary Method for HQPM (MOEA-PM): Fang et al. [25] presented an improved multi-objective optimization method for high-utility pattern mining that included three new objectives. The MOEA-PM method may uncover high-utility patterns without needing minimal support, minimal occupation, or minimum utility. NSGA-II has been extended in the planned work. As a multi-objective optimal solution for high-utility pattern mining (HUPM), the authors contend that this is the first study to combine three measures: support, occupancy, and utility value. In order to ensure that the community is evenly distributed over the feasible optimal solution, two kinds of population initiation processes are designed. To speed up the convergence of the computation, an auxiliary tool is constructed, taking the model's properties into consideration. The results of experiments conducted on datasets taken from the real world demonstrate that the proposed three-objective problem model combined with the MOEA-PM algorithm has the potential to find patterns in transaction datasets that are both highly useful and occur frequently, while still maintaining a level of comprehensiveness that is satisfactory. MOEA-PM exceeds state-of-the-art MOEA-based HQPM algorithms in terms of both the efficiency with which they converge and the quality of the results they produce.

Data Sanitization Model Based on a Multi-objective PSO Algorithm to Mine HUIs in PPDM (MOPSO-Based Data Sanitization Model): In last decades, one of the most significant challenges has been data protection (PPDM), which not only conceals data but also provides information that is necessary for making decisions. This algorithm presents a sanitization technique that takes into consideration, to discover optimal solutions for PPDM, four side effects based on multi-objective PSO and hierarchical clustering methods that have been used. A data sanitization model that is based on a multi-objective PSO (MOPSO) algorithm was recommended by Wu et al. [26] in order to mine HUIs in PPDM. However, since dominance relations are required to be used in order to optimize the transactions for removal, the MOPSO approach cannot be applied directly to a PPDM problem. As a consequence of this, a technique for PPDM sanitization that is based on hierarchical clustering has been developed. During the stage of processing, the items need to be added to the list of private information before the method of data sanitization may take place. During the evolution phase, the particles are reviewed in order to obtain optimal solutions for the subsequent iteration. Both the present single-objective strategy, cpGA2DT, and the multi-objective strategy, NSGA2DT, are outperformed by the suggested method in terms of concealing failure, absent cost, artificial cost, and dataset dissimilarity. By deleting more duplicate information from the database, the strategy that was recommended helps raise the dissimilarity across the datasets.

Multi Objective Evolutionary Approach to Discover the High Expected Utility Patterns Mining (MOEA-HEUPM): The multi-objective evolutionary method to identify the high expected utility patterns mining (MOEA-HEUPM) framework in a restricted time-period from an uncertain dataset was suggested by Ahmed et al. [27] in the year

2020. In order to effectively mine the intriguing high expected utility patterns (HEUPs) in a limited amount of time based on a multi-objective evolutionary framework, they consider utility and uncertainty to be the majority objects. The advantages of the developed model, which are referred to collectively as MOEAHEUPM, allow for the discovery of profitable HEUPs in an uncertain environment without the need for pre-defined threshold values (i.e., minimal utility and minimum uncertainty). In order to demonstrate the MOEA-efficacy, HEUPM's two different encoding approaches were taken into consideration throughout its development. The MOEA-HEUPM model that was created allows for the set of non-dominated HEUPs to be identified in a short amount of time, which facilitates decision-making. Tchebycheff weight-based technique is utilized in conjunction with the utility and uncertainty (multi-objective) ideas in order to locate non-dominated solutions in an efficient manner. Second, in order to produce a diversity of solutions that are highly convergent, we use two different encoding strategies, namely binary encoding and value encoding. This allows us to reach high levels of both variety and convergence. The MOEA/D methodology is used in the recommended method for determining evolution progress. Following the completion of MOEA and repeated D's evolutionary process, the final population is generated and produced. Experiments are then carried out in order to demonstrate the efficiency and usefulness of the proposed model in comparison to the general and conventional U-Apriori and EFIM model in terms of convergence, hypervolume, and the number of motifs that were identified.

3.4 Hybrid Approaches

Bio-Inspired Based High Utility Itemset Mining Framework (Bio-HUIF): A bio-inspired HUIM framework was presented by Song and Huang [28] to identify HUIs, and the authors provided a bio-inspired algorithm-based HUIM framework (Bio-HUIF). This model utilizes a roulette wheel to determine the beginning focus of another population instead of simply choosing HUIs with the highest expected utility in the existing population. Bio-HUIF-PSO, Bio-HUIF-GA, and Bio-HUIF-BA are the three HUIM methods based on Bio-HUIF that have been proposed. Evolutionary Algorithms are all examples of these. A starting point for the next population could be determined based on the usefulness of each newly discovered HUI in comparison to the combined utility of all newly discovered HUI. To begin the process of mining HUIs, the original dataset is first transformed to just a bitmap. The collection contains as many 1-HTWUIs as there are encoding vectors to represent each person in it. As part of the initial dataset scan, the 1-HTWUIs are computed using the TWU model. After that, a bitmap representation is generated by using the PEVC pruning technique. Finally, a comprehensive collection of HUIs is compiled for analysis. The proposed approach beats two previous bio-inspired techniques, HUPEumu-GRAM and HUIM-BPSO, as well as two state-of-the-art HUIM techniques, IHUP, in terms of the runtime, the number of HUIs created, and the velocity at which they converge.

Grid Based Multi-objective Particle Swarm Optimization algorithm (GMPSO): A method called GMPSO [29] was developed by Tsu-Yang Wu et al. that employs a grid-based technique to find the best sanitization candidates in 2019. Two methods are used by the GMPSO to upgrade the finest during the evolutionary phase. To further speed up the evolutionary process, the pre-large idea is used herein to reduce the number of database scans required for each evolutionary stage. Prior to processing, the frequent and pre-large itemsets are gathered and organized into lists called FI (Set of frequent itemsets) and PF (Set of pre-large itemsets). PPDM's evolution method uses two strategies to develop non-dominant solutions during the evolution phase: global best (gbest) and personal best (pbest). Using the concept of pre-large, the process may be accelerated. GMPSO's experimental results indicate that it does a good job of concealing hidden information (fail to hide) but only rarely achieves optimal results in terms of missing or artificial expenditures. Due to the trade-off between side effects as well as the NSGA-II-based approach and cpGA2DT, the GMPSO still has a modest database divergences (Dis) impact. For four adverse effects, GMPSO beats the other two methods and provides greater versatility.

Top Non-Redundant High Utility Association Rule Mining (TNR-HUARM): In 2020, Krishna and Ravi [30] presented top non-redundant HUI mining (TNR-HUARM) approaches employing BDE and ABDE systems. Using a true online retail database, TNR-value-based HUARM's customer segmentation is tested. Binary Differential Evolution and Adaptive Binary Differential Evolution are the most successful non-redundant HUAR miners. These miners are efficient in terms of rule generation, convergence rate, and memory use. The preceding study demonstrates the versatility and strength of BDE. ABDE and BDE-based TNR-HUARM miners were statistically similar in seven major comparisons. The authors also considered using TNR-HUARM to categorize customers based on value. This study's smart allocation and management of shelf space may benefit the retail sector, potentially increasing ROI. This retail business study also analyzes transactional information to evaluate which items may create large amounts of cash if provided together. According to the findings, the BDE-based TNR-HUARM algorithm performed superiorly than the ABDE-based TNR-HUARM algorithm across all seven datasets in terms of its numerical performance. However, it has come to our attention that the use of a t-test does not result in the rejection of the null hypothesis. As a direct consequence of this, statistical equivalence was shown to exist between rule miners that were based on differential evolution and adaptive differential evolution for six out of the seven datasets. When the suggested algorithms were compared against two algorithms that are considered to be state-of-the-art, the results were inconsistent.

4 Discussion

In the preceding part, we examined evolutionary algorithms, including GA, Swarm intelligent algorithms, multi-objective optimization, and hybrid HUI mining techniques.GA-based algorithms produce the next population through different procedures, with each individual representing a solution. Meta-heuristic GA-based approaches employ crossover, mutation, and selection to address challenging optimization issues. These genetic procedures create new generations. They employed fitness to minimize disguising failure, missing costs, and false costs. GA-based techniques have trouble allocating starting chromosomes in later evolution. Obtaining GA parameters is not easy. EC-based on Swarm algorithms have been proposed to effectively mine HUIs. Bio-inspired and population-based techniques identify optimum solutions by updating particle velocity. SI-based algorithms can be simply developed without setting crossover and mutation rates. PPDM's sensitive data is sanitized using a hierarchical MOPSO structure. It cannot be directly used for PPDM since dominance relationships must be used to generate optimal transactions for deletion. The MOPSO framework uses a grid-based algorithm to achieve un-dominated solutions in PPDM by adopting pre-large ideas and updating gbest and pbest values in the evolution process. It reduces failure, missed costs, and fake costs. The HUIMAF-based heuristic technique searches a huge space to identify optimum solutions quickly. SO-based algorithms are faster, find more HUIs, and converge faster than GA-based methods. Some information may be needed to find all HUIs in the dataset. To solve the foregoing restrictions, EC-based ant colony optimization algorithms are suggested, which effectively mine HUIs and ensure the whole set of HUIs in the dataset. However, setting the heuristic function properly is difficult. Previous research focused on frequent or HUIs. They combine support and usefulness. It impacts mining performance. MO EC-based approaches consider support and utility concurrently to mine frequent HUIs without establishing minimum support and utility thresholds. Consider the dataset's closed itemsets to expand this work. Optimizing huge datasets is computationally expensive. An MOEA-based technique is presented to mine HUIs from large-scale sparse MOPs. HUIM's bio-inspired methods enhance optimum diversified solutions. Rather than sustaining ideal levels in the following population. A second HUIM system, based on the Optimal solution, mines HUIs utilizing nectar sources and bitmap architecture. A multi-objective EC-based framework is suggested to mine HEUPs from an unpredictable environment in a short period. An optimization model based on grey wolf behaviors is suggested to mine HUIs with few parameters and great accuracy. An EC method based on BDE and ABDE is presented to mine HUIs from online shopping.

5 Opportunity and Future Directions

Evolutionary approaches-based high-utility itemsets mining is a promising field that includes using evolutionary algorithms to find high-utility itemsets. There are many opportunities and future directions for this field, such as mining high-utility item sets in large datasets, combining multiple evolutionary algorithms, using domain knowledge, dealing with uncertain data, making parallel and distributed evolutionary algorithms, and combining machine learning techniques. With more study and development, this field could help solve complex problems in fields like healthcare, finance, and e-commerce in a more accurate and efficient way. In healthcare, evolutionary approaches can be used to analyze medical data and identify disease patterns, which can assist in disease diagnosis and treatment. In finance, high-utility itemset mining used to analyze financial data and identify trading patterns, which can assist in making investment decisions. In marketing and e-commerce, high-utility itemsets mining utilized to analyze customer data and identify customer behavior patterns, which can assist in developing personalized marketing strategies and improving customer experience.

6 Conclusion

A taxonomy of evolutionary computing for HUI mining was presented in this paper as part of the study. Both a high-level and a more in-depth description of the evolutionary computation-based HUI mining approaches can be found in this article. In this study, we gave a comprehensive review of a range of approaches that may be used to mine high-utility item sets utilizing evolutionary methods. Among the evolutionary techniques that were utilized were GA, SO, multi-objective optimization, and hybrid approaches. Other evolutionary strategies that were used were inspired by nature. The paper also included a discussion on the various HUI mining strategies that are available. In addition, the study provided end-users with insights into the construction of suitable algorithms for mining high-utility item sets using evolutionary computation-based approaches.

References

1. Agrawal, R., Srikant, R.: Fast algorithms for mining association rules. In: Proceedings of 20th International Conference very large data bases, VLDB **1215**, 487–499 (1994)
2. Han, J., Pei, J., Yin, Y.: SIGMOD conference - mining frequent patterns without candidate generation. ACM SIGMOD Rec. **29**(2), 1–12 (2000). https://doi.org/10.1145/335191.335372
3. Chan, R., Yang, Q., Shen, Y.D.: Mining high utility itemsets. In: Third IEEE international Conference on Data Mining, p. 19 (2003)
4. Lin, C.W., Hong, T.P., Wong, J.W., Lan, G.C., Lin, W.Y.: A GA-based approach to hide sensitive high utility itemsets. Sci. World J. 804629 (2014). https://doi.org/10.1155/2014/804629
5. Liu, M., Qu, J.: Mining high utility itemsets without candidate generation. In: Proceedings of the 21st ACM International Conference on Information and Knowledge Management, pp. 55–64 (2012)
6. Fournier-Viger, P., Chun-Wei Lin, J., Truong-Chi, T., Nkambou, R.: A survey of high utility itemset mining. In: Fournier-Viger, P., Lin, J.-W., Nkambou, R., Vo, B., Tseng, V.S. (eds.) High-Utility Pattern Mining. SBD, vol. 51, pp. 1–45. Springer, Cham (2019). https://doi.org/10.1007/978-3-030-04921-8_1
7. Dasseni, E., Verykios, V.S., Elmagarmid, A.K., Bertino, E.: Hiding association rules by using confidence and support. In: Moskowitz, I.S. (ed.) IH 2001. LNCS, vol. 2137, pp. 369–383. Springer, Heidelberg (2001). https://doi.org/10.1007/3-540-45496-9_27
8. Hong, T.-P., Lin, C.-W., Yang, K.-T., Wang, S.-L.: Using TF-IDF to hide sensitive itemsets. Appl. Intell. **38**(4), 502–510 (2013)
9. Atallah, M., Bertino, E., Elmagarmid, A., Ibrahim, M., Verykios, V.: Disclosure limitation of sensitive rules. In: Proceedings 1999 Workshop on Knowledge and Data Engineering Exchange (KDEX'99) (Cat. No. PR00453), pp. 45–52 (1999)
10. Daniel, E.O.L.: Knowledge discovery as a threat to database security. In: Proceedings of the 1st International Conference on Knowledge Discovery and Databases, vol. 107, p. 516 (1991)
11. Poli, R., Kennedy, J., Blackwell, T.: Particle swarm optimization. Swarm Intell. **1**(1), 33–57 (2007)
12. Zhang, X., Tian, Y., Jin, Y.: Approximate non-dominated sorting for evolutionary many-objective optimization. Inf Sci (NY) **369**, 14–33 (2016)
13. Fieldsend, J.E., Singh, S.: Pareto evolutionary neural networks. IEEE Trans. Neural Netw. **16**(2), 338–354 (2005). https://doi.org/10.1109/tnn.2004.841794

14. Ponsich, A., Jaimes, A.L., Coello, C.A.: A survey on multiobjective evolutionary algorithms for the solution of the portfolio optimization problem and other finance and economics applications. IEEE Trans. Evol. Comput. **17**(3), 321–344 (2013). https://doi.org/10.1109/tevc.2012.2196800
15. Zhang, Q., Fang, W., Sun, J., Wang, Q.: Improved genetic algorithm for high-utility itemset mining. IEEE Access **7**, 176799–176813 (2019). https://doi.org/10.1109/access.2019.2958150
16. Javangula, V.: Mining of high utility item sets using genetic algorithm. Turk. J. Comput. Math. Educ. (TURCOMAT) **12**(9), 2437–2448 (2021)
17. Wu, J.M., Zhan, J., Lin, J.C.: An ACO-based approach to mine high-utility itemsets. Knowl. Based Syst. **116**, 102–113 (2017). https://doi.org/10.1016/j.knosys.2016.10.027
18. Pazhaniraja, N., Sountharrajan, S., Sathis Kumar, B.: High utility itemset mining: a Boolean operators-based modified grey wolf optimization algorithm. Soft. Comput. **24**(21), 16691–16704 (2020). https://doi.org/10.1007/s00500-020-05123-z
19. Pazhaniraja, N., Sountharrajan, S.: High utility itemset mining using dolphin echolocation optimization. J. Ambient. Intell. Humaniz. Comput. **12**(8), 8413–8426 (2020). https://doi.org/10.1007/s12652-020-02571-1
20. Arunkumar, M.S., Suresh, P., Gunavathi, C.: High utility infrequent itemset mining using a customized ant colony algorithm. Int. J. Parallel. Prog. **48**(5), 833–849 (2018). https://doi.org/10.1007/s10766-018-0621-7
21. Song, W., Li, J., Huang, C.: Artificial fish swarm algorithm for mining high utility itemsets. In: Advances in Swarm Intelligence, pp. 407–419 (2021)
22. Fang, W., Zhang, Q., Lu, H., Lin, J.C.-W.: High-utility itemsets mining based on binary particle swarm optimization with multiple adjustment strategies. Appl. Soft. Comput. **124**, 109073 (2022). https://doi.org/10.1016/j.asoc.2022.109073
23. Cao, H., Yang, S., Wang, Q., Wang, Q., Zhang, L.: A closed itemset property based multi-objective evolutionary approach for mining frequent and high utility itemsets. In: 2019 IEEE Congress on Evolutionary Computation (CEC), pp. 3356–3363 (2019).https://doi.org/10.1109/CEC.2019.8789985
24. Tian, Y., Zhang, X., Wang, C., Jin, Y.: An evolutionary algorithm for large-scale sparse multiobjective optimization problems. IEEE Trans. Evol. Comput. **24**(2), 380–393 (2020). https://doi.org/10.1109/tevc.2019.2918140
25. Fang, W., Zhang, Q., Sun, J., Wu, X.: Mining high quality patterns using multi-objective evolutionary algorithm. IEEE Trans. Knowl. Data Eng. **34**(8), 3883–3898. https://doi.org/10.1109/tkde.2020.3033519
26. Coello, C.A.C., Lechuga, M.S.: MOPSO: a proposal for multiple objective particle swarm optimization. In: Proceedings of the 2002 Congress on Evolutionary Computation. CEC 2002 (Cat. No. 02TH8600), vol. 2, pp. 1051–1056 (2002)
27. Ahmed, U.L., Jerry, C.-W., Srivastava, G., Yasin, R., Djenouri, Y.: An evolutionary model to mine high expected utility patterns from uncertain databases. IEEE Trans Emerg. Top Comput. Intell. **5**(1), 19–28 (2021). https://doi.org/10.1109/tetci.2020.3000224
28. Song, W., Huang, C.: Mining high utility itemsets using bio-inspired algorithms: a diverse optimal value framework. IEEE Access **6**, 19568–19582 (2018). https://doi.org/10.1109/access.2018.2819162
29. Wu, T.Y., Lin, J.C., Zhang, Y., Chen, C.H.: A grid-based swarm intelligence algorithm for privacy-preserving data mining. Appl. Sci. 9(4), 774 (2019). https://doi.org/10.3390/app9040774
30. Krishna Vadlamani, G.J.R.: Mining top high utility association rules using binary differential evolution. Eng. Appl. Artif. Intell. **96**, 103935-NA (2020). https://doi.org/10.1016/j.engappai.2020.103935

A GPU-Based Artificial Orca Algorithm for Solving Traveling Salesman Problem

Lydia Sonia Bendimerad(✉), Habiba Drias, Maya Houacine, and Lydia Messaoudene

LRIA, USTHB, BP 32 El-Alia Bab-Ezzouar, Algiers, Algeria
{lbendimerad,hdrias}@usthb.dz

Abstract. The present paper proposes to solve a complex discrete problem known as Travelling Salesman Problem (TSP) based on a recent swarm intelligence algorithm called Artificial Orca Algorithm (AOA). The AOA is inspired by the lifestyle of orcas and their living behavior. This algorithm proves its efficiency in solving continuous optimization problems. To extend the application of this algorithm, we propose a discrete version of AOA, using the swap operator in the fundamental phases of AOA while respecting its basic concepts. However, the larger the TSP sample size and the population of AOA, the higher the running time. For this reason, a GPU-based AOA is suggested based on the Master-Worker paradigm. To test the efficiency of the proposed approaches, we apply the two versions of adapted AOA on some benchmark instances of TSPLIB. The results show the proposed discrete AOA's efficiency, especially with integrating the master-worker paradigm through GPU for the gain in running time.

Keywords: Swarm Intelligence · Artificial Orca Algorithm · Traveling Salesman Problem · Discretization · GPU · Master-Worker Paradigm

1 Introduction

In Artificial Intelligence, combinatorial optimization problems (COPs) [14] are prevalent. Problems in industry, medicine, agriculture, finance, and other real-world areas can be modeled as combinatorial optimization problems. These problems can be tackled through exact and approximate methods. Depending on the studied problem, several methods are proposed to solve COPs because of their multiple uses in real-life disciplines [3,8].

The Traveling Salesman Problem (TSP) [10] is a combinatorial optimization problem classified as NP-Hard(Non-Deterministic Polynomial-Hard). The TSP attracts a lot of researchers because it is adaptable and useful in different domains, and the more its size grows, the more difficult it becomes to solve. Given a series of cities and a list of distances between each pair, the TSP is defined as follows: *what is the shortest possible route that visits each city exactly*

H. Drias et al. (Eds.): AID 2022, CCIS 1852, pp. 58–70, 2023.
https://doi.org/10.1007/978-981-99-4484-2_5

once and returns to the origin city? The definition of the problem, at first sight, seems simple, but for a set of "**n**" cities, the complexity of this problem is of the order of $O(n!)$.

The TSP remains very practical to use; we find it in several real application domains, such as logistics [4], to optimize the route of movement of trucks for delivery, medical ambulances for vaccination, and even for the planning of rounds for public transport services in large and small cities. We also find the application of TSP for the optimization of drone routes [9]. This problem is adapted to several applications [11], such as PCB routing and electronic circuit design in the industrial field.

Due to the importance of TSP in the literature, researchers are constantly proposing new methods to solve it. In the last few years, Swarm Intelligence Algorithms (SIAs) have been highly praised by researchers in solving this problem. Based on 2-OPT, 3-OPT heuristics, swap operator, swap mutation sequences, and/or DE/best/2 mutation mechanism, several discretizations of continuous SIAs were proposed, such as Discrete Particle Swarm Optimization [1,18,20], Discrete Bat Algorithm [12], Discrete Elephant Herding Optimization [5], Discrete Grey Wolf Optimizer [13], Discrete Sparrow Search Algorithm [19], Discrete Cuckoo Search Algorithm [15] and so on. All these methods have been proven on benchmarks, but the running time remains a constraint when the size of the TSP sample increases.

This paper aims to propose a discretization of a recent continuous swarm intelligence algorithm called Artificial Orca Algorithm (AOA) [2], to solve the Travelling Salesman Problem. In addition to the discretization of AOA, in order to overcome the problem of running time, using the graphic unit processor (GPU), a parallel version of AOA is proposed based on the master-worker paradigm [7]. The emergence of the Graphic Processor Unit (GPU) comes back to 3D modeling needs for real-time rendering, especially for video games. Since its advent in the 70s, this component was only used for graphic purposes, but in 2007 Nvidia released a programming language called CUDA for "Compute Unified Device Architecture". CUDA uses a specific language similar to C/C++ programming language, which allows launching parallel executions thanks to the particular architecture of GPU composed of a multitude of threads and thus makes programs faster.

The remainder of this paper is organized into five sections. The following Section presents a formal definition of the traveling salesman problem. Section 3 offers the original version of the Artificial Orca Algorithm. The discretization of AOA based on the swap operator is described in Sect. 4. Section 5 presents the parallel AOA based on GPU. Before ending with a conclusion in Sect. 7, the experimental study is presented in Sect. 6.

2 The Traveling Salesman Problem

The Traveling Salesman Problem [6] can be used in different domains for planning or scheduling purposes. Since its complexity is factorial, exact methods are less efficient for large instance sizes. For this reason, researchers suggest new methods for solving this problem. Several variants of TSP exist in the literature: Symmetric Travelling Salesman Problem, Asymmetric Travelling Salesman Problem, Multiple Travelling Salesman Problem, and so on. In this contribution, to observe AOA's efficiency in the problem, we tackle the symmetric Traveling Salesman Problem(STSP). The Symmetric Traveling Salesman Problem is modeled as an undirected weighted graph G = (V, E, c) such that:

- The "V" is the set of vertices that represent the cities to be visited.
- The "E" is the set of arcs representing the path between two cities.
- The "c" is the cost function on the edges (weights of arcs). For example, this cost function can be represented by the time of displacement or the distance between cities.

Based on these definitions, the graph G can be formulated as a matrix such that the first row and the first column contain the vertices(cities) and, at the intersection of each two vertices, is given the cost of displacement "c" between them. For a set of **"n"** cities, the mathematical formulation of TSP is the following:

$$Determine\ x_{i,j} \forall i, j \in n\, and\, i \neq j$$

$$Min\mathbf{z} = \sum_{i=1}^{n} \sum_{i=1}^{n} c_{i,j} \times x_{i,j} \tag{1}$$

Subject to:

$$\sum_{j=1}^{n} x_{i,j} = 1 \forall i \in 1, 2, ..n$$
$$\sum_{i=1}^{n} x_{i,j} = 1 \forall j \in 1, 2, ..n$$

where, $x_{i,j}$ is 1 if the salesman visits city j from city i, otherwise 0. Based on the definition of TSP, which aims to find the shortest path starting from a city and returning to that same city by passing through all the other cities once. The solution of a TSP is represented as a vector representing the ordered sequence of all the cities to visit and ends with the starting city. Thus, the objective of the salesman is to find a complete tour (solution) defined as follows:

$$Min\mathbf{z} = \sum_{i=1}^{n-1} c_{i,i+1} + c_{n,1} \tag{2}$$

3 Original Artificial Orca Algorithm

In the current work, we choose to discretize a recent Swarm Intelligence Algorithm called Artificial Orca Algorithm (AOA) proposed by Bendimerad and Drias [2] in 2021. The artificial Orca Algorithm mimics the social organization of orcas and their living behavior. The population of orcas is organized into several clans, and each clan consists of a set of pods. Each pod comprises a group of artificial orcas directed by a "matriarch" considered as the fittest solution in a pod. In addition to this, each hierarchical level is characterized by a degree of closeness. AOA balances two fundamental phases of swarm intelligence algorithms: *Intensification* and *Diversification* searches.

The Artificial Orca Algorithm (AOA) follows a series of steps to find the best solution to a given problem. First, the empirical parameters of the algorithm, such as the population size, wavelength L, wave period T, minimum and maximum frequency f_{min} and f_{max}, are defined, and the orcas' population is initialized. In the second step, the fitness of each orca is calculated, and the pods are sorted based on the fitness value of their artificial orcas. Then, an intensification search is performed to update the artificial orcas using either an echolocation search, with equations Eq. 3, Eq. 4, and Eq. 5, or a Cooperation Update, with equations Eq. 6, Eq. 7, and Eq. 8. Next, a diversification search is carried out, updating the worst artificial orcas of each pod using equation Eq. 9. In step 5, the stopping criteria are updated, and the population is evaluated by calculating the fitness value of its individuals and sorting them. If the stopping criteria are met, the best individual in the population is returned; otherwise, the algorithm is restarted from the intensification phase.

$$f_{group} = f_{min} + \alpha \times (f_{max} - f_{min}) \tag{3}$$

$$v_{p_i}^t = v_{p_i}^{t-1} + f_{pi} \times D_p + f_c \times D_c + f_{pop} \times D_{pop} \tag{4}$$

$$x_{p_i}^t = x_{p_i}^{t-1} + v_{p_i}^t \tag{5}$$

$$x_{temp,p_i}^t = A \times \sin(\frac{2 \times \pi}{L}) x_{p_i}^{t-1} \times \cos(\frac{2 \times \pi}{T}) t_x \tag{6}$$

$$x_{m,p}^t = \frac{\sum_{j=1}^{n} x_{temp,p_j}}{n} \tag{7}$$

$$x_{p_i}^t = x_p^* - \beta \times x_{m,p}^t \tag{8}$$

$$x_{new,p_i}^t = \frac{\gamma \times x_{pop_{rand1}}^t + \omega \times x_{C_{rand2}}^t}{2} \tag{9}$$

In these equations, α ,γ, and ω are randomly generated numbers between 0 and 1. The variable t represents the current iteration, and $v_{p_i}^t$ corresponds to the velocity of the i-th artificial orca in the pod p. The variables f_{min} and f_{max} represent the minimum and maximum frequencies, respectively. They are used to generate a random frequency, f_{group}, for the pod (f_{pi}), clan (f_c), and population ($fpop$) within the frequency range. It's important to note that the distances D_{pi}, D_c, and D_{pop} correspond to the distance between each orca and the matriarch of the pod, the clan to which it belongs, and the entire population, respectively. The variable A is specific to the modeling problem, while L and T represent the wavelength and wave period, respectively. x_p^* refers to the matriarch of the current pod p, while $x_{p_i}^t$ denotes the position of the i-th artificial orca in that pod. The new solution for the i-th individual is x^t_{new,p_i} and it is obtained using $x^t_{pop,rand1}$, a random individual from the population at position rand1, and $x^t_{c,rand2}$, a random individual from the clan c of the current pod at position rand2. These steps's are summerized in Algorithm 1.

Algorithm 1. Original Artificial Orca Algorithm

```
Initialisation
Initialise the population of orcas respecting the distance between individuals in clans and pods.
Define empirical parameters : T, f_min, f_max
Evaluation
Calculate the fitness of all the orcas in the population
while Stopping criterion is not reached do
    Sort all the artificial orcas in the pods following their fitness values
    Launch Intensification search: Update the orcas of the population.
    Evaluate the fitness of the pods according to the newly updated individuals
    Sort the pods of each clan
    Launch Diversification search
    Update the stopping criterion
    Evaluate the fitness of the new orcas
end while
Output:best orca of all the population
```

4 Discrete AOA for the TSP

4.1 Representation of the Solution

A solution represents a path (the order of cities to visit) that starts and ends at the same position. We have represent these positions in an array where each element corresponds to the *id* of a position(defined in the input data). If we have "n" positions, our array is composed of "n+1" elements because we must always return to the starting position at the end.

- *Example*: Here is an example that represents one of the possible solutions: Let the points x_1, x_2 and x_3.
  A potential solution could be represented as follows: $X = [2, 3, 1, 2]$.

4.2 Distance Between Two Solutions

The distance between two solutions (Orcas) is calculated using the Hamming distance. It allows us to quantify the distance between two sequences of symbols. In our case, this distance is calculated between two solutions containing the same elements. If two elements in the same position have different *id*, the Hamming distance initialized at 0 is incremented by looking at two solutions.

- *Example*: The hamming distance between two solutions $A = [2, 3, 1, 2]$ and $B = [1, 3, 2, 1]$ is $Distance(A, B) = 3$

4.3 Discrete Echolocation Search

In the original AOA, this phase allows the artificial orcas to get closer to the prey (matriarch) based on velocity (Eq. 4). Keeping this logic in the discrete version of AOA, each artificial orca can get closer *velocity times* either to the matriarch of the pod, the clan, or the population based on their frequencies, as described in Algorithm 2.

Algorithm 2. Discrete Echolocation phase

Generate the pod, the clan and population frequencies f_{pi}, f_c *and* f_{pop}
if (f_{pi} is bigger then f_c *and* f_{pop}) **then**
Determine permutations between the matriarch of the pod and the current artificial orca
end if
if (f_c is bigger then f_{pi} *and* $fpop$) **then**
Determine permutations between the matriarch of the clan and the current artificial orca
end if
if (f_{pop} is bigger then f_{pi} *and* f_c) **then**
Determine permutations between the matriarch of the population and the current artificial orca
end if
Calculate velocity v_i (Eq.4)
for i in range(0,v_i) **do**
    performs permutation i in the current solution
end for

4.4 Discrete Cooperation Update

The Eq. 8 allows calculating a new solution from the best orca in the pod and the temporary solution that results from the equations Eq. 6 and Eq. 7 representing the wave washing technique of orcas in pods. In discrete AOA, Eq. 8 simulates the permutations applied to the temporary solution to get closer to x_p^*. This phase is described in Algorithm 3.

Algorithm 3. Discrete Cooperation phase

For each pod, calculate the temporary solution "$x_{m,p}^t$".
Calculate the swap sequence (Permutations) that allows going from the temporary solution to the best solution in the pod
Apply the swap sequence to each artificial orca of the pod to get closer to the best solution

4.5 Discrete Diversification Phase

The diversification phase calculates $x_{new,pi}$ following Eq. 9 based on γ, ω and random orca from clan $x_{C_{rand2}}$and population $x_{pop_{rand1}}$. In this step, the artificial orcas of the worst pod in each clan are updated by $x_{new,pi}$. In the current case of study, to do this update, $x_{new,pi}$ is constructed and not calculated as described in Algorithm 4.

Algorithm 4. Discrete Diversification search

Initialize $x_{new,pi}$
for (**do** i in range (0,n))
  if ($\gamma > \omega$) **then**
  insert the position i of $x_{C_{rand2}}$in $x_{new,pi}$
  else
  insert the position i of $x_{pop_{rand1}}$ in $x_{new,pi}$
  end if
end for

5 Parallel Artificial Orca Algorithm

5.1 GPU Architecture

The emergence of the Graphic Processor Unit (GPU) comes back to 3D modeling needs for real-time rendering, especially for video games. Since its advent in the 70s, this component was only used for graphic purposes. However, in 2007 Nvidia released a programming language called CUDA [16] for "Compute Unified Device Architecture", which is a GPGPU technology (General -Purpose Computing on Graphics Processing Units), i.e., using a (GPU). CUDA uses a specific language similar to C/C ++ programming language, which allows launching parallel executions thanks to a particular architecture to launch parallel executions and thus makes programs faster. CUDA is invoked by a CPU program based on "Kernels" functions. These Kernels are launched simultaneously using threads. CUDA also provides Synchronization threads and a shared memory. The architecture launched by CUDA is Heterogeneous, and the code is executed first in a CPU serially and calls the kernels found in the GPU. GPU parallelize the kernels by running them in different threads. These threads are contained in blocks that are in grids.

5.2 Master-Worker Paradigm

The master-worker, also called master-slave [17], is a parallel programming paradigm with two main actors: the master and the worker. The master releases the main calculations by generating several sub-problems that the worker must solve in parallel. The two actors can interact thanks to the exchange of data in memory. Thus the master launches the sub-problems on the workers in parallel, and then each worker returns the results to the master.

5.3 Description of Proposed GPU-AOA

The traveling salesman problem is a complex problem classified as NP-Hard. Proposing a swarm intelligence algorithm to solve it increases the quality of the solution, but large dataset instances still need to be revised in terms of running time. To tackle this issue, a parallel Artificial Orca Algorithm is proposed. This formalism launches the update of orcas in parallel using GPU and based on the Master-Worker paradigm. As mentioned, the master executes the workers and the latter responds with results. In our model, The master is performed on the CPU while the worker is offloaded to the GPU. Contrary to the original AOA, here, the master initializes the population of artificial orcas, the velocity of each artificial orca, the cooperation vector, and the fitness of each artificial orca on the CPU. These data are copied to the memory of the GPU. Then, the master simultaneously evaluates each artificial orca on $\mathbf{N}(N = \#clan \times \#pod \times \#orcas)$ threads. It's followed by the execution of $\#pod \times \#clan$ thread to calculate the pod cooperation solution, **N** thread for parallel execution of the intensification search, and finally $\#clan$ thread to launch the diversification searches. The data is updated on GPU by the different workers established by the master. The results are then returned to the CPU (Master). This process is repeated as long as the stop criterion is not reached. This process is described in Fig. 1, and Algorithm 5.

6 Experiments and Results

This section presents an experimental study of the proposed discrete AOA and GPU-AOA to solve TSP. Let's note that the study is based on benchmark instances of TSPLIB[1]. The proposition is developed in C++ programming language for discrete AOA and C-CUDA programming language for GPU-AOA. The simulation was performed on a machine with a CPU host with a Core(TM) 64 i7-3770 K and a clock speed of 3,5 GHz and 16 GB of Random Access Memory, and the GPU device is an NVIDIA Quadro 500, where each block consists of 256 threads. Several experiments are conducted to choose the best parameters for the proposed approach. Thus the number of clans $\#Clan = 15$, $\#Pod = 5$, $\#Orca = 15$, the minimum and maximum frequencies were set respectively to 0 and 1, while the wave period T was set to 1000 and the stopping criteria was set to 1000 iterations. In this set of experiments, we have carried out 100 executions for each instance of TSPLIB in order to present the average obtained results and the running time of each discrete AOA and GPU-AOA. Table 1 shows the obtained results on ten instances of TSPLIB. In addition to the average obtained results, the optimum of each instance as presented in the TSPLIB benchmark is presented (See Footnote 1). It is clear from the results that both the serial and parallel proposed approaches of discrete AOA don't reach the optimum while presenting a good performance. Figure 2, demonstrates the running time of serial discrete AOA and GPU-based AOA. This figure clearly shows that the

[1] http://elib.zib.de/pub/mp-testdata/tsp/tsplib/tsplib.html.

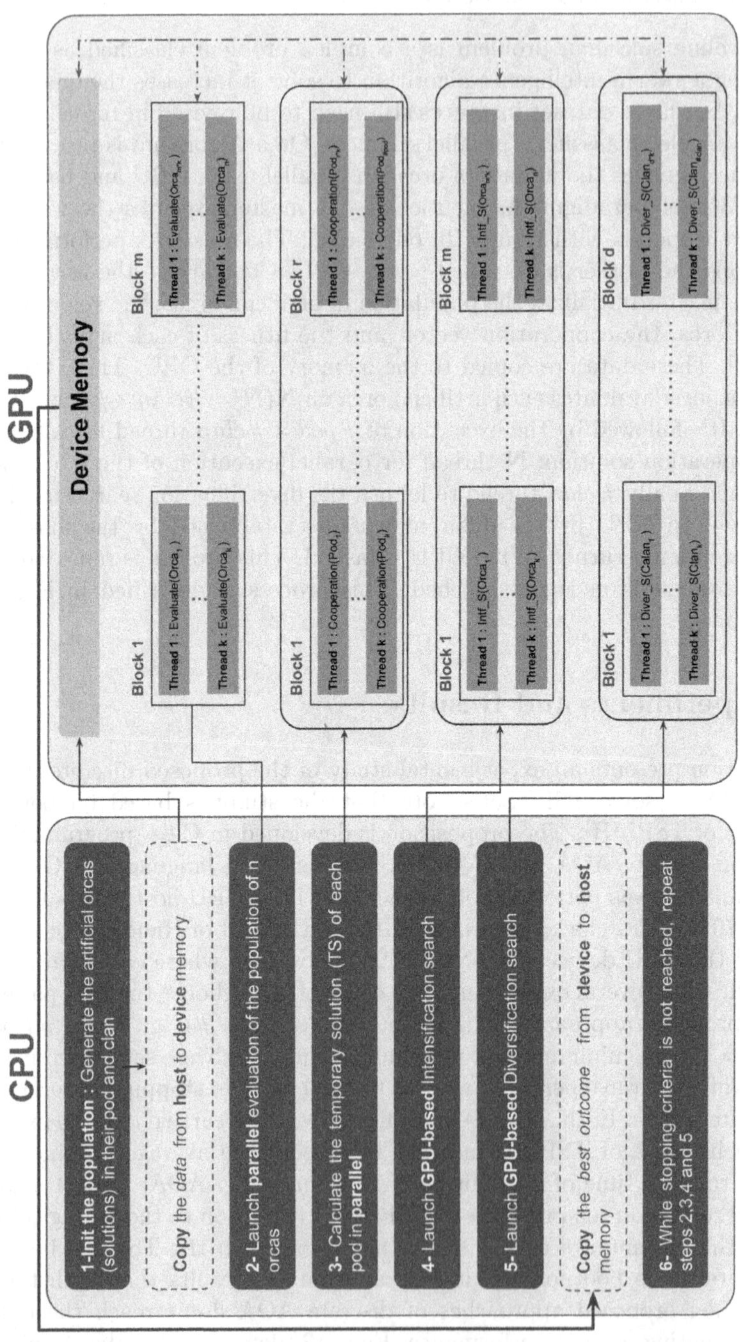

Fig. 1. The Master-worker Paradigm principle for GPU-AOA.

Algorithm 5. Parallel Discrete Artificial Orca Algorithm for Travelling Salesman Problem

```
Initialisation
Initialise the population population of N orcas respecting the distance between individuals in clans and pods.
Define empirical parameters : T, f_min, f_max
Initialise the velocity of each artificial orca : V
while Stopping criterion is not reached do
    cudaMemcpy(population,cudaMemcpyHostToDevice)
    cudaMemcpy(V,cudaMemcpyHostToDevice)
    cudaMemcpy(cooperation,cudaMemcpyHostToDevice)
    cudaMemcpy(fitnesses,cudaMemcpyHostToDevice)
    Launch N thread for parallel evaluation of each artificial orca in the device memory
    Launch #pod × #clan thread to calculate the pods temporary solution
    Launch N thread for parallel Intensification Search
    Launch #clan thread for Diversification Search
    cudaMemcpy(population,cudaMemcpyDeviceToHost)
    cudaMemcpy(V,cudaMemcpyDeviceToHost)
    cudaMemcpy(cooperation,cudaMemcpyDeviceToHost)
    cudaMemcpy(fitnesses,cudaMemcpyDeviceToHost)
    Select the best artificial orca (Solution) of the current iteration based on their fitness values
    Update the stopping criterion
end while
Output:best orca of all the population
```

GPU approach based on the master-worker paradigm took less running time than the serial approach. These results confirm the ability of GPUs to minimize running time.

Table 1. The obtained Results by Directe AOA and GPU-AOA on TSP benchmark.

Bechmark Instance	**st70**	**pr152**	**pr144**	**pr136**	**pr124**
Optimum	675	73682	58537	96772	59030
Average DAOA	720,405	74852,325	59412,362	97663,125	61032,235
Average GPU-AOA	712,85	74638,325	58956,869	97853,785	60956,263
Bechmark Instance	**pr107**	**gil262**	**eil76**	**d198**	**bier127**
Optimum	44303	2378	538	15780	118282
Average DAOA	44511,6	2631,5	558,205	16780,02	119212,086
Average GPU-AOA	44403,23	2486,1	542,14	16325,522	118356,36

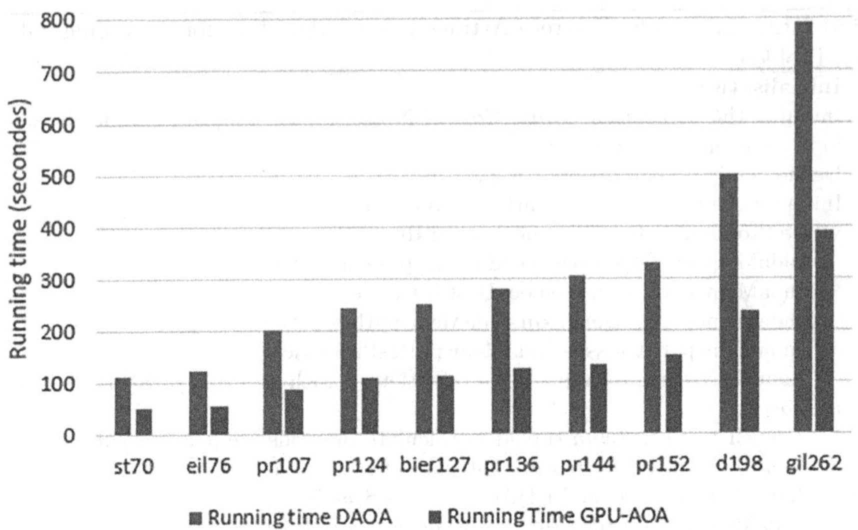

Fig. 2. The average running time obtained by Directe AOA and GPU-AOA.

7 Conclusion

This study focuses on solving the Traveling Salesman Problem (TSP), which is an NP-hard combinatorial optimization problem. The aim is to evaluate the effectiveness of the Artificial Orca Algorithm (AOA), a recent swarm intelligence algorithm. To solve the TSP, we proposed a discrete version of AOA, and a parallel version based on the GPU and Master-Worker paradigm to overcome time constraints. The TSPLIB benchmark was used to test the simulation results, which were then compared to the optimal solution. Our comparison demonstrated the performance of both the serial and parallel approaches of the discrete version of AOA, and the speed of the parallel method. In the future, we plan to use clustering to divide TSP instances into sub-problems to be solved in parallel, and then compare this approach with the current methods proposed.

References

1. Akhand, M., Akter, S., Rashid, M.: Velocity tentative particle swarm optimization to solve tsp. In: 2013 International Conference on Electrical Information and Communication Technology (EICT), pp. 1–6. IEEE (2014)
2. Bendimerad, L.S., Drias, H.: An artificial orca algorithm for continuous problems. In: Abraham, A., Hanne, T., Castillo, O., Gandhi, N., Nogueira Rios, T., Hong, T.-P. (eds.) HIS 2020. AISC, vol. 1375, pp. 700–709. Springer, Cham (2021). https://doi.org/10.1007/978-3-030-73050-5_68

3. Bendimerad, L.S., Drias, H.: Intelligent contributions of the artificial orca algorithm for continuous problems and real-time emergency medical services. Evol. Intell. 1–36 (2023)
4. Filip, E.: The travelling salesman problem and its application in logistic practice (2011)
5. Hossam, A., Bouzidi, A., Riffi, M.E.: Elephants herding optimization for solving the travelling salesman problem. In: Ezziyyani, M. (ed.) AI2SD 2018. AISC, vol. 912, pp. 122–130. Springer, Cham (2019). https://doi.org/10.1007/978-3-030-12065-8_12
6. Ilavarasi, K., Joseph, K.S.: Variants of travelling salesman problem: a survey. In: International Conference on Information Communication and Embedded Systems (ICICES2014), pp. 1–7 (2014). https://doi.org/10.1109/ICICES.2014.7033850
7. Kechid, A., Drias, H.: GPU-based bat algorithm for discovering cultural coalitions. In: Wotawa, F., Friedrich, G., Pill, I., Koitz-Hristov, R., Ali, M. (eds.) IEA/AIE 2019. LNCS (LNAI), vol. 11606, pp. 470–482. Springer, Cham (2019). https://doi.org/10.1007/978-3-030-22999-3_41
8. Khelfa, C., Khennak, I., Drias, H., Drias, Y., Belharda, Y., Smail, M.: Slime mould algorithm for solving ambulance dispatching problem. In: Abraham, A., Hanne, T., Gandhi, N., Manghirmalani Mishra, P., Bajaj, A., Siarry, P. (eds.) Proceedings of the 14th International Conference on Soft Computing and Pattern Recognition (SoCPaR 2022), pp. 822–831. Springer, Cham (2023). https://doi.org/10.1007/978-3-031-27524-1_80
9. Kim, S., Moon, I.: Traveling salesman problem with a drone station. IEEE Trans. Syst. Man Cybern. Syst. **49**(1), 42–52 (2019). https://doi.org/10.1109/TSMC.2018.2867496
10. Lawler, E.L., Lenstra, J.K., Rinnooy Kan, A.H., Shmoys, D.B.: Erratum: the traveling salesman problem: a guided tour of combinatorial optimization. J. Oper. Res. Soc. **37**(6), 655–655 (1986)
11. Matai, R., Singh, S.P., Mittal, M.L.: Traveling salesman problem: an overview of applications, formulations, and solution approaches. In: Traveling Salesman Problem, Theory and Applications, vol. 1 (2010)
12. Osaba, E., Yang, X.S., Diaz, F., Lopez-Garcia, P., Carballedo, R.: An improved discrete bat algorithm for symmetric and asymmetric traveling salesman problems. Eng. Appl. Artif. Intell. **48**, 59–71 (2016). https://doi.org/10.1016/j.engappai.2015.10.006, https://www.sciencedirect.com/science/article/pii/S0952197615002353
13. Panwar, K., Deep, K.: Discrete grey wolf optimizer for symmetric travelling salesman problem. Appl. Soft Comput. **105**, 107298 (2021). https://doi.org/10.1016/j.asoc.2021.107298, https://www.sciencedirect.com/science/article/pii/S1568494621002210
14. Rahman, M.A., Sokkalingam, R., Othman, M., Biswas, K., Abdullah, L., Abdul Kadir, E.: Nature-inspired metaheuristic techniques for combinatorial optimization problems: Overview and recent advances. Mathematics **9**(20) (2021). https://doi.org/10.3390/math9202633, https://www.mdpi.com/2227-7390/9/20/2633
15. Reda, M., Onsy, A., Elhosseini, M.A., Haikal, A.Y., Badawy, M.: A discrete variant of cuckoo search algorithm to solve the travelling salesman problem and path planning for autonomous trolley inside warehouse. Knowl.-Based Syst. **252**, 109290 (2022). https://doi.org/10.1016/j.knosys.2022.109290, https://www.sciencedirect.com/science/article/pii/S0950705122006463
16. Tan, Y., Ding, K.: A survey on GPU-based implementation of swarm intelligence algorithms. IEEE Trans. Cybern. **46**(9), 2028–2041 (2015)

17. Tangherloni, A., Rundo, L., Spolaor, S., Cazzaniga, P., Nobile, M.S.: Gpu-powered multi-swarm parameter estimation of biological systems: A master-slave approach. In: 2018 26th Euromicro International Conference on Parallel, Distributed and Network-based Processing (PDP), pp. 698–705 (2018). https://doi.org/10.1109/PDP2018.2018.00115
18. Wang, K.P., Huang, L., Zhou, C.G., Pang, W.: Particle swarm optimization for traveling salesman problem. In: Proceedings of the 2003 International Conference on Machine Learning and Cybernetics (IEEE cat. no. 03ex693), vol. 3, pp. 1583–1585. IEEE (2003)
19. Zhang, Z., Han, Y.: Discrete sparrow search algorithm for symmetric traveling salesman problem. Appl. Soft Comput. **118**, 108469 (2022). https://doi.org/10.1016/j.asoc.2022.108469, https://www.sciencedirect.com/science/article/pii/S1568494622000321
20. Zhong, Y., Lin, J., Wang, L., Zhang, H.: Discrete comprehensive learning particle swarm optimization algorithm with metropolis acceptance criterion for traveling salesman problem. Swarm Evol. Comput. **42**, 77–88 (2018). https://doi.org/10.1016/j.swevo.2018.02.017, https://www.sciencedirect.com/science/article/pii/S2210650216304680

Mushroom-like Structure Design Using Particle Swarm Optimization Algorithm to Improve the Performance of a Microstrip Antenna

Abdelmalek Louaifi(✉), Zineb Laieb, and Youssef Lamhene

University of Science and Technology Houari Boumediene, Algiers, Algeria
maleklou0@gmail.com

Abstract. In this paper, we want to improve the performance of a microstrip patch antenna resonating at 5.8 GHz by using a mushroom-like electromagnetic bandgap (EBG) structure. For this purpose, the particle swarm optimization (PSO) algorithm is used to optimize the dimensions of the structure in order to cover the frequency band of interest. The optimization and simulation of the antenna have been done using MATLAB and CST MICROWAVE STUDIO. The obtained results show an improvement in the designed antenna's return loss, bandwidth, and gain.

Keywords: Electromagnetic band gap (EBG) · Mushroom-like structure · Particle swarm optimization (PSO) · Microstrip antenna

1 Introduction

Antennas are essential to establish a communication link between wireless devices. Nowadays, their presence is notable in all fields, especially microstrip antenna, which is low profile, cheap to fabricate, and compatible with integrated circuits. The conventional microstrip antenna is a metal plate of arbitrary shape placed above a ground plane and separated by a dielectric substrate. The excitation is often from a microstrip line or a coaxial probe. Nevertheless, the microstrip antenna suffers disadvantages such as low gain, narrow bandwidth, and surface wave excitation [1].

Surface waves are electromagnetic waves that are not radiated and remain on the surface of the antenna, which leads to a deterioration of the radiation. Electromagnetic bandgap (EBG) metamaterials are a solution to eliminate them. EBG structures are defined as an artificial arrangement of periodic (sometimes non-periodic) materials, which allows the elimination of electromagnetic waves in a certain frequency band. The best-known one is the mushroom-like structure proposed by Sievenpiper in 1999 [2], which is a periodic arrangement of metal plates connected by a via (vertical interconnect access) to the ground plane.

Due to the complex behavior of EBGs, which usually requires a long parametric study to design with the desired characteristics, stochastic methods are an interesting choice for the modeling and design of these structures. The use of metaheuristic algorithms

H. Drias et al. (Eds.): AID 2022, CCIS 1852, pp. 71–79, 2023.
https://doi.org/10.1007/978-981-99-4484-2_6

such as the genetic algorithm (GA) or particle swarm optimization (PSO) is common in engineering and in particular in antenna design, where in [3] the spacing in an antenna array is optimized using the particle swarm optimization algorithm to maximize the difference between the gain peak of the main lobe and the highest side lobe, in [4] the genetic algorithm is used to design an EBG structure with a band gap that covers the resonant frequency of 5. 8 GHz of a microstrip antenna.

In this work, the number of candidates is limited due to the slow simulation. Therefore, the best choice is the PSO algorithm due to its simplicity and fast convergence to an optimal solution compared to other metaheuristic algorithms. First a mushroom-like EBG structure is designed using CST Microwave studio linked to a PSO algorithm in MATLAB, then the optimized structure is incorporated into a 5.8 GHz microstrip antenna to improve its return loss, bandwidth, and gain.

2 Generalities

To simulate the antenna radiation, we use the CST Microwave studio software, which is a full wave electromagnetic simulator based on the finite integration technique (FIT) that solves the integral form of Maxwell's equations.

Below we give a non-exhaustive description of electromagnetic bandgap structures and some of the antenna parameters for a better understanding of the study.

2.1 Electromagnetic Bandgap Structure

Electromagnetic bandgap can offer a distinct characteristic in controlling the propagation of electromagnetic waves. They can act like a perfect magnetic conductor that does not exist in nature. EBG materials are also known for preventing the propagation of electromagnetic waves in a certain frequency band. EBG materials are classified based on their arrangement into (1, 2 or 3) dimensional structures [5]. The 2D planar arrangement is the preferred one in antenna design, where we find different configurations like the mushroom-like structure, the uni-planar (UC-EBG) design, the frequency selective surface (FSS), and more.

Mushroom-like Structure. The mushroom-like structure is a periodic arrangement of metal plates of different shapes (square, circular, hexagonal…etc.) connected to the ground by a via. The operating mechanism of this structure can be explained by an array of parallel resonant LC circuits (Fig. 1) that block the flow of current around the structure in a certain forbidden frequency band, where the inductance is generated by the current through the vias, while the capacitance is generated by the gap between adjacent patches.

Dispersion Diagram. The dispersion diagram is a representation of the propagation constant versus frequency [5]. The dispersion analysis simulates an infinite periodic unit cell by applying the periodic boundary to it. The bandgap of EBG structures is usually determined from their dispersion diagram, which is considered as an accurate representation to distinguish the frequency band where the surface waves are eliminated.

2.2 Antenna Parameters

Return Loss. The return loss or reflection coefficient of an antenna is a figure that indicates the proportion of electromagnetic waves arriving at the port that are rejected as a ratio against those that are accepted.

For maximum energy, it is desirable to have a return loss close to zero or the lowest possible in decibels.

Bandwidth. The bandwidth is defined as the range of frequencies within which performances of the antenna are within an acceptable value of those at the resonance frequency. It is typically taken at the −10 dB frequency band of the return loss.

Gain. Antenna gain tells us the power transmitted by an antenna in a specific direction compared to an isotropic antenna. This specification describes how strong a signal an antenna can send out or receive in a specified direction.

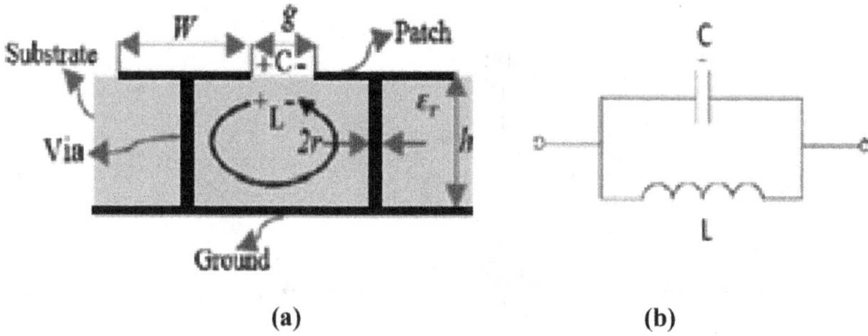

Fig. 1. EBG unit cell (a) mushroom-like EBG parameters (b) lumped element equivalent circuit

3 Optimized EBG Structure Using PSO

The mushroom-like EBG (Fig. 2) can be investigated using the eigenmode solver of the CST MWS, where the bandgap for surface wave suppression is visible in the dispersion diagram. To do so, we use MATLAB to apply the PSO algorithm and to control CST through the VBA macro language in CST MWS, the mushroom unit cell parameters are then optimized. Figure 3 shows the flowchart of the proposed PSO algorithm for mushroom-like structure optimization.

The particle swarm optimization (PSO) algorithm was proposed in 1995 [6]. It has found a growing interest in engineering due to its simplicity and low computational cost, which make it suitable for solving a wide range of problems. PSO is inspired by the social behavior of bird swarm. It uses candidate solutions as particles that move in a search space to find the best solution, where each particle adjusts its traveling position and velocity according to its current position and velocity, personal best position, and other particles position with the global best parameter.

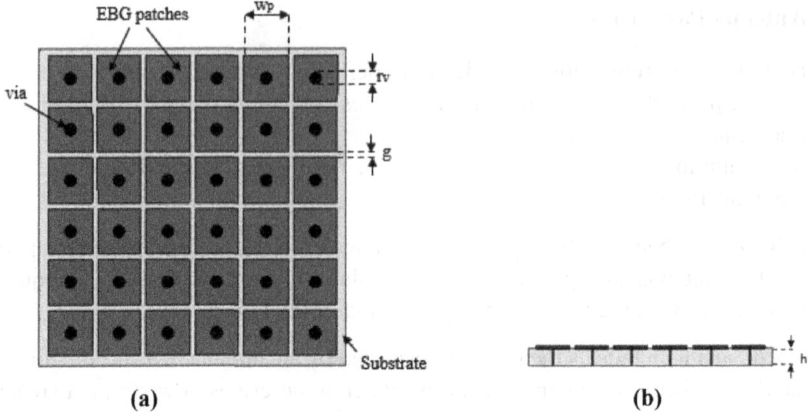

Fig. 2. Mushroom-like structure (a) Top view (b) Side view.

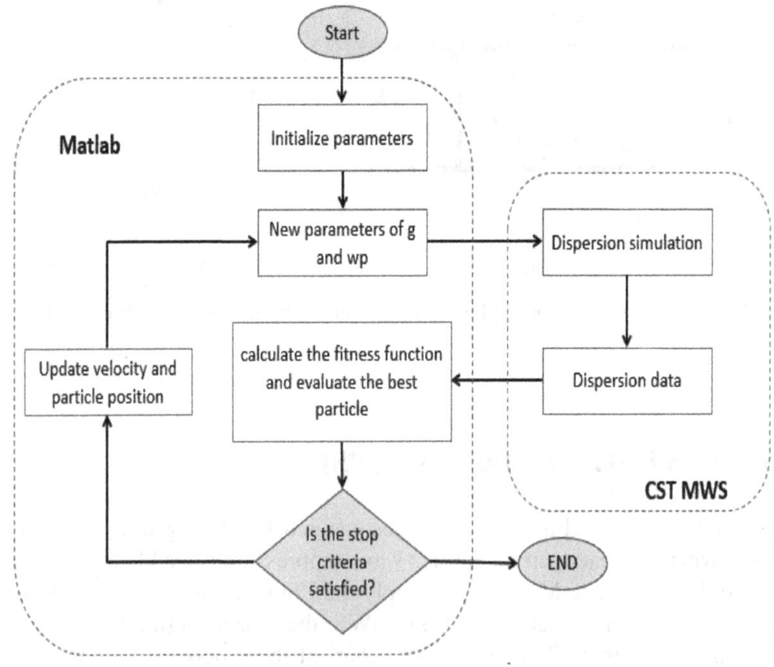

Fig. 3. Flowchart of the proposed PSO for EBG optimization.

We use the particle swarm optimization algorithm to determine the best patch size w_p and gap g between adjacent patches, which are selected as state variables, while other parameters are kept constant, with a via radius $r_v = 0.5$ mm, a substrate with a relative permittivity $\varepsilon_r = 4.3$, and a height h equal to 2.6 mm (Table 1).

The patch size w_p is defined within the range of [5, 7] mm, while the gap varies between [0.4, 1.2] mm with a precision of two decimals. The number of particles is set at 30 units, and the total number of iterations is equal to 20.

The PSO algorithm is applied to search for the global minimum in the search space. The fitness function is divided into two parts, where the first part is set to center the band gap around the resonance frequency $f_c = 5.8$ GHz, while the second part is defined to search for the largest possible band gap. The fitness function is defined as follows:

$$fit = \left(\frac{f_{max} + f_{min}}{2} - f_c\right)^2 - \left(\frac{f_{max} - f_{min}}{f_c}\right) \quad (1)$$

where f_{max} is the intersection frequency between the light line and the second mode of the dispersion diagram, while f_{min} is the highest frequency reached by the first mode. The two frequencies define the upper and lower limits of the bandgap.

Table 1. Mushroom unit cell parameters.

Parameters	Value
wp	[5, 7] mm
g	[0.4, 1.2] mm
h	2.6 mm
ε_r	4.3

The best particle at the end of the simulation resulted in a patch size wp = 6.62 mm and a gap g equal to 0.86 mm. The dispersion diagram of the best solution is depicted in Fig. 4. The band gap is visible between [4.6, 6.9] GHz. No surface wave can propagate in the EBG structure inside this bandgap.

4 Microstrip Antenna with an Optimized EBG

Three rows of the optimized mushroom-like structure surround the radiating microstrip patch, which has a dimension of 11.4 × 6.8 mm and is excited by a 0.5 radius probe, as depicted in Fig. 5. The performances of the antenna are simulated and compared to a conventional one without EBG elements.

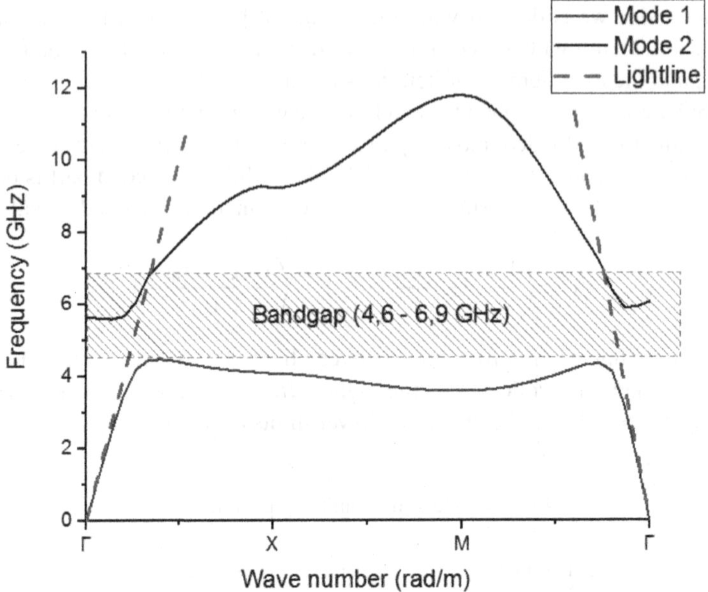

Fig. 4. Dispersion diagram of the optimized mushroom-like structure.

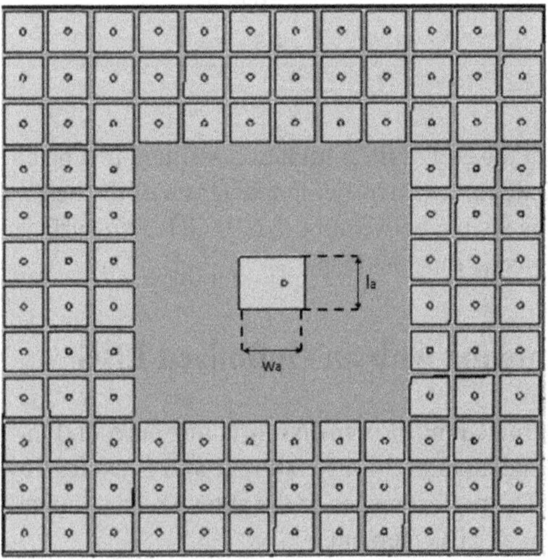

Fig. 5. Microstrip antenna geometry with EBG elements.

5 Results

The simulated return loss of the two antennas is shown in Fig. 6. At the resonance frequency, the conventional antenna has a minimum of −22 dB and a bandwidth of 400 MHz, while the microstrip antenna surrounded by the optimized mushroom-like

Table 2. Designed antenna parameters.

Parameters	Value
wa	11.4 mm
la	6.8 mm
h	2.6 mm
ε_r	4.3
wp	6.62
g	0.86

elements has a return loss of −35 dB and an important improvement in the bandwidth with 540 MHz, which allows it to cover a larger frequency range.

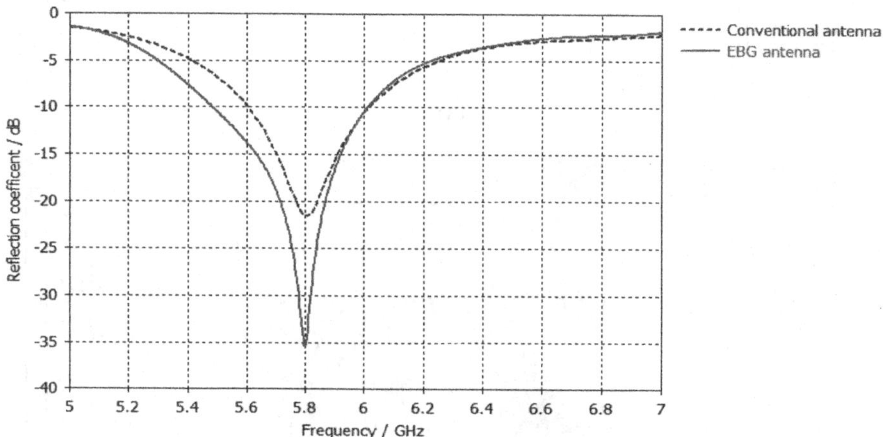

Fig. 6. Simulation of the return loss of the two antennas.

The farfield simulation of the two antennas depicted in Fig. 7 shows a superior gain for the microstrip antenna with EBG elements, where it reaches 6.1 dB, against 4.9 dB for the conventional one. This difference is due to the incorporation of the mushrooms EBG and the successful suppression of surface waves.

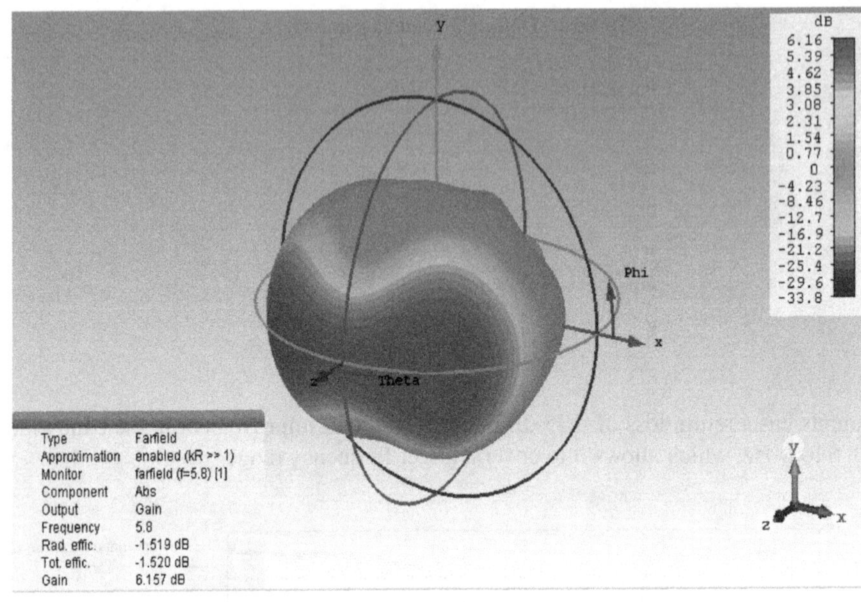

(a)

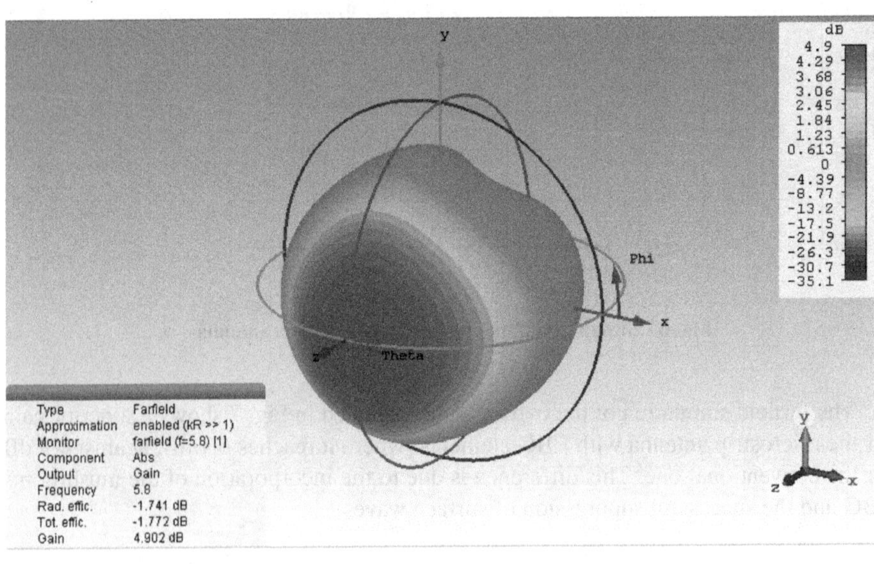

(b)

Fig. 7. 3D farfield simulation of the gain (a) antenna with EBG elements (b) conventional microstrip antenna.

Table 3. Proposed antenna comparison with related works on 5.8 GHz antennas

Related works	[4]	[7]	This work
Dielectric	RT/Duroid 6010	RT/Duroid 6006	FR-4
Relative permittivity	10.2	6.15	4.3
Return loss (dB)	−42	−32	−35
Bandwidth	417	400	540
Gain (dB)	8	6.4	6.16

6 Conclusion

This paper investigates the use of the particle swarm optimization algorithm to design a mushroom-like structure with a band gap covering the frequency band around 5.8 GHz. Firstly, the optimal EBG is determined, and then it is combined with a microstrip antenna to suppress the surface waves.

Overall, the obtained results show an improvement in the return loss, larger bandwidth, and a superior gain compared to a conventional microstrip antenna resonating at 5.8 GHz, which makes this antenna a good candidate for Wi-Fi and WiMAX antenna application.

References

1. Balanis, C.A.: Antenna Theory: Analysis and Design, Wiley, 4th edition (2016)
2. Sievenpiper, D., Zhang, L., Broas, R.F., Alexopolous, N.G., Yablonovitch, E.: High-impedance electromagnetic surfaces with a forbidden frequency band. IEEE Trans. Microw. Theory Tech. **47**(11), 2059–2074 (1999)
3. Lee, K.C., Jhang, J.Y.: Application of particle swarm algorithm to the optimization of unequally spaced antenna arrays. J. Electromagn. Waves Appl. **20**(14) (2012)
4. Melouki, N., Hocini, A., Denidni, T.A.: Performance enhancement of a compact patch antenna using an optimized EBG structure. Chin. J. Phys. **69**, 219–229 (2020)
5. Yang, F., Rahmat-Samii, Y.: Electromagnetic Band Gap Structures in Antenna Engineering. Cambridge (2008)
6. Kennedy, J., Eberhart, R.: Particle swarm optimization. In: Proceedings of ICNN 1995-International Conference on Neural Networks, vol. 4, pp. 1942–1948. IEEE (1995)
7. Da Silva, J.L., et al.: Performance of microstrip patch antenna due EBG/PBG arrangements insertion. Microw. Opt. Technol. Lett. **58**(12), 2933–2937 (2016)

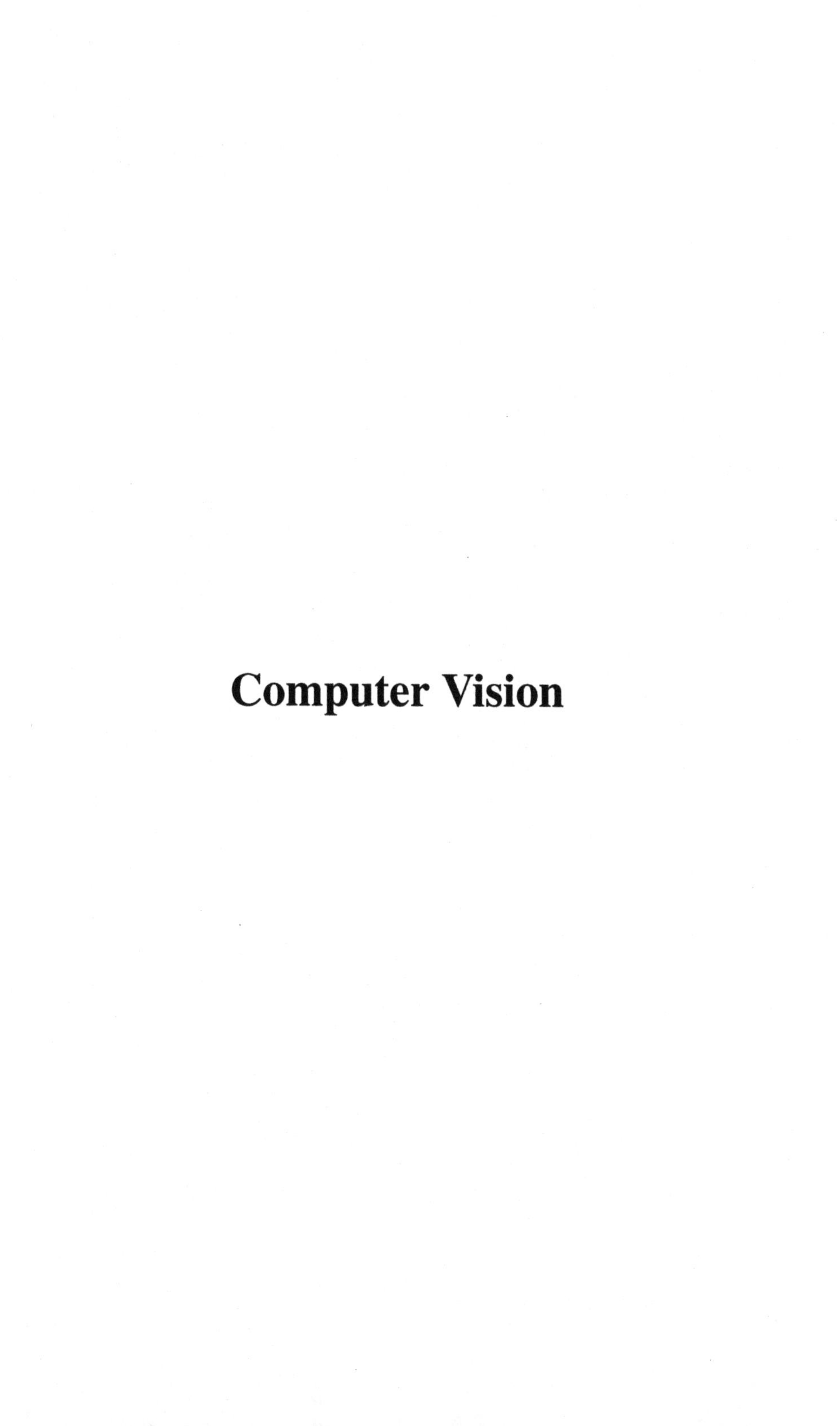

Computer Vision

Improving Thermal Object Detection for Optimized Deep Neural Networks on Embedded Devices

Naoual El-Djouher Mebtouche[1(✉)], Nadia Baha[1], Nassim Kaddouri[1], Abderrahim Zaghdar[1], and Abou Bakr Essadiq Redjil[2]

[1] Laboratory of Research in Artificial Intelligence (LRIA), Faculty of Computer Science, University of Science and Technology Houari Boumediene (USTHB), Algiers, Algeria
{nmebtouche,nbahatouzene}@usthb.dz

[2] Faculty of Physics, University of Science and Technology Houari Boumediene (USTHB), Algiers, Algeria

Abstract. Detecting objects during the dark is critical for autonomous driving, Lately, thermal cameras have become popular, yet object detectors show low performance on thermal images. In this paper, we aim to improve the capacity of deep neural networks to detect objects from thermal images and run in a restricted environment. The main contributions of this work are 1) Optimize a famous object detector to run on an embedded device. 2) propose a set of improvements to improve the feature extraction from thermal images. Comprehensive experiments were conducted on Utokyo dataset [1] and USC thermal drone dataset [2]. The proposed approach achieves higher precision and near real-time speed.

Keywords: Object Detection · Thermal Imaging · Deep Neural Networks · Feature Extraction

1 Introduction

Robust object detection is critical for autonomous driving such as pedestrian and car detection [1] or for security such as UAV detection [2,3]. The detection must be robust across various illumination conditions, including daytime, and nighttime. For this reason, thermal cameras became popular. Despite that famous object detectors perform poorly on thermal sources. This is due to the difficulty of extracting significant features from thermal images. Besides that, they require a considerable quantity of data and high-performing GPUs. Unfortunately, thermal data suffer from scarcity.

The main contributions of this work are described here as: 1. We present an optimization of a famous architecture implemented on an embedded device. 2. We propose a number of modules added to the architecture to boost the detection results from thermal cameras. 3. We present a data augmentation strategy to

H. Drias et al. (Eds.): AID 2022, CCIS 1852, pp. 83–94, 2023.
https://doi.org/10.1007/978-981-99-4484-2_7

overcome the lack of thermal data. 4. We present a set of improvements to thermal images to increase the detection of objects from thermal sources.

The rest of the paper is organized as follows. Section 2 presents the related work. In Sect. 3 The proposed approach is explained in detail. In Sect. 4 Experimental results of the proposed approach are presented. Finally, in Sect. 5 conclusion and future work are presented.

2 Related Works

Object detection achieved great performance in color images such as RCNN [4] and YOLO [5]. Unfortunately, these models perform poorly when fed thermal images. In this section, we review the different methods for object detection from thermal images.

Approaches such as [1,6] propose to detect objects by fusing color and thermal sources. Thermal images are used to complement color images. However, these techniques do not use the full potential of thermal images and cannot detect objects from thermal sources only. Other methods [7] attempt to use the knowledge learned from the color domain and transfer it to the thermal domain. Recently, authors in [8] modified an architecture by adding additional layers to learn more useful features from thermal images. In [9] authors employed several networks to detect objects in thermal sources. Authors in [10] proposed merging features extracted by many layers in the network to boost the detection results. Authors in [11] proposed an interesting method to improve the detection by combining K-means and a deep learning-based object detector. These last works have shown advancement in the detection results. However, they raise the complexity of the models, they also require heavy training and high-performing GPUs and thus cannot be used on embedded devices.

Questions arise. How to build a deep neural network that is able to: 1) Detect objects on thermal images? 2) Being able to run in real time on embedded environement? 3) How to improve feature extraction on an optimized network?

In this work we propose a new approach to detect objects from thermal images using an optimized neural network. Not only the network can learn from thermal images but also runs in an embedded device. The novelty of this work is to propose a set of improvement to increase the feature extraction of thermal images.

3 Proposed Approach

In this section, we present our detailed approach to improve thermal object detection. The proposed approach consists of two axes: First, We modify and optimize a deep learning-based object detector so it can run fast in an embedded device. The second axis consists of increasing the extraction of thermal features. For this aim, we propose a set of improvements to increase the neural network capacity of extracting thermal features.

3.1 Architecture Optimization

YOLO-V3 [12] object detector has a high level of accuracy but is relatively slow. Tiny YOLO-V3 [13] was built to be faster than YOLO-V3. Tiny-YOLO-V3 shows the best trade-off speed/accuracy reported in the literature [14]. In this work, tiny YOLO-V3 was chosen to work on. However, tiny YOLO-V3 remains relatively slow. To overcome this, we propose to reduce the computational time of tiny YOLO-V3. Figure 1 shows the architecture of tiny YOLO-V3. Specifically, we use a technique called pruning [15]. Pruning consists of removing irrelevant parts from the network and reducing the redundancy of parameters. This encourages the network to be lighter and faster with fewer parameters to tune during training. This optimization strategy allows the network to train on smaller datasets which is an issue as previously mentioned.

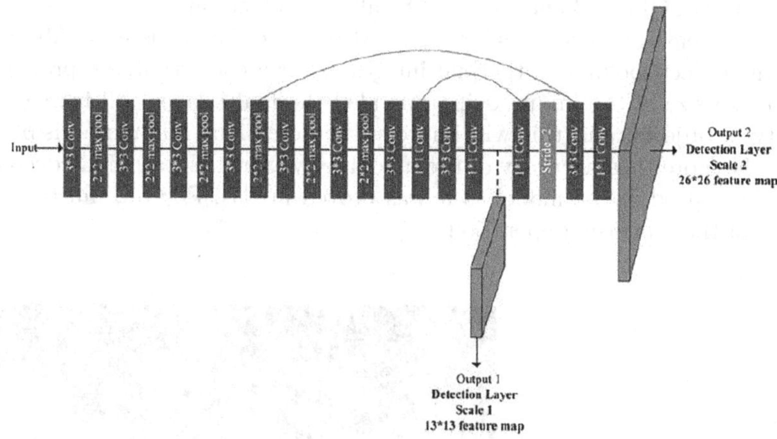

Fig. 1. Proposed Optimized Architecture

3.2 Thermal Channel Duplication

Each color image contains 3 channels Red, Green, and Blue. Thermal images only contain one channel and are represented in grayscale. Using a single channel in the network will limit the feature extraction. To overcome this problem, we propose to duplicate the thermal images 3 times and use 3 channels to process thermal images as color ones. This means that each channel will provide a new set of features to be extracted from the network. This operation will greatly improve the detection results. Figure 2 illustrates the difference in the number of input channels.

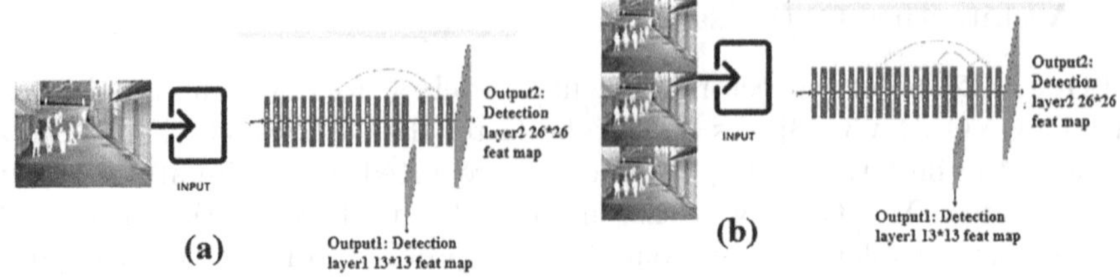

Fig. 2. (a) 1 channel input thermal in the network. (b) duplicated 3 channel thermal images in the network

3.3 Increasing the Input Size

YOLO v3 and Tiny YOLO V3 can detect objects at multi scales [12,13], unfortunately, tiny YOLO-V3 encounters difficulty to detect small objects [16]. This difficulty increases with thermal images. Also this difficulty is encountered by a human subject looking at thermal images. To overcome that, we propose to increase the size of the input. Using upscaled thermal images will increase the visibility of objects, and this will improve the detection. The more visible the objects the more thea accuracy of the model. However, this technique decreases slightly the speed of the model as it was proved in [17]. Figure 3 illustrates an example of the increasing operation.

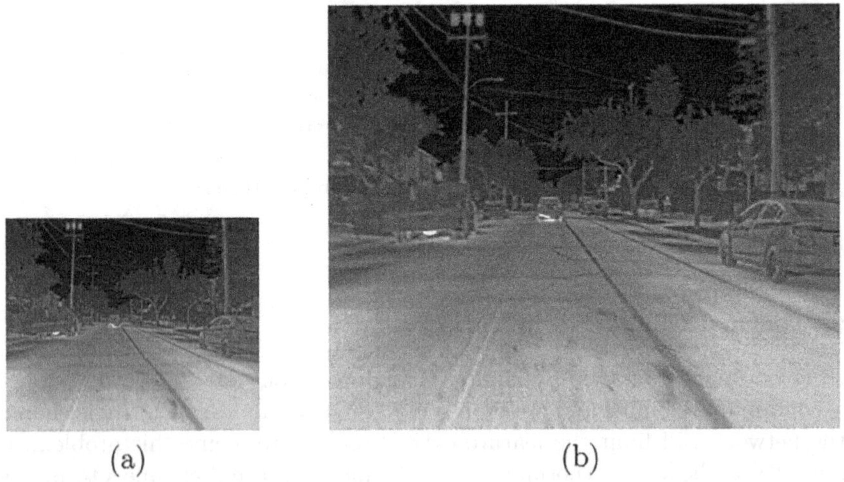

Fig. 3. Increasing the input size of thermal images.

3.4 Thermal Contrast Enhancement

Objects in thermal images are challenging to detect. To remedy this, we enhance thermal images, by improving the contrast. There are several methods for enhancing contrast in images. In this work, we use the CLAHE algorithm [18]. CLAHE algorithm uses small patches of the image, called tiles. The benefit of using CLAHE is that it runs instantly, and it preserves the natural objects' boundaries without increasing noise. Recently, CLAHE was used in deep neural networks [19] and has boosted the ability of deep neural networks to extract significant features.

3.5 Red Channel Pretrained Weights

Using pre-trained weights has proved to be important in model convergence in the RGB domain. However, there are no pre-trained weights available for the thermal domain. To remedy that we propose a novel training strategy to generate pre-trained weights for thermal images. We train the proposed architecture with red channels. The idea is that in the light spectrum red signal is the closest to the infrared thermal one. This strategy is susceptible to increase detection results. In this paper, we generate the weights from Pascal VOC dataset [20]. The strategy is detailed as follow: First, we select the 4 object categories from Pascal VOC dataset that are most common in thermal images. Namely, car, person, bicycle, and person. After that, for each image from the dataset, we split the images into red, green, and blue channels. Finally, we train Yolo-T3C with the red channel images.

3.6 Data Augmentation

Deep neural networks require a large amount of data to train on, however lack of data is one of the most common challenges in building deep learning models. Data augmentation is a technique to overcome the scarcity of data. It consists of creating new samples in the training set from the original available data. Data augmentation helps increase the precision of deep learning models. In the problem of object detection not all data augmentation techniques are suitable [3,21] (such as rotation, color change, noise...). For augmenting the thermal dataset, we use horizontal flipping to augment the training set and annotations. This technique multiplies the samples by a factor of 2. Figure 4 shows the results of the flipping operation on a sample image.

4 Experimental Results

In this section, we present the different experimentations to evaluate the proposed approach quantitatively, qualitatively, and comparatively.

Fig. 4. Illustration of the Horizontal flipping.

4.1 Datasets

Multi-Class Thermal Objects: Utokyo object detection dataset [1] contains a total of 7512 images. The dataset contains five classes (person, car, bike, stop, cone). Mono-Class Thermal Objects: The USC thermal drone dataset [2] consists of eight thermal videos of drones in an urban environment. This dataset is challenging as the drones may appear small and hidden.

4.2 Implementation Details

In this work, two hardware environments were used one for training and one for inference. For training, we used the Google Colaboratory platform with these characteristics: NVIDIA Tesla T4 GPU and 16 Go RAM. For the inference phase, we used the Nvidia Jetson Nano Developer Kit, with these characteristics: NVIDIA Maxwell 128 cores GPU, 1.43 GHz Quad-core ARM A57 CPU, 4 Go RAM, and Ubuntu 18.04 OS. We implemented our approach using the publicly available Pytorch [22] framework with Darknet [17] and OpenCV. With the following parameters: Learning rate: 0.001, Decay:0.0005, Batch-size: 64, iterations: 10000

4.3 Evaluation Metrics

To evaluate of the proposed approach, measurements for both precision and speed were used. The precision measures: average precision (AP), mean average precision (mAP), and miss rate (MR). The precision measures are to maximize except the missing rate is to minimize. The speed measures: frame per second (FPS), time detection in milliseconds (D/ms). The FPS is to maximize while the time detection is to minimize.

4.4 Quantitative Evaluation

First, we consider the basic tiny-YOLO-3, with the following parameters. 208$*$208$*$1, channel input dimensions. This architecture will be considered the baseline to compare with.

Effect of Increasing Channel Duplication. We experiment the effect of increasing the number of input channels from 1 to 3. We compare two baseline versions the first with 1 channel and a the second with 3 channels, which we named mini-YOLO-3C. Table 1 presents the obtained results from tiny-YOLO-3 baseline and mini-YOLO-3C.

Table 1. Results of increasing the number of channels

Configuration	Canal	mAP	MR	FPS	D/ms
Baseline	1	15.35%	83%	62	1.08
mini-YOLO-3C	3	19.84%	79%	61	1.32

According to Table 1, we notice a clear improvement in the level of mAP which increases by more than 4% and the MR decreases by 4%, Also, we notice a comparable D/ms and FPS. Increasing the number of channel to 3 increase the detection results. In the following experiments, mini-YOLO-3C configuration will be used.

Effect of Upscaling the Input. For this experiment, we will increase the input size by a factor of 2 from 208 * 208 to 416 * 416. We called this architecture configuration YOLO-T3C. The comparison results between mini-YOLO-3C and YOLO-T3C are shown in Table 2.

Table 2. Results of increasing the input size

Configuration	Input size	mAP	MR	FPS	D/ms
mini-YOLO-3C	208×208	19.84%	79%	**61**	1.32
YOLO-T3C	416×416	31.02%	**70%**	20	3.34

From Table 2 we obseve that mini-YOLO-3C is faster than the YOLO-T3C configuration. However, the YOLO-T3C configuration outperforms mini-YOLO-3C by around 11% in mAP and around 8% in MR and stays fast with 20 FPS. For the rest of the experiments, YOLO-T3C configuration is used since it represents the best trade-off between accuracy and speed.

Effect of Red Channel Pre-trained Weights. For this experiment, we use the best configuration which is YOLO-T3C and we perform different training sessions: the first without pre-trained weights (from scratch) and the second with pre-trained weights from imagnet, and finally with Red channel weights using the strategy described in Sect. 3.5. Results are shown in Table 3.

From Table 3, we notice that learning with pre-trained RGB weights reduces mAP and increases MR compared to training from scratch. Training from scratch gives better results than pre-trained RGB weights. Pretrained RGB weights are

Table 3. Results of proposed red pre-trained weights

Training from	mAP	MR
scratch	31.02%	70%
RGB pretrained	23.80%	79%
red-channel	**33.24%**	**67%**

not effective on thermal images. We also observe an improvement of mAP and MR measures with the Red channel pre-trained weights outperforming the two other training strategies. This proves that Red channels and thermal images share common features.

Effect of Thermal Contrast Enhancement. For the experiment, we trained the model on the original Utokyo dataset and with the enhanced thermal images obtained by applying the process described in Sect. 3.4 (on the same dataset). The obtained results are shown in Table 4.

Table 4. Results of thermal enhancement

Contrast	mAP	MR
without	33.24%	67%
With	**35.86%**	**65%**

We notice from Table 4 that the contrast enhancement brings an improvement to the global mAP and MR.

Effect of the Augmentation on the Detection Results. We experiment with different data augmentation strategies and observe their effects on detection. We compare the obtained results of training the network without augmentation, then with the auto-augment algorithm [21], and with the proposed augmentation technique described in Sect. 3.6. Auto-augment algorithm is an augmentation technique where the algorithm selects automatically the augmentation techniques according to the dataset. The results are displayed in Table 5.

Table 5. Results of Data Augmentation

	mAP	MR
without data augmentation	35.86%	65%
Auto-augment	36.84%	65%
proposed augmentation	**38.76%**	**63%**

From Table 5, we notice that learning with the proposed augmentation technique reduces MR and increases mAP compared to training with no augmentation or with auto-augment. Training with auto augment gives comparable results to not using augmentation. mAP and MR measures are improved using the proposed augmentation technique outperforming the two other training strategies.

Multi Class Thermal Object Detection. Table 6 shows obtained accuracy results in AP on the different classes of the Utokyo dataset.

Table 6. Detailed Results of our approach on Utokyo object categories

	mAP	bike	car	car_stop	color_cone	person
Yolo-T3C	**38,76%**	28.12%	**49.2%**	13.18%	**38.2%**	**65.12%**

From Table 6, we notice the highest AP results for the classes person, car, and color-cone followed by bike and car-stop. We also observe a considerable gap between person and car-stop. The AP measure is higher when the object emits more thermal signal objects such as persons and cars, while the AP value is lower in objects that emit less thermal radiation such car-stop.

Drone Detection Results. We evaluate our approach on a single-class dataset. For this, we train the network on the drone detection dataset. this dataset contains drones as one single class. Drone detection is particularly difficult because drones are small objects and can easily blend into the background. The results obtained are presented in Table 7.

Table 7. Results of Drone detection

	AP	MR
Yolo-T3C	**77.02%**	**22%**

According to Table 7, we observe a high rate of mAP with 77.02% and an MR at 22%. These results show the effectiveness of the approach for drone detection from thermal images. It also shows that the approach gives better results at single-class object detection.

Comparative Evaluation. This section shows a comparison between the proposed approach and the Tiny-YOLO-V3 architecture [13]. Table 8 compares the speed and accuracy results obtained on the Utokyo dataset, by the proposed YOLO-T3C, tiny-YOLOv3, and tiny-YOLOv3E, tiny-YOLOv3E is en enhanced version of basic tiny-YOLOv3, trained with only some of strategies proposed in

Table 8. Comparative Results with state-of-the-art

Model	mAP	MR	FPS	D/ms
tiny-YOLO-V3	20.7%	78%	**59**	**1.37**
tiny-YOLO-V3E	31.57%	69%	18	3.59
YOLO-T3C	**38,76%**	**63%**	**20**	**3.01**

this paper, namely: increasing the input to 3 channels, increasing the input size, and the contrast enhancement.

According to Table 8, the proposed YOLO-T3C is faster than tiny-YOLOV3E. Also, it appears that the proposed YOLO-T3C is more performant than its counterparts tiny-YOLOv3E and tiny-YOLOv3 in terms of mAP and accuracy. Our proposed architecture also is trained faster than both tiny-YOLO-V3E and tiny-YOLOv3.

4.5 Qualitative Evaluation

Figure 5 illustrates object detection results obtained by our approach on an example from Utokyo. left represents the detection results obtained from YOLO-T3C. Right represents the detection results obtained with Tiny-YOLO-V3.

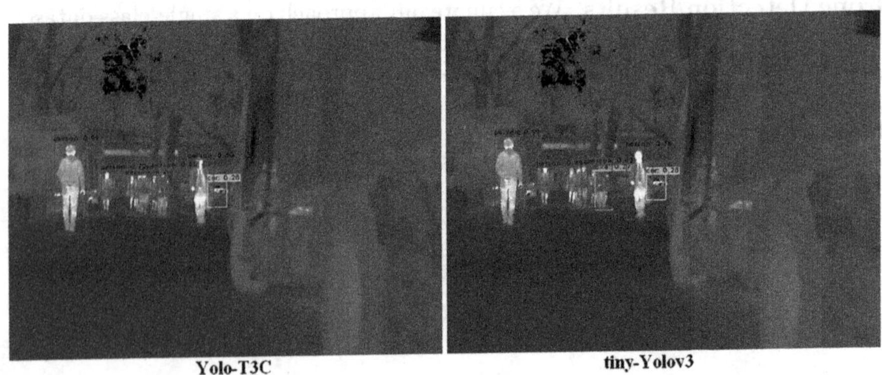

Fig. 5. Detection results on a sample image from the Utokyo dataset. Left results obtained with our appraoch. Right results obtained with tiny-YOLO-V3E

From Fig. 5, we observe that YOLO-T3C can detect more objects in the image with a total of 7 objects out of 7 with correct labels. While tiny-TOLO-V3 labels wrongly a person as a bike. This shows the effectiveness of YOLO-T3C to detect objects from thermal sources.

Figure 6 shows the detection results of the proposed approach on samples from the USC dataset.

Fig. 6. Detection results on a sample image from the USC thermal dataset

From Fig. 6, we observe that the model performs well in the USC dataset. We notice that the detector can detect drones even when not sufficiently visible (image on the left). These observable results show that the model can detect drones in thermal images.

5 Conclusion

In this paper, we have addressed the problem of improving object detection from thermal images on an optimized deep neural network. First, we used pruning on the tiny-YOLO-v3 model to obtain an optimized version of it that can run in real-time on a Jetson nano. Then, we made a set of improvements to increase the detection results on thermal images. Namely: 1) Increasing the number of channels, 2) increasing the input size, 3) using Red-Channel pre-trained weights,4) increasing the contrast of the thermal images, and 5) augmenting the thermal dataset. We carried out several experiments to evaluate our model named YOLO-T3C on the UTokyo and USC datasets. These results show that the proposed YOLO-T3C model learns well from thermal images. In future work, we plan to increase further the capability of the network to extract significant features from thermal images.

References

1. Takumi, K., Watanabe, K., Ha, Q., et al.: Multispectral object detection for autonomous vehicles. In: Proceedings of the Thematic Workshops of ACM Multimedia, Mountain View, CA, USA (2017)
2. Wang, Y., Chen, Y., Choi, J, C, C., Kuo, J.: towards visible and thermal drone monitoring with convolutional neural networks. APSIPA Trans. Signal Inf. Process. **8**, E5 (2019)
3. Mebtouche, N.ED., Baha, N.: Robust UAV detection based on saliency cues and magnified features on thermal images. Multimedia Tools Appl. (2022)
4. Girshick, R., Donahue, J., Darrell, T., Malik, J.: Rich Feature hierarchies for accurate object detection and semantic segmentation. In: IEEE Conference on Computer Vision and Pattern Recognition, pp. 580–587 (2014)

5. Redmon, J., Divvala, S., Girshick, R., Farhadi, A.: You only look once: unified, real-time object detection. In: Proceedings of the IEEE Conference on Computer Vision and Pattern Recognition, pp. 779–788 (2016)
6. Mebtouche, N.E.-D., Baha, N.: Robust object detection based on deep neural network and saliency features from visible and thermal images. In: AI2SD 2020. AISC, vol. 1418, pp. 529–540. Springer, Cham (2022). https://doi.org/10.1007/978-3-030-90639-9_43
7. Kieu, M., Bagdanov, A.D., Bertini, M.: Bottom-up and layer-wise domain adaptation for pedestrian detection in thermal images. In: ACM Transactions on Multimedia Computing, Communications and Applications, New York, NY, USA. ACM (2020). 19 pages
8. Zhang, H., Xg, H., Zhu, L.: Detecting small objects in thermal images using single-shot detector. Autom. Control. Comput. Sci. **55**, 202–211 (2021)
9. Li, S., Li, Y., Li, Y., Li, M., Xu, X.: YOLO-FIRI: improved YOLOv5 for infrared image object detection. IEEE Access **9**, 141861–141875 (2021)
10. Cao, Y., Zhou, T., Zhu, X., Su, Y.: Every feature counts: an improved one-stage detector in thermal imagery. In: Proceedings of the IEEE 5th International Conference on Computing Communication (ICCC), pp. 1965–1969 (2019)
11. Manssor, S.A.F., Sun, S., Abdalmajed, M., et al.: Real-time human detection in thermal infrared imaging at night using enhanced Tiny-yolov3 network. J. Real-Time Image Proc. **19**, 261–274 (2022)
12. Redmon, J., Farhadi, A.: Yolov3: an incremental improvement. arXiv preprint arXiv:1804.02767 (2018)
13. Adarsh, P., Rathi, P., Kumar, M.: YOLO v3-Tiny: Object Detection and Recognition using one stage improved model. In: 6th International Conference on Advanced Computing and Communication Systems (ICACCS) (2020)
14. Pan, H., Shi, Y., Lei, X., et al.: Fast identification model for coal and gangue based on the improved tiny YOLO v3. J. Real-Time Image Proc. **19**, 687–701 (2022)
15. Wang, Z., Li, C., Wang, X.: Convolutional neural network pruning with structural redundancy reduction. In Proceedings of the IEEE/CVF Conference on Computer Vision and Pattern Recognition, pp. 14913–14922 (2021)
16. Zhang, Y., Shen, Y., Zhang, J.: An improved tiny-yolov3 pedestrian detection algorithm. Int. J. Light. Electron. Optics. **183**, 17–23 (2019)
17. Alexey, A. B., Redmon, J.: Darknet (2020)
18. Reza, A.M.: Realization of the Contrast Limited Adaptive Histogram Equalization (CLAHE) for real-time image enhancement. J. VLSI Signal Process. Syst. Signal Image Video Technol. **38**(1), 35–44 (2004). https://doi.org/10.1023/B:VLSI.0000028532.53893.82
19. Aulia, S., Rahmat, D.: Brain tumor identification based on VGG-16 architecture and CLAHE method. Int. J. Inform. Vis. (JOIV) **6**(1), 96–102 (2022)
20. Everingham, M., et al.: The pascal visual object classes challenge: a retrospective. Int. J. Comput. Vision **111**, 1 (2015)
21. Cubuk, ED., Zoph, B., Mané, D., Vasudevan, V., Le, QV.: AutoAugment: learning augmentation strategies from data. In: IEEE/CVF (CVPR) Conference on Computer Vision and Pattern Recognition (2019)
22. Paszke, A., et al.: Automatic differentiation in pytorch (2017)

An Enhanced Blood Cell Counting System Using Swin Transformer with Dynamic Head and KNN Model

Mohamed Ait Mehdi[1(✉)], Khadidja Belattar[2], and Feriel Souami[1]

[1] LRIA, USTHB, Algiers, Algeria
maitmehdi@usthb.dz, feryel.souami@gmail.com
[2] Computer Science Department, University of Algiers, Algiers, Algeria
k.belattar@univ-alger.dz

Abstract. The blood cell count is a valuable feature that is usually measured with specialized tools for diagnosis and monitoring purposes. However, the conventional counting methods are limited by their performance. Hence arise the need for a rapid and effective detection and counting system using the blood cell images. In this article, we propose an automatic approach for the blood cell enumeration using swin transformer with dynamic head detector and KNN model. The experimental results show that our proposed approach, "SwinT-Dyhead+KNN" can significantly improve the blood cell detection and counting tasks using the blood cell count dataset (BCCD).

Keywords: Blood cell counting · Blood cell detection · Swin transformer · Dynamic head · Object detection · KNN model

1 Introduction

The blood testing is a crucial task in the healthcare field to diagnose and treat a range of blood conditions and diseases. In the pathology laboratories, the specialists undertake the test by examining and counting the number of red blood cells (RBC), white blood cells (WBC) and platelets. This allows the doctors to confirm or assume a specific disease according to the alterations presented in the count [4].

Generally speaking, the blood cell enumeration can be mainly established either by manually utilizing a hemocytometer, or by using the blood smear sample under a microscope. Such task is laborious, subjective, time-consuming and error-prone [16]. Addressing these issues and relying on imaging technologies and artificial intelligence techniques, a simple, rapid and effective blood cell recognition process could be achieved.

Several research studies have been reported in the literature to facilitate the process of the blood cell counting from the blood cell images. In the last decades, almost every automatic blood cell recognition system has exploited different image processing algorithms for the blood cells counting step. Some of these approaches use a circular Hough transform [1,5], the watershed transformation [13,20] and the segmentation algorithms [7] allowing blood cell counting

H. Drias et al. (Eds.): AID 2022, CCIS 1852, pp. 95–106, 2023.
https://doi.org/10.1007/978-981-99-4484-2_8

improvement. But, on the whole, the blood cell counting performance can not meet the requirements in areas with high cell overlap.

Machine learning models are also proposed to address the blood cell counting problem. In [19], the authors used spectral angle imaging and SVM to automatically count the red blood cells. In [10], the leukocyte (WBC) counting is accomplished based on PCA of the image hue features. Similar to the previous study, Habibzadeh et al. [12] combined the SVM, CNN and PCA models to perform the automatic counting of the white blood cells. Another work [24] was proposed by Romero et al., who employed the morphological operations, the Hough transform, the K-means algorithm and the watershed method to count the group of overlapped red blood cells.

In recent years, deep learning-based object detectors have been successfully applied to different medical applications, including COVID-19 recognition [2], ophthalmic disease detection [25], pneumonia detection [29], breast cancer detection [14], tuberculosis disease diagnosis [11], colon cancer detection [23], and the skin lesion recognition [22].

In the context of the blood cell detection and counting tasks, Zhang et al. [30] employed YOLOv3 detector and image density estimation method to count the red and white blood cells in microscopic images. The proposed method shows an improved counting accuracy on the complete blood count dataset.

The tiny YOLO architecture is also adapted in [3] to detect different blood cells. The detected blood cells are introduced to the KNN model and the thresholding method by intersection over union (IOU) measure to count the blood cells. The proposed method was evaluated on the blood cell count dataset and achieved 96.09% accuracy in counting RBC, 86.89% accuracy in counting WBC and 96.36% accuracy in counting platelets.

In [27], Xia et al. investigated the fully automatic WBC counting method based on microscopy image analysis using Faster-RCNN model. The overall recognition accuracy of the adapted model is 98.4% on the complete blood count dataset (of 364 images).

Another method proposed by [6] suggested an automated real-time complete blood cell count and malaria pathogen detection using a modified version of YOLO. Since the model is embedded in Raspberry Pi 3 platform, its architecture is reduced in size. The mean average precision (mAP) of the system is about 95% on the created dataset containing nine types of cells (basophil, eosinophil, neutrophil, lymphocyte, monocyte, thrombocyte, infected RBC, healthy RBC, platelet clump) with a number of 319,997 cells.

Following the previous work, Dralus et al. [9] presented an automatic method to estimate the blood cells using the RetinaNet architecture. The authors assessed the quality of the detection and cell counting methods using 230 blood cell images. The average accuracy, recall and F1-score of the blood cell counting are 92.37%, 91.28% and 91.82%, respectively.

Jiang et al. [15] suggested attention-guided YOLO to improve the blood cell detection and counting performance. The mAP of the blood cell counting has an improvement of 7.10% on the blood cell count dataset.

Based on the studies mentioned above, it should be noticed that most of these solutions focus on improving the quality of the blood cell detection and counting results. However, they are impacted by the unbalanced distribution of red blood cells, white blood cells and platelets. Specifically, the RBCs are characterized by their high density and different sizes, whereas the distribution of WBC and platelet tends to be sparse. Furthermore, they require a massive training time beforehand.

In this research, we used the KNN model with the swin transformer and dynamic head detector to improve the detection and counting of the blood cells.

The rest of the paper is organized as follows. Section 2 describes the used materials and methods for the blood cell counting process. Section 3 reports the obtained experimental results, followed by the discussion of the most important findings of the developed system. Section 4 concludes the present work.

2 Materials and Methods

In this section, the image dataset and the proposed system for the blood cell counting are presented.

2.1 Image Dataset

In this study, we employed the blood cell count dataset[1] (BCCD) for the cell detection and counting tasks. It consists of 364 blood cells images (with a resolution of 640 × 480 pixels) belonging to three classes, namely: RBC, WBC and Platelets. In order to improve the performance of both tasks, we performed the data augmentation by applying the flipping, rotation, brightness-enhancement and exposure-adjustment operations on the original dataset.

2.2 Proposed System

The article in hand presents the use of the swin transformer with dynamic head and KNN model for the counting of the blood cells. The whole process of the counting includes four steps, as outlined in Fig. 1. These stages are detailed in the following.

Image Sampling. In the data sampling step, we use 70% of the data for the model training while the remaining 20% and 10% served as the validation and test set, respectively.

Blood Cell Training. To generate the model and make detection on the blood cell images, we adopt the swin transformer as a backbone [18], feature pyramid network (FPN) [17]-based neck and dynamic head [8]. Figure 2 shows the adapted architecture of the model.

[1] https://public.roboflow.com/object-detection/bccd.

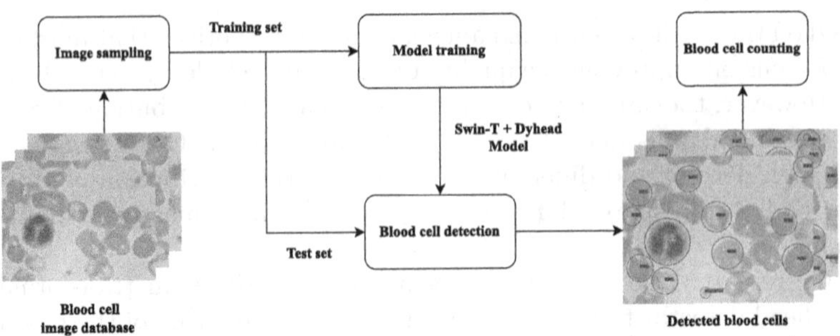

Fig. 1. The proposed system

Swin Transformer Module: is a network operating on the input RGB image (of height H and width W) according to four stages. Each one is repeated several (2x, 2x, 6x and 2x, respectively) times.

- In the first stage, perform a linear embedding mapping on the raw-valued feature of the non-overlapping patches (with size $\frac{H}{2^{l+1}} \times \frac{W}{2^{l+1}} \times 2^{l-1}C$). It yields C-dimensional feature. Then, process the output feature vector through the first swin transformer block.
- In the second stage, apply the patch merging and feature transformation methods. The former is based on merging the stack of patches generating a pyramidal feature hierarchy.
- The remaining stages use the same principle as in the first and the second ones.

The output resolution in each stage is $\frac{H}{2^{l+1}} \times \frac{W}{2^{l+1}} \times 2^{l-1}C$, where l denotes the stage level. According to the number of layers, the embedding size parameter C and the number of heads, we can distinguish the tiny swin transformer (swin-T), small swin transformer, baseline swin transformer and large swin transformer. However, relying on small, baseline or large versions for the blood cell detection and counting are conceptually time-consuming. Hence, we propose a tiny version for the blood cell detection and counting tasks.

FPN Module: in this module, the feature maps computed from the last three stages C_2, C_3, C_4 of the swin transformer module are aggregated. It produces pyramid features of five levels; P_2, P_3, P_4, P_5, P_6. The P_4 is produced using 1×1 convolution (conv) followed by 3×3 conv on the feature map M_4 (which is computed in C_4). P_5 and P_6 are obtained via 3×3 stride-2 conv on P_4 and P_5, respectively. While P_3 is computed from C_3 by using 1×1 conv and lateral connections with an upper sampling from the previous layer M_4 followed by 3×3 conv. The same principle is applied for P_2 computation. All the feature levels have 256 channels and $\frac{H}{2^{l+1}} \times \frac{W}{2^{l+1}}$ feature map resolution, where l refers to the pyramid level.

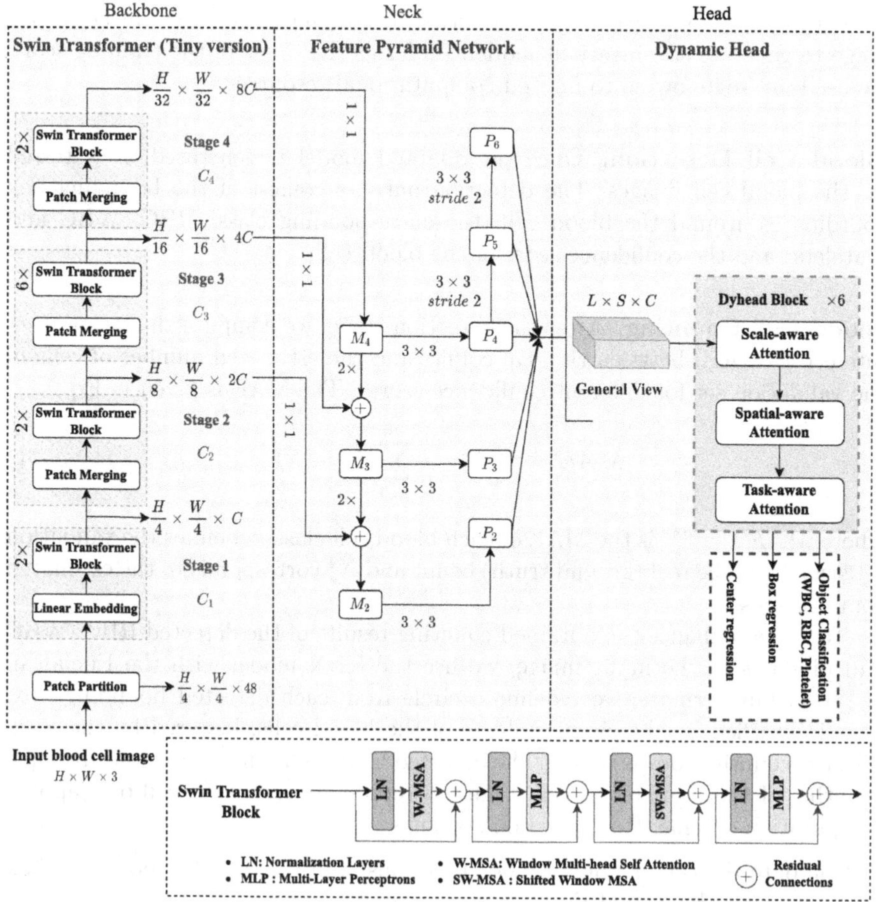

Fig. 2. The adapted SwinT-Dyhead architecture

Dynamic Head Module: allows a unified detection by combining self-attention matrices between feature levels, among spatial locations and within output channels. The model represented the five levels of the feature maps by 3-dimensional feature tensor of shape $(level, space, channel)$. The *level* dimension represents the number of levels in the computed pyramid, while the *space* and *channel* dimensions correspond to the size $(height \times width)$ and the number of channels of the median level feature, respectively. For each tensor dimension, the self-attention is calculated, giving scale-aware attention, spatial-aware attention and task-aware attention. The final output of the dynamic head (denoted as Dyhead) is the combination of the computed self-attentions. The Adaptive Training Sample Selection (ATSS) [31] is also used to train the dynamic head for the classification, localization and the center regression tasks.

During the model learning, the multi-scale training is also introduced in this stage to generate size-invariant model. As far as the range of the training scale, we used [384-640] owing to limited computational resources.

Blood Cell Detection. Once the adapted model is generated, it is tested on the blood cell images. The detection outputs consist of the bounding box coordinates around the blood cell, the corresponding class (RBC, WBC and platelets) and the confidence score of the blood cell.

Blood Cell Counting. After the detection stage, we compute the mean absolute error (MAE) between the real counts and the estimated number of cells in the validation set for different confidence scores. The MAE is given in Eq. 1.

$$MAE^{cell\_class} = \frac{1}{n}\sum_{i=1}^{n}|N_g^i - N_e^i| \quad (1)$$

where MAE^{cell_class} is the MAE of each blood cell class, n defines the validation set size, N_g^i is the real (ground truth) count and N_e^i corresponds to the estimated count of cells.

To better enhance the obtained counting results of the detected RBC, WBC and platelets in the input image, we use the KNN model with the Euclidean distance. Furthermore, we redefine a circle from each detected bounding box. This is justified by the circular shape of the blood cells. Inspired by the work [21], the counting idea is to filter the detected blood cells and remove the multiple counting of the same blood cell. Figure 3 represents the blood cell overlapping computation scheme. It is based on six steps:

1. Compute the center point c_i and the radius r_i of the detected bounding box b_i, using the Eq. 2 and Eq. 3, respectively.

$$c_i = (\frac{x_1 + x_2}{2}, \frac{y_1 + y_2}{2}) \quad (2)$$

$$r_i = \frac{\min\left(|x_1 - x_2|, |y_1 - y_2|\right)}{2}\varepsilon \quad (3)$$

Where (x_1, y_1), (x_2, y_2) are the top left and bottom right coordinates of the bounding box i and ε is a value that adjusts the size of the circle.

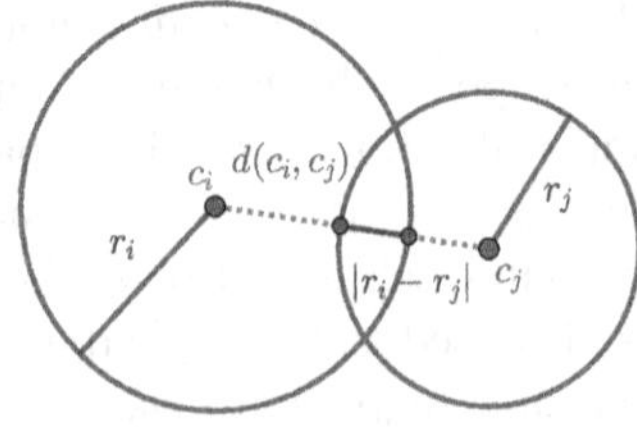

Fig. 3. The blood cell overlapping computation scheme

2. Find the nearest neighbor bounding box j of the actual one; i
3. Determine the Euclidean distance between both centers of the bounding box j and i
4. Compute the overlapping distance of the bounding box i and j
5. Compute the overlapping ratio formula given in the Eq. 4

$$ratio = \frac{|r_i - r_j|}{d(c_i, c_j)} \tag{4}$$

6. Compare the computed overlapping ratio with a given threshold which is empirically defined as 10%. When the ratio has a smaller value than the threshold, so update the RBC, WBC and platelet counts; otherwise, run the steps (2–6).

The same process is repeated for each detected bounding box in the input blood cell image.

3 Experimental Study

All the experiments showcased in this section were carried out on a Google Colaboratory platform with 12GB memory and free K80/T4 GPU. Python programming language was employed to develop the different techniques of the blood cell counting task.

3.1 Hyper-parameter Setting

For the sake of fine-tuning the model hyper-parameters and identify the optimal ones, we carried out extensive tests on the developed system to get better counting performance. Empirically speaking, we have set the batch size to 2 and the number of epochs to 12. For the optimizer, we employed AdamW. We have also opted for the initial learning rate to be 5×10^{-5} and the decay of 0.1 at the training epochs 8 and 11.

Concerning the detection confidence score $\in [0.3, 0.6]$, we have set it for RBC class to the value of 0.42, while for the WBC 0.6 we used and 0.46 for the platelet cells since they best represent the final blood cell counting results. The Fig. 4(a) shows the MAE evolution with the variation of the confidence scores using SwinT-Dyhead detector.

Another important hyper-parameter for the counting method is epsilon. We computed the MAE change according to the epsilon with values ranging from 0.10 to 0.45. The results shown in Fig. 4(b) allow to determine the adequate epsilon for the RBC, WBC and platelets counting which are set to 0.25, 0.25 and 0.45, respectively.

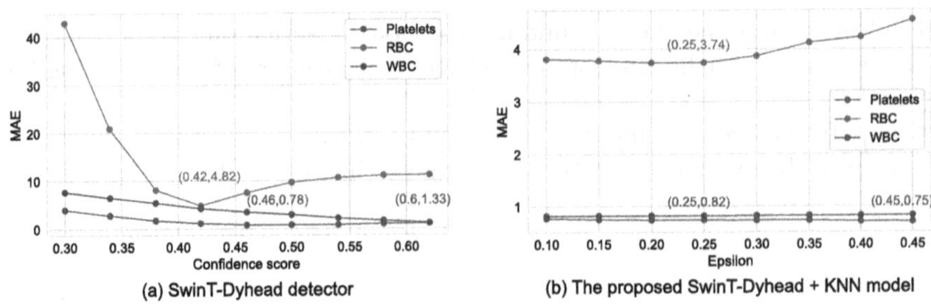

Fig. 4. MAE of the blood cell counting using different: (a) Confidence scores, (b) Epsilon values

3.2 Detection and Counting Results

In this section, we report the detection and counting results of the proposed approach. Figure 5 illustrates the classification loss, localization loss and centerness regression loss functions of the SwinT-Dyhead detector. We observe that the model has more stable curve in the classification task than those of the localization and centerness. It converges to a value of 0.17 after epoch 9 for the training and validation sets in the classification task. Regarding the loss curve of the training and validation data for both localization and centerness tasks, the SwinT-Dyhead model is fluctuating considerably, and it yields the training and validation loss of about 0.3 and 0.59, respectively.

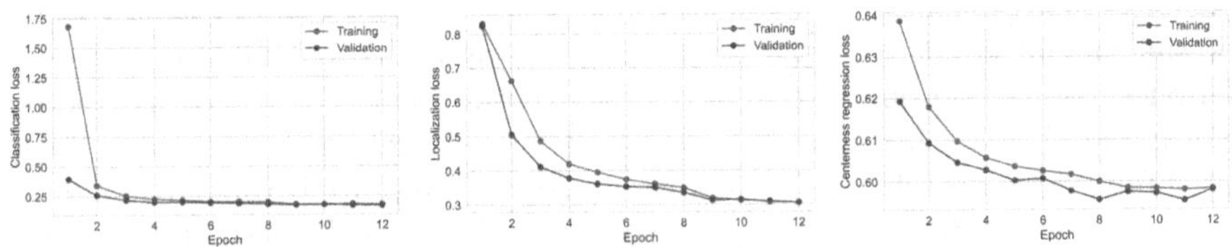

Fig. 5. Loss curves of the proposed SwinT-Dyhead detector

The proposed detection approach is also evaluated using the Frame-Per Second (FPS) metric. It defines how fast the object detector processes the input image and recognizes the desired output. The higher FPS value is, the faster recognition would be. It achieves the FPS value of 2.1.

The Table 1 presents the evaluation metrics (in terms of the number of parameters; PN, AP, AP_{50}, AP_{75}, AP_S, AP_M and AP_L) of the blood cell detection obtained with the swinT-Dyhead and the most recent models [26,28,30] in the literature for the blood cell detection.

From the obtained results shown in Table 1, it is well seen that SwinT-Dyhead detector outperforms the other implemented blood cell detection-based all of

Table 1. Comparison of the blood cell detectors

Model	PN	AP	AP_{50}	AP_{75}	AP_S	AP_M	AP_L
YOLOv3 [30]	62 M	45.9%	86.7%	45.3%	22.6%	50.4%	48.2%
YOLOF [26]	42 M	57.5%	89.0%	65.7%	43.8%	57.9%	47.3%
TE-YOLOF-B3 [28]	**16.76 M**	58.4%	90.6%	66.0%	66.0%	66.0%	66.0%
SwinT-Dyhead (ours)	42.37 M	**62.5%**	**92.2%**	**72.7%**	**48.0%**	**64.1%**	**48.3%**

YOLOv3, YOLOF and TE-YOLOF-B3 in terms of detection quality. However, TE-YOLOF-B3 offers a reduced computational complexity compared to the proposed detectors.

Figure 6 provides the obtained visual results from the application of the detector "SwinT-Dyhead" and proposed SwinT-Dyhead+KNN approach on some test blood cell images. For the WBC and platelets counting, both approaches have given similar results in almost cases (Fig. 6(a), Fig. 6(b) and Fig. 6(d)). When comparing RBC, the model shows a correct counting of 2 samples from 4 images and some false positive cells as illustrated in images (b) and (c). In overall, it yields detection AP_{50} values of 83.7%, 85.9% and 97.1% for the platelets, RBC, and WBC classes, respectively.

As seen from the figure, the proposed SwinT-Dyhead+KNN approach outperformed the SwinT-Dyhead detector in terms of the count.

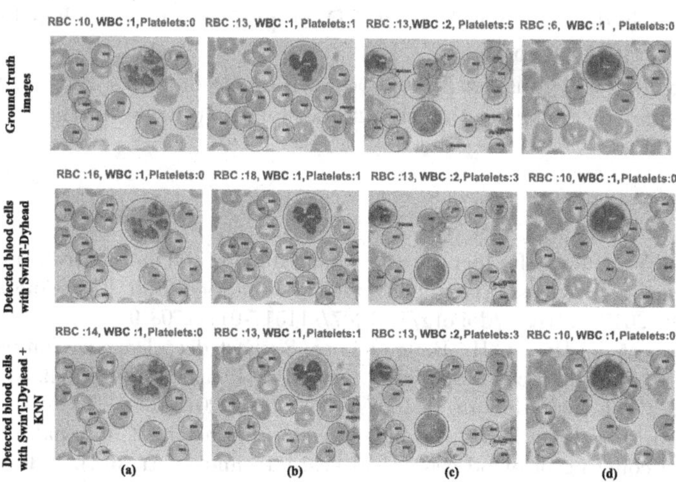

Fig. 6. The blood cell detection and counting results of the proposed approach

We also compare the proposed SwinT-Dyhead+KNN counting approach to the SwinT-Dyhead detector and KNN with IOU-based counting algorithm [3], as illustrated in Fig. 7. It is clear from the figure that the proposed approach has successfully improved the counting of the RBC compared to those obtained with

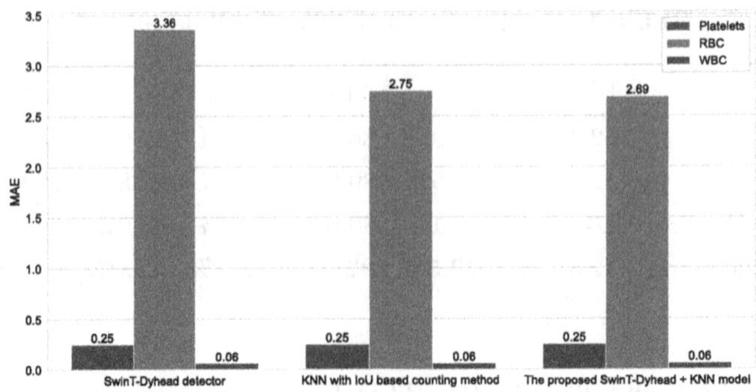

Fig. 7. Comparing the MAE value of the counting methods

SwinT-Dyhead detector and KNN with IOU-based counting model. It attains the MAE value of 2.69, whereas there is no improvement in the counting of the WBC and platelets for all three methods.

4 Conclusion

In this paper, we present a blood cell counting system based on the swin transformer with dynamic head and KNN model. The objective is to facilitate and enhance the identification and counting of the RBCs, WBCs, and platelets. The proposed method is evaluated on BCCD. It performs better when identifying the RBCs, WBCs, and platelets.

In future, we will consider large blood cell image datasets. Further work will focus on using the density estimation model for the purpose of the comparison.

References

1. Acharya, V., Kumar, P.: Identification and red blood cell automated counting from blood smear images using computer-aided system. Med. Biol. Eng. Comput. **56**(3), 483–489 (2017). https://doi.org/10.1007/s11517-017-1708-9
2. Al-antari, M.A., Hua, C.H., Bang, J., Lee, S.: Fast deep learning computer-aided diagnosis of covid-19 based on digital chest x-ray images. Appl. Intell. **51**(5), 2890–2907 (2021). https://doi.org/10.1007/s10489-020-02076-6
3. Alam, M.M., Islam, M.T.: Machine learning approach of automatic identification and counting of blood cells. Healthcare Technol. Lett. **6**(4), 103–108 (2019). https://doi.org/10.1049/htl.2018.5098
4. Bijlani, R.: Fundamentals Physiology A Textbook for Nursing Students. Jaypee Brothers Medical Publishers (2001). https://books.google.dz/books?id=Di_FswEACAAJ
5. Chadha, G.K., Srivastava, A., Singh, A., Gupta, R., Singla, D.: An automated method for counting red blood cells using image processing. Procedia Comput. Sci. **167**, 769–778 (2020). https://doi.org/10.1016/j.procs.2020.03.408, international Conference on Computational Intelligence and Data Science

6. Chowdhury, A.B., Roberson, J., Hukkoo, A., Bodapati, S., Cappelleri, D.J.: Automated complete blood cell count and malaria pathogen detection using convolution neural network. IEEE Robot. Autom. Lett. **5**(2), 1047–1054 (2020). https://doi.org/10.1109/LRA.2020.2967290
7. Cruz, D., et al.: Determination of blood components (wbcs, rbcs, and platelets) count in microscopic images using image processing and analysis. In: 2017IEEE 9th International Conference on Humanoid, Nanotechnology, Information Technology, Communication and Control, Environment and Management (HNICEM), pp. 1–7 (2017). https://doi.org/10.1109/HNICEM.2017.8269515
8. Dai, X., et al.: Dynamic head: unifying object detection heads with attentions. In: 2021 IEEE/CVF Conference on Computer Vision and Pattern Recognition (CVPR), pp. 7369–7378 (2021). https://doi.org/10.1109/CVPR46437.2021.00729
9. Dralus, G., Mazur, D., Czmil, A.: Automatic detection and counting of blood cells in smear images using retinanet. Entropy **23**(11) (2021). https://doi.org/10.3390/e23111522
10. Garcia-Lamont, F., Alvarado, M., Cervantes, J.: Systematic segmentation method based on pca of image hue features for white blood cell counting. PLOS ONE **16**(12), 1–17 (12 2022). https://doi.org/10.1371/journal.pone.0261857
11. Guo, Z., Wang, J., Wang, J., Yuan, J.: Lightweight yolov4 with multiple receptive fields for detection of pulmonary tuberculosis. Comput. Intell. Neurosci. **2022**, 9465646 (2022). https://doi.org/10.1155/2022/9465646
12. Habibzadeh, M., Krzyżak, A., Fevens, T.: White blood cell differential counts using convolutional neural networks for low resolution images. In: Rutkowski, L., Korytkowski, M., Scherer, R., Tadeusiewicz, R., Zadeh, L.A., Zurada, J.M. (eds.) ICAISC 2013. LNCS (LNAI), vol. 7895, pp. 263–274. Springer, Heidelberg (2013). https://doi.org/10.1007/978-3-642-38610-7_25
13. Hari, J., Prasad, A.S., Rao, S.K.: Separation and counting of blood cells using geometrical features and distance transformed watershed. In: 2014 2nd International Conference on Devices, Circuits and Systems (ICDCS), pp. 1–5 (2014). https://doi.org/10.1109/ICDCSyst.2014.6926205
14. Hassan, N.M., Hamad, S., Mahar, K.: Mammogram breast cancer CAD systems for mass detection and classification: a review. Multimed. Tools Appl. **81**(14), 20043–20075 (2022). https://doi.org/10.1007/s11042-022-12332-1
15. Jiang, Z., Liu, X., Yan, Z., Gu, W., Jiang, J.: Improved detection performance in blood cell count by an attention-guided deep learning method. OSA Continuum **4**(2), 323–333 (2021). https://doi.org/10.1364/OSAC.413787
16. Kaza, N., Ojaghi, A., Robles, F.E.: Virtual staining, segmentation, and classification of blood smears for label-free hematology analysis. BME Front. **2022**, 9853606 (2022). https://doi.org/10.34133/2022/9853606
17. Lin, T.Y., Dollar, P., Girshick, R., He, K., Hariharan, B., Belongie, S.: Feature pyramid networks for object detection. In: Proceedings of the IEEE Conference on Computer Vision and Pattern Recognition (CVPR), July 2017. https://doi.org/10.1109/CVPR.2017.106
18. Liu, Z., et al.: Swin transformer: hierarchical vision transformer using shifted windows. arXiv preprint arXiv:2103.14030 (2021). https://doi.org/10.48550/ARXIV.2103.14030
19. Lou, J., Zhou, M., Li, Q., Yuan, C., Liu, H.: An automatic red blood cell counting method based on spectral images. In: 2016 9th International Congress on Image and Signal Processing, BioMedical Engineering and Informatics (CISP-BMEI), pp. 1391–1396 (2016). https://doi.org/10.1109/CISP-BMEI.2016.7852934

20. Monteiro, A.C.B., Iano, Y., França, R.P.: Detecting and counting of blood cells using watershed transform: an improved methodology. In: Iano, Y., Arthur, R., Saotome, O., Vieira Estrela, V., Loschi, H.J. (eds.) BTSym 2017, pp. 301–310. Springer, Cham (2019). https://doi.org/10.1007/978-3-319-93112-8_31
21. Moon, J., Lim, S., Lee, H., Yu, S., Lee, K.B.: Smart count system based on object detection using deep learning. Remote Sens. **14**(15) (2022). https://doi.org/10.3390/rs14153761
22. Nie, Y., Sommella, P., O'Nils, M., Liguori, C., Lundgren, J.: Automatic detection of melanoma with yolo deep convolutional neural networks. In: 2019 E-Health and Bioengineering Conference (EHB), pp. 1–4 (2019). https://doi.org/10.1109/EHB47216.2019.8970033
23. Pacal, I., Karaman, A., Karaboga, D., Akay, B., Basturk, A., Nalbantoglu, U., Coskun, S.: An efficient real-time colonic polyp detection with yolo algorithms trained by using negative samples and large datasets. Comput. Biol. Med. **141**, 105031 (2022). https://doi.org/10.1016/j.compbiomed.2021.105031
24. Rondón, M.F.R., Rosas, L.M.S., Rozo, L.X.B., Castellanos, A.M.: Algorithm for detection of overlapped red blood cells in microscopic images of blood smears. Dyna (Medellin, Colombia) **83**, 188–195 (2016). https://doi.org/10.15446/dyna.v83n198.47177
25. Santos, C., Aguiar, M., Welfer, D., Belloni, B.: A new approach for detecting fundus lesions using image processing and deep neural network architecture based on yolo model. Sensors **22**(17) (2022). https://doi.org/10.3390/s22176441
26. Shakarami, A., Menhaj, M.B., Mahdavi-Hormat, A., Tarrah, H.: A fast and yet efficient yolov3 for blood cell detection. Biomed. Signal Process. Control **66**, 102495 (2021). https://doi.org/10.1016/j.bspc.2021.102495
27. Xia, T., Jiang, R., Fu, Y.Q., Jin, N.: Automated blood cell detection and counting via deep learning for microfluidic point-of-care medical devices. IOP Conf. Ser. Mater. Sci. Eng. **646**(1), 012048 (2019). https://doi.org/10.1088/1757-899X/646/1/012048
28. Xu, F., Li, X., Yang, H., Wang, Y., Xiang, W.: Te-yolof: tiny and efficient yolof for blood cell detection. Biomed. Signal Process. Control **73**, 103416 (2022). https://doi.org/10.1016/j.bspc.2021.103416
29. Yao, S., Chen, Y., Tian, X., Jiang, R.: Pneumonia detection using an improved algorithm based on faster r-cnn. Comput. Math. Methods Med. **2021**, 8854892 (2021). https://doi.org/10.1155/2021/8854892
30. Zhang, D., Zhang, P., Wang, L.: Cell counting algorithm based on yolov3 and image density estimation. In: 2019 IEEE 4th International Conference on Signal and Image Processing (ICSIP), pp. 920–924 (2019). https://doi.org/10.1109/SIPROCESS.2019.8868603
31. Zhang, S., Chi, C., Yao, Y., Lei, Z., Li, S.Z.: Bridging the gap between anchor-based and anchor-free detection via adaptive training sample selection. In: 2020 IEEE/CVF Conference on Computer Vision and Pattern Recognition (CVPR), pp. 9756–9765 (2020). https://doi.org/10.1109/CVPR42600.2020.00978

Object Local Aspect Aided CNN for Recognition

Brahim Remmouche(✉), Salah-Eddine Maoudj, and Mokhtar Taffar

LaRIA Laboratory, Computer Science Department, University of Jijel, BP 98 Ouled Aissa, Jijel, Algeria
brahim.remmouche@univ-jijel.dz

Abstract. Object recognition is a subfield of computer vision that refers to the ability to identify objects in images. The existing methods in the literature can be classified into two main approaches, the classic approach based on a combination of local visual characteristics and classifiers, and the new approach based on deep learning. Each approach has its advantages and drawbacks. In this paper, we aim to improve the object recognition process in the case of occluded objects, from which both approaches suffer. To do this, we propose a CNN model guided by visual local aspect which describes the appearance of objects in the scene. The proposed model proved its effectiveness in the recognition of objects, especially in the case of occluded objects, and it reaches an acceptable rate of accuracy that outperforms a simple CNN.

Keywords: Local feature · SIFT · Visual aspect · Classifier · SVM · CNN · Object recognition · Occulted objects recognition

1 Introduction

Computer vision and image analysis for object recognition are interdisciplinary scientific and applicative fields that deal with how models and algorithms acquire high-level understanding from images or videos. One of their major disciplines is object recognition, which refers to the ability to identify objects in a scene based on visual cues. Several object recognition methods have been proposed in the last two decades. These methods can be classified into two main categories of approaches: the classical approach combining the local visual features and the classifiers, and the new deep approach based on the convolutional neural networks [1].

The classical approach can be effective in the case of object recognition in complex or cluttered images or where objects are partially occluded [2], but it also has many drawbacks. One of them is the manual extraction of features [3]. Moreover, these methods have shown poor performance in multi-object recognition cases [4]. Although these approaches have dominated the field of object recognition, the appearance of convolutional neural networks [5] has completely changed the performance of algorithms dedicated to computer vision, in particular those intended for object detection, where some models have become the standards and essential references for tasks upstream of object classification.

H. Drias et al. (Eds.): AID 2022, CCIS 1852, pp. 107–119, 2023.
https://doi.org/10.1007/978-981-99-4484-2_9

This great enthusiasm for deep learning models has enabled them to go further in their architectures.

Due to the great success of deep convolutional neural networks (DCNN) in object classification tasks, the use of local detectors with standard classifiers has become almost inefficient for detection, recognition, tracking, etc. But like any approach, DCNN models have their own drawbacks. Among them, we can mention the poor performance in recognizing occluded objects [6]. Another disadvantage is when the classes of objects are too similar in their overall structure, like in animal classification, where the objects have approximately the same length, width, and shape. These cases can be mitigated by going deeper into the architectures with very fine tuning of the network hyperparameters [7]. All of this brings us to another more technical issue related to the huge amount of parameters that a network can contain, which restricts the use of the model in low-computational devices, both during the training and the testing and even during its real integration.

To avoid the problems mentioned above, and especially to solve the case of the recognition of occluded objects, we propose a convolutional neural network (CNN) with two inputs: one for the original image and the other for the part of the image that has the highest density of visual contents modeled by SIFT [8] appearance features belonging to the object. To decide whether a visual aspect point belongs to the object or not, we train an SVM classifier [9]. The purpose of using a two-input CNN network is to give the model the ability to capture both global and local information: the global information from the whole image and the local one from the partial image.

The rest of the paper is organized as follows. Section 2 provides an overview of related work. Section 3 presents a brief comparison between the classical approach and CNN. Section 4 describes the model we propose, followed by a presentation of the experimental results obtained by our model in Sect. 5. In Sect. 6, we discuss the performance, advantages and drawbacks of our model, and finally, Sect. 7 concludes this work.

2 Related Works

Many contributions in the computer vision area have been made to tackle different object recognition tasks, particularly in the case of occlusion. The recent works of the decade tried to solve the problem by using DCNN and the most recent using recurrent neural networks (RNN), e.g., for occulted object tracking, and their variants.

DeVries and Taylor in [10] used the simple regularization technique of randomly masking out square regions to improve the robustness and overall performance of convolutional neural networks. They claim that their approach can be combined with other regularizers and existing data augmentation techniques to further enhance model performance.

Yun et *al.* in [11] propose the CutMix augmentation strategy: patches are cut and pasted among training images where the ground truth labels are also mixed proportionally to the area of the patches. They state that the CutMix strategy outperforms the state-of-the-art augmentation strategies on CIFAR and ImageNet classification tasks by efficiently using training pixels and retaining the regularization effect of regional dropout.

Cao et *al.* in [12] propose a novel context feature pyramid network architecture that is guided by attention (ACFPN) to address the contradicting requirement between feature map resolution and receptive field on high-resolution input images for object detection and to improve the discriminative ability of feature representations. This model incorporates attention-guided multi-path features to extract discriminative data from various large receptive fields using two modules. The first is the Context Extraction Module (CEM), which explores massive amounts of contextual information from numerous receptive fields. The second module, called Attention-guided Module (AM), uses the attention mechanism to adaptively capture the salient dependencies over objects. It is stated that the modules can be easily integrated into existing object detection and segmentation networks and end-to-end trained.

Aslan et *al.* in [13] compare Convolutional Neural Network (CNN) with Histogram of Oriented Gradients (HOG)-Support Vector Machine (SVM) in human detection, and conduct these comparisons for complete occlusion status. The authors state that CNN is more successful since it identifies more across the video in a noisy and complete occlusion scenario. In the absence of occlusion, HOG-SVM yields more successful outcomes. However, when real-world applications are considered CNN produces more optimum results.

H. Zhang et *al.* propose in [6] a new convolutional neural network (CNN) model for traffic object detection by using multi-scale local and global feature representation (MFR). The proposed model is made up of two parts: a region proposal network that creates candidate object regions and an object detection network that integrates multi-scale features and global information, called MFR-CNN. These two components are jointly optimized. The trained system can detect real-world traffic objects accurately, especially small objects and heavily occluded objects.

Z. Zhang et *al.* in [14] present the DeepVoting deep network, which is useful for semantic part detection under partial occlusion. It incorporates robustness and explainability so that the whole pipeline can be jointly optimized. Specifically, it adds two layers after the intermediate features of a deep network, e.g., the pool-4 layer of VGGNet. Local visual cue evidence is extracted by the first layer, and a voting mechanism is performed by the second layer by utilizing the spatial relationship between visual cues and semantic parts.

Wang et *al.* in [15] propose a solution to detect partially occluded objects using CompositionalNets by segmenting the context during training via bounding box annotations. They use the segmentation to learn a context-aware CompositionalNet that disentangles the representation of the context and the object. They extend the part-based voting scheme in CompositionalNets to vote for the corners of the object's bounding box. They state that this enables the model to reliably estimate bounding boxes for partially occluded objects.

Xu et *al.* in [16] propose the GC-FRCN (Generative feature completing Faster RCNN) occluded object detection algorithm, which consists of the OSGM (Occlusion Sample Generation Module) and OSIM (Occlusion Information Module) (Occlusion Sample Inpainting Module). To increase the diversity of occlusion scenarios in the training dataset, the OSGM specifically mines and discards feature points with high category responses on the feature map. In order to improve feature quality by repairing the noisy object feature, OSIM develops an implicit mapping connection from an occluded feature map to a real feature map in an adversarial manner. The authors claim that the GC-FRCN has strong robustness for occlusion at various scales and can detect objects with local external occlusion successfully.

Dong et *al.* in [17] describe a CNN-based ellipse detector, Ellipse R-CNN, for representing and inferring occluded objects as ellipses in images of strongly occluded items in cluttered environments, such as fruit clusters in trees, which are difficult to segment. Based on the Mask R-CNN architecture, they present an ellipse regression that is reliable and compact for elliptical object recognition. Even when several elliptical objects are obscured by other nearby objects, their approach can still determine their parameters. They combine the U-Net structure for learning various occlusion patterns to compute the final detection score and use enhanced feature regions for the regression stage for better occlusion handling.

3 CNN vs. Classical Approach

Until the beginning of the last decade, the classical approach based on classifiers and local detectors dominated the object recognition domain. Its process can be divided into two steps: extracting features from data using local descriptors (like SIFT, SURF, and HOG) [18], then the image classification based on these features using a machine learning classifier (like SVM, KNN, etc.) [9]. This approach seemed effective until the AlexNet [5] model was proposed. It is the first CNN that won the ImageNet Large Scale Visual Recognition Challenge (ILSVRC) [19]. Since then, these models have dominated most computer vision applications.

The deep and convolutional neural model or deep learning approach in general automatically extracts features from data in the form of a network internal representation [1], which is a great advantage over the classical approach that extracts these features manually using local descriptors [18]. CNNs also perform well in terms of multi-object recognition when the availability of training data and computational resources is guaranteed.

Regarding the disadvantage of the CNN in the object recognition process [20], it can perform a bad classification in the case of occluded objects [6]. Once the CNN accepts the entire image, this could mislead the model when the object is partially hidden. On the other hand, the classical approach can be regularly performed in these cases because some features will appear in the non-occluded part of the object, which will not affect the recognition process.

4 Proposed Model

In this section, we present the proposed model for recognizing partially occluded objects. The model is built around a CNN network guided by the visual local aspect of the objects to identify. The visual local aspects of an object are defined by the visual contents of its local parts. These local aspects are detected and extracted using the SIFT detector. Our approach uses two classification models: an SVM classifier and a CNN network with two inputs, see Fig. 1. Thus, the SVM classifier distinguishes between the visual appearances that belong to the object and the others that are nonobject. Then, it selects the best aspects belonging to the object ordered by their magnitude, calculates the average of their positions, and crops a region of the image centered on the barycenter. The proposed CNN has two inputs: one input for the original image and the other for the cropped image. The two images are exposed to separate convolutions to generate two feature maps that will be flattened and concatenated into a single vector. The last one feeds the fully connected layers.

The idea of using two inputs for the CNN network, where the second input is a part of the first, is that the model can learn global information from the whole image and local information from the cropped image. This local information that describes the aspect of the object is usually located in the region of the image where the density of the object's appearance is highest.

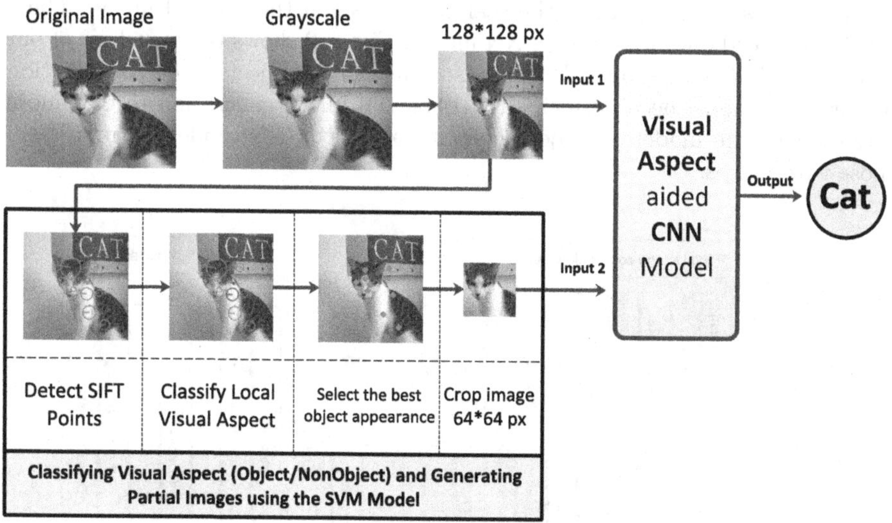

Fig. 1. General view of our local visual aspect aided CNN model for recognition.

4.1 SVM Model

The SVM classifier is mainly dedicated to the visual aspect of object selection. Its role is to decide whether an extracted feature belongs to the object or not. To construct the SVM model for visual content classification, two steps are required: (i) object content detection, and (ii) SVM model learning.

To detect the aspect features of objects, we used the scale-invariant feature transform (SIFT) algorithm [8]. According to the study work in [18], SIFT can perform better in our case than other detectors where the algorithm generates keypoints that are invariant to changes in uniform scale, orientation, and illumination, but also invariant to partial affine distortions in-plane 2D of the image. Each keypoint is represented by a 128-element descriptor containing elementary information about the detected patch of the object.

Once visual contents of objects have been detected and extracted, they feed the SVM model defined around a polynomial kernel. The result is a trained SVM that distinguishes the visual contents of objects (e.g., dog and cat aspects) from nonobjects.

4.2 CNN Model

The second model is the basis of the proposed method. It uses the first model that extracts the part of the image likely to contain the detected object. This new image is obtained from the region of interest localized through the local features describing a similar aspect to the searched object in the original image. These two images feed our two inputs CNN model. Figure 2 shows the structure of our proposed CNN model aided by the visual aspect of objects. The construction of our CNN model needs principally: (i) partial image generation to give more attention to the model on object content, and (ii) CNN model learning from those two images.

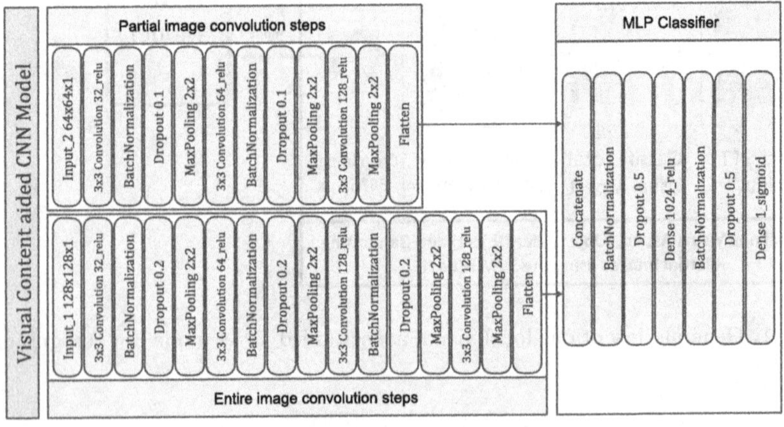

Fig. 2. Architecture of the proposed CNN model aided by the visual aspect of objects.

The generation of partial images is done automatically using the SVM model. In this step, we used several aspect feature parameters. After generating the visual features, we used their corresponding descriptors to classify whether or not each feature has the aspect of the searched object, in other words, whether each feature belongs to the object or not. Then, the best visual contents with the highest magnitude are selected and their coordinates are used to calculate the average position. Finally, the image centered on this barycenter is cropped to 64×64 px.

The CNN model is trained from the original images and their corresponding partial images where the objects are scaled to give CNN more attention to the presence of the object.

5 Experimental Results

5.1 Dataset and Training

To train and test our model, we used the Kaggle Dogs-Vs-Cats dataset[1]. This dataset contains only two classes of objects (dogs and cats), and they are very similar in their overall shape, thereby adding an additional difficulty in distinguishing their aspects. The efficiency of the proposed model compared to a simple CNN can be seen when it can achieve better performance on this type of dataset.

In order to validate the superiority of our model over a simple CNN in the case of occulted objects, we built a database of hundreds of images from the Kaggle Dogs-Vs-Cats dataset. The objects in the images have been covered and partially occluded. By randomly choosing the regions of the objects, these regions are hidden by a part of their respective image backgrounds in order to increase the power of occultation and camouflage.

We used a binary SVM classifier with a polynomial kernel. SVM is useful for learning and constructing the hyperplane that separates explicitly the variability interclass of objects but also for classifying aspect features of objects, where in our case, features belong to two classes: object class (e.g., dogs and cats in the same class) and nonobject class. It is a simple and efficient machine learning algorithm that can perform binary or multiple classifications with few learning data.

During the learning process, we first selected images manually from Kaggle Dogs-Vs-Cats dataset as a training set. For each image, we detected and extracted all the interesting features describing different aspects. Then we went through each of them and decided whether it was an important object appearance or not for training. As mentioned previously, each object aspect is presented by a descriptor of a 128-histogram of gradient orientations. The next step is to feed the aspect descriptors with their labels to the SVM for learning.

After automatically generating partial images, each image and its part in the training set are normalized between 0 and 1 and given to the two CNN inputs,

[1] https://www.kaggle.com/competitions/dogs-vs-cats.

where they are separately exposed to convolution operations. Finally, they are concatenated into fully connected layers to provide a single output. Thus, CNN should learn to distinguish between dog and cat object classes.

5.2 Data Considerations

As mentioned earlier, we created a simple CNN to compare its performance with our proposed model. Both models are trained on the Kaggle Dogs-Vs-Cats dataset. We divided the data into two parts: 16000 images for the training set and 4000 images for the validation set.

5.3 Evaluation of the SVM Model

In this series of evaluations, we estimate the performance of the SVM model in terms of accuracy, precision, recall, and F1 score. The evaluation values obtained in these terms are expressed as:

$$Accuracy = \frac{TP + TN}{TP + FP + TN + FN} = \frac{825}{1030} = 80\% \tag{1}$$

The **accuracy** of a model is given by the number of correct predicted keypoints out of the total number of keypoints.

$$Precision = \frac{TP}{TP + FP} = \frac{582}{671} = 86.7\% \tag{2}$$

The **precision** estimates the proportion of correctly predicted keypoints belonging to the object to all predicted keypoints belonging to the object.

$$Recall = \frac{TP}{TP + FN} = \frac{582}{698} = 83.3\% \tag{3}$$

The **recall** expresses the proportion of keypoints predicted as correctly belonging to the object to all keypoints really belonging to the object.

$$F1\ score = \frac{2 * Precision * Recall}{Precision + Recall} = 84.96 \tag{4}$$

F1 score is the metric that calculates the harmonic mean between the precision and recall values.

Where

TP: True Positive expresses the number of keypoints predicted as belonging to the object, and really belonging to it.

TN: True Negative is the number of keypoints that were predicted not to belong to the object, and that they really do not belong.

FP: False Positive estimates the number of keypoints that were predicted to belong to the object, and that they do not belong.

FN: False Negative gives the number of keypoints that were predicted as not belonging to the object when in fact they do belong.

So we randomly selected 50 images and fed them to the model. The model generates an average of 20 visual aspect points for each image, and this procedure gives us the results described as a confusion matrix given by Table 1.

Table 1. The confusion matrix reports the performance of the SVM.

	Predicting object aspects	Predicting nonobject aspects
Belongs to the object	582	116
Does not belong to the object	89	243

5.4 Evaluation and Comparison of Proposed CNN

As we see in the curves of Fig. 3, the models perform well on the training set where the value of the validation accuracy for both models is close to the training accuracy and increases regularly. However, our model outperforms the simple CNN model in training accuracy and validation with significant results.

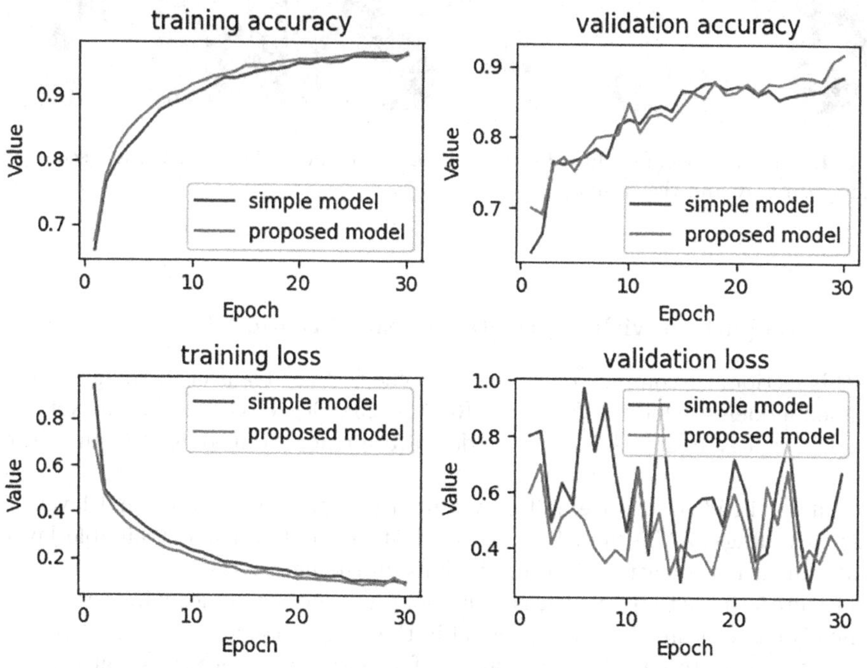

Fig. 3. Evolution of accuracy and loss during training and validation for both models.

Case of Non-Occluded Objects: To test the performance of the models on data they have never seen before, we reserved 5000 images for the test set and fed them to the models. Our model outperforms the simple CNN model on the test set, where it achieves 92% accuracy versus 88% reached by the other model.

Case of Occluded Objects: As mentioned in Sect. 5.1, and for testing purposes, we partially covered hundreds of images of the dataset in order to feed both models. Our model outperforms the Simple CNN model even in the case of partially occluded objects when it reaches an accuracy of 87%, whereas the Simple CNN reaches only 62%. Figure 4 shows some correct detections of partially occluded objects.

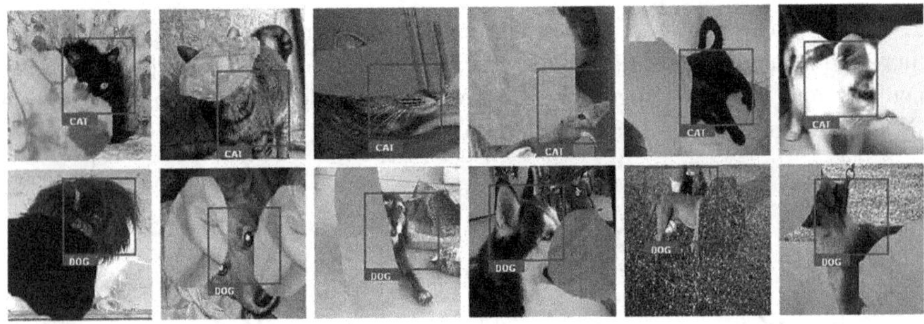

Fig. 4. Some images of occluded objects (Dogs and Cats) where our model recognizes them correctly and the simple CNN fails.

5.5 Comparison with Some State-of-the-Art Models

In this section, we compare our model to some popular transfer learning [21] pre-trained models, including VGG [22], ResNet [23], DenseNet [24], MobileNet [25], and EfficientNet [26]. All these models are already trained on the ImageNet dataset.

The main idea is to freeze the weighted pre-trained convolutional layers to take advantage of the model to extract features and add new trainable layers that will turn old features into predictions on the new dataset.

Figure 5 shows that EfficientNet develops an accuracy performance of 97.74% which is higher than that of our model in the case of non-occlusion. However, in occluded object recognition, our model offers an accuracy of 87% slightly higher than that of EfficientNet and which exceeds clearly other models.

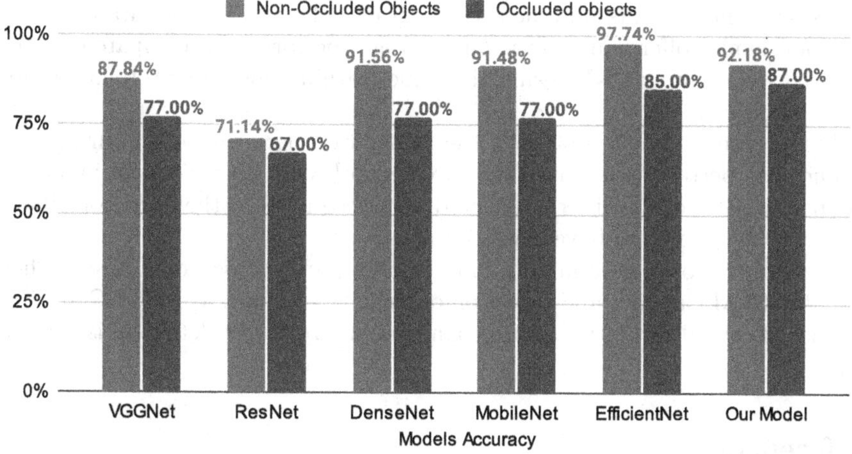

Fig. 5. Comparison of our CNN model with state-of-the-art models.

6 Discussion

As we claimed earlier, the proposed model works well in the case of partially occluded objects, where it outperforms the CNN model by a percentage of 25%. This can be explained by the impact of the visual aspect features of the object. The learned object visual traits contributed to guiding the CNN model toward the non-occluded part of the objects in images and extracting meaningful information from these parts.

The limitation that we can highlight for our model is the poor performance in the case of multi-object recognition. The reason is that the SVM classifier used cannot distinguish whether the visual aspects belong to different objects. It is a 2-class classifier that only distinguishes between objects (dogs and cats) and nonobject parts. Moreover, although the SVM classifier has proven its efficiency in object recognition, its learning through local characteristics remains a limit because the manual choice of object and nonobject visual content is delicate to ensure an impartial model on the one hand, and a balanced distribution between intra-class and inter-class on the other hand.

7 Conclusion

In this paper, we have studied the feasibility of guiding a CNN model by visual aspect features in order to improve the process of object recognition, especially in the case of occluded objects. We have developed a CNN network with two inputs: the first for the original image, and the second for a part of it cropped to the region with the highest density of visual content features belonging to the object. To recognize these visual aspects of objects, we learned a 2-class SVM classifier.

Experimental results obtained on the Kaggle Dogs-Vs-Cats dataset showed that our model offers an additional accuracy performance compared to that achieved by a simple CNN, using the same learning and test protocol on non-occluded objects.

In the case of occulted objects, the recognition performance of our model is significantly better, proof that the CNN network with an additional input containing the parts of the objects detected and recognized by the SVM contributed to driving our model to have this accuracy.

For future work, we aim to build a model purely based on CNNs without using the SVM classifier and test it on other datasets, such as MSCOCO [27], in the case of occluded multi-object recognition, where object detection is a crucial step.

References

1. Dhillon, A., Verma, G.: Convolutional neural network: a review of models, methodologies and applications to object detection. Progress Artif. Intell. **9**, 85–112 (2020)
2. David, P., DeMenthon, D.: Object recognition in high clutter images using line features. In: Tenth IEEE International Conference on Computer Vision (ICCV'05), vol. 1. 2, pp. 1581–1588 (2005)
3. O'Mahony, N., et al.: Deep learning vs. traditional computer vision. In: Advances In Computer Vision: Proceedings of the 2019 Computer Vision Conference (CVC), vol. 1 1, pp. 128–144 (2020)
4. Deselaers, T., Keysers, D., Paredes, R., Vidal, E., Ney, H.: Local representations for multi-object recognition. In: Michaelis, B., Krell, G. (eds.) DAGM 2003. LNCS, vol. 2781, pp. 305–312. Springer, Heidelberg (2003). https://doi.org/10.1007/978-3-540-45243-0_40
5. Krizhevsky, A., Sutskever, I., Hinton, G.: Imagenet classification with deep convolutional neural networks. Advances In Neural Information Processing Systems. 25 (2012)
6. Zhang, H., Wang, K., Tian, Y., Gou, C., Wang, F.: MFR-CNN: incorporating multi-scale features and global information for traffic object detection. IEEE Trans. Veh. Technol. **67**, 8019–8030 (2018)
7. Wang, Y., Zhang, H., Zhang, G.: cPSO-CNN: an efficient PSO-based algorithm for fine-tuning hyper-parameters of convolutional neural networks. Swarm Evol. Comput. **49**, 114–123 (2019)
8. Lowe, D.: Distinctive image features from scale-invariant keypoints. Int. J. Comput. Vision **60**, 91–110 (2004)
9. Sha'Abani, M., Fuad, N., Jamal, N., Ismail, M.: kNN and SVM classification for EEG: a review. In: ECCE2019, pp. 555–565 (2020)
10. DeVries, T., Taylor, G.: Improved regularization of convolutional neural networks with cutout. ArXiv Preprint ArXiv:1708.04552 (2017)
11. Yun, S., Han, D., Oh, S., Chun, S., Choe, J., Yoo, Y.: Cutmix: Regularization strategy to train strong classifiers with localizable features. In: Proceedings of the IEEE/CVF International Conference On Computer Vision, pp. 6023–6032 (2019)
12. Cao, J., Chen, Q., Guo, J., Shi, R.: Attention-guided context feature pyramid network for object detection. ArXiv Preprint ArXiv:2005.11475 (2020)

13. Aslan, M., Durdu, A., Sabanci, K., Mutluer, M.: CNN and HOG based comparison study for complete occlusion handling in human tracking. Measurement **158**, 107704 (2020)
14. Zhang, Z., Xie, C., Wang, J., Xie, L., Yuille, A.: Deepvoting: a robust and explainable deep network for semantic part detection under partial occlusion. In: Proceedings of the IEEE Conference On Computer Vision And Pattern Recognition, pp. 1372–1380 (2018)
15. Wang, A., Sun, Y., Kortylewski, A., Yuille, A.: Robust object detection under occlusion with context-aware compositionalnets. In: Proceedings of the IEEE/CVF Conference on Computer Vision And Pattern Recognition, pp. 12645–12654 (2020)
16. Xu, C., Yuen, P., Lang, W., Xin, R., Mao, K., Jiang, H.: Generative detect for occlusion object based on occlusion generation and feature completing. J. Visual Commun. Image Representation **78**, 103189 (2021)
17. Dong, W., Roy, P., Peng, C., Isler, V.: Ellipse R-CNN: learning to infer elliptical object from clustering and occlusion. IEEE Trans. Image Process. **30**, 2193–2206 (2021)
18. Routray, S., Ray, A., Mishra, C.: Analysis of various image feature extraction methods against noisy image: SIFT, SURF and HOG. In: 2017 Second International Conference On Electrical, Computer And Communication Technologies (ICECCT), pp. 1–5 (2017)
19. Russakovsky, O., Deng, J., Su, H., Krause, J., Satheesh, S., Ma, S., Huang, Z., Karpathy, A., Khosla, A., Bernstein, M., Berg, A.C., Fei-Fei, L.: ImageNet large scale visual recognition challenge. Int. J. Comput. Vision **115**(3), 211–252 (2015). https://doi.org/10.1007/s11263-015-0816-y
20. Arkin, E., Yadikar, N., Xu, X., Aysa, A., Ubul, K.: A survey: object detection methods from CNN to transformer. Multimed. Tools Appl., 1–31 (2022)
21. Hussain, M., Bird, J., Faria, D.: A study on cnn transfer learning for image classification. In: UK Workshop On Computational Intelligence, pp. 191–202 (2018)
22. Simonyan, K., Zisserman, A.: Very deep convolutional networks for large-scale image recognition. ArXiv Preprint ArXiv:1409.1556 (2014)
23. He, K., Zhang, X., Ren, S., Sun, J.: Deep residual learning for image recognition. Proceedings of the IEEE Conference on Computer Vision and Pattern Recognition, pp. 770–778 (2016)
24. Huang, G., Liu, Z., Van Der Maaten, L., Weinberger, K.: Densely connected convolutional networks. In: Proceedings of the IEEE Conference on Computer Vision and Pattern Recognition, pp. 4700–4708 (2017)
25. Howard, A., et al.: Mobilenets: efficient convolutional neural networks for mobile vision applications. ArXiv Preprint ArXiv:1704.04861 (2017)
26. Tan, M., Le, Q.: Efficientnet: rethinking model scaling for convolutional neural networks. In: International Conference on Machine Learning, pp. 6105–6114 (2019)
27. Lin, T.-Y., et al.: Microsoft COCO: common objects in context. In: Fleet, D., Pajdla, T., Schiele, B., Tuytelaars, T. (eds.) ECCV 2014. LNCS, vol. 8693, pp. 740–755. Springer, Cham (2014). https://doi.org/10.1007/978-3-319-10602-1_48

Development of a Haptic Device-Based Serious Game for Cognitive Rehabilitation

Amel Smaili[1], Litissia Medgueb[1](✉), Nouara Achour[1], M. Z. Amrani[1], Abdelghani Daoudi[1], and Selmane Derder[2]

[1] LabLRPE USTHB University, Bab Zouar, Algiers, Algeria
Litissia59@hotmail.com

[2] Health Centre of kinesitherapy and Rehabilitation, Ouled Fayet, Algiers, Algeria

Abstract. In order for patients to achieve their maximum potential for physical, cognitive and psychological functions in an interesting and enjoyable way, serious games-based rehabilitation was introduced to the healthcare sector during the last few years. And although serious games do not always require the use of virtual reality, the immersion in a virtual world reinforces the patient's sense of presence and the real time auditory, visual and/or haptic feedback may result in increased motivation and effort during the rehabilitation. In this paper we present the development of a maze application using the Phantom Omni as its control device that provides real time haptic feedback, which can be used as a complementary exercise for cognitive rehabilitation. The application design was based on our findings from literature studies and informal interviews with medical personnel and patients. A study was also conducted on 11 test subjects to evaluate the usability of the application; the obtained results were satisfactory and showed that the system has the potential of being an innovative experience for the said subjects as well as a stimulating and encouraging exercise complement to the traditional methods of rehabilitation. As for validation tests, further data acquisition functions will be implemented in order to conduct a full validity test of the developed system

Keywords: Cognitive Rehabilitation · Cognitive Remediation · Virtual Reality · Haptic · Immersion · Serious Games · Phantom Omni · Maze

1 Introduction

Cognition incorporates different cognitive processes that allow us to gather and acquire knowledge about our environment (to understand, remember, think and decide) to control and manipulate it. Cognition and its aspects have an important role in human behavior according to Bandura [1], who states that interaction must be understood as a reciprocal determinism of personal cognition and emotions, environmental, and behavioral factors.

Hence, if cognitive problems occur, it is really important to deal with them since they will seriously impact human comportment and hinder communication and human

A. Smaili and L. Medgueb—contributed equally to the work and serve as co-first authors.

H. Drias et al. (Eds.): AID 2022, CCIS 1852, pp. 120–133, 2023.
https://doi.org/10.1007/978-981-99-4484-2_10

interaction with the environment. One of the most common treatments for these problems is cognitive rehabilitation, which is a set of exercises given by a therapist to help the brain regain its normal function.

To ensure the effectiveness of cognitive rehabilitation, it must be done repetitively for each exercise, which is going to be hard for the patients to maintain their interest. One of the best solutions that researchers have found to keep the patients motivated is the use of virtual reality and serious games.

Virtual reality (VR) is a recent tool in the healthcare industry (since the early 1990s [2]) that allows for a more objective evaluation and intensive rehabilitation under ecological conditions. VR also allows the patient to be immersed in a ludic and attractive environment, simplified and specially adapted to his physical and cognitive limitations. The artificial environment is designed with hardware and software; it is presented to the user in a way that it appears as a realistic environment that is more or less close to reality, with a degree of immersion that differs according to the hardware used. This immersive experience ranges from simple keyboard and mouse interaction to full auditive, visual, and haptic immersions. Figure 1 represents an example of a virtual rehabilitation system "SaboVR" [3].

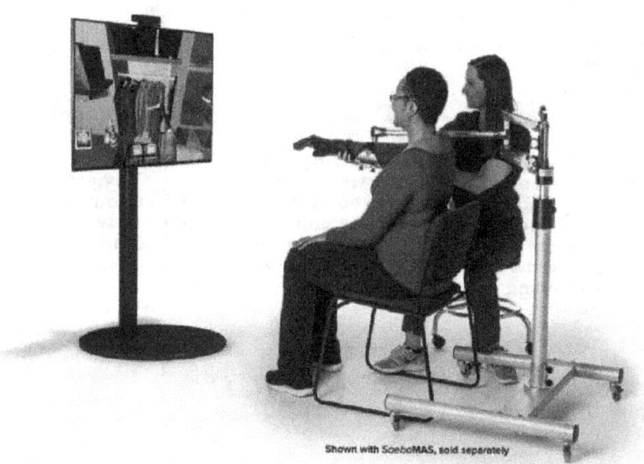
Shown with SaeboMAS, sold separately

Fig. 1. Example of a virtual rehabilitation system "SaboVR".

Serious games are games that use their "ludic" features of motivation, commitment, and enjoyability for serious purposes.

While designing a serious game and to ensure its smooth functioning and effectiveness, it is always necessary to refer to the basic elements that Brian Winn has specified: learning, story-telling, gameplay, user experience, and technology [4].

Serious games are used in various sectors to facilitate learning and training. Indeed, they are widely used in medical applications, primarily in rehabilitation.

Therefore, the use of serious games combined with virtual reality will make rehabilitation exercises much more enjoyable and motivating, which will increase patient adherence to treatment.

This work aims to develop a serious game application with the use of virtual reality dedicated to cognitive rehabilitation, where the patient performs by playing with a virtual reality device that is in our case a haptic device.

2 Motivation and Exercise Selection

Cognitive impairment can easily interfere with the patient's normal functioning in relationships, at work and in school. Thus, cognitive remediation is often necessary as it can interrupt the diminishment of cognitive skills [5].

The remediation exercises typically focus on specific cognitive functions, where tasks are repeated at increasing degree of difficulty. And each exercise can work one or several functions at a time [6].

One common exercise is the maze navigation which makes use of a range of key cognitive skills [7] and can produce many other benefits. Moreover, performing it using the Phantom Omni can enhance the already existing aspects shown in Fig. 2, which motivated us more to turn this 2D paper-pencil exercise into a 3D VR application to offer the patients a better experience during their rehabilitation.

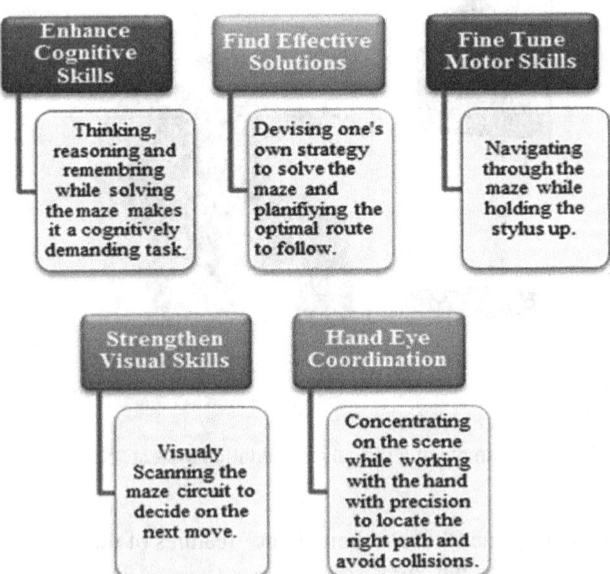

Fig. 2. Maze solving actions and their resulting benefits.

Based on the patient's profile, it is up to the specialist doctor to determine the exercise characteristics (section IV.C.7). Generally, the patient's goal is to complete a maze without colliding with its walls, entering a dead-end, backtracking or going over the same path twice. The time it takes to complete the task can also be used to measure cognitive efficiency.

3 Related Works

By seeing the impact of Rehabilitation on patients' daily life, maintaining their interest during the rehabilitation process is a crucial matter. Therefore, serious games and virtual reality for rehabilitation have been the object of several research works.

Martha Gustavsson et al. [8] explored participants' experiences and perceptions of using a commercial fully immersive head-mounted VR gaming system as a means of rehabilitation for chronic stroke.

Atif Alamri et al. [9] designed a haptic virtual rehabilitation system based on five common exercices that can be used for both diagnosis and rehabilitation of patients with hand impairments.

Y F Hendrawan [10] implemented the Growing Tree Method to build a Maze Game on Android that can generate maze layouts dynamically.

Bowen Xiao et al. [11] designed a virtual reality rehabilitation system for upper limbs that inhibits compensatory movement based on Kinect.

Michele Pirovano et al. [12] used computational intelligence to design a self-adaptive game for rehabilitation at home by monitoring the patient's performance and postures and adapting the gameplay accordingly.

Stéphane Gobron et al. [13] presented a process pipeline using haptic-based serious games for leg rehabilitation with a series of physical exercises in order to identify gaming properties and attributes that health specialists recognized as potentially useful for rehabilitation.

Xiyuan Hou and Olga Sourina [14] used both haptic and EEG devices to develop a "Basket" serious game for post-stroke rehabilitation in which the patient's level changes not only according to his in-game score but also his mental state by implementing emotion recognition algorithms.

In summary, the work presented in this paper builds on previous research to explore how virtual reality and serious games contribute to improving rehabilitation outcomes. While earlier work focused solely on the practical attributes of their developed games and systems, we prioritized the designing phase of our application while focusing both on the exercise's therapeutic benefits and the user interface by setting a more attractive 3D environment, which can enhance the patients' adherence to their rehabilitation even more.

4 Materials and Methods

4.1 Participants

In total, eleven participants (6 females) between the age of 13 and 62 years participated in this study. The participants included one stroke patient, 2 therapists and eight healthy subjects. Most of the testing was conducted in a clinic using our own hardware.

4.2 System Components

Figure 3 shows the implementation tools used in this study and the overall interactions within the system.

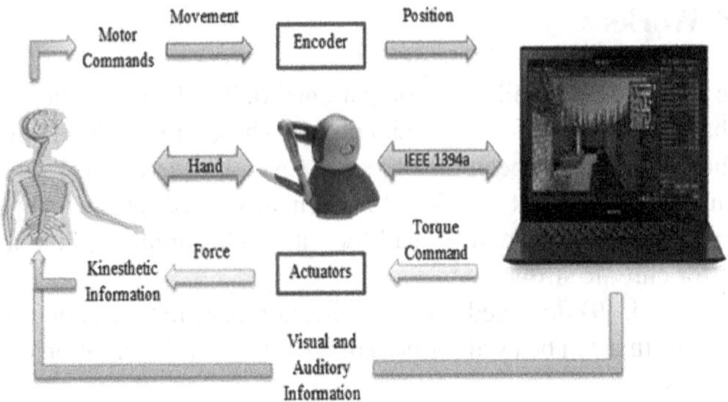

Fig. 3. The components required for the implementation of the system

The haptic device provided is the Phantom Omni developed by SensAble Technologies which is a Pen-based master device that allows interaction with the virtual environment through tools, like a stylus in this case [15]; it uses encoders to track the user's displacement of the end effector and three brushed DC motors to display forces up to 3.3N [16]. A FireWire IEEE 1394a port ExpressCard is used to connect the Phantom Omni to our computer. As for the software, Unity3D was used to develop the application and Visual Studio 2019 for the IDE with C# as a programming language. In addition, the virtual interface is displayed to the user on the computer monitor and the audio is emitted through external or built-in speakers.

4.3 Game Design and Implementation

As mentioned in Sect. 2 , the rehabilitation exercise selected was the Maze. The patients' goal is to reach the lake by clearing the maze situated in the forest while trying to avoid the walls and dead-ends. In that regard, several functions and characteristics were added when designing the application.

Stages. To match the patient's level of cognitive and motor ability and reduce the ceiling and floor effects the maze exercise should have different levels of increasing degree of difficulty (maze's complexity) (Fig. 4).

Fig. 4. Examples of mazes from two different levels

Additionally, to prevent the practice effect that can hinder the cognitive objective of the exercise [17] every level should have several mazes with the same difficulty but different circuits that can be loaded randomly with every play.

Haptic Feedback. Using the force feedback and restricting the haptic device workspace to the maze's base limits prevent the player from physically going through the walls or reaching the end from the outside. Another use of haptic feedback is the vibrations generated when the player is close to the walls, which help him improve his focus, avoid collisions and get him back on track with better precision [18].

Interface Design. In order to motivate the patient to do the exercise, it is important to provide him with a pleasant environment to play in. As preferences differ, we used a common relaxing theme which is nature. And for a better immersion, we decided to go with a first-person view with a mini-map to the side that will guide the patient and help him plan his route, as shown in Fig. 5.

Fig. 5. Game View

User Interface. As this is a cognitive rehabilitation application, the UI should be straightforward and clear while matching the overall theme (Fig. 6, 7, 8, 9).

Fig. 6. The application's main menu interface

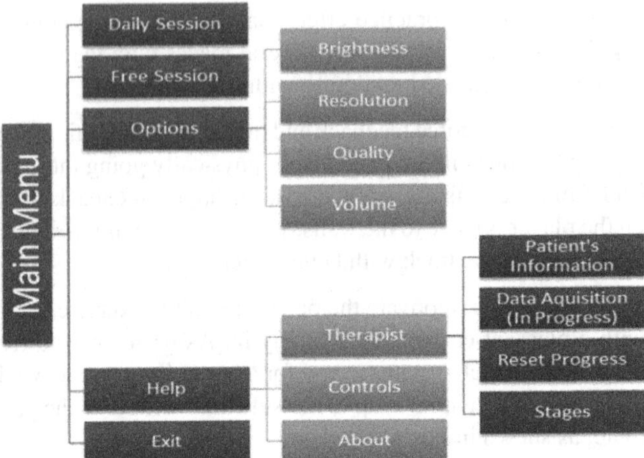

Fig. 7. Main Menu Diagram

Daily Session. Generally, cognitive rehabilitation isn't limited to a short period [19]. In order to allow gradual progress to be made, it is important to respect the schedule set by the therapists. In that regard, the exercise was split into two moods. The daily session (DS) mood is made to showcase the patient's progress; it can only be accessed once the period's duration set by the therapist is up. Additionally, to motivate the patient to perform the exercise regularly, a level up system, that can be incremented only once DS is cleared, was implemented.

Free Session. The free session mood allows the patient to access the exercise whenever he feels like doing extra sets between two daily sessions.

Fig. 8. Free Session Completion Interface

Patient's Information. Since abilities and rehabilitation needs differ from a patient to another, it is up to the therapist to customize the rehabilitation program of each patient by filling in the user information chart presented in Fig. 9.

The input fields include the name of the patient, the number of DS that need to be completed to level up, the exercise frequency (time between each DS) and the patient's level.

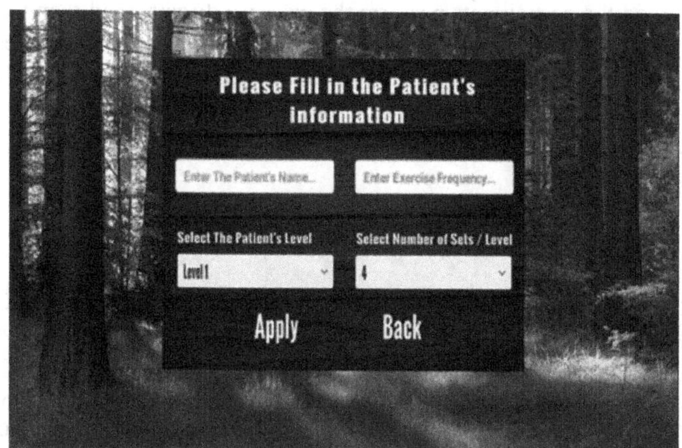

Fig. 9. Patient's program information fill-in interface

Controls. To navigate the maze the movement of the virtual player corresponds, on the same scale, to the movement of the physical stylus of the Phantom Omni. The y-movement in the virtual environment was restricted which means that the only possible movements are the ones in accordance to the x- and z- axis (Fig. 10).

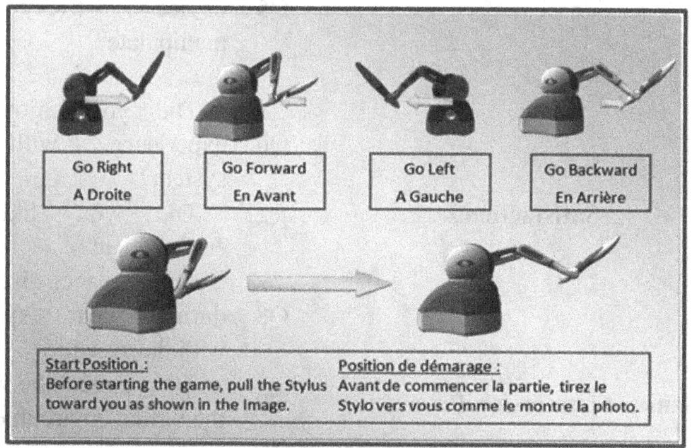

Fig. 10. In-game player controls with the Phantom Omni

5 Results and Discussion

For the evaluation of our application, we conducted a usability test that is regarded as the most efficient method for the evaluation of an application or software. To accomplish this, we observed the participants perform the exercise directly, and then we attempted to identify the difficulties they faced by asking them a few questions. The questions were specifically designed according to the ISO 9241–11 standard and Vruse [20] to measure effectiveness, satisfaction, learnability, efficiency and the sense of immersion/Presence of the application as listed in Table 1.

Table 1. The questions table

		Questions
Effectiveness	Q1	Did you find the task difficult?
	Q2	Did you experience frustration or lack of orientation during your experience with the system?
Learnability	Q3	Is the information provided by the system clear?
	Q4	Were you able to control the system?
	Q5	Did you find the system device tricky to manipulate?
Satisfaction	Q6	Did you enjoy your experience with the system?
	Q7	Did you like the environment?
	Q8	Did you feel discomfort during your experience with the system?
Sense of immersion/Presence	Q9	Did you feel the walls of the virtual environment?

5.1 Stroke Patient

Mr. Y is a patient with hemiplegia who is used to traditional rehabilitation exercises, he is in an advanced state of rehabilitation, therefore, he is able to pick up and hold the Phantom Omni stylus. He has trouble controlling the movement of his left hand (shaky hand) which leads to a lack of precision in performing certain tasks with it. Mr. Y is not used to the computer.

Once the game concept was explained, he tried the system with two medium difficulty levels using his left hand. The time spent on each trial was noted, as shown in Fig. 11, 12.

Mr. Y quickly grasped the game's concept, finding that level 2 was quite easy, and asked us to improve the level to a higher difficulty. He encountered some difficulties while using the Phantom Omni which was understandable as it was his first time using such a device, despite that, it didn't take him long to get better at handling it, which can be seen in the time difference achieved between tests 1 and 2 for the two levels as shown in diagrams 1 Fig. 16 and 2 Fig. 17.

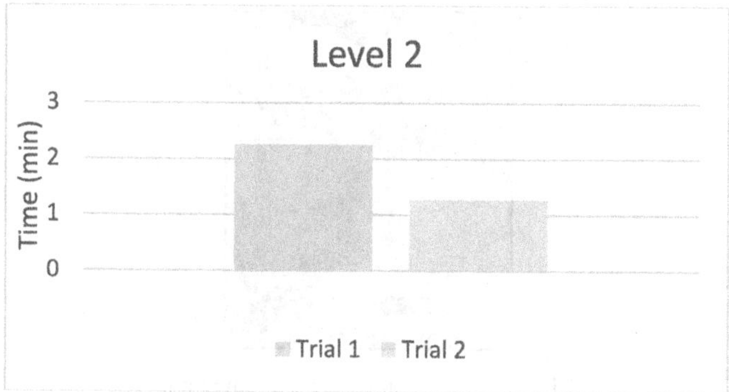

Fig. 11. Trials time for level 2

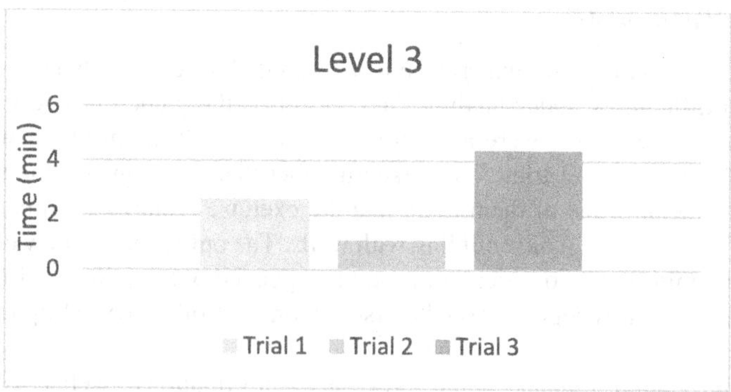

Fig. 12. Trials time for level 3

As for the environment, Mr. Y liked it; he even enjoyed and felt comfortable during this experience.

For the last test, Mr. Y was getting tired, so he lowered his arm as shown in Fig. 13, thus making the handling of the Phantom Omni a bit more delicate, he can't control nor perform the large movements that the arm is in charge of, leading to difficulties in covering the entire workspace (he can't reach easily the left or right side of the maze), which explains the 4 min he did in this test. So, to perform the "Maze" exercise, the arm can be used in different ways; however, its most natural mode of operation is the control and execution of the larger movements by the upper arm, while the lower arm and wrist are used for the finer movements.

According to Mr. Y, the maze exercise differs from traditional rehabilitation exercises, it is even more interesting since it helps cognition as well as hand motor skills, it also may limit the anxiety disorders usually experienced by the patient due to the comparison between his pre-and post-stroke state. He adds that by using this application, he won't get bored as during the rehabilitation he does with the therapist, which shows that the objective of our application has been achieved (Fig. 13).

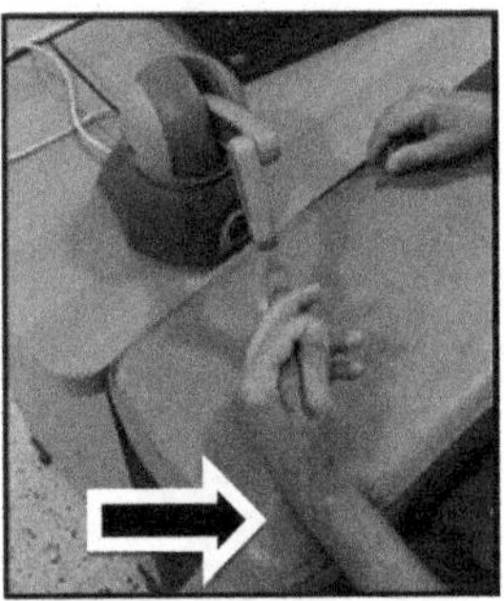

Fig. 13. Mr.Y using the Phantom Omni

5.2 Other Participants

The participants had no prior experience using haptic devices or virtual environments; they had no difficulties understanding the concept of the game and the virtual environment. On average, they were able to manipulate the Phantom Omni without any problems after only 1 to 3 tries. They liked the fact that they can feel the walls when they run into them. Some of them think that the exercise requires good concentration and focus if they want to avoid colliding with walls. The only problem they encountered was using the mini-maps for orientation, some depended only on the mini-map during the game and the others depended on the first-person controller view. Despite this, all of the participants enjoyed this experience.

Table 2 provides a summary of the participants' information as well as their answers to the questions set in Table 1 (Fig. 14).

At the end of this test and according to the answers of the participants we can say that our application is usable because it meets all the criteria ("Effectiveness", "Satisfaction"

Table 2. The answers table

Name (Mr, Mrs)	Age	Participant nature	Results								
			Q1	Q2	Q3	Q4	Q5	Q6	Q7	Q8	Q9
M. Yasser	13 yo	healthy person	NO	YES	YES	YES	NO	YES	YES	NO	YES
S. Amel	22 yo	healthy person	NO	YES	YES	YES	NO	YES	YES	NO	YES
M Litissia	23 yo	healthy person	NO	YES	YES	YES	NO	YES	YES	NO	YES
M Belkacem	25 yo	healthy person	NO	YES	YES	YES	NO	YES	YES	NO	YES
T. Sarah	26 yo	healthy person	NO	YES	YES	YES	NO	YES	YES	NO	YES
D. Sakina	36 yo	healthy person + therapist	NO	YES	YES	YES	NO	YES	YES	NO	YES
L. Nedjoua	45 yo	healthy person + therapist	NO	YES	YES	YES	NO	YES	YES	NO	YES
A. Kahina	53 yo	healthy person	NO	YES	YES	YES	NO	YES	YES	NO	YES
S Hocine	59 yo	healthy person	NO	YES	YES	YES	NO	YES	YES	NO	YES
M. Kamel	59 yo	healthy person	NO	YES	YES	YES	NO	YES	YES	NO	YES

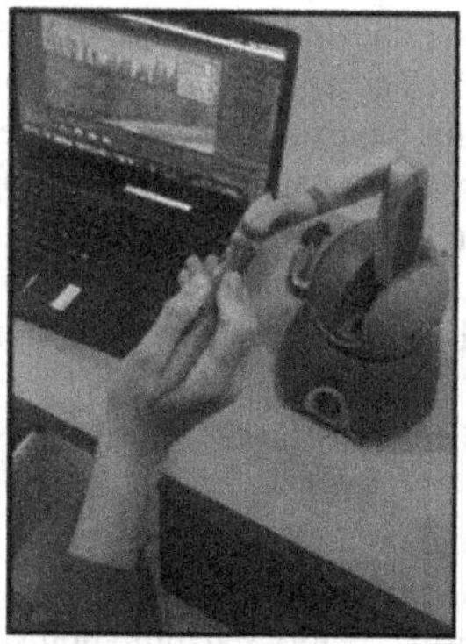

Fig. 14. One of the participants Ms.D testing the application

"Learnability" and "efficiency" "Sense of immersion/Presence") that the ISO 9241–11 standard and Vruse has specified to evaluate usability.

6 Conclusion and Future Work

In this study, we designed and developed a haptic technology-based serious game meant to be used as a complementary exercise for cognitive and upper limb rehabilitation.

The exercise choice relied on the data collected from previous research that proved the maze's cognitive and motor benefits. Moreover, the overall design was set to enhance the advantages virtual reality and serious games have to offer when included in the healthcare sector and rehabilitation's programs.

The usability assessment has shown that the proposed maze application maintains the user interest during the task performance, thereby it can improve the patient's motivation and exercise intensity and strengthen treatment compliance throughout the rehabilitation period.

Nevertheless, although the application was designed for both clinical and home based rehabilitation, the latter cannot be applied until a full and effective validation test is run. On that account, further data acquisition functions will be implemented including: number of collisions (fine motor skills assessment), task completion time (ability efficiency assessment), and an image of the patient's traveling path (cognitive functions assessment). Furthermore, to optimize the application efficiency, we plan on adding a maze generator function to avoid creating several different mazes for every level manually.

References

1. Bandura, A.: Social Learning Theory, Englewood Cliffs. Prentice-Hall, N.J. (1977)
2. Keshner, E.A.: Virtual reality and physical rehabilitation: a new toy or a new research and rehabilitation tool?. J. NeuroEng. Rehabil. **1**(1), 1–2 (2004)
3. Saebo, V.R.: Saebo. https://www.saebo.com/shop/saebovr/
4. Winn, B.M.: The design, play, and experience framework. In : Handbook of Research on Effective Electronic Gaming in Education. Pennsylvanie : IGI Global, pp. 1010–1024 (2009)
5. What is Cognitive Remediation Therapy? on Lifeskills South Florida. https://www.lifeskillssouthflorida.com/mental-health-blog/what-is-cognitive-remediation-therapy/
6. Best, M.W., et al.: Motivation and engagement during cognitive training for schizophrenia spectrum disorders. Schizophrenia Res. Cogn. **19**, 100151 (2020)
7. Kirsch, P., et al.: Brain activation during mental maze solving. Neuropsychobiology (2006)
8. Gustavsson, M., et al.: Virtual reality gaming in rehabilitation after stroke. Disabil. Rehabil. **44**(22), 6759–6765 (2022)
9. Alamri, A., et al. : Haptic virtual rehabilitation exercises for post-stroke diagnosis. IEEE Trans. Instrum. Measurement **57**(9), 1876–1884 (2008)
10. Hendrawan, Y.F.: A maze game on android using growing tree method. In: Proceedings of International Joint Conference on Science and Technology (2017)
11. Xiao, B., et al.: Design of a virtual reality rehabilitation system for upper limbs that inhibits compensatory movement. Med. Nov. Technol. Dev. **13**, 100110 (2022)
12. Pirovano, M., et al.: Self-adaptive games for rehabilitation at home. In: Proceedings of IEEE Conference on Computational Intelligence and Games (CIG), pp. 179–186 (2012)
13. Gobron, S.C., et al. : Serious games for rehabilitation using headmounted display and haptic devices. In: Augmented and Virtual Reality: Second International Conference, AVR 2015, Lecce, Italy, August 31-September 3, 2015, Proceedings 2. Springer International Publishing, pp. 199–219 (2015)
14. Hou, X., Sourina, O.: Emotion-enabled haptic-based serious game for post stroke rehabilitation. In: Proceedings of the 19th ACM Symposium on Virtual Reality Software and Technology, pp. 31–34 (2013)
15. O'Malley, M.K., Gupta, A.: Haptic interfaces. In: HCI Beyond the GUI, pp. 25–64 (2008)

16. O'Malley, M.K., et al.: Improved haptic fidelity via reduced sampling period with an FPGA-based real-time hardware platform. J. Comput. Inf. Sci. Eng. (2009)
17. Sanderson-Cimino, M., et al.: Practice effects in mild cognitive impairment increase reversion rates and delay detection of new impairments. Front. Aging Neurosci. **14** (2022)
18. Achour, N., Daoudi, A.: Haptic interface design to virtual environments. In: Proceedings of Control and Decision Conference, p. 1473 – 1476. China (2012)
19. Studios, Twinlight. Cognitive Rehabilitation: How Long And Effective Is It?, Haym Salomon Home for Nursing & Rehabilitation (2021). https://www.haymsalomonhome.com/cognitive-rehabilitation/. Accessed 18 Oct 2021
20. Kalawsky, R.S.: VRUSE—a computerised diagnostic tool: for usability evaluation of virtual/synthetic environment systems. Appl. Ergon. Conf. 14 (1997)

Artificial Intelligence Applications

A Robust Biometric Identification System Using ECG Statistical Features and SVM

Amel Benabdallah and Abdelghani Djebbari(✉)

Laboratory of Biomedical Engineering, Faculty of Technology, University of Tlemcen, Tlemcen, Algeria
{amel.benabdallah,abdelghani.djebbari}@univ-tlemcen.dz

Abstract. Recently, various attempts have been undertaken to build trustworthy biometric identification systems based on physiological signals, such as the Electrocardiogram (ECG) signal.

Biometric systems based on ECG signals may be categorized according to data acquisition, preprocessing stages, feature extraction, and classification approaches. Among these stages, feature extraction has a substantial influence on biometric performance.

The current study presents a biometric identification system based on ECG. The research leverages the distinct heartbeats of ECGs and their statistical measurements as a feature set for classifying ECGs. We included and validated a support vector machine classifier for ECG classification through 10-fold cross-validation which reached trustworthy obtained results 95.40% and up to 99% for MIT–BIH and ECG–ID databases respectively.

Keywords: Biometrics · Electrocardiogram · heartbeats · cross–validation · biometric · recognition

1 Introduction

In recent years, there has been growing interest in biometric systems as a means of identifying individuals, owing to their high level of accuracy and dependability. One of the latest biometric identification techniques is based on electrocardiogram (ECG) data, which provides a unique set of characteristics for each individual, including waveform morphology, amplitude, and duration, as first proposed by Biel et al. [6]. In contrast to other biometric traits, such as facial or voice recognition, which can be susceptible to forgery, ECG biometrics are difficult to counterfeit due to their distinct nature and widespread usage, as noted by Ingale et al. [16], and can offer a high level of security in identification systems, as highlighted by Pelc *et al.* [25]. In addition, ECG signals can be obtained in real-time and through a non-invasive modality, making them a desirable option for numerous applications.

Several research investigations have been undertaken in this area to explore the usefulness of ECG biometrics for person identification. ECG biometrics have

H. Drias et al. (Eds.): AID 2022, CCIS 1852, pp. 137–147, 2023.
https://doi.org/10.1007/978-981-99-4484-2_11

the potential to improve the security and accuracy of identifying systems in a variety of applications, including healthcare, banking, and access control. Despite the encouraging findings, some obstacles, including inter-individual variability and noise in ECG readings, must be addressed. As a result, additional study is required to investigate the potential of ECG biometrics and build more strong and trustworthy identification systems.

One recent study proposed a deep learning-based approach for ECG biometric recognition, using a convolutional neural network (CNN) to automatically extract features from ECG signals and a multi-layer perceptron (MLP) for classification [27]. Another study proposed a method for ECG biometric recognition based on a combination of time-domain and frequency-domain features, achieving high recognition rates using a support vector machine (SVM) classifier [18]. In addition, some studies have explored the use of ensemble learning for ECG-based biometric recognition, combining multiple classifiers to improve performance. For example, one study proposed an ensemble of SVM classifiers based on different feature sets, achieving high recognition rates with reduced error rates [8].

An electrocardiogram (ECG) is a physiological signal obtained by placing conventional electrodes on the patient's chest and limbs. The P-wave, QRS complex, and T-wave are the primary components of the ECG signal and depict the electrical activity of the heart throughout distinct periods of the cardiac cycle. Several research investigations depend on the ECG signal's fiducial points in connection to its generating waves P, Q, R, S, and T [14]. ECG features are manually recovered using fiducial approaches, which utilize time domain analysis and local ECG wave qualities such as amplitude, maximum and minimum peaks, and segmentation. These features are gathered as a vector for classification purposes and integrated with machine learning methods such as template matching and dimension reduction [23]. These components' shape, amplitude, and duration may be utilized to extract traits that are unique to a person.

However, the neuroplasticity of neurotransmitter channels may explain the influence of aging on specific ECG characteristics. Despite this, research on the biometric analysis of ECG has demonstrated the presence of temporal-amplitude domain characteristics that are constant and alter little over time [26].

QRS Complex Slope. The slope of the QRS complex represents the speed of cardiac depolarization. This feature has been shown to be very distinguishable for biometric identification.

R-peak Amplitude. The amplitude of the R-peak, which shows maximal ventricular depolarization, may potentially be employed as a biometric trait.

Overall, the reliable features extracted from ECG signals for biometric identification determine the efficacy of the developed algorithm. Indeed, features that are distinctive, stable, and reproducible over time are essential for trustworthy biometric identification.

These techniques evaluate the full signal to extract morphological features independently from any characteristic point [5,15,17]. Instead, other methods focus on holistically evaluating an ECG, often by using time or frequency analysis to derive the feature.

Statistical analysis approaches for ECG biometrics have recently been addressed. Alotaiby *et al.* used the mean, standard deviation, median, maximum value, minimum value, range, interquartile range, interquartile first quarter (Q1), interquartile third quarter (Q3), kurtosis, and skewness of the ECG signal for feature extraction and a random forest classifier on the PTB–ECG database. The authors achieved an average accuracy of 99.61%.

The paper is organized as follows. Section 1 provides an overview of relevant works on ECG biometrics and their achievements. Section 2 discusses the principles of ECG as well as the signal preprocessing techniques employed in data representation and analysis. Then, we address the suggested time domain statistical analysis model for three heartbeats segmented from ECG signals, employing QRS complex analysis as an anchor to sliced ECG, and we include the Hurst–exponent feature in the machine learning classifier template. Section 4 covers experimental information such as the dataset being used, recognition results using cross-validation, and a comparison analysis. Finally, we establish a conclusion on the basis of the findings from the study.

2 Materials and Methods

This section describes two publicly accessible referenced datasets that were used in biometric ECG experiments. ECG biometric investigations frequently use in-person, on-the-person, and off-the-person data acquisition techniques. A block diagram, as shown in Fig. 1, describes the major processes in the biometric framework.

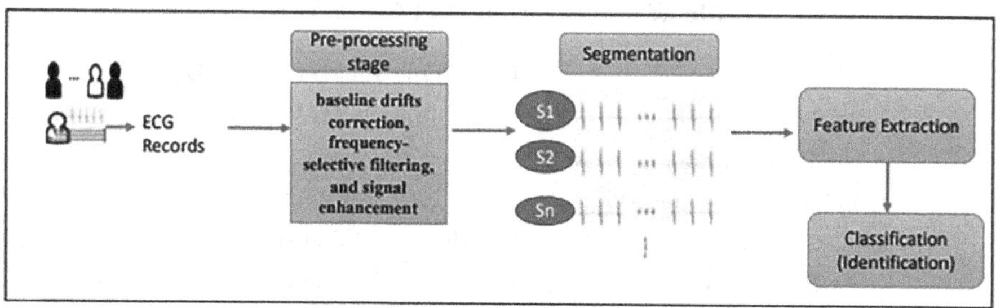

Fig. 1. A block diagram of the proposed ECG–based biometric framework

2.1 Dataset

The lack of benchmarked datasets for ECG biometrics is a major challenge. Many ECG biometric approaches have been validated using the Physionet ECG datasets, which were initially developed for medical research. Indeed, public datasets for biometric research that use off-the-person and on-the-person ECG data acquisition techniques, such as the ECG–ID and MIT–BIH Arrhythmia databases, have been put forward.

The ECG–ID Database. This database [21] is dedicated to aiding research into the use of the ECG for biometric purposes. Its recordings for normal ECG include a total of 310 ECG recordings from 90 individuals and are available on Physionet's website [13]. The database contains between 2 and 20 recordings for each individual, collected over six months. A limb-clamp electrode at the wrists was used to collect the signals from Lead I. These ECG signals were digitized 500 Hz at a 12–bit resolution with an amplitude range of ±10mV range, of 1 min for each segment. Each ECG signal segment had a length of 1 min. This database [21] is devoted to fostering studies on the use of the ECG for biometric applications. Its normal data sets contain 310 ECG recordings from 90 people and are accessible on the Physionet website. [13]. The database comprises 2 to 20 recordings for each participant, gathered over a six-month period. The signals from Lead I were collected using a limb-clamp electrode at the wrists. These ECG signals were digitized 500 Hz, with a 12-bit resolution and an amplitude range of ±10**mV**, of 1-minute duration.

The MIT–BIH Arrhythmia Database. This collection includes 48 half-hour ECG recordings from 47 distinct people. The MIT–BIH Arrhythmia Database is ideal for evaluating the proposed ECG biometric approach due to its universality [12, 16, 22].

A short description of the main parameters used in this paper is presented in Table 1.

Table 1. Parameters of the ECG datasets

Parameters	ECG-ID DB	MIT-BIH DB
Leads	I-lead filtered	MLII Lead
Total number of records	20	47
Number of heartbeats	3	3
Sampling rate	500 Hz	360 Hz
Record time	1min	1min
Electrode placement	Wrist	Chest
Health condition	Healthy	Arrhythmia

2.2 Data Preprocessing

Signal processing techniques, such as filter designs [19] and Fourier Transforms [7], have been widely used to enhance ECG biometrics in the literature.

While several pre-processing approaches are used to improve signals, three process operations are often advised for boosting ECG data before beginning classification, namely, baseline drift correction, frequency-selective filtering, and signal enhancement [21]. Indeed, preprocessing is a key step in preparing data for classification. Thus, ECG signals were preprocessed through filtering as illustrated in Fig. 2.

ECG signals from the ECG-ID and MIT-BIH Arrhythmia databases are considered for processing. Power interferences, baseline drift, and EMG interferences all have an effect on ECG signals [11]. As a result, various research projects have been conducted on denoising ECG signals using bandpass filters, low pass filters, and wavelet transforms [1,11]. In this study, as a first experiment, we used a 60–Hz notch filter to reduce electrical power interferences from MIT–BIH Arrhythmia Database [4] ECG signals. The ECG signals are then detrended and smoothed using a wavelet-based (Daubechies 6) baseline removal approach.

We employed a low-pass filter in the second experiment to decrease high-frequency noise induced by external interferences and muscular activity [11]. In this paper, we create a bandpass filter with a passband frequency range of [0.5, 40] Hz to accentuate QRS complexes while reducing drift and any high-frequency noise, as well as a notch filter to eliminate powerline interference 60 Hz.

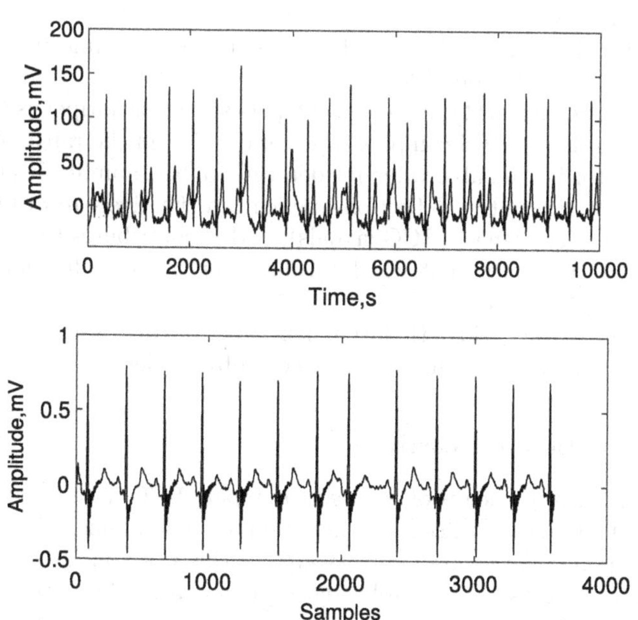

Fig. 2. Pre–processing process for ECG–ID and MIT–BIH signals

2.3 Statistical Analysis and Feature Extraction

The feature extraction process is critical in deciding the performance of ECG-based biometric devices. Fiducial and non-fiducial features may be extracted using different approaches. The following features have been extracted. The mean and median are used to determine the central tendency of the ECG signal, whereas the root mean square is used to assess the statistical dispersion.

Higher-Order Statistics (HOS) are used to quantify the sharpness of the peak and the asymmetry of the ECG signal distribution through kurtosis and skewness. As supplementary data, we give the lowest value, peak value, and peak-to-peak amplitude.

Basic Statistics. The basic statistics include mean, root mean square (RMS), shape factor, minimum, variance, median, and peak–to–peak value.
Root Mean Square (RMS) provides a novel alternative measure of ventricular repolarization, as expressed in Table 2.
Variance This parameter measures the variability in the electrical activity during the depolarization phase.
Higher–order statistics (HOS) characterizes non–Gaussian and nonlinear processes.
Kurtosis, fourth moment of a signal, measures the tailedness of the probability distribution of a signal.
Skewness, third moment of a signal, represents the asymmetry of a signal's distribution of samples around R–peaks.
The Hurst-exponent (H), indicates the persistence or antipersistence degree of a time–series. For a QRS complex time-series, H is in the range of $[\mathbf{0,1}]$.

This indicator is a reliable value for determining the amplitude and frequencies of positive and negative deflections, which can effectively record the properties of the processed signals (ECG signals), and it contributes to the formation of a robust feature vector that will be utilized for the identification procedure relying on an SVM classifier.

In this study, we consider that the class label of each instance corresponds to three ECG heartbeats segmented for each subject identity.

2.4 Segmentation of Heartbeats

A sliding window approach is often used to prepare ECG data for classification, in which the ECG data is sliced depending on a window time using the R-peak as an anchor point. We focused our research in this work on QRS complexes to segment all heartbeats. This enables data augmentation by generating several data samples, with each slice of data serving as a sample for each individual while also serving as input for machine learning training.

The QRS complex is a prominent characteristic of a typical ECG, consisting of three clearly identifiable graphical deflections. It is often regarded as the most visible and significant component of ECG tracing [19]. Obviously, when massive amounts of ECG data are recorded, we require suitable equipment with a large storage capacity to analyze this data for biometric purposes.

Table 2. Extracted time domain statistical features

Mean	$\mu = \sqrt{\frac{1}{N}\sum_{n=1}^{N} x_i}$
STD	$std = \sqrt{\frac{1}{N}\sum_{n=1}^{N}(x_i - \mu)^2}$
Min	$mn = min(x_i)$
Max	$mx = max(x_i)$
Kurtosis	$K = \frac{E(x_i-\mu)^4}{\sigma^4}$
Skewness	$skw = \frac{E(x_i-\mu)^3}{\sigma^3}$
Variance	$v = \frac{1}{N}\sum_{n=1}^{N}(x_i(n) - \mu)^2$
Root Mean Square	$X_{SF} = \frac{x_{rms}}{\frac{1}{N}\sum_{i=1}^{n}\lvert x_i\rvert}$
Mode	$x = argmaxxiP(X = xi))$
Hurst–Exponent	$\mathbb{E}\left[\frac{R(n)}{S(n)}\right] = Cn^H$ as $n \to \infty$

2.5 Multi Classification Step and Identification

Different machine learning algorithms have been applied for the classification of ECG biometric signals, including multi-class SVM, K-nearest neighbor algorithms, principal component analysis, and artificial neural networks [24]. However, the performance of these classifiers remains inefficient for a large database of input signals.

Cortes and Vapnik [9] employed the Support Vector Machine (SVM) classifier as a binary classification technique. In this study, we utilize 10 folds cross-validation to accomplish multi-class classification using a Support Vector Machine (SVM). We select kernel functions and adjust their parameters to achieve optimal accuracy [3]. The created system employs the one-vs-one paradigm to divide a multi-class classification task into one binary classification task for each pair of classes. As a result, we implement the SVM with a linear kernel function, as specified in (1);

$$K(x_i, x_j) = x_i^T x_j \tag{1}$$

The classifier achieves an accuracy of 99% for the ECG–ID database with a generalized classification error equal to 95.40% for MIT–BIH Arrhythmia database.

Table 3. The developed biometric model in comparison with other reported framework recognition.

Studies	Approach	Datasets	Classifier	Results
Li and et al. (2020) [20]	Truncated 40% from R–R interval as heartbeat	5 datasets	Cascaded Convolutional Neural Network	94.3%
Dalal and et al. (2021) [2]	time-frequency analysis of segment of an ECG signal around the R-peak	PTB ECG–ID	CNN models	99.90% 94.18%
Fatimah and al. [10]	Fourier decomposition and phase transform on one or more heartbeats	MIT-BIH, ECG-ID and CYBHi	Random forest and SVM	97.92% 98.45% 91.07%
Our method	***Time–domain analysis of short three heartbeats ECG segments using Husrt–exponent with statistical features***	***MIT–BIH ECG–ID***	***SVM with 10 folds Cross Validation***	***95.40% up to 99%***

3 Results and Discussion

In this section, we present the experimental setup of training and testing procedures, and performance analysis.

3.1 Developed Biometric Framework

This study investigated how the time-domain representation of a short heartbeat of an ECG signal could be viable and effectively used for biometric recognition, employing multi-classification techniques with 10-fold cross-validation to improve the acceptability and usability of this modality for healthcare applications.

3.2 Multi–Classification Step

The overall recognition for both data was quite good for multi-classification using support vector machine (SVM), with 10 folds cross-validation (Fig. 3).

A 10-fold cross-validation procedure was used to reduce the training set's generalization error. The final classification accuracy results are obtained using the average of the ten distinct results provided by the cross-validation test, which achieved 95.40% and 99%for MIT-BIH and ECG–ID databases, respectively, as shown in Fig. 4.

We compared our method's findings to the state of the art for both the MIT–BIH and ECG-ID databases. Table 3 compares the obtained findings with state-of-the-art methodologies that evaluated their framework biometric systems, utilizing heartbeat segmentation, which was determined to be successful.

Using lengthy ECG signals yields superior results even for a limited number of individuals, as shown in citebenabdallah2022biometric. We can see from the results shown in Table 3 that the established biometric algorithm accurately identifies all participants from both databases. The developed technique enables efficient feature extraction, rating, and identification.

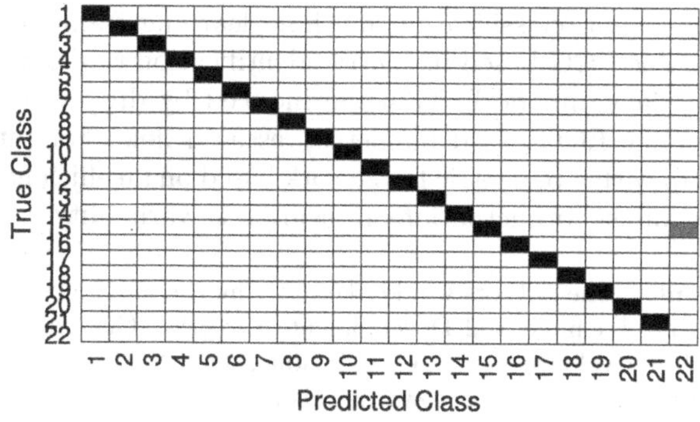

Fig. 3. Confusion Matrix Chart for ECG–ID recognition

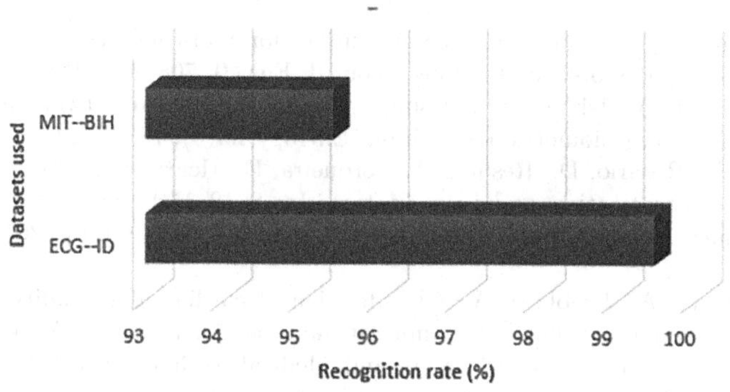

Fig. 4. Recognition rate of both data-sets

4 Conclusion

The ECG is a physiological signal that measures the electrical activity of the heart. Aside from its utility in medical diagnostics, the ECG might be a useful alternative to traditional biometrics for safeguarding the system against fraudulent assaults because to its vitality features. ECG-based biometric identification is used in a wide range of applications all around the globe. Machine learning is often used to construct more accurate and robust scoring models for ECG-based biometric identification in order to achieve a high user recognition rate. This study presents a high-dimensional collection of patients drawn from well-known ECG datasets (ECG-ID and MIT-BIH). Furthermore, we show that most current machine learning-based identification algorithms employ a large chunk of the ECG signal to attain a high detection rate. We, on the other hand, employed a brief segment of ECG signals around the QRS complexes to achieve good detection accuracy in both sets (normal and/or aberrant ECG signals), exceeding current state-of-the-art approaches. It is possible to infer that the time-domain representation of a small segment of an ECG signal is essential in the biometric framework, enabling us to improve recognition results.

Then, using a multi-classification machine learning framework with cross-validation, a reliable ECG-based biometric identification rate was attained. Furthermore, the variance in the ECG signal induced by diverse heart diseases is a major issue in the ECG-based biometric research field. For future work, we intend to come up with a biometric framework based on an efficient deep-learning machine that is robust to fluctuations in heart rate variability.

Acknowledgments. The authors would like to thank the Directorate–General of Scientific Research and Technological Development (Direction Générale de la Recherche Scientifique et du Développement Technologique, DGRSDT, URL:www.dgrsdt.dz, Algeria) for the financial assistance towards this research.

References

1. Ahlstrom, M., Tompkins, W.: Digital filters for real-time ecg signal processing using microprocessors. IEEE Trans. Biomed. Eng. **9**, 708–713 (1985)
2. AlDuwaile, D.A., Islam, M.S.: Using convolutional neural network and a single heartbeat for ecg biometric recognition. Entropy **23**(6), 733 (2021)
3. Barros, A., Rosário, D., Resque, P., Cerqueira, E.: Heart of iot: Ecg as biometric sign for authentication and identification. In: 2019 15th International Wireless Communications & Mobile Computing Conference (IWCMC), pp. 307–312. IEEE (2019)
4. Benabdallah, A., Djebbari, A.: Classification of cardiac abnormality using ECG and HRV signals by linear discriminant analysis. In: Khelassi, A. (ed.) International Congress on Health Sciences and Medical Technologies 2021. Knowledge Kingdom Publishing (2021). https://doi.org/10.26415/978-9931-9446-5-2, www.eurl-knowking.dz
5. Benouis, M., Mostefai, L., Costen, N., Regouid, M.: ECG based biometric identification using one-dimensional local difference pattern. Biomed. Signal Process. Control **64**, 102226 (2021). https://doi.org/10.1016/j.bspc.2020.102226
6. Biel, L., Pettersson, O., Philipson, L., Wide, P.: ECG analysis: a new approach in human identification. IEEE Trans. Instrum. Meas. **50**(3), 808–812 (2001). https://doi.org/10.1109/19.930458
7. Chen, P.Y., Chang, M.J., Tu, K.C., Yu, S.S., Liu, C.C.: Study of using fourier transform to capture the ecg signals between awakeness and dozing. In: 2016 International Symposium on Computer, Consumer and Control (IS3C), pp. 1055–1058. IEEE (2016)
8. Chiu, J.K., Chang, C.S., Wu, S.C.: Ecg-based biometric recognition without qrs segmentation: a deep learning-based approach. In: 2021 43rd Annual International Conference of the IEEE Engineering in Medicine & Biology Society (EMBC), pp. 88–91. IEEE (2021)
9. Cortes, C., Vapnik, V.: Support-vector networks. Mach. Learn. (1995). https://doi.org/10.1007/BF00994018
10. Fatimah, B., Singh, P., Singhal, A., Pachori, R.B.: Biometric identification from ecg signals using fourier decomposition and machine learning. IEEE Trans. Instrum. Meas. **71**, 1–9 (2022)
11. Gilani, S.O., Ilyas, Y., Jamil, M.: Power line noise removal from ecg signal using notch, band stop and adaptive filters. In: 2018 International Conference on Electronics, Information, and Communication (ICEIC), pp. 1–4. IEEE (2018)

12. Goldberger, A.L., et al.: Physiobank, physiotoolkit, and physionet: components of a new research resource for complex physiologic signals. Circulation **101**(23), e215–e220 (2000)
13. Goldberger, A., et al.: PhysioBank, PhysioToolkit, and PhysioNet: components of a new research resource for complex physiologic signals. Circulation [Online]. **101**(23), e215–e220
14. Hammad, M., Luo, G., Wang, K.: Cancelable biometric authentication system based on ECG. Multimed. Tools Appl. **78**(2), 1857–1887 (2018). https://doi.org/10.1007/s11042-018-6300-2
15. Hegde, C., Prabhu, H.R., Sagar, D.S., Deepa Shenoy, P., Venugopal, K.R., Patnaik, L.M.: Statistical analysis for human authentication using ECG waves. In: Dua, S., Sahni, S., Goyal, D.P. (eds.) ICISTM 2011. CCIS, vol. 141, pp. 287–298. Springer, Heidelberg (2011). https://doi.org/10.1007/978-3-642-19423-8_30
16. Ingale, M., Cordeiro, R., Thentu, S., Park, Y., Karimian, N.: ECG biometric authentication: a comparative analysis. IEEE Access **8**, 117853–117866 (2020). https://doi.org/10.1109/ACCESS.2020.3004464
17. Kaur, G., Singh, D., Simranjeet: Electrocardiogram (ecg) as a biometric characteristic: A review (2015)
18. Khan, M.U., Aziz, S., Iqtidar, K., Saud, A., Azhar, Z.: Biometric authentication system based on electrocardiogram (ecg). In: 2019 13th International Conference on Mathematics, Actuarial Science, Computer Science and Statistics (MACS), pp. 1–6. IEEE (2019)
19. Kim, S.K., Yeun, C.Y., Damiani, E., Lo, N.W.: A machine learning framework for biometric authentication using electrocardiogram. IEEE Access **7**, 94858–94868 (2019)
20. Li, Y., Pang, Y., Wang, K., Li, X.: Toward improving ecg biometric identification using cascaded convolutional neural networks. Neurocomputing **391**, 83–95 (2020)
21. Lugovaya T.S: Biometric human identification based on electrocardiogram. [Master's thesis] Faculty of Computing Technologies and Informatics, Electrotechnical University "LETI", Saint-Petersburg, Russian Federation
22. Moody, G.B., Mark, R.G.: The Impact of the MIT-BIH Arrhythmia Database (June), 45–50 (2001)
23. Nait-ali, A., Biometric, W., Meets, S.: Hidden Biometrics
24. Patro, K.K., Reddi, S.P.R., Khalelulla, S.E., Rajesh Kumar, P., Shankar, K.: Ecg data optimization for biometric human recognition using statistical distributed machine learning algorithm. J. Supercomputing **76**, 858–875 (2020)
25. Pelc, M., Khoma, Y., Khoma, V.: ECG signal as robust and reliable biometric marker: datasets and algorithms comparison. Sensors (Switzerland) **19**(10) (2019). https://doi.org/10.3390/s19102350
26. Srivastva, R., Singh, A., Singh, Y.N.: Plexnet: a fast and robust ecg biometric system for human recognition. Inf. Sci. **558**, 208–228 (2021)
27. Wang, D., Si, Y., Yang, W., Zhang, G., Liu, T.: A novel heart rate robust method for short-term electrocardiogram biometric identification. https://doi.org/10.3390/app9010201. www.mdpi.com/journal/applsci

DISS: A Discrete Input-Space Sampling Path Planning and Obstacle Avoidance Strategy for Swarm Robotics

Naila Aziza Houacine(✉) and Habiba Drias

LRIA, USTHB, Algiers, Algeria
{nhouacine,hdrias}@usthb.dz

Abstract. In this research, the path planning and obstacle avoidance problem for Swarm Robotics is addressed. Our contribution consists in a Discrete adaptation of the well-known Input-Space Sampling method (DISS). The DISS is integrated into a Swarm Intelligence approach, named Multi-Bee Swarm Optimization (MBSO) that must be embedded into autonomous mobile robots. The MBSO algorithm, in turn, is multi-swarm adaptation of the well-known Bee Swarm Optimization. It aims to resolve the Target Detection Problem by exploring a 2D discrete, complex, and unknown environment. Thus, the search strategy must be provided with an adequate path planning and obstacles avoidance strategy which is a determinant factor to the robots' efficiency in their search mission. The experimental results show that, by varying the obstacle density in the search environments MBSO's performances are not much affected. Our path planning and obstacle avoidance strategy offer an efficient and effective navigation capability to the robots of MBSO.

Keywords: Autonomous Robots · Path planning · Obstacle Avoidance · Discrete Input Space Sampling · Swarm Robotics · Dynamic Target Detection Problem

1 Introduction

Autonomous robots, as one of the cornerstones of AI, include the Swarm Robotics (SRs) field, where SRs is a research field that focuses on the combination of Swarm Intelligence (SI) and robotics. Boosted by the development of Artificial Intelligence, SRs has achieved considerable progress offering parallelism, robustness, flexibility and scalability. Especially that nowadays we are facing too many dangerous and inaccessible missions for human beings, such as the planet's exploration, the search for victims in disasters, the detection of radioactive sources, the location of anti-personnel mines and bombs, and so on [2]. All these problems share some common characteristics that can be summarized as: a large area with multiple targets that must be reached with no map of the search environment, a complex, unknown, and possibly dangerous area for any living being [15] that we may shorten into the Target Detection Problem

H. Drias et al. (Eds.): AID 2022, CCIS 1852, pp. 148–161, 2023.
https://doi.org/10.1007/978-981-99-4484-2_12

(TDP). So, sending an Intelligent Swarm of Robots to face such problems was the most suitable and reasonable option.

One of the most interesting Swarm Intelligence (SI) approaches we find the Bee Swarm Optimization (BSO) [3] that mimic the Bees behavior in its pollen foraging to resolve the Target Detection Problem, which is of discrete nature. The BSO algorithm follow a search strategy based on the diversification and intensification processes to calculate the next position to relocate each bee in order to converge to the targets. However, in order to enhance it efficiency and cover more search space at a time, a multi-swarm adaptation of BSO, called MBSO is proposed. In addition, to implement this technique into real robots, it must be equipped with a path planning and obstacle avoidance policy. Hence, the robots will safely and rapidly navigate from their current position to the ones calculated by MBSO.

In fact, path planning is a key task for the motion planners of autonomous mobile robots. Collision-free path planning means: (1) avoiding collisions between obstacles and the robots and (2) optimizing the path according to predefined constraints like path length or smoothness [9]. This problem have been proven to be NP-Hard [13], such as it consist of finding a safe and short path from an initial position A to a goal position B among an exponential number of possible paths. Depending on the robot's environment, we may deal with a discrete or continuous navigation. Such as within continuous environments the robots try to move through some short moves, calculating a velocity and direction based on the goal position and the obstacles around. In the other side, within discrete environments, the robots navigate from box to box through map's grid. Another important parameter to consider is whether it is an active path planning, which means the robots navigate in an unknown area with limited sponsors' perception range and gradually build the path between their current and destination positions. Or the environment's map is known so the robots compute their entire path before starting their motion.

In this article, we consider the environment to be a discrete 2D grid that contains randomly positioned targets that emit a signal on a fixed range and random obstacles of different sizes and shapes. A swarm of omnidirectional robots is considered with a limited range of perception while exploring a complex and unknown environment. We propose a discrete adaptation of the path planning and obstacle avoidance algorithm, Discrete Input-Space Sampling (DISS). Then, this method is integrated in the enhanced Swarm Intelligence algorithm BSO, Multi-Bee Swarm Optimization, in order to resolve the Target Detection Problem (TDP) by multiple swarms of robots. We conducted a series of experiments to evaluate the performance of the DISS-MBSO. We first evaluated the impact of the density of the obstacles on the MBSO-DISS algorithm, and then, we evaluated the impact of the environment's size and targets number on the MBSO algorithm and compare it with the performances of the original BSO.

This paper is structured as follows. In the next Section, we present some related works about the path planning issue and the TDP. In the Third section, we propose the Discrete Input-Space Sampling method is described. Then, the fourth section is dedicated to the MBSO algorithm for TDP and its combination with the DISS framework. The obtained results of the conducted experiments on the environments complexity are exposed and discussed in the fifth section. At last, a conclusion summarizes the contributions of this work and proposes some future works.

2 Related Works

When we do not have access to the entire map, the robots need an active path planning strategy. Hence, algorithms like A^* and *Djikstra* are not suitable. There are a number of path planning techniques that process the path gradually, i.e., as the robot advances and discovers its environment.

The literature shows a variety of those obstacle avoidance strategies to solve the collision issue. *O. Khatib* was the first to propose a **Potential Field** method based on attractive force towards the goal position and repulsive force of obstacles [8], the closer the obstacle the stronger the repulsive force. In [12], the authors propose a discrete artificial potential field method for obstacle avoidance. They also define an extra potential function that repels the robot from the local minimum using a virtual obstacle.

The suggested method in [5], is a simple **Fuzzy Logic Controller** that determines the robot's collision-free path in order to smoothly avoid the obstacles. And Finally, there is the **Input Space Sampling** (ISS) planning method for obstacle avoidance that was first presented by the authors in [6]. It estimates a set of potential admissible paths according to the robots' local view and select the local optimal one and repeat this process until it reach the goal position. This last approach was widely used and tested on recent real mobile robots with continuous motion [7].

On the other side, the state-of-the-art of Swarm Intelligence approaches for the resolution of the Target Detection Problem shows that only few algorithms consider obstacles in their search environment. Therefor, very few search approaches provide a path planning and obstacle avoidance strategy. Among those adapted for Robotic constraints we find:

Artificial Potential Fields (APF) approaches [10], this method considers two vectors of local forces that influence the robot movements such that close targets emit attractive forces, while nearby robots and obstacles emit repulsive forces.

An enhanced APF-based approach for autonomous mobile robots that search for targets in unknown complex environments is provided in [11]. It can program a legitimate, workable, and quick path from the robot's starting point to the desired position. The authors redefined the repulsive potential field and improved the wall-following method to solve oscillation problem. But the APF has a well-known drawback which consist of getting the robots stuck in local optimum.

Adaptive Robotic Particle Swarm Optimization (A-RPSO) [2] is an improved version of the original PSO. The A-RPSO method provides an obstacle avoidance strategy included in the update's velocity equation. The motion of the robot is guided by its personal best intuition, the global best intuition of the entire swarm, and the attempt of driving away from close obstacles. Each of those parameters are weighted in order to calculate the robot's direction and velocity at each iteration. This method do not guarantee a safe path or the avoidance of oscillation.

Multi-swarm hybrid of FruitFly Optimization Algorithm and Particle Swarm Optimization (MFPSO) [14] aims at finding a single target in unknown environments. This metaheuristic avoids premature convergence by the independence of the swarms of robots and the evasion of obstacles through the Multi-Scale Cooperative Mutation (MSCM) as an evacuation mechanism from stagnation. However, MSCM is not adapted for high obstacle density and rapidly becomes computationally expensive.

3 Proposed Adaptation of the DISS

As a result of the demonstrated effectiveness, safety, speed, and flexibility of the ISS method for autonomous mobile robots, we have decided to incorporate it into our robot's path planning. However, given that we are working with discrete environments, we must establish the subsequent ideas:

- Direction: The concept of direction involves partitioning a robot's immediate environment into four 90° zones: North-East, North-West, South-East, and South-West. To determine the robot's field of view, a 90° angle is selected based on the location of the destination point P_{dest} with respect to the robot's current position P_{cur}.

- Accessible positions: The robot view is limited by the sensor's range of perception. Thus accessible positions are the ones included within this range in the robot view's direction.

- Admissible paths: A path is admissible when it is obstacle-free. For that, we exploited *Bresenham's* algorithm [1] to extract successive positions of a straight line and check if it contains obstacles. In principle, the path is constructed as a set of k waypoints and can be denoted as $Path = wp_1, wp_2, ...wp_k$, where wp_1 is equal to P_{cur} and wp_k to an admissible intermediate position P_t.

- Optimal admissible path: The criteria to choose the best path from the admissible ones is by calculating the distance remaining between an intermediate position P_t and the destination position P_{dest}, using the Euclidean distance.

Accordingly, the collision-free path planning algorithm can be resumed in Algorithm 1. At each iteration t of the target search process, each robot has a current position P_{cur} and calculates its next destination P_{dest} through algorithm MBSO. Those are the inputs parameter for the proposed DISS. So the DISS method starts with estimating the destination position direction. Then, it samples the area in that direction into some potential paths, the accessible intermediate positions in the robot's local view border are called "accessible positions". But the robot has to evaluate each one in order to eliminate the ones that contains obstacles. The resulting set of paths are safe paths, also known as "Admissible paths". Finally, from the set of admissible paths, the robot estimates the path's quality in terms of distance, so it selects the path that locally minimizes the distance to the destination position. Each robot repeats this process through intermediate positions until it reaches the destination position.

Algorithm 1: Discrete Input Space Sampling path planning

```
Input: P_cur : robot's current position, P_dest : robot's destination position;
       MaxVelocity : robot's maximum velocity;
Output: GlobalPath: path from initial position to destination;
begin
    Initialization:
    Initialize the step counter t ← 0;
    Initialize the intermediate position of the t^th step P_t ← P_cur;
    Initialize the robot's perception range R;
    while P_t <> P_dest and t < MaxVelocity do
        D ← Determine the direction to take;
        Positions ← get accessible positions in direction D in range R;
        SubPaths ← get admissible paths from P_t to Positions;
        optimalSubPath ← get optimal admissible path from SubPaths;
        GlobalPath ← GlobalPath ∪ optimalSubPath;
        P_{t+1} ← Last position of optimalSubPath;
        t ← t + 1;
    return GlobalPath;
```

Furthermore, one iteration of the path planing process is illustrated in Fig. 1, where the robot is the yellow point, and the destination is represented by the red cross. The Figure shows the iterative process from the robot estimation of the direction, as NE, to the selection of the optimal sub-path. It also gives a global overview from the first to the last iteration that allows the robot to reach the destination position.

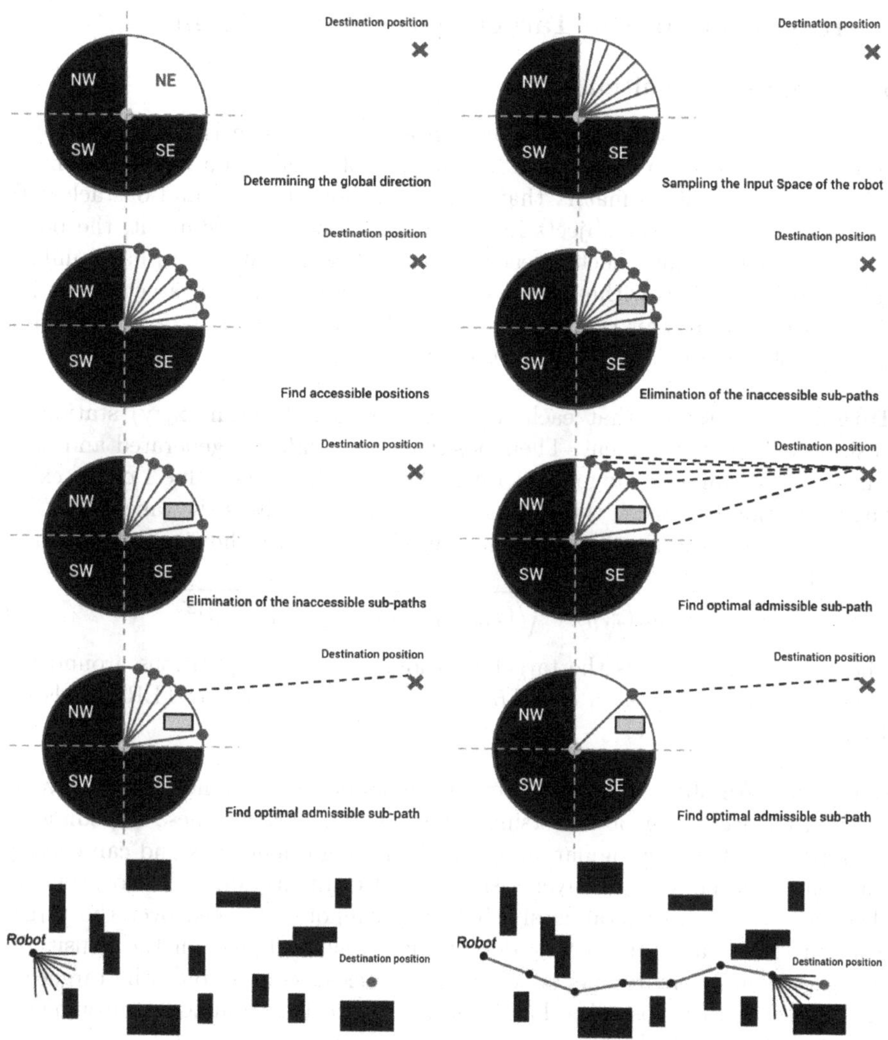

Fig. 1. Graphical explanation of an iteration of the ISS method.

There are some cases where a robot may be stuck in a local optimum or oscillates into the same subset of positions. The DISS addresses this issue by two mechanisms:

(1) When the robot is trapped into a position almost surrounded by obstacles, like a corner, it enlarges its action angle to 180° and even to 270°, if necessary.
(2) DISS memorizes its lasts positions so it can avoid oscillating too long in the same area. This process is exploited to eliminate the last already visited positions and take another random direction.

4 Resolution of the Target Detection Problem

4.1 Problem Definition

The Target Detection Problem in a discrete environment consists of a multi-robot system cooperating to search a known number of targets in a limited unknown 2D environment, like a matrix that can hold robots, targets, and obstacles. To distinguish the different objects in the discrete search environment, the boxes can take several values, such as each position of coordinate (x, y) has a unique value. Positive values within the range]0 - 1[to represent the target's emission signal, the value 1 is for target positions, and negative values (-1) for obstacles. The rest of the area is neutral and takes the value 0.

Target: We assume that each target is considered as an (x, y) stationary position of the environment. Their positions are randomly generated and have a fixed signal emission range. This range decreases from the value 1 of the exact target position to 0 when the distance to the target exceeds the range size. The Eq. 1 represents the Euclidean distance used to simulate the signal emission of a target.

$$Signal(x, y) = \sqrt{(x_{target} - x)^2 + (y_{target} - y)^2} \quad (1)$$

where (x_{target}, y_{target}) is the target position, (x,y) is the positions around the target such as $|x_{target} - x| \leq TER$ and $|y_{target} - y| \leq TER$. TER stands for Target Emission Range.

Obstacle: An obstacle is an object that hinders a robot's motion by preventing it from occupying or traversing a particular location. These impediments are represented as rectangular shapes with varying dimensions and can overlap with one another to form diverse shapes and configurations. The locations of obstacles are generated randomly, but they cannot be placed over the target position. There are three categories of environments based on the density of obstacles: Simple environments (without obstacles): contain only the target(s). Environments with obstacles: low density of obstacles. Complex environments: high density of obstacles.

Robots: In this work, multiple omnidirectional mobile robots are used for the resolution of the TDP. Each robot is defined by its position and performance. It occupies a single position defined by its coordinates (x, y) of the environment. It is assumed that each robot is capable of determining its position in relation to the environment, enabling it to update and share this information with other robots based on the search strategy. The performance of each robot is assessed using the fitness function. The fitness function's values range from 0 to 1, higher values indicates that the robot is closer to the target. A fitness value of 1 indicates that the robot has successfully located the target. The sensors of the robots have a limited range of perception, with a radius of 10 squares around each robot. To gradually develop a path between the robot's current and destination positions, each robot must have a strategy for path planning and obstacle avoidance.

4.2 Original Bee Swarm Optimization (BSO)

The Swarm Intelligence-based approach Bees Swarm Optimization (BSO) [3] is inspired by the behavior of the worker bees. It models a swarm of artificial bees cooperating together to solve general optimization problems. BSO is characterized by a set of concepts such as:

- **Sref:** is the reference solution. It is initialized randomly at the start of the search, then updated by the best solution in terms of quality or diversity.

- **Flip:** is the reversal frequency. It determines the number of dimensions to invert in the Sref to obtain a set of solutions equidistant from Sref.

- **Local Search:** Each bee performs a local search from its personal solution and evaluates neighboring solutions, keeping only the best one. This process consists of the intensification step of the BSO.

- **MaxChances:** Each solution has a maximum number of chances to be chosen as the reference solution at each iteration. This parameter avoids stagnation and prevents the search strategy from getting stuck in a local optimum.

- **Dance Table:** The "Dance" table is the common repository for all the bees in the swarm to record their best local solutions. At each iteration, the best solution in terms of quality is automatically selected from the table Dance as the new Sref. Except in the case of stagnation, which means the same solution is taken as the Sref beyond "MaxChances" times, where the new Sref is then chosen according to the criterion of diversity.

Algorithm 2: Flip

```
Input: Flip, Sref;
Output: solutionsSet : set of solutions equidistant from Sref;
Initialization:
h ← 0 ;
solutionsSet ← {} ;
while size(searchspace) < k and h < Flip do
    s ← Sref; p ← 0;
    repeat
        s ← Inverse(s, s[Flip * p + h]);
        p ← p + 1;
    until Flip * p + h > n
    solutionsSet ← solutionsSet ∪{s} ;
    h ← h + 1;
end
return solutionsSet;
```

The Algorithm 3 describes the different steps of the BSO approach. Where n is the size of a solution and $\#Bees$ the number of bees in the swarm.

Algorithm 3: Bee Swarm Optimization

```
Input: tmax, Flip, MaxChances, #Bees;
Output: Sref : the best solution found;
Initialization:
Initialize the generation counter : t ← 0;
Initialize the reference solution Sref ;
while t < tmax do
    Insert Sref in the taboo list ;
    SearchArea ← get search area from Sref using Algorithm 2 ;
    foreach i ← 1 to #Bees do
        Position the i-th bee : x_i^t ← SearchArea_i^t ;
        Local search on the i-th bee: x_i^t ;
        Evaluate the fitness of the i-th bee : f(x_i^t);
        Insert the local best solution of the i-th bee in table Dance ;
    end
    Sref ←Choose the best quality solution from the table Dance ;
    if Sref.chances > MaxChances then
        Sref ←Choose the best diversity solution from the table Dance ;
    end
end
return Sref;
```

4.3 Proposed Multi-Bee Swarm Optimization (MBSO)

In this paper we propose a multi-swarm based version of the original BSO algorithm. Instead of having only one swarm of bees that cooperate to search the optimal solution, this approach works with a number $\#Swarms$ of swarms where each swarm is composed of a number $\#Bees$ of bees. In MBSO each swarm s has its own reference solution $Sref_s$ and only communicates with the artificial bees of its swarm through the table $Dance_s$. While the principle of the $Flip$, $Localsearch$, and $MaxChances$ parameters remain the same as for BSO.

The Algorithm 4 describes the proposed MBSO algorithm. Where n is the size of a solution, $\#Swarms$ the number of swarms, and $\#Bees$ the number of bees in each swarm.

Algorithm 4: Multi-Bee Swarm Optimization

Input: $tmax, Flip, MaxChances, \#Bees, \#Swarms$;
Output: $Sbest$: the best solution found;
Initialization:
Initialize the generation counter : $t \leftarrow 0$;
Initialize the reference solution of each swarm $Sref_s$;
while $t < tmax$ **do**
  foreach *swarm s in #Swarms* **do**
    Insert $Sref_s$ in the taboo list ;
    $SearchArea_s \leftarrow$ get search area from $Sref_s$ using Algorithm 2 ;
    foreach $i \leftarrow 1$ *to* $\#Bees$ **do**
      Calculate the next position $x^t_{s,i}$ From $SearchArea^t_{s,i}$;
      Plan the path from $x^{t-1}_{s,i}$ to $x^t_{s,i}$ using Algorithm ??;
      local search on the i-th bee of swarm s: $x^t_{s,i}$;
      Evaluate the fitness of the i-th bee of swarm s : $f(x^t_{s,i})$;
      $Dance_s \leftarrow$ Insert the local best solution of bee i swarm s ;
    end
    $Sref_s \leftarrow$Choose the best quality solution from the table $Dance_s$;
    if $Sref_s.chances > MaxChances$ **then**
      $Sref_s \leftarrow$Choose the best diversity solution from $Dance_s$;
    end
    if $Sref_s$ *is better than* $Sbest$ **then**
      $Sbest \leftarrow Sref_s$;
    end
  end
end
return $Sbest$;

5 Experiments and Results

The simulation environment are 2D matrix with random obstacle and target positions in addition to the random size of the rectangular obstacles.

First, we started with the MBSO parameters setting. Using the Genetic self-parameterizer [4], so a solution for the Genetic Algorithm (GA-parameterizer) is a specific parameterizing of the MBSO algorithm. The solution (Chromosome) is a vector of parameters where each parameter represents a "Gene". Hence, the crossover and mutation operators are applied to the different values of each parameter. We tuned the MBSO parameters and found the best parameter settings to be: #Swarms = 5, #Bees = 5, $Flip$ = 20, and $MaxChances$ = 2.

Then, in order to validate the effectiveness of the DISS-MBSO search algorithms, we experimented it by varying some external parameters relative to the environment and the targets.

5.1 A. Influence of the Environment's Size

For these experiments, the robots must find a total of 5 targets. The different tested environments have a square shape with the side length equal to: 50, 100, 200, 400, 600, 800, 1000, 1500, 3000, 5000 boxes. We undertook 40 executions per environment size (10 executions on 4 different datasets), which amounts to a total of 400 executions for each environment type (Simple, With obstacles, and complex ones).

The obtained results of the DISS-MBSO are shown in Fig. 2. The left line chart represents comparative results of the DISS-MBSO iterations number when varying the environment size within simple, with obstacles, and complex environments. It has been noted that increasing the obstacle density has a slight impact on the proposed approach, requiring the robots to expend more effort. For instance, DISS-MBSO takes up to 30 iterations to navigate in complex environments, whereas it requires less than 20 iterations for other types of environments. However, from the right line chart, we remark that the execution time is not impacted by the raise of environment complexity, performing the search mission within a maximum of 15 to 17.5 s for all three environment types.

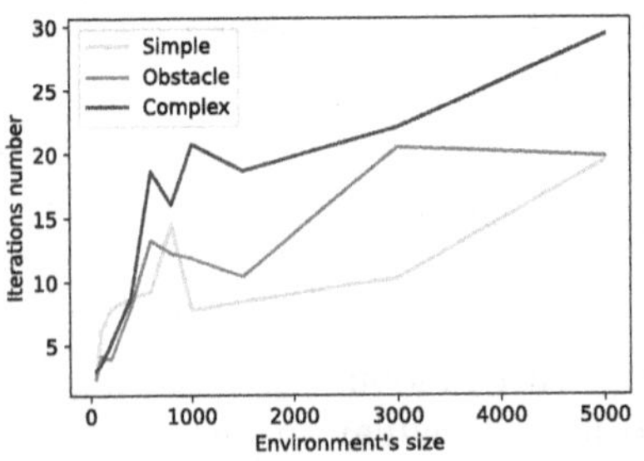

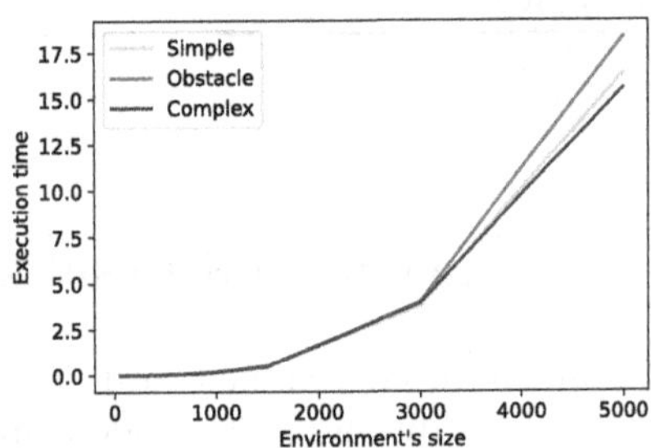

Fig. 2. Impact of the environment's size of the DISS-MBSO method in various obstacle density environments.

The obtained results of the compared methods on environments with obstacles are shown in Fig. 3. The comparative results show that the proposed MBSO algorithm performs better than the classical BSO. It obtains higher success rate in less iterations in most environment sizes, even if the execution time of MBSO is slightly higher than the one of BSO when dealing with big environments, it is still very small. On the other hand, we notice that varying the environment size increases affect the compared approach, making the robots furnish more efforts. In fact, the original BSO finds less than 20% of the targets within big environment (5 000 × 5 000), while it does not go under the 70% for the proposed MBSO. However, from the to other line charts, we remark that the bigger the search space the longer the search time and the iterations number.

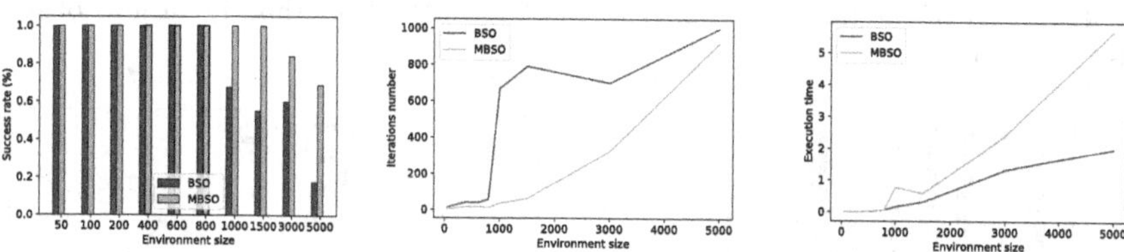

Fig. 3. Impact of the environment's size of the DEHO-DISS method in various obstacle density environments.

5.2 B. Influence of the Target's Number

In order to study the influence of the target's number present in our environments on the behavior of DISS-MBSO, we have set the size of the environments to 500 × 500 squares and a the target's signal emission range to a radius = 50. We have taken the following set of target's number 1, 3, 5, 7, 9, 11, 13, 15.

As a consequence, the results of the tests comes from the executions on 32 environments (4 per number of targets), which corresponds to 320 a total of executions per environment type.

Figure 4 exhibits the evolution of the iterations number on the left line chart, whereas the execution time is illustrated on the right line charts. We observe that increasing the obstacle density does not influence the DISS-MBSO efficiency and effectiveness when increasing the targets' number to be reached during the search mission. The execution time reach a maximum of around 19 iterations within no more than 0.1 s for all the environment types.

Figure 5 exhibits the evolution of the success rate, the iterations number, and the execution time are illustrated on the charts from the left to the right. We observe that the targets' number to be reached during the search mission does not influence the BSO and MBSO effectiveness. Whereas, it induce an augmentation in the furnished efforts by the two algorithms. More precisely, BSO is the one that performs the more iterations reaching an average of 80 iterations compared to the MBSO that doesn't exceed the 30 iterations. Concerning the execution time, the two approaches have very similar behavior achieving less than 0.06 s even when searching for 15 targets.

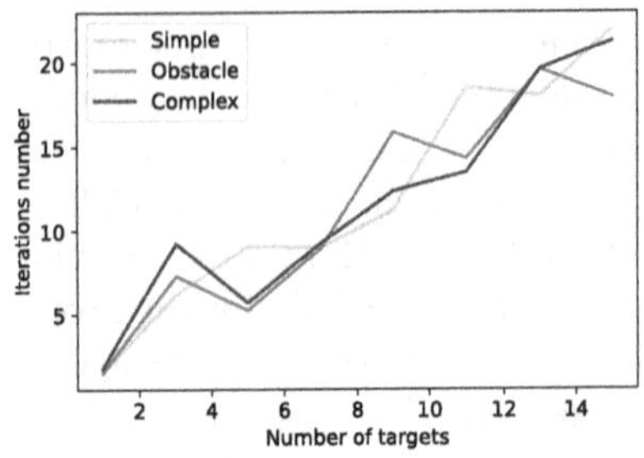

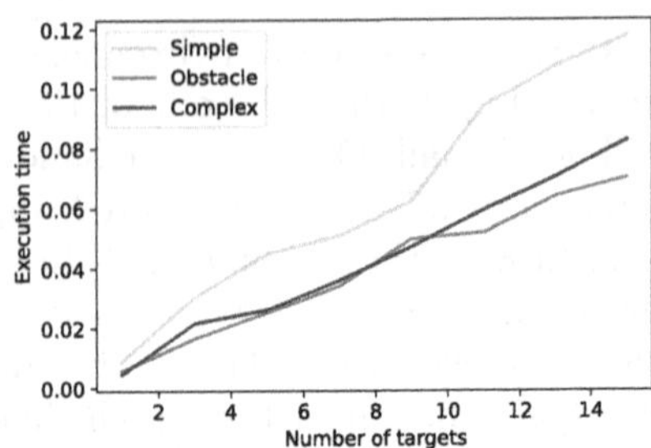

Fig. 4. Impact of the targets' number of the DISS-MBSO method in various obstacle density environments.

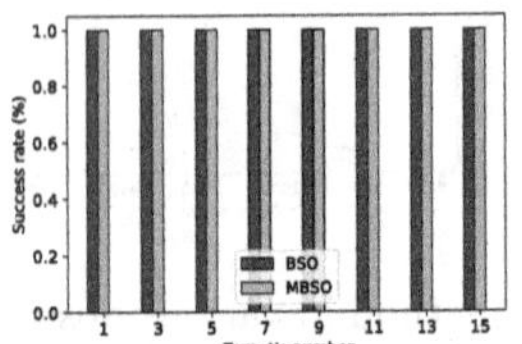

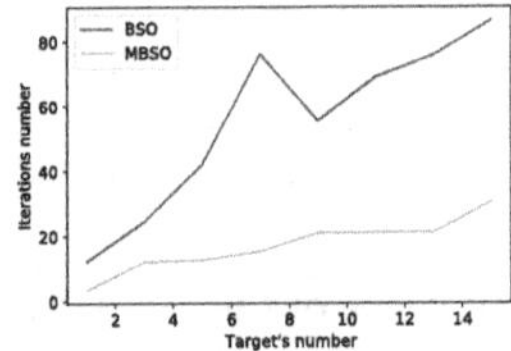

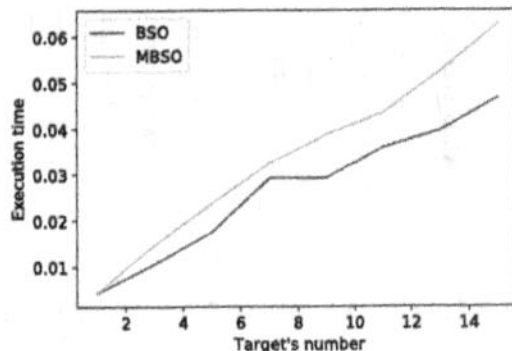

Fig. 5. Impact of the targets' number of the DEHO-DISS method in various obstacle density environments.

6 Conclusion

In this article, we proposed a discrete adaptation of the Input-Space Sampling algorithm for the SRs, namely DISS. We also integrated this path planning and obstacle avoidance strategy into the MBSO search approach in order to effectively tackle the TDP. Numerous experiments to study the DISS-MBSO performances were conducted within different environment types (Simple, With obstacles, and Complex environments). The proposed approach have also been tested with various number of targets and environment sizes. From the presented results, we conclude that on the one hand, the MBSO algorithm offers more exploration capabilities which leads to better results. On the other hand, the DISS policy allows the MBSO search algorithm to move quickly regardless of the obstacles' density. This performance may be explained by the gradual elimination of possible paths, which greatly reduces the execution time in addition to the two escape mechanisms from local optima and oscillation. Also, the DISS approach has a considerable advantage of portability, such as it may be adapted to any SI or SR approach since it is an independent framework.

References

1. Bresenham, J.E.: Algorithm for computer control of a digital plotter. IBM Syst. J. **4**(1), 25–30 (1965). https://doi.org/10.1147/sj.41.0025

2. Dadgar, M., Jafari, S., Hamzeh, A.: A PSO-based multi-robot cooperation method for target searching in unknown environments. Neurocomputing **177**, 62–74 (Feb 2016). https://doi.org/10.1016/j.neucom.2015.11.007
3. Drias, H., Sadeg, S., Yahi, S.: Cooperative bees swarm for solving the maximum weighted satisfiability problem. In: Cabestany, J., Prieto, A., Sandoval, F. (eds.) IWANN 2005. LNCS, vol. 3512, pp. 318–325. Springer, Heidelberg (2005). https://doi.org/10.1007/11494669_39
4. Houacine, N.A., Drias, H.: Self-parameterized swarm intelligence algorithms for targets' detection in complex and unknown environments. In: Abraham, A., Hanne, T., Castillo, O., Gandhi, N., Nogueira Rios, T., Hong, T.-P. (eds.) HIS 2020. AISC, vol. 1375, pp. 690–699. Springer, Cham (2021). https://doi.org/10.1007/978-3-030-73050-5_67
5. Jin, S., Choi, B.-J.: Fuzzy logic system based obstacle avoidance for a mobile robot. In: Kim, T., Adeli, H., Stoica, A., Kang, B.-H. (eds.) CA/CES3 -2011. CCIS, vol. 256, pp. 1–6. Springer, Heidelberg (2011). https://doi.org/10.1007/978-3-642-26010-0_1
6. Kelly, A., Stentz, A.: Rough terrain autonomous mobility-part 1: a theoretical analysis of requirements. Auton. Robot. **5**(2), 129–161 (1998). https://doi.org/10.1023/a:1008801421636
7. Khaksar, W., Sahari, K.S.M., Hong, T.S.: Application of sampling-based motion planning algorithms in autonomous vehicle navigation. In: Autonomous Vehicle. InTech, September 2016. https://doi.org/10.5772/64730
8. Khatib, O.: Real-time obstacle avoidance for manipulators and mobile robots. In: Proceedings. 1985 IEEE International Conference on Robotics and Automation. Institute of Electrical and Electronics Engineers (1985). https://doi.org/10.1109/robot.1985.1087247
9. Larsen, L., Kim, J., Kupke, M., Schuster, A.: Automatic path planning of industrial robots comparing sampling-based and computational intelligence methods. Procedia Manufacturing **11**, 241–248 (2017). https://doi.org/10.1016/j.promfg.2017.07.237
10. Li, G., Tong, S., Cong, F., Yamashita, A., Asama, H.: Improved artificial potential field-based simultaneous forward search method for robot path planning in complex environment. In: 2015 IEEE/SICE International Symposium on System Integration (SII). IEEE, December 2015. https://doi.org/10.1109/sii.2015.7405075
11. Li, H.: Robotic path planning strategy based on improved artificial potential field. In: 2020 International Conference on Artificial Intelligence and Computer Engineering (ICAICE), pp. 67–71 (2020). https://doi.org/10.1109/ICAICE51518.2020.00019
12. Park, M.G., Lee, M.C.: A new technique to escape local minimum in artificial potential field based path planning. KSME Int. J. **17**(12), 1876–1885 (2003). https://doi.org/10.1007/bf02982426
13. Surynek, P.: Abstract path planning for multiple robots: a theoretical study (2010). https://doi.org/10.1.1.173.4771. https://citeseerx.ist.psu.edu/viewdoc/download?doi=10.1.1.173.4771&rep=rep1&type=pdf
14. Tang, H., Sun, W., Yu, H., Lin, A., Xue, M., Song, Y.: A novel hybrid algorithm based on PSO and FOA for target searching in unknown environments. Appl. Intell. **49**(7), 2603–2622 (2019). https://doi.org/10.1007/s10489-018-1390-0
15. Trianni, V., Campo, A.: Fundamental collective behaviors in swarm robotics. In: Kacprzyk, J., Pedrycz, W. (eds.) Springer Handbook of Computational Intelligence, pp. 1377–1394. Springer, Heidelberg (2015). https://doi.org/10.1007/978-3-662-43505-2_71

Advancements in Digital Soil Mapping: From Data Acquisition to Uncertainty Estimation - A Comprehensive Review

Widad Hassina Belkadi[1(✉)] and Yassine Drias[2]

[1] LRIA, USTHB, BP 32 El Alia, Bab Ezzouar, 16111 Algiers, Algeria
wbelkadi@usthb.dz

[2] University of Algiers, 02 rue Didouche Mourad, 16000 Algiers, Algeria
y.drias@univ-alger.dz

Abstract. Soil is a crucial ecosystem component, supporting plant growth and contributing to environmental quality. Digital maps of soil properties play a critical role in effective soil conservation planning and management. This paper comprehensively reviews recent developments in Digital Soil Mapping (DSM) models from 2017 to 2022, focusing on sustainable agriculture and environmental management. We outline the DSM process, starting with data acquisition and explaining the soil-forming factors and the SCORPAN model. We examine different data sources used in DSM and their applications. We then discuss the methods for mapping soil, including geostatistical, machine learning, and deep learning, highlighting their strengths and limitations. We also explore the introduction of transfer learning in DSM and its potential for enhancing accuracy. Additionally, we review how recent studies validate and estimate uncertainty in their results. To analyze current trends in DSM, we perform statistical analysis on the reviewed works. Finally, we compare the findings of several exploratory studies and identify remaining challenges and future opportunities in DSM research. Overall, this review provides valuable insights into recent developments in DSM and their potential applications in soil management and conservation.

Keywords: Digital soil mapping · Machine learning · Deep learning · Transfer learning · Remote sensing · SCORPAN · Climate change

1 Introduction

According to the Food and Agriculture Organization of the United States (FAO), Russia and Ukraine are among the world's top producers of agricultural products, and both countries are net exporters of such products [11]. However, the ongoing war between the two nations has resulted in significant global food security challenges. As such, the focus is now on improving soil capability and conditions to increase agricultural production, with soil being a crucial natural resource that contains various metals, nutrients, and minerals essential for plant

H. Drias et al. (Eds.): AID 2022, CCIS 1852, pp. 162–177, 2023.
https://doi.org/10.1007/978-981-99-4484-2_13

growth [32]. Proper soil management is critical to sustainably utilizing these features, but poor management can lead to many problems. Thus, a spatially accurate soil information map is necessary to address these issues.

Traditionally, soil mapping relied on soil surveys, which can be labor-intensive, time-consuming, expensive, and require expert knowledge. However, Digital Soil Mapping (DSM) has emerged as a solution to these challenges, utilizing advanced technology such as geographic information systems, geostatistics, machine learning, remote sensing, and high-performance computing to estimate soil properties by integrating soil survey data [7,16].

This review paper will focus on the latest research in digital soil mapping from 2017 to 2022. To limit the scope of our work, we will adopt the following structure:

- In Sect. 2, we will provide a comprehensive background for DSM by defining the process using the SCORPAN model.
- Next in Sect. 3, we will explain DSM from the initial step of "Data acquisition" We will cite several data sources and available datasets to illustrate this process. In Sect. 4, we will outline the mapping techniques used in DSM, with a detailed overview of deep learning techniques recently gaining popularity. We will also analyze the various validation and interpretability methods used in respectively Sect. 5 and Sect. 6.
- Then, we will discuss and compare the results in Sect. 7. To conclude, we will suggest recommendations for addressing DSM's challenges and future outlook in Sect. 8.

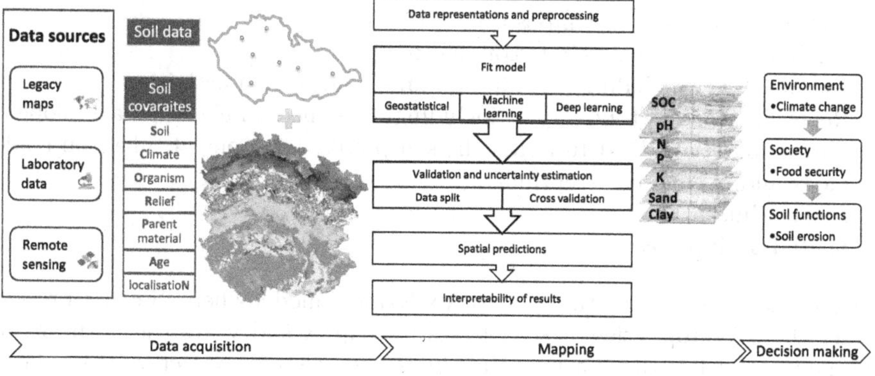

Fig. 1. General framework of digital soil mapping adapted from [4].

2 Background on Digital Soil Mapping

2.1 Environmental Definition of DSM

Digital soil mapping (DSM), or pedometric mapping, is used to extract the relationship between soil attributes and soil-forming factors. The output of DSM is a digital map that displays the georeferenced soil database, revealing the spatial arrangement of soil types and/or characteristics [10].

In recent years, DSM has focused on mapping soil organic matter (SOM) content due to its crucial role in soil health, global climate, and food security. Soil organic carbon (SOC), the primary component of SOM, is essential in maintaining soil quality [41]. The depletion of SOM can lead to accelerated microbial decomposition and oxidation of SOM to CO_2, which increases atmospheric CO_2 concentrations and contributes to global warming. As a result, SOM content is a critical factor in sustainable land management practices and is a major focus of DSM research.

In addition to SOM content, DSM can map other important soil properties such as soil texture, pH, nutrient content, and water-holding capacity. Having access to comprehensive soil data can aid farmers in making informed choices regarding crop management, soil conservation, and nutrient management. Furthermore, DSM can be utilized for identifying areas of high soil erosion risk, which can be targeted for conservation measures to prevent soil loss and degradation.

2.2 Mathematical Model of DSM

The DSM methodology was formalized on [16]. The Scorpan model was presented by the authors as an empirical and quantitative correlation between a soil characteristic and its spatially implicit formative factors [16]. The following observable soil factors can influence the soil processes expressed as observed soil proprieties [10]:

- Soil 'S' represents the composition of the soil,
- Climate 'C' such as precipitation and temperature,
- Organism 'O', including vegetation, fauna, and human activities.
- Relief 'R' includes topography, including differences in elevation and slope,
- Parent materials 'P' determines the soil profile development, like iron oxide index and magnetic susceptibility,
- Age or time 'A,'
- Spatial position 'N.'

Equation 1 represents the SCORPAN formula model where: S can represent either the soil proprieties or soil classes to map, x and y are the positions of the point, and f is the function that links the SCORPAN factors with the S proprieties and an error term 'e' is added that could include the spatial trends that are not captured by the predictive factors [10].

$$S(x, y) = f(\mathrm{s}_{(\mathrm{x,y})}, \mathrm{c}_{(\mathrm{x,y})}, \mathrm{o}_{(\mathrm{x,y})}, \mathrm{r}_{(\mathrm{x,y})}, \mathrm{p}_{(\mathrm{x,y})}, \mathrm{a}_{(\mathrm{x,y})}, \mathrm{n}_{(\mathrm{x,y})}) + \mathrm{e}_{(\mathrm{x,y})} \quad (1)$$

Figure 1 showcases the DSM framework, which entails a sequence of steps. Firstly, SCORPAN factors and soil data are collected from proximally or remotely sensed sources. Next, a mapping model is developed and trained using these data. The model is then validated and interpreted before it is used to generate spatial predictions of soil properties. In the following sections, we will review these steps in detail.

3 Data Acquisition

DSM uses data from various sources to generate soil information in a database. This section defines data types needed in DSM, including primary and auxiliary data, and explains the impact of these covariates on soil properties prediction. In addition, we also review some data sources of each data type.

3.1 Data Types

Primary Data. In order to predict soil characteristics accurately, we require reliable ground truth information about soil variables. Soil profiles collected in the field provide the primary source of soil information and are considered the most dependable. A soil profile reflects the chemical composition (pH, organic carbon content, etc.), physical attributes (texture, color, structure, etc.), and biological components (roots, earthworms, etc.) of the soil at a specific spatial location.

Moreover, the existing soil information can also serve as a covariate in DSM [16]. For example, soil properties and classes like texture, bulk density, and clay mineralogy can account for the variability in soil organic carbon (SOC).

Auxiliary Data. Auxiliary data refers to any additional information that can be used to support the DSM methodology and improve the accuracy of predictions. In the case of SCORPAN factors, auxiliary data can include a wide range of variables that are not directly related to soil properties but can affect the formation of soil characteristics.

- Climate (C) can explain soil functions and threats of soil as soil particle loss, weathering, erosion of soil, and soil fertility [10]. The main climatic variables that affect soil formation are precipitation and temperature.
- Organisms (O), including vegetation cover, can enrich SOC by various mechanisms such as adding organic material and conserving soil moisture [16].
- Relief (R), also known as topography, refers to the composition of the land surface. Terrain parameters based on digital elevation models (DEMs) have been commonly used as covariates in DSM [8,26,39].
- Parent material (P) is an essential initial soil material that determines the soil profile development as well as the physical properties of soils. It affects soil formation by the strength of weathering, the nutrients contained for the plant to utilize, and the particle size included.
- Age (a) or time, It takes time for soil-forming processes to manifest their effects; this explains why age may vary from a few years to several thousand years. Some studies like [42] considered phonological variables.
- Location (n) The soil is a continuum in which the soil properties of a particular location depend on its geographical location and the soil properties of adjacent areas [10].

3.2 Data Sources

Spectroscopy denotes the investigation of the interaction between matter and electromagnetic radiation. When light passes through a substance, it can be either absorbed, reflected, or transmitted through the material. In soil science, absorption spectroscopy is widely used to analyze the spectral reflectance of different radiations based on the corresponding wavelength. The unique combination of these spectral reflectances, also known as a spectrum signature, allows us to identify an object precisely. We can determine the chemical composition and structure of the soil under study by analyzing the spectrum signatures of soils using proximal sensors in the laboratory and field or remote sensors.

The U.S. Geological Survey (USGS) defines remote sensing as "the process of detecting and monitoring the physical characteristics of an area by measuring its reflected and emitted radiation at a distance typically from a satellite (spaceborne) or aircraft (airborne)" [36]. Remote sensing images provide information as a stack of images encapsulating different spectral bands. There are two types of remote sensing images: multispectral and hyperspectral imagery. Multispectral sensors typically have 3 to 10 distinct band measurements on each pixel of the image they produce. On the other hand, hyperspectral sensors are narrower than multispectral sensors and measure energy across numerous bands. Hyperspectral images can contain hundreds of continuous spectral bands, which increases their ability to be used in artificial intelligence and machine learning.

Furthermore, using different combinations of spectral bands enables the calculation of indices that can provide essential insights into the health of an ecosystem. For example, the normalized difference vegetation index (NDVI) is commonly used to assess vegetation health by measuring the difference in reflectance between the visible and near-infrared bands. The range of NDVI values is typically from -1 to 1, where higher values are indicative of more vigorous vegetation. Other vegetation indices, such as the enhanced vegetation index (EVI) and the green chlorophyll index (GCI), can provide complementary information on vegetation health and productivity.

Primary Data Sources. We can utilize existing legacy soil profiles, but more precise characteristics can be determined in a laboratory from soil samples. Primary data can be obtained from various sources. In studies such as [2,3,8], national soil information services were considered, while others such as [21] used soil information from university institutes. Remote sensing presents possibilities for expanding current soil survey datasets. By minimizing the requirement for extensive, time-consuming, and expensive field surveys, these techniques allow for the mapping of hard-to-reach regions. Additionally, there are publicly available soil spectra libraries that can be used. The following are some commonly used sources of soil data.

- The Rapid Carbon Assessment (RaCA) dataset, which provides information on soil carbon stocks in the United States.

- Land Use/Cover Area frame Statistical Survey (LUCAS) containing approximately 20,000 points of Europe's topsoil.
- Africa soil information service (AfSIS). which offers soil information for Sub-Saharan Africa.
- World Soil Information (ISRIC) providing more than 70 datasets for DSM.
- FAO SOILS PORTAL which is a comprehensive database for global soil information.

Auxiliary Data Sources. Unlike soil profile data, auxiliary data is already available and ready to use. Many free, open-source databases for remote sensing images are available today. In particular, the following datasets are rich in auxiliary data:

- The MARS dataset provides information about the annual phenological calendar in order to put in relation climate attributes with vegetation cycles [10].
- The EU Digital Elevation Model (DEM), with a resolution of 90m, is one of the most consistent and detailed sources of terrain information [10].
- Moderate Resolution Imaging Spectroradiometer (MODIS) viewing the entire Earth's surface every 1–2 days, mainly explored for monitoring vegetation activity via NDVI.

4 Mapping Methods

In the field of soil mapping, various techniques have been utilized to tackle the prediction and classification of soil characteristics and classes. In the following sections, we will discuss these models in detail.

4.1 Geostatistical Methods

Traditionally, many studies have created DSM models using conventional DSM techniques such as geostatistical-based spatial interpolation. In this framework of techniques, a sample of soil properties is modeled as the sum of the linear combinations of environmental covariates and spatial autocorrelation (stochastic) residuals [38]. An often-used geostatistical technique is kriging, and its variants: ordinary kriging and residual kriging [5], regression kriging [6]. Geostatistical models offer various benefits, such as explicitly modeling spatial variability and spatial autocorrelation, as well as enabling measurement of the uncertainties linked with predictions [38]. However, they have several limitations, such as data distribution assumptions, the need for larger sample sizes, data transformations, and the inability to handle non-linear relationships [9].

4.2 Machine Learning Methods

Various machine learning (ML) methods categories have been applied to predict and classify soil characteristics/classes in soil mapping. Linear modeling techniques such as partial least squares regression (PLSR) have been found to be appropriate for small, relatively homogeneous datasets [31]. This algorithm has been explored in [30–32,40,45]. Multiple linear regression (MLR) is another example of a linear model used in DSM, as shown in [22,32]. Support vector machines (SVM), also known as support vector regression (SVR) when applied to solve regression problems, have been used in [22,30,34,40]. Distance-based algorithms such as k-Nearest Neighbors (kNN) have also been used in DSM, such as in [30,34,41]. Other algorithms have been performed, such as in [35], where the authors report the development of a new memory-based learning approach named LGR (Local Gaussian Regression) that outperformed PLSR.

Tree-based learners are the most commonly used learners in the DSM literature. Different categories of tree-based learners were explored in DSM, including decision tree C5.0 used in [34], CART regression tree tested in [23], and random forests (RF) tested in all ML studies reviewed in this paper. ISRIC tested a variant of RF named quantile random forest (QRF) in [29] to predict soil properties on a global scale and gave satisfying results, as shown in other works such as [4,15,30]. Other tree-based algorithms commonly used in DSM are Boosted Regression Tree (BRT) in [12], cubist in [30], and gradient boosting in [14,34]. Several works [30,34,40,44] have aimed to test and compare various ML algorithms in DSM. In these studies, tree-based methods outperform the others, especially RF and QRF algorithms.

4.3 Deep Learning Methods

Feedforward Deep Learning. Several deep learning (DL) models have been developed for soil mapping. For example, the authors of [2,3] focused on the region of Scotland. In [3], a digital mapping approach was employed to produce fuzzy maps of soil classes using an artificial neural network (ANN) model. The models developed in [2] were considered accurate enough to produce carbon stock maps. Another study [21] explored a Deep Neural Network (DNN) approach for estimating soil organic carbon (SOC) across South Africa using remote sensing Sentinel-3 data. The authors compared the model's results to other ML models, such as RF, ANN, and SVM, and found that the DNN performed better.

Furthermore, some studies have combined ANN/DNN models with different methods to produce more efficient maps of soil properties. For example, the authors of [8] estimated soil organic matter (SOM) by developing a hybrid framework of Radial Basis Function (RBF) networks and ordinary kriging methods.

Convolutional Neural Networks. Convolutional Neural Networks (CNN) have been proven effective in DSM, as demonstrated by various studies. Firstly, in [25], the authors proposed a multi-task CNN architecture that can predict multiple soil properties simultaneously using a single model. They showed that

CNNs are more effective than conventional methods like PLS regression and Cubist regression tree, particularly the multi-tasking model. They tested the model on the LUCAS soil database and another smaller database with spectral data. Secondly, in [26], the authors aimed to improve prediction accuracy over traditional DSM models by adding contextual spatial information. They accomplished this by designing a CNN model that takes an input as a covariate image and examines spatial context information. They also used a multi-task CNN to estimate the organic carbon in different soil depth ranges. In [39], the authors developed a multi-task CNN model to map SOC using multi-source spectral data of the Hunter Valley area, Australia. They considered the uncertainty of SOC measurement when calibrating the model, which was a key contribution. Another study [42] also used multi-task CNNs, but with multiple covariates (SCORPN of SCORPAN model) compared to the previous ones that used fewer covariates [26,39]. In [45], the authors developed a deeper architecture ResNet that uses a multi-task deep CNN (DCNN) in addition to two single-task DCNNs and trained them on the LUCAS dataset.

Recurrent Neural Networks. Hyperspectral images consist of spectral data taken directly from satellite radiometry. The authors of [19] demonstrated that this spectral data could be considered sequential. Recurrent neural networks (RNNs) are DL models capable of handling this data type. Unlike a feedforward neural network, an RNN can process sequential inputs using a recurrent hidden state, whose activation at each step depends on the previous step's state [19]. Among different types of RNN models, Long-Short Term Memory (LSTM) and Gated Recurrent Unit (GRU) are the two most well-known. Various works [13,20,33] have achieved good results by treating the spectral data sequentially and using LSTM for hyperspectral image classification. Inspired by these works, DSM researchers have also employed this approach [32,41]. The proposed framework in [32] is based on Principal Component Analysis (PCA), which reduces the dimensions of hyperspectral data, and LSTM, which predicts the soil characteristics from the spectral data of the LUCAS dataset. Another interesting contribution was made by [41], where an extensive soil spectral library was utilized to comprehensively assess and compare ML algorithms and spectral pretreatment techniques of soil spectra data for SOC concentration prediction. In this work, LSTMs have been identified as the most suitable algorithm.

4.4 Transfer Learning

Soil spectra are typically measured in a laboratory setting. Nevertheless, implementing a calibration model created from the soil database to spectral information acquired from the proximal or remote sensing can present difficulties. Transfer learning (TL) can bridge this gap and allow the calibration model to be transferred from one sensor to another [17]. TL aims to transfer knowledge from a source domain to a target domain [43]. One method of TL is to fine-tune the network weights by training the network with newly available data. The first case study to adopt CNN-based TL for soil spectroscopy was [17]. The purpose of the study was to explore how transfer learning could be employed to improve soil clay mapping accuracy using hyperspectral imagery. A 1D-CNN was trained and evaluated using many spectra measured in the laboratory (LUCAS dataset) and then fine-tuned with remote sensing hyperspectral imagery dataset. Finally, the fine-tuned model was applied to the entire hyperspectral image to obtain the soil clay content map in the study area. The authors of [24] aimed to explain and evaluate the effectiveness of TL to "localize" global soil spectral datasets. They first trained the model with a significant volume of data that covered many cases. Then they fine-tuned the model with a small amount of local data. Similarly, a recent investigation by [31] employed a strong and reliable deep transfer learning approach to transfer valuable information from vast soil spectroscopy libraries (SSL) located in China, Sweden, and the USA. This information was used to produce local estimations of SOC at either the farm or field level.

5 Validation and Uncertainty Estimation in DSM

Model validation aims to compare the predictions of a model with a set of real and unknown data to evaluate the accuracy and predictive ability of the model. Validation can be done by splitting the data or using cross-validations and then calculating specific quality parameters of the multivariable model, known as evaluative metrics. Several examples of metrics exist, such as root mean square error ($RMSE$) and coefficient of determination (R^2), to assess relevance and accuracy.

Apart from assessing the model's efficiency, it is considered good practice to measure its degree of uncertainty [1]. There are two main types of uncertainty: epistemic (model uncertainty) and aleatoric (data uncertainty) [1]. Model uncertainty arises when the test and training data do not match, while data uncertainty arises due to overlapping classes or noise in the data [28]. However, estimating the uncertainty of knowledge is much more complicated than estimating the uncertainty of the data. Uncertainty estimation and quantification (UQ) have been extensively studied in DNN, and predictions made without UQ are usually not trustworthy [1]. The three most popular uncertainty estimation models are Monte Carlo (MC) dropout, the Bootstrap model, and the GMM [1]. Quantification of uncertainty provides upper and lower bounds of the estimated output variables [1]. In [21,23,26], the upper and lower bounds of the SOC map generated by each model were determined using a typical standard deviation of ± 1.64 on the bootstrap sample of the input data with a significance level of 90% confidence interval. Model uncertainty was studied in [41]. Some works, such as [29,37], calculated the prediction interval range probability (PICP). PICP is the percentage of observations covered by the defined prediction interval. Ideally, the PICP should be close to 0.9, indicating that the uncertainty is being assessed correctly [29].

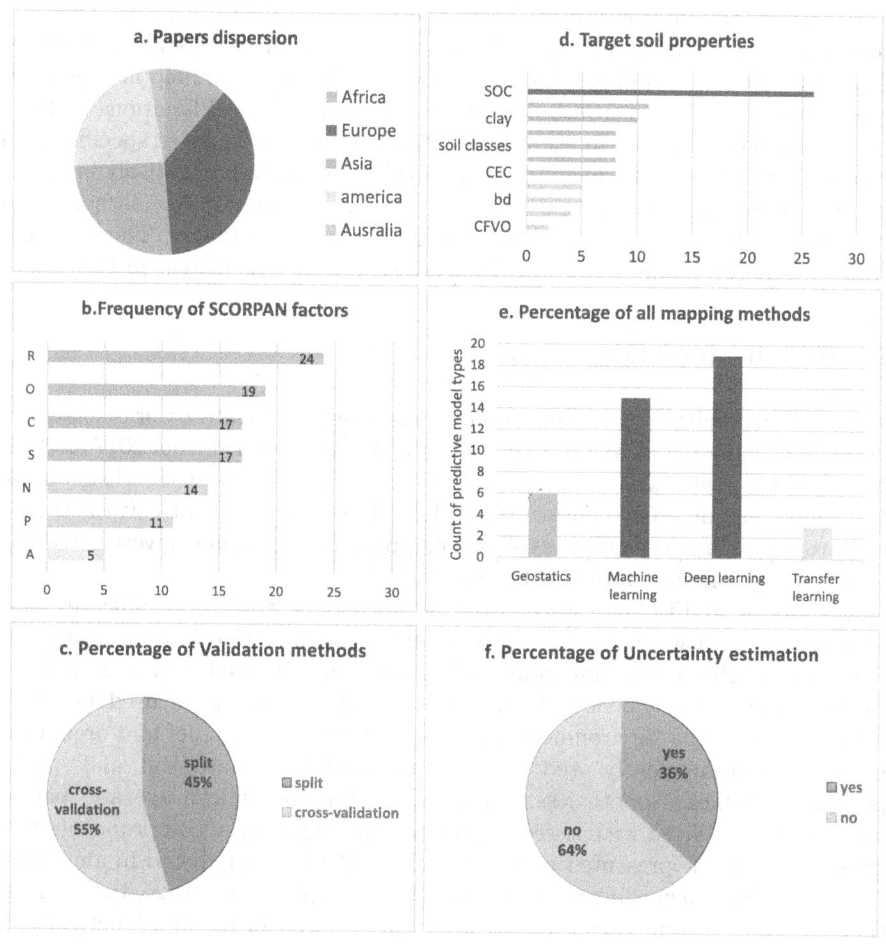

Fig. 2. Summary of statistical study results of the reviewed works.

6 Interpretability of Results in DSM

Model interpretability aims to comprehend and clarify the decision-making process of ML and DL models during predictions. It enables users to query the model's decisions and determine the crucial attributes and reasons behind the predictions. As a result, it is a vital step that can contribute to creating new insights to improve our understanding of soils.

For most ML algorithms, such as linear, tree-based, and distance-based methods, the importance of variables is easy to determine. For instance, the Random Forest (RF) model has an essential function known as Gini impurity, which helps users identify the contribution of each predictor to the model's overall performance [21].

However, DL models are often considered "black boxes" because they fail to quantify the importance of variables for regression or classification tasks. Therefore, several techniques have recently been proposed to help interpret DL predictions [21]. One such technique is SHApely Additive exPlanations (SHAP) [18], which has been used in [21,27,45]. The SHAP method assigns specific mean values to each variable to demonstrate how they positively or negatively influence the model's output [21]. The basis of this technique is rooted in the mathematical principles of Shapley values, which originate from game theory. These studies show that it is possible to move towards interpretable DL models in DSM.

7 Results and Discussion

In this study, we have reviewed a comprehensive set of the latest works related to DSM, which amounted to approximately 40 papers published from 2017 to 2022. To present a statistical overview of the studies, we analyzed the distribution of papers over different continents, evaluated the frequency of covariates and soil properties used in DSM, explored mapping methods, and investigated the validation techniques employed by the studies.

As shown in Fig. 2a, the distribution of papers worldwide indicates that Europe and Asia were the most extensively studied continents. The European dataset LUCAS was the most commonly used in the reviewed studies. In Fig. 2b, we presented the frequency of different SCORPAN covariates used in DSM, which revealed that environmental covariates representing relief and organisms were the most frequently used variables, followed by climate, soil, and spatial position variables. Nonetheless, covariates that represent the age and parent material were utilized with lower frequency. The frequency of soil properties targeted in DSM was presented in Fig. 2d, where SOC was predicted in almost all reviewed works. Regarding mapping methods, as depicted in Fig. 2e, we observed that DL and ML approaches constituted the majority of mapping methods. In contrast, geostatistics methods were scarcely used in the DSM process. Transfer learning was not given much consideration in the reviewed studies. Furthermore, we found that most studies validated their models using the data split method, and the remaining used cross-validation, as shown in Fig. 2c. Additionally, we found that around 35% of the studies estimated the uncertainty despite its significance in DSM.

Furthermore, it is worth noting that ML and DL algorithms have significantly improved the accuracy of DSM models for predicting soil properties content in recent years. In this regard, we compared the outcomes of numerous experimental studies that utilized the LUCAS dataset to map SOC, considered the most estimated soil property. Root mean square error ($RMSE$) and coefficient of determination (R^2) were reviewed as the most commonly used evaluation metrics to assess the relevance and accuracy of the models.

Table 1 summarizes the performance of seven models developed in recent studies, including [25,32,37,45], ranked in descending order by R^2 from the most accurate to the least accurate. In [37], the authors used LUCAS dataset

Table 1. Comparison of R^2 and $RMSE$ of prediction of SOC using LUCAS dataset.

Model	Covered countries	R^2	$RMSE$
1D multi-LucasResNet-16([45])	All	0.955	19.130
1D LucasResNet-16 ([45])	All	0.952	19.837
1D LSTM ([32])	All	0.940	23.250
PLSR ([45])	All	0.906	27.732
SVM ([45])	All	0.906	27.618
2D CNN ([25])	All	0.880	32.140
2D multi-CNN ([25])	All	0.690	16.820
2D multi-CNN ([37])	France	0.15	18.65
Random Forests ([37])	France	0.12	24.91

covering only France, and the 2D multitask-CNN performed better than the RF in both R^2 and $RMSE$. The other models were used with the entire LUCAS dataset, and the best model was the 1D multitask LucasResNet-16 [45], which performed better than PLSR, SVM, and also the single-task LucasResNet-16 of the same work. The 2D multi-CNN model [25] had a slightly lower R^2 compared to the other studies [45], but the $RMSE$ was the best of all the models. The 1D LSTM [32] also gave good results in terms of R^2 and $RMSE$. It is worth noting that the deeper layers of the CNN and LSTM architectures allow them to capture more complex structures, making them more effective in predicting SOC content in DSM models. Additionally, multitask DL models have shown better performance than single-task DL models because the former takes into account correlations between soil properties.

In summary, comparing these models highlights the potential of ML and DL algorithms in improving the accuracy and relevance of DSM models, particularly in predicting SOC content. However, as shown in Table 1, the $RMSE$ values obtained by the models are still relatively high, indicating that there is still room for improvement in DSM models.

8 Conclusions and Future Trends

Based on the reviewed literature, we draw the following conclusions:

- DSM has gained significant attention in Europe, Asia, the United States, and South Africa. At the same time, North Africa has not been explored due to the lack of soil profile datasets. To address this limitation, one possible solution is to leverage remote sensing data or transfer learning approaches from regions with similar covariates.
- The lack of covariates limits the prediction accuracy of DSM models. Therefore, technological advances are needed to better represent soil-forming factors like parent material and age, such as satellite-based remote sensing sources providing temporal information.

- Most studies focused on mapping SOC/SOM, while other soil properties essential for soil functions and land management have received less attention. Further efforts are needed to predict these properties using DSM.
- Geostatistics and ML models have traditionally been used in DSM, but DL has recently emerged as a promising technique. CNN and RNN models, particularly LSTM, have outperformed other methods in several works. Combining traditional models with DL techniques can yield better results.
- TL is a new trend in DSM, particularly when dealing with a lack of local data. It shows potential to improve prediction accuracy, and more research is needed to explore this technique further.
- Validating mapping results and estimating explicit uncertainty have become important tasks in DSM. Cross-validation and external datasets are recommended to prove the accuracy and reliability of DSM models.

Overall, In this review, we aimed to provide an overview of the current state-of-the-art in DSM using ML, DL, and TL techniques. By synthesizing and analyzing the literature, we identified the main trends and challenges in DSM and the most promising ML and DL algorithms for predicting soil properties. Our review highlights these advanced techniques' potential to improve DSM models' accuracy and relevance. We hope our work can contribute to advancing the field of DSM and inspire future research in this area.

References

1. Abdar, M., et al.: A review of uncertainty quantification in deep learning: techniques, applications and challenges. Inf. Fusion **76**, 243–297 (2021)
2. Aitkenhead, M., Coull, M.: Mapping soil profile depth, bulk density and carbon stock in Scotland using remote sensing and spatial covariates. European J. Soil Sci. **71**(4), 553–567 (2020). https://doi.org/10.1111/ejss.12916
3. Aitkenhead, M.J., Coull, M.C.: Digital mapping of soil ecosystem services in Scotland using neural networks and relationship modelling—Part 1: Mapping of soil classes. Soil Use and Management **35**(2), 205–216 (June 2019)
4. Žížala, D., et al.: High-resolution agriculture soil property maps from digital soil mapping methods, Czech Republic Catena 212 (May 2022). https://doi.org/10.1016/j.catena.2022.106024
5. Alsamamra, H., Ruiz-Arias, J.A., Pozo-Vázquez, D., Tovar-Pescador, J.: A comparative study of ordinary and residual kriging techniques for mapping global solar radiation over southern Spain. Agricultural and Forest Meteorology **149**(8), 1343–1357 (August 2009). https://doi.org/10.1016/J.AGRFORMET.2009.03.005
6. Bangroo, S.A., Najar, G.R., Achin, E., Truong, P.N.: Application of predictor variables in spatial quantification of soil organic carbon and total nitrogen using regression kriging in the North Kashmir forest Himalayas. CATENA 193 (October 2020). https://doi.org/10.1016/J.CATENA.2020.104632
7. Chen, S., et al.: Digital mapping of GlobalSoilMap soil properties at a broad scale: a review. Geoderma 409 (March 2022). https://doi.org/10.1016/j.geoderma.2021.115567

8. Dai, F., Zhou, Q., Lv, Z., Wang, X., Liu, G.: Spatial prediction of soil organic matter content integrating artificial neural network and ordinary kriging in Tibetan Plateau. Ecological Indicators **45**, 184–194 (2014). https://doi.org/10.1016/j.ecolind.2014.04.003
9. Dash, P.K., Panigrahi, N., Mishra, A.: Identifying opportunities to improve digital soil mapping in India: a systematic review, vol. 28. Geoderma Regional, Elsevier B.V., Mar. 01 (2022). https://doi.org/10.1016/j.geodrs.2021.e00478
10. Dobos, E., Carré, F., Hengl, T., Reuter, H., Tóth, G.: Digital soil mapping as a support to production of functional maps, vol. 22123 (2006)
11. FAO: The importance of Ukraine and the Russian Federation for global agricultural markets and the risks associated with the war in Ukraine. FAO (June 2022). https://www.fao.org/3/cb9013en/cb9013en.pdf
12. Gebauer, A., Gómez, V.M.B., Ließ, M.: Optimisation in machine learning: an application to topsoil organic stocks prediction in a dry forest ecosystem. Geoderma 354 (November 2019). https://doi.org/10.1016/j.geoderma.2019.07.004
13. Hang, R., Liu, Q., Hong, D., Ghamisi, P.: Cascaded recurrent neural networks for hyperspectral image classification. IEEE Trans. Geosci. Remote Sens. **57**(8), 5384–5394 (2019). https://doi.org/10.1109/TGRS.2019.2899129
14. Hengl, T., et al.: SoilGrids250m: Global gridded soil information based on machine learning. PLoS ONE **12**, 2 (February 2017). https://doi.org/10.1371/journal.pone.0169748
15. Heuvelink, G.B.M., et al.: Machine learning in space and time for modelling soil organic carbon change. European Journal of Soil Science **72**(4), 1607–1623 (July 2021). https://doi.org/10.1111/ejss.12998
16. McBratney, A.B., Mendonça Santos, M.L., Minasny, B.: On digital soil mapping. Geoderma **117**(1), 3–52 (2003). https://doi.org/10.1016/S0016-7061(03)00223-4
17. Liu, L., Ji, M., Buchroithner, M.: Transfer learning for soil spectroscopy based on convolutional neural networks and its application in soil clay content mapping using hyperspectral imagery. Sensors (Switzerland) **18**, 9 (September 2018). https://doi.org/10.3390/s18093169
18. Lundberg, S.M., Lee, S.I.: A unified approach to interpreting model predictions. In: Advances in Neural Information Processing Systems, vol. 30 (2017)
19. Mou, L., Ghamisi, P., Zhu, X.X.: Deep recurrent neural networks for hyperspectral image classification. IEEE Trans. Geosci. Remote Sens. **55**(7), 3639–3655 (2017). https://doi.org/10.1109/TGRS.2016.2636241
20. Ndikumana, E., Minh, D.H.T., Baghdadi, N., Courault, D., Hossard, L.: Deep recurrent neural network for agricultural classification using multitemporal SAR Sentinel-1 for Camargue, France. Remote Sensing 10, 8 (August 2018). https://doi.org/10.3390/rs10081217
21. Odebiri, O., Mutanga, O., Odindi, J.: Deep learning-based national scale soil organic carbon mapping with Sentinel-3 data. Geoderma 411 (April 2022). https://doi.org/10.1016/j.geoderma.2022.115695
22. Ottoy, S., van Meerbeek, K., Sindayihebura, A., Hermy, M., van Orshoven, J.: Assessing top- and subsoil organic carbon stocks of low-input high-diversity systems using soil and vegetation characteristics. Sci. Total Environ. **589**, 153–164 (2017). https://doi.org/10.1016/j.scitotenv.2017.02.116
23. Padarian, J., Minasny, B., McBratney, A.B.: Chile and the Chilean soil grid: A contribution to GlobalSoilMap. Geoderma Regional **9**, 17–28 (June 2017). https://doi.org/10.1016/J.GEODRS.2016.12.001

24. Padarian, J., Minasny, B., McBratney, A.B.: Transfer learning to localise a continental soil vis-NIR calibration model. Geoderma **340**, 279–288 (2019). https://doi.org/10.1016/j.geoderma.2019.01.009
25. Padarian, J., Minasny, B., McBratney, A.B.: Using deep learning to predict soil properties from regional spectral data. Geoderma Regional 16 (March 2019). https://doi.org/10.1016/j.geodrs.2018.e00198
26. Padarian, J., Minasny, B., McBratney, A.B.: Using deep learning for digital soil mapping. SOIL **5**(1), 79–89 (2019). https://doi.org/10.5194/soil-5-79-2019
27. Padarian, J., McBratney, A.B., Minasny, B.: Game theory interpretation of digital soil mapping convolutional neural networks. Soil **6**(2), 389–397 (2020)
28. Phan, B.T.: Bayesian deep learning and uncertainty in computer vision. Master's thesis, University of Waterloo (2019)
29. Poggio, L., et al.: SoilGrids 2.0: producing soil information for the globe with quantified spatial uncertainty. SOIL **7**(1), 217–240 (2021). https://doi.org/10.5194/soil-7-217-2021
30. Rudiyanto, B.M., Setiawan, B.I., Saptomo, S.K., McBratney, A.B.: Open digital mapping as a cost-effective method for mapping peat thickness and assessing the carbon stock of tropical peatlands. Geoderma **313**, 25–40 (2018). https://doi.org/10.1016/j.geoderma.2017.10.018
31. Shen, Z., et al.: Deep transfer learning of global spectra for local soil carbon monitoring. ISPRS J. Photogramm. Remote. Sens. **188**, 190–200 (2022). https://doi.org/10.1016/j.isprsjprs.2022.04.009
32. Singh, S., Kasana, S.S.: Estimation of soil properties from the EU spectral library using long short-term memory networks. Geoderma Regional 18 (September 2019). https://doi.org/10.1016/j.geodrs.2019.e00233
33. Su, H., Zhang, T., Lin, M., Lu, W., Yan, X.H.: Predicting subsurface thermohaline structure from remote sensing data based on long short-term memory neural networks. Remote Sensing of Environment 260 (July 2021). https://doi.org/10.1016/j.rse.2021.112465
34. Taghizadeh-Mehrjardi, R., et al.: Synthetic resampling strategies and machine learning for digital soil mapping in Iran. Eur. J. Soil Sci. **71**(3), 352–368 (2020). https://doi.org/10.1111/ejss.12893
35. Tziolas, N., Tsakiridis, N., Ben-Dor, E., Theocharis, J., Zalidis, G.: A memory-based learning approach utilizing combined spectral sources and geographical proximity for improved VIS-NIR-SWIR soil properties estimation. Geoderma **340**, 11–24 (2019). https://doi.org/10.1016/j.geoderma.2018.12.044
36. U.S.G.S: What is remote sensing and what is it used for?. https://www.usgs.gov/faqs/what-remote-sensing-and-what-it-used
37. Wadoux, A.M.J.C.: Using deep learning for multivariate mapping of soil with quantified uncertainty. Geoderma **351**, 59–70 (2019). https://doi.org/10.1016/j.geoderma.2019.05.012
38. Wadoux, A.M.J.C., Minasny, B., McBratney, A.B.: Machine learning for digital soil mapping: Applications, challenges and suggested solutions, vol. 210. Earth-Science Reviews, Elsevier B.V., Nov. 01 (2020). https://doi.org/10.1016/j.earscirev.2020.103359
39. Wadoux, A.M.J.C., Padarian, J., Minasny, B.: Multi-source data integration for soil mapping using deep learning. SOIL **5**(1), 107–119 (2019). https://doi.org/10.5194/soil-5-107-2019
40. Wang, K., Qi, Y., Guo, W., Zhang, J., Chang, Q.: Retrieval and mapping of soil organic carbon using sentinel-2A spectral images from bare cropland in autumn. Remote Sens. 13, 6 (March 2021). https://doi.org/10.3390/rs13061072

41. Wang, S., et al.: Using soil library hyperspectral reflectance and machine learning to predict soil organic carbon: Assessing potential of airborne and spaceborne optical soil sensing. Remote Sens. Environ. 271 (March 2022). https://doi.org/10.1016/j.rse.2022.112914
42. Yang, L., Cai, Y., Zhang, L., Guo, M., Li, A., Zhou, C.: A deep learning method to predict soil organic carbon content at a regional scale using satellite-based phenology variables. Int. J. Appl. Earth Observ. Geoinf. 102 (October 2021). https://doi.org/10.1016/j.jag.2021.102428
43. Yuan, Y., Zheng, X., Lu, X.: Hyperspectral image superresolution by transfer learning. IEEE J. Selected Top. Appl. Earth Observ. Remote Sens. **10**(5), 1963–1974 (2017). https://doi.org/10.1109/JSTARS.2017.2655112
44. Zhang, M., Zhang, M., Yang, H., Jin, Y., Zhang, X., Liu, H.: Mapping regional soil organic matter based on sentinel-2a and modis imagery using machine learning algorithms and google earth engine. Remote Sens. **13**, 15 (August 2021). https://doi.org/10.3390/rs13152934
45. Zhong, L., Guo, X., Xu, Z., Ding, M.: Soil properties: their prediction and feature extraction from the LUCAS spectral library using deep convolutional neural networks. Geoderma 402 (November 2021). https://doi.org/10.1016/j.geoderma.2021.115366

Online Book Selling Dapp Based on Smart Contracts

Hanane Echchaoui(✉) and Rachid Boudour

Embedded Systems Laboratory, Badji Mokhtar Annaba-University, BO 12, 23000 Annaba, Algeria
hanane_ech@yahoo.fr

Abstract. Smart contracts are the wave of the future. The idea behind them is to allow people who don't know or trust each other to do business together without the need for a middleman. Since their appearance in the blockchain, smart contracts extended usability for a wide range of applications, from financial transactions to everyday agreements. This work explored mainly the smart contract and addressed the problem of lengthy and costly payment processes, including some obstructive steps to settle a transaction and additional fees to pay for payment gateways. To shorten this lengthy process, we implemented data exchange between a smart contract and the user interface that supports custom ether and token purchases in a form of an online book-selling system. Our results indicate the viability and efficiency of the Dapp. Finally, we have demonstrated through this work that smart contracts can extend the usability of blockchain technology to other fields.

Keywords: Blockchain · Smart contract · online bookselling

1 Introduction

Blockchain is an intriguing technology that was created as the backbone of Bitcoin and it is commonly associated with cryptocurrency. However, since its inception, it has been constantly evolving and becoming much more than just a secure way to transfer digital currencies. The development of the technology has occurred over a series of three generations, each with its distinctive approaches to Blockchain. "Blockchain 1.0 refers to digital currency, Blockchain 2.0 to digital finance, and Blockchain 3.0 to digital society [1]". The second generation of blockchain technology gave rise to the blockchain known as Ethereum. It is the most often used blockchain for creating smart contracts and non-cryptocurrency applications [2].

The emergence of smart contracts broadened the potential for employing blockchain in several industries and changed people's perceptions of its potential beyond its use in digital currency to include a variety of possible applications in various industries such as healthcare, insurance, voting, social services and artist royalties [3–5]. E-commerce is one of the important areas in which these possibilities can be implemented. It has taken notice of the growing significance of blockchain technology in the global economy.

Major brands such as Microsoft, Twitch and Overstock from around the world are allowing customers to pay with cryptocurrencies for their services. However, Blockchain

H. Drias et al. (Eds.): AID 2022, CCIS 1852, pp. 178–191, 2023.
https://doi.org/10.1007/978-981-99-4484-2_14

offers innovative business opportunities beyond cryptocurrencies. The advantages of blockchain in e-commerce range from more efficient and affordable corporate operations to enhanced data security and better customer services.

Although blockchain technology has enormous potential, its adoption of the technology is still in its infancy. It is only logical for researchers and scholars to adopt blockchain and test its applicability in different sectors. In this respect, this work presents the potential that blockchain has in the e-commerce sector and aims to combine the competence of decentralized applications (Dapps) and smart contracts and apply them in an e-commerce application.

The main objectives of this study are to examine how blockchain technology and smart contracts can be employed in e-commerce, evaluate the advantages and limitations of incorporating these technologies and contribute to the advancement of the e-commerce industry by adopting new innovative technologies.

The rest of the paper is organized as follows. Section 2 gives an overview of blockchain technology and smart contracts and their development process and it presents some related works. The design of the e-commerce application is presented in Sect. 3. Section 4 shows the implementation and evaluation of the system. Section 5 concludes the paper.

2 Basic Concepts and State of the Art

2.1 Blockchain Technology

Blockchain technology was created by Satoshi Nakamoto in 2008 as a distributed ledger [6]. It is a new digital technology that combines cryptography, data management, networking, and incentive mechanisms to verify, execute, and record transactions between parties. Transactions are added to the blockchain ledger by proposing parties, and the processing nodes within the blockchain system verify their integrity before recording them in new blocks on the ledger. The blockchain ledger content is replicated across many distributed processing nodes, which operate the blockchain system jointly without the central control of a single trusted third party. However, the blockchain system ensures that all nodes eventually reach a consensus on the integrity and shared content of the blockchain ledger.

Blockchain is a new and dependable technology that aids in data security, preservation, and reliability. it is a distributed temper-resistant network that allows for storing data and transactions [7].

2.2 Smart Contract

Despite what many people believe, smart contracts are not a novel concept that was pioneered by the Ethereum Blockchain Platform, they date back to the 1990s when computer scientist Nick Szabo introduced the word [8]. A smart contract is a self-executing contract where the conditions of the agreement between the two parties are directly encoded into lines [9]. The agreements and underlying code are distributed throughout a decentralized blockchain network where transactions are traceable and irreversible, and the code regulates their execution [9]. Smart contracts store data that can be used to record information, facts, associations, balances and any other information necessary to implement the logic of real-world contracts. They can also be described as sets of computer code that are preserved on the blockchain network and specifies the terms that all parties to the contract must consent to. A smart contract is created following these steps:

1. Choosing the suited platform:

   Choosing a platform is the first step to developing a smart contract. Owing to the raising interest in blockchain and smart contracts in the last years, a wide variety of platforms exist, from which we can site: Ethereum, Bitcoin, Stelar and Neo. Each platform has its strength and weaknesses that should be considered before choosing between them.
2. Choosing the appropriate tools:

   Developing smart contracts require development tools. They can be subcategorized into:

   - Wallets: a browser plugin that serves as a service or program that stores information for cryptocurrency transactions. Examples of wallets include: Metamask, Coinbase Wallet, MyEther wallet, Wallet Connect, Binance Chain Wallet
   - IDEs: integrated development environments that can be downloaded or run from browsers. They are used to interact with the Testnet Remix Browser IDE, Visual Studio Code,
   - Programming languages: choosing the programming language depends on the choice of the platform. For instance, Ethereum uses the programming Solidity and Neo supports a wide range of programming languages exists from which we can cite: java, C# and Python.
   - Testnets and frameworks: It enables developers to upload tests, and interact with smart contracts without incurring gas costs. Robsten Test Network, Kovan Test Network, Rinkeby Test Network, Hardhat and Truffle are a few of the most used test networks.

3. Developing the smart contract:

   - Open-source library: using open-source and tested libraries such as OpenZeppelin minimises the risk of vulnerabilities in the application
   - Using Oracles: they enhance the capabilities of blockchain networks by granting access to all necessary external resources.

4. Testing the smart contract:

   - Creating a wallet at the chosen tool
   - Adding Dummy Crypto to the Wallet
   - Writing the smart contract and creating a file with the extension.sol (example: Mycontract.sol)
   - Smart Contract Code to Create ECR20 Tokens
   - Using the test net to check and eliminate errors
   - Compile the smart contract

5. Deploy the Contract (Fig. 1)

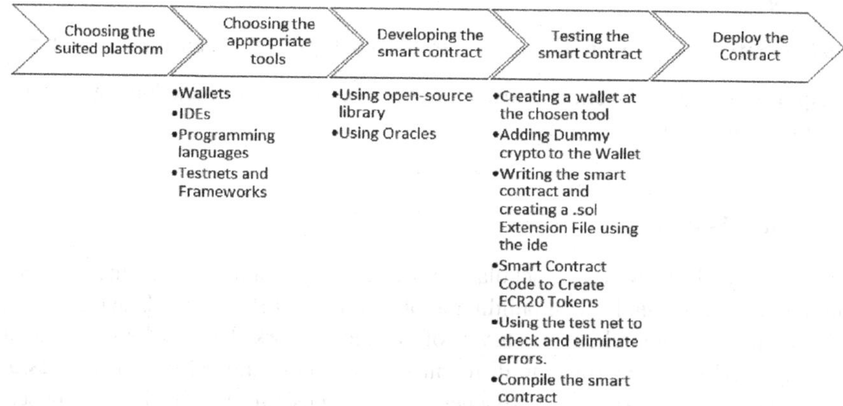

Fig. 1. Steps to developing a smart contract

The growth of the e-commerce industry in recent years led to the need for more efficient and secure payment systems. Blockchain and smart contracts have emerged as potential solutions for the challenges that face traditional existing systems offering several advantages such as transparency, trust and efficiency [10, 11]. However, there are challenged by some limitations like their complexity and social acceptance that can impede their integration and adoption into real-world applications.

2.3 Decentralized Applications (Dapp)

A DApp is, essentially, a computer program that exists and runs on a blockchain. All web applications consist of two parts: the "front-end" (on the computer) and the "back-end" (on the respective servers). The particularity of DApps is that their back-end part exists on a blockchain. This means that, by definition, no individual or group controls a DApp [12]. Dapps have a significantly distinct architecture from conventional applications. The most significant distinction is that in contrast to centralized applications, client-side applications communicate directly with the blockchain rather than a database. Dapps are generally composed of:

Front-end is the part that the users interact with directly and is usually developed using web technologies such as HTML.

Back-end is the part that is in charge of managing data storage, interacting with other services or networks, and carrying out any processing. It consists of smart contracts that are deployed on a blockchain. Additionally, it might include servers, databases, and APIs that give the system more functional.

Dapps offer several advantages:

Resistance to Censorship and Shutdown. Since there is no third party to control the application

Data Security. Data is stored on a decentralized network which ensures its protection

Transparency. All transactions and activities are visible on the blockchain, giving users greater trust and security.

2.4 Related Works

Throughout the last few years, scholars and researchers gained increasing interest in using blockchain technology in building applications in different fields and areas. Lin et al. provided a comprehensive survey of academic work that employs Blockchain technology and smart contracts in different sectors and examined the advantages and disadvantages of the existing approaches [13]. Bhanushali et al. in [14] proposed a blockchain-based application for buying and selling properties using smart contracts. The purpose was to make the process convenient and transparent. The system consists of two phases: the first one is the contract deployment the second is for buying, selling and storing these transactions in the blockchain. BookChain is a decentralized book-sharing application based on blockchain and smart contract technology presented in [15]. The aim was to enhance trust among borrowers and minimise the potential of losing books without the need for a third party. The experimental results show its efficiency and low cost. Rehman et al. introduced in [16] a blockchain-based e-payment system for E-commerce applications. The system makes use of Ethereum smart contracts to address the weaknesses of existing systems in terms of privacy and security. The transactions and trading of goods are accomplished without the involvement of a third party. Chiu et al. put in place an e-Library system called LibBlock [17]. The system incorporates smart contracts and IPFS to create a powerful, decentralized, adaptable, and customizable e-Library. This combination allowed, based on the experimental results, for tight record keeping and easy scaling. A decentralized marketplace application in an Ethereum smart contract format was proposed in [18] to address the shortcomings of the current online marketplace. The goal was to prevent the merchant from being blocked, keep them from being treated unfairly by centralized systems and maximise user data privacy. Khan et al. designed [19] a blockchain and smart contract system that ensures the correct and secure data transfer against cybersecurity breaches in e-commerce platforms that can be extended to other fields of application. A novel blockchain-based decentralized e-commerce transaction system was proposed by Xiao et al. using IPFS for storage Multi-Criteria Decision Making (MCDM) for reputation value calculation [20] to promote the stable operation of e-commerce systems. Priyadarsh et al. described a decentralized marketplace application based on Ethereum Smart Contract that promotes transparent trading and addresses four key issues: private payment, preserving privacy, user control, and sharing incentives [21]. Lastly, Zhang et al. described a decentralized food delivery system based on blockchain technology and smart contracts. The purpose was to automate the delivery process and ensures its security and transparency [22].

Table 1. Provides a summary of the related works discussed above, as well as the tools used to conduct each work.

Table 1. Related works

Reference	Author	Title	Tools
[13]	Lin et al.	A survey of application research based on blockchain smart contract	
[14]	Bhanushali et al.	BlockChain to Prevent Fraudulent Activities: Buying and Selling Property Using BlockChain	Ethereum Angular Truffle framework Ganache-CLI Metamask Solidity
[15]	Zeng et al.	BookChain: Library-free Book Sharing Based on Blockchain Technology	Apache Tomcat FISCO BCOS
[16]	Rehman et al.	Cyber Security Intelligence and Ethereum Blockchain Technology for E-commerce	Ethereum IPFS Web3.js
[17]	Chiu et al.	LibBlock - Towards Decentralized Library System based on Blockchain and IPFS	Ethereum IPFS
[18]	Prasad et al.	A Decentralized Marketplace Application on The Ethereum Blockchain	Ethereum BigChainDB IPFS Web3.js NodeJS Rinkeby
[19]	Khan et al.	Revolutionizing E-Commerce Using Blockchain Technology and Implementing Smart Contract	Ethereum Solidity
[20]	Xiao et al.	A Novel Decentralized E-Commerce Transaction System Based on Blockchain	Ethereum IPFS MCDM
[21]	Priyadarsh et al.	Web3.0 E-Commerce Decentralized Application	Ethereum MoralisDB
[22]	Zhang et al.	A Peer-to-Peer Smart Food Delivery Platform Based on Smart Contract	Blockchain Smart contract

3 Proposed System

The goal of this project is to build a decentralized application that will remove third parties and automate e-commerce processes, which can be done using a system based on blockchain principles and smart contracts that promise easy transactions, fast and secure for all online interactions. In addition to eliminating the necessary infrastructure used to manage payments, smart contracts can build mutual trust between buyers and sellers, and thus mitigate the need to give intermediaries sensitive personal and financial information to be authorized to use payment platforms that are not under the control of their users.

The objective is to build a system capable of implementing data exchange between a smart contract and customer currencies and supporting purchases by ETH (cryptocurrency of the Ethereum network) and custom tokens. This system will have the same functionalities as the conventional systems used, but with cheaper and faster payment processing with Blockchain.

Before the design process of the system, the question of why using blockchain in e-commerce is needed should be answered. E-commerce embracing blockchain technology results in a mutual gain for both the buyer and the seller. Along with providing security to the transactions, it reduces costs and transaction time, increases efficiency and improves customer service.

- Security: blockchain offers a high level of security for transactions and sensitive data for both parties from scams and attacks, which will benefit the customer by protecting his information and privacy and the merchant by attracting more clients by offering a safer commerce environment.
- Cost reduction: blockchain, is a peer-to-peer technology, that gives businesses the ability to cut down the cost of multiple sub-services such as banks.
- Trustworthiness: blockchain provides customers with peace of mind and the assurance that they are buying from legitimate sources with whom they can entrust both their sensitive and personal information and the authenticity of the products.
- Transparency: owing to its decentralized nature, blockchain provides the proper level of transparency for e-commerce, prohibits altering transactions between buyer and seller and ensures complete product traceability.
- Time-saving: by cutting down middlemen, blockchain makes the transaction faster and occurs almost instantaneously.

3.1 System Design

System Architecture. Figure 2 depicts an architecture diagram for the proposed system. This system is mainly composed of three layers:

- The Storage level is where the smart contract, data and all transactions are stored securely.
- Service level: users are given access to the essential bookselling system features and function through the service level. Each node of the Ethereum user nodes has a copy of the blockchain.

- Application level: the front-end of the system that allows customers to utilize it adequately (Dapp).

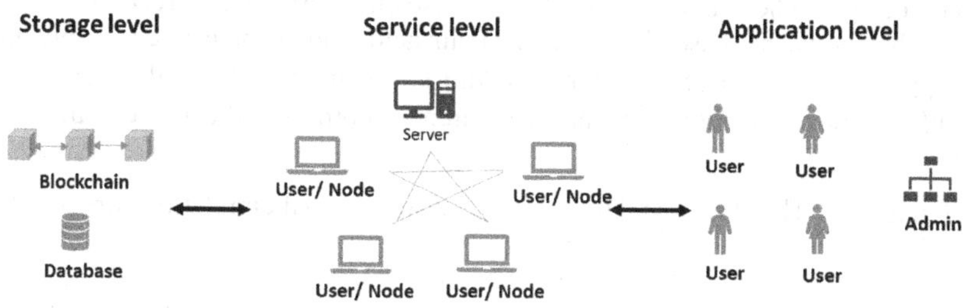

Fig. 2. System architecture

The designed smart contract resides on the blockchain ledger. When a transaction is invoked, the according method is executed on the validating parties. Access to the contract is given to the participants using their user credentials.

The data used in the experiment are shown in the UML diagrams described below.

Use Case Diagram. The use case diagram shown in Fig. 3 describes the functions and the scope of the system in addition to the interactions between the system and its actors. The system has two main actors: the user and the admin.

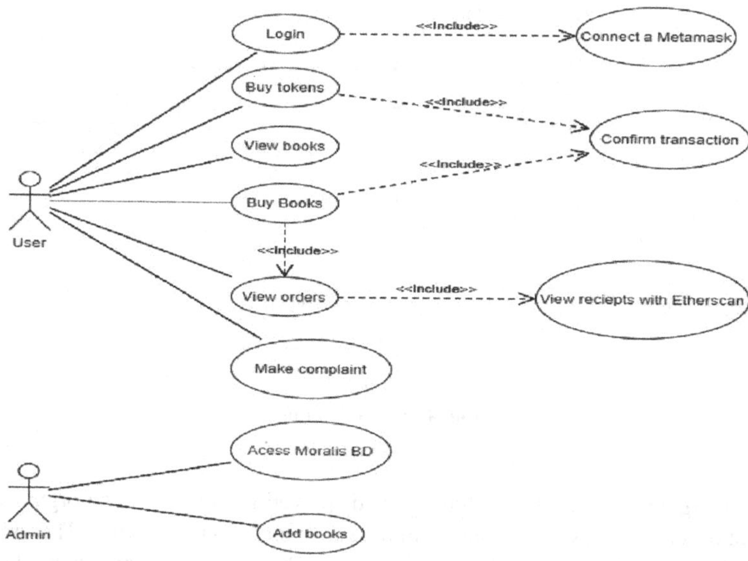

Fig. 3. Use case Diagram

In the buy tokens use case, the main actor (user) buys tokens in exchange for ether to purchase books. The user must be logged in to have access to this option. The Dapp asks the customer to enter the number of tokens they want to buy in exchange for ether then, the user clicks on the "Buy" button and confirms the transaction. The user gets the balance in Dapp so he can buy books. He can also check transaction receipts.

In the buy books use case, the user is the main actor and the objective is to buy books. The Dapp asks the customer to enter his address. The user clicks on the "Buy" button and confirms the transaction. He can view purchased orders and can check transaction receipts.

Class Diagram. The classes and interfaces of systems and their relationships are shown in Fig. 4:

- The class User: as soon as the user is connected, all his data on the channel is instantly synchronized in the Moralis database.
- The class Book: this class was designed to store the details of books. All the books are imported from the class into the interface.
- The class ethTransaction: each transaction will be stored here; this class is automatically created by the Moralis database.
- The class ethtransfer: every ether transfer will be stored here; this class is also created automatically by the Moralis database.

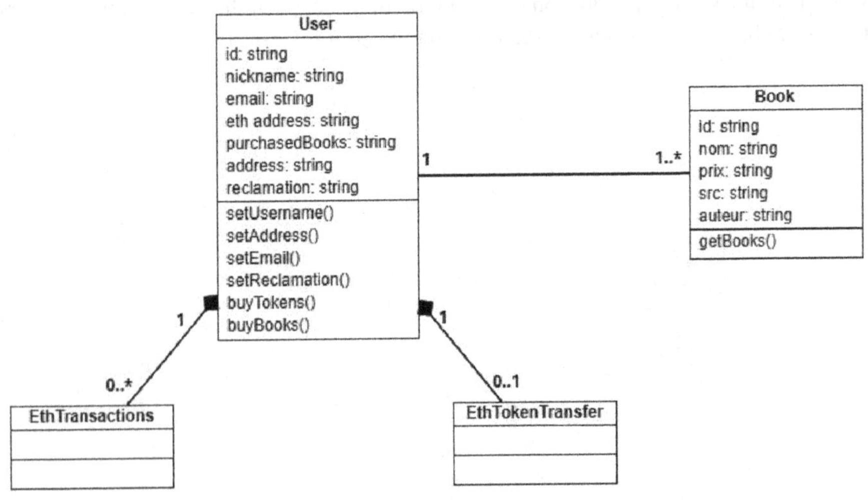

Fig. 4. Class diagram

Activity Diagram. The activity diagram is displayed in Fig. 5, it is an organizational chart that describes the system flow from the start point to the endpoint. The user must log in to the system to have the ability to browse books, buy tokens and buy books. After the purchase is made, the customer will have the ability to view his orders and make comments or complaints.

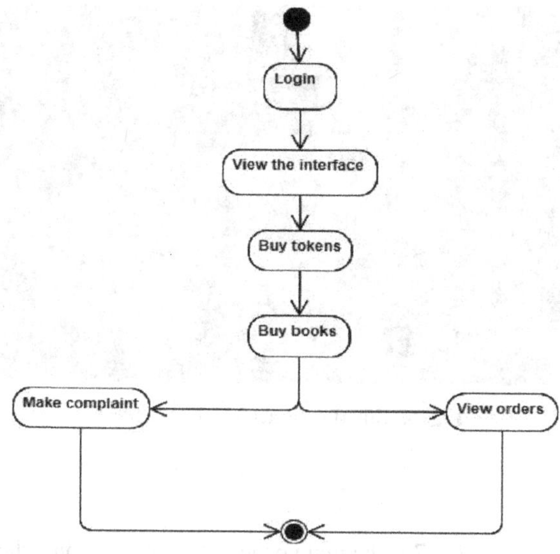

Fig. 5. Activity diagram

4 Experimental Results

The system is an e-commerce Dapp and its business logic is built based on the Ethereum smart contract. It is an online bookstore where customers can buy books and pay with special tokens.

4.1 Back-End

The system is deployed and tested using the Rinkeby test net. First, Metamask was used to create an account in the system's network and collect fake Ether. Then, a new file called "Money.sol" was created for the smart contract code which was used to combine different OpenZeppelin contracts as shown in Fig. 6. This contract allows for mining tokens with the help of the erc20 standard which ensures that all mined tokens are compliant and compatible with the Ethereum blockchain and also checks if the amount which is required to send is equal to the token amount needed. After that, either funded account on this network is needed and obtained using Moralis. A new file with the address and the private key of the node is created. Hardhat is used to compile the contract. A ContractFactory in ethers.js is an abstraction used to deploy new smart contracts, so Money here is a factory for instances of our Money contract. When using the ContractFactory plugin and hardhat-ethers contract, instances are connected to the first signer by default.

Calling deploy() on a ContractFactory will initiate the deployment and return a Promise that resolves to a Contract object. This is the object that has a method for each of the smart contract functions.

```
pragma solidity ^0.8.4;

import "@openzeppelin/contracts/token/ERC20/ERC20.sol";
import "@openzeppelin/contracts/access/Ownable.sol";

contract Money is ERC20, Ownable {
    constructor() ERC20("Money", "DA") {}

    function mint( uint256 amount) public payable {
        require(msg.value == amount * 0.0000038 ether,"invalid
        _mint(msg.sender, amount);
    }
    receive() external payable{}
    fallback() external payable{}
}
```

Fig. 6. Smart contract Money.sol file

4.2 Front-End

The home page shown in Fig. 7 is the main page of the application, where users can log in, start the purchase process, buy tokens or simply check the books that the platform provides.

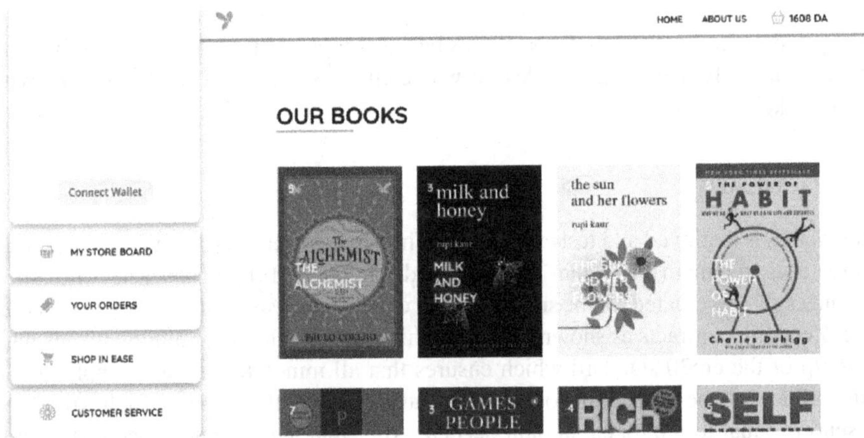

Fig. 7. Home page

When a user logs the DApp using cryptocurrency wallet authentication, the address of this wallet will be automatically saved in the Moralis database with all the data configured, such as token balance and transaction history. The user will then have the ability to buy tokens in exchange for ether. The tokens are then used to buy books. The seller does not require having money in his wallet to complete the transaction since the transferred amount is exact and there is no need to transfer the change from the seller to a buyer.

Figure 8 illustrates some of the screenshots of different pages of the application.

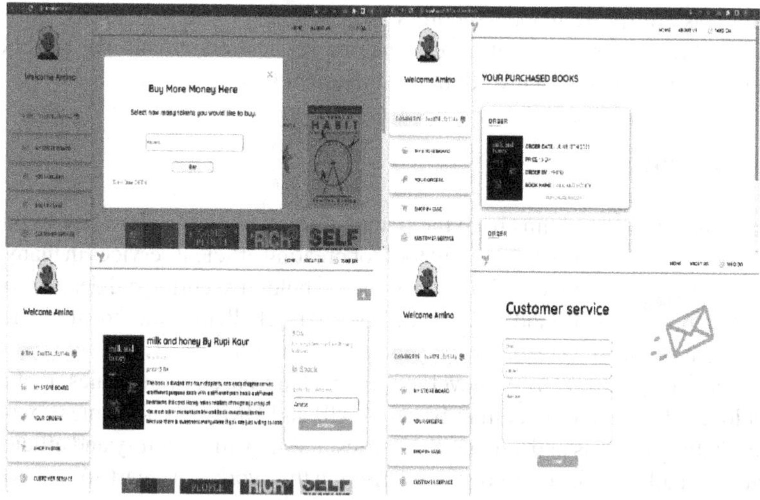

Fig. 8. System screenshots

Despite their benefits, using blockchain technology and smart contract in e-commerce also has some challenges and limitations that must be considered.

For instance, blockchain-based e-commerce systems can face scalability issues due to their limited capacity to handle a high volume of transactions in real-time [23]. Additionally, for blockchain-based e-commerce systems, the lack of interoperability is a problem because various blockchain platforms and protocols aren't always compatible with one another. Finally, Because of the ongoing evolution of the regulatory landscape surrounding blockchain technology, both consumers and businesses may experience uncertainty in adopting it.

Smart contracts are run on a blockchain network which makes them susceptible to security risks. Smart contracts might contain coding flaws or vulnerabilities that hackers could use to gain access without authorization or tamper with the contract's execution. They may be the target of attacks like denial-of-service attacks or replay attacks [24] that can prevent or affect the execution of the contract.

Standardization is required for the creation and use of smart contracts to reduce these risks. Smart contracts can be developed securely and reliably with clear specifications and coding standards. The adoption of standards can also encourage interoperability and make it easier to integrate smart contracts with other platforms and systems.

Decentralized applications have some limitations that could impact their overall functionality and societal acceptance. After their deployment, Dapps can be hard to update or modify and since maintenance is a critical part of their development, this can make them exposed to attacks. Dapps are also vulnerable to network congestion due to their decentralized structure, which can cause delays and higher transaction costs. Moreover, the lack of user experience with Dapps could make it challenging for them to navigate and use Dapps effectively because they are still relatively new.

As long as efforts are made to address and overcome these limitations, Dapps will continue to draw the attention of developers and researchers around the world due to their tremendous potential to revolutionize numerical fields.

5 Conclusion

Smart contracts in blockchains have the potential to revolutionize how we do business online. Thus, a smart contract is a useful tool for creating efficient services in many areas. Blockchains have proven their effectiveness in the field of security and decentralization in diverse applications around the world. The main challenge was to implement the data exchange between a smart contract and a client interface and also to support ether purchases and custom tokens, to develop a blockchain-based online sales application. We developed design and modelling based on UP and UML. To implement our Dapp, we used a battery of tools and languages. Our results show the viability and efficiency of our system. Finally, we have demonstrated through this work that smart contracts extend the usability of blockchain technology to different fields.

This is a work in progress, it met the objective of showing the applicability of smart contracts in the field of e-commerce.

In future work, we will conduct many experiments to evaluate the performance of our Dapp to analyze the main activities. Therefore, the response times of these actions are the key indices to evaluate the performance of the system.

References

1. Coghill, J.G.: Blockchain and its implications for libraries. J. Electr. Resour. Med. Libr. **15**, 66–70 (2018)
2. Alharby, M., Van Moorsel, A.: Blockchain-based Smart Contracts: A systematic mapping study. arXiv preprint arXiv:1710.06372 (2017)
3. Liang, X., Zhao, J., Shetty, S., Liu, J., Li, D.: Integrating blockchain for data sharing and collaboration in mobile healthcare applications. In: 2017 IEEE 28th Annual International Symposium on Personal, Indoor, and Mobile Radio Communications (PIMRC), pp. 1–5. IEEE, Montreal (2017)
4. Agate, V., De Paola, A., Ferraro, P., Lo Re, G., Morana, M.: SecureBallot: a secure open source e-voting system. J. Netw. Comput. Appl. **191**, 103165 (2021)
5. Shen, B., Xu, X., Yuan, Q.: Selling secondhand products through an online platform with blockchain. Trans. Res. Part E Logist. Trans. Rev. **142**, 102066 (2020)
6. Nakamoto, S.: Bitcoin: a peer-to-peer electronic cash system. SSRN Electr. J. (2008)
7. Jiang, J., Chen, J.: Framework of a blockchain-supported e-commerce platform for small and medium enterprises. Sustainability. **13**, 8158 (2021)
8. Szabo, N.: Formalizing and securing relationships on public networks. First Monday **2** (1997)
9. Mohanta, B.K., Panda, S.S., Jena, D.: An overview of smart contract and use cases in blockchain technology. In: 2018 9th International Conference on Computing, Communication and Networking Technologies (ICCCNT), pp. 1–4. IEEE, Bengaluru (2018)
10. Ryan, P.: Smart contract relations in e-commerce: legal implications of exchanges conducted on the blockchain. Technol. Innov. Manag. Rev. **7**, 14–21 (2017)
11. Ismanto, L., Ar, H.S., Fajar, A.N., Sfenrianto, Bachtiar, S.: Blockchain as an e-commerce platform in Indonesia. J. Phys. Conf. Ser. **1179**, 012114 (2019)

12. Zhang, W., Anand, T.: Blockchain and Ethereum Smart Contract Solution Development: DAPP programming with solidity, 1st edn. Apress Media LLC, New York, NY (2022)
13. Lin, S.-Y., Zhang, L., Li, J., Ji, L.-li, Sun, Y.: A survey of application research based on blockchain smart contract. Wirel Netw. **28**, 635–690 (2022)
14. Bhanushali, D., Koul, A., Sharma, S., Shaikh, B.: Blockchain to prevent fraudulent activities: buying and selling property using blockchain. In: 2020 International Conference on Inventive Computation Technologies (ICICT), pp. 705–709. IEEE, Coimbatore (2020)
15. Zeng, J., Dai, X., Xiao, J., Yang, W., Hao, W., Jin, H.: BookChain: library-free book sharing based on blockchain technology. In: 2019 15th International Conference on Mobile Ad-Hoc and Sensor Networks (MSN), pp. 224–229. IEEE, Shenzhen (2019)
16. Rehman, M.-ur-, Arain, A.A., Khoso, F.H., Hussain, Z., Lakhan, A.: Cyber security intelligence and ethereum blockchain technology for e-commerce. Int. J. Emerg. Trends Eng. Res. **9**, 967–972 (2021)
17. Chiu, W.-Y., Meng, W., Li, W.: Libblock - towards decentralized library system based on blockchain and IPFS. In: 2021 18th International Conference on Privacy, Security and Trust (PST), pp. 1–9. IEEE, Auckland (2021)
18. Ranganathan, V.P., Dantu, R., Paul, A., Mears, P., Morozov, K.: A decentralized marketplace application on the Ethereum blockchain. In: 2018 IEEE 4th International Conference on Collaboration and Internet Computing (CIC), pp. 90–97. IEEE, Philadelphia (2018)
19. Khan, M.M., RoJa, N.T., Almalki, F.A., Aljohani, M.: Revolutionizing e-commerce using blockchain technology and implementing the smart contract. Secur. Commun. Netw. **2022**, 1–8 (2022)
20. Xiao, Y., Zhou, C., Guo, X., Song, Y., Chen, C.: A novel decentralized e-commerce transaction system based on Blockchain. Appl. Sci. **12**, 5770 (2022)
21. Priyadarsh, S.S., Ashutosh, K., Brindha, R.: Web3.0 e-commerce decentralized application. SSRN Electr. J. (2022)
22. Zhang, L., Kim, D.: A peer-to-peer smart food delivery platform based on Smart Contract. Electronics **11**, 1806 (2022)
23. Zhou, Q., Huang, H., Zheng, Z., Bian, J.: Solutions to the scalability of Blockchain: a survey. IEEE Access. **8**, 16440–16455 (2020)
24. Duan, L., Sun, Y., Zhang, K., Ding, Y.: Multiple-layer security threats on the Ethereum blockchain and their counter measures. Secur. Commun. Netw. **2022**, 1–11 (2022)

A Survey on Recent Optimization Strategies in Ambulance Dispatching and Relocation Problems

Celia Khelfa(✉) and Ilyes Khennak

Laboratory for Research in Artificial Intelligence, USTHB, Algiers, Algeria
{ckhelfa,ikhennak}@usthb.dz

Abstract. The COVID-19 pandemic disrupted and posed significant challenges to the healthcare transportation system. Since the pandemic spread around the world in February 2020, the Emergency Medical Services (EMS), which is the first healthcare provider at an emergency site and the system responsible for sending adequate care in a minimum amount of time, has been confronted with a massive number of emergency calls and a limited capacity of existing facilities (ambulances, hospitals). The challenge of EMS was to develop practical and effective methods for ensuring the quality of the service under various conditions in order to save people's lives. The main focus of this study is to provide an overview and a discussion of modern modeling approaches designed in the literature to tackle problems with ambulance location and relocation as well as dispatching decisions. However, it reviews recent work on static and dynamic ambulance location problems. In this way, it is crucial to emphasize that the dynamic location of EMS is currently a relevant topic, given its influence on the outcomes of the healthcare system. Various significant contributions were proposed, including an analysis of summarized models, a presentation of recent approaches, and a recommendation for future advancements.

Keywords: Healthcare transportation · COVID-19 · EMS · Location and relocation decisions · Static and dynamic ambulance location

1 Introduction

2020 has seen a significant influence on daily life brought on by the Coronavirus Disease (COVID-19) pandemic. During the three years of the pandemic, reports from numerous areas worldwide indicated significant increases in EMS call volume, which put a lot of pressure on the EMS dispatch center [1]. The researchers predict that a new variety of Covid-19 resistant to current natural and vaccination immunity may cause future pandemics [3]. Plans and policies for the EMS must consider the feasibility of different interventions and improve their ability to respond efficiently to emergency calls that can impact people's lives. Response time can be used to gauge the effectiveness of an emergency medical system. The placement of ambulance stations, the number of ambulances and other vehicles to place at each station, the scheduling of employees, and many other decisions

H. Drias et al. (Eds.): AID 2022, CCIS 1852, pp. 192–203, 2023.
https://doi.org/10.1007/978-981-99-4484-2_15

are made within the EMS. In addition, the EMS services should act swiftly and decisively, making good decisions while offering their patients real-time services.

In a medical emergency response system, the location of ambulance stations and the allocation of ambulances to these stations are critical problems in developing an EMS system capable of responding to emergency calls and covering as many individuals as possible. Dispatching strategies have a substantial impact on the system's ability to meet future demand. In practice, the easiest and most popular strategy is to send the closest idle vehicle to serve an emergency call. The "closest idle ambulance" policy is not always the most effective method because it will only serve the nearest resort, which can lead to a decline in coverage, especially when resources are limited [19]. Until recently, most of the work focused on tactical and strategic strategies. At the strategic level, the locations of the ambulance stations are determined while considering constraints on coverage. Note that the region is covered if an idle ambulance can get there within a certain amount of time [20]. These choices lead to the construction or rental of warehouse facilities, which must be long-lasting and able to hold the necessary resources, such as emergency vehicles [2]. In contrast, tactical decisions specify mid- or short-term decisions such as the location of the standby sites as well as crew pairing and scheduling. A lot of efforts have been dedicated to the development of approaches to address operational decisions, such as relocation strategies and vehicle dispatching. Therefore, real-time decisions have become the primary focus of study, and dynamic models that handle relocation and dispatch decisions are gaining popularity.

This survey aims to provide a comprehensive overview of static and dynamic ambulance location problems, their applications, and recent advancements. As shown in Fig. 1, we reviewed 20 documents from recent publications to identify knowledge gaps and suggest future research directions. The paper is organized as follows: Section 2 describes the EMS procedure. Section 3 presents the most common mathematical models used for solving the problem. Section 4 reviews recent important approaches to static ambulance locations. Section 5 surveys current dynamic relocation strategies, offline redeployment, and real-time ambulance relocation. Section 6 presents conclusions and research perspectives.

2 Emergency Medical Services

EMS plays an essential role in modern health systems [18]. It is in charge of the pre-hospital component which includes responding to emergency calls, sending medical care as quickly as possible, and ensuring the safe transportation of patients to the appropriate hospitals. EMS transportation problem can be divided into three categories: (1) Covering problems that aim to minimize the response time to any future emergency. (2) Ambulance dispatching problems are solved by dispatching vehicles to reach the accident scene or a patient. (3) Vehicle allocation problems guarantee satisfactory service reliability for a specified geographic number of facilities with a finite number of vehicles.

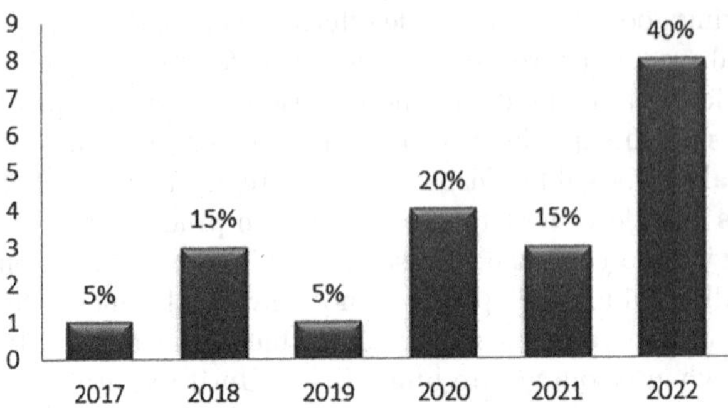

Fig. 1. Selected publications related to the emergency transportation problem.

In such a context, the procedure leading to the intervention of a paramedic team, as described in Fig. 2 consists of the following steps: (1) the reception of calls and the request for necessary information to determine which type of ambulance is the best to send to the emergency site, (2) the dispatch of vehicles and for that, there are different procedures to decide which ambulance could serve a particular emergency, (3) the ambulance traveling to the emergency, (4) on-site treatment and pre-hospital care, (5) then if necessary, the patient is assigned and moved to a hospital. After transporting the patient to the hospital, the vehicle should position itself at a particular point to improve coverage when some ambulances become busy or return to their original location. The EMS systems typically incorporate several specialized medical units to perform different jobs [28]. Advanced Life Support (ALS) and Basic Life Support (BLS) are the two common types of ambulances.

The EMS must be flexible and robust to quickly send an ambulance to the emergency site. This expectation is difficult to realize because of limited resources and stringent government budgets. A key indicator of these performance goals is the medical response time, which is among the most important predictive factors for patient survival [21].

3 Mathematical Optimization Models for Ambulance Location Problem

In this section, we discuss the modeling of the problem. Although it is difficult to review all available models for solving the ambulance location problem, only the frequently employed ones are discussed in this study. For each of these models, the set of demand zones is represented by I and The set of ambulances able to respond to emergency calls is represented by J. The travel times, including a fixed pre-trip delay, from all potential base locations $j \in J$ to demand locations $i \in I$ are given by t_{ij}. Most models employ a target response time r that must be met to cover a demand location. In other words, a demand point $i \in I$ is

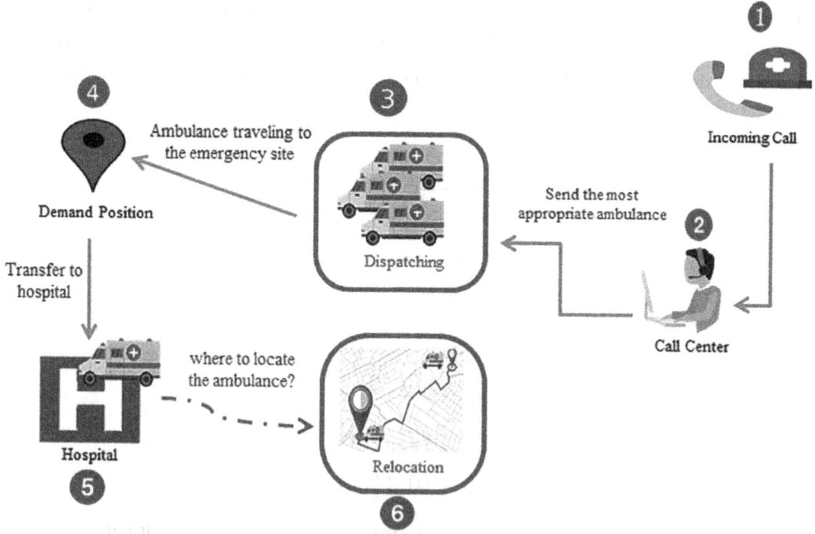

Fig. 2. EMS chain of events.

said to be covered by site $j \in J$ if and only if $t_{ij} \leq r$, which represents the potential base locations that cover demand location $i \in I$. To specify how many ambulances are present in the base location $j \in J$, all introduced models employ integer variables called x_j. When x_j equals 0, base location $j \in J$ is not opened.

3.1 Set Covering Location Problem (SCLP)

SCLP [9] considers a set covering problem to determine the location of emergency facilities. The objective function in Equation (1) minimizes the total number of facilities used. Each demand node is covered by the limitations (2) with the coverage matrix J_i. The formulation of this problem is as follows:

Minimize

$$\sum_{j \in J} x_j \tag{1}$$

Subject to

$$\sum_{j \in J_j} x_j \geq 1 (i \in I) \tag{2}$$

$$x_j \in \{0, 1\} (j \in J) \tag{3}$$

3.2 Maximal Covering Location Problem (MCLP)

MCLP [8] maximizes the weighted number of demand locations that are covered by at least one ambulance. In this model, d_i denotes the demand for vertex i, which is maximized by (4), p is the number of available vehicles, and y_i is a decision variable that is equal to 1 if node i is covered and 0 otherwise. According to (5), every demand location must be covered by a base that is occupied.

Maximize

$$\sum_{i \in I} d_i y_i \tag{4}$$

Subject to

$$\sum_{j \in J_i} x_j \geq y_i, \forall i \tag{5}$$

$$\sum_{j \in J} x_j \leq p, \forall j \tag{6}$$

$$x_j \in \{0, 1\}, \forall j \tag{7}$$

$$y_i \in \{0, 1\}, \forall i \tag{8}$$

The number of vehicles and home stations required may be determined using SCLP for strategic and tactical planning. In contrast, MCLP is an operational model that calculates vehicle distribution to home stations.

3.3 Dynamic Model

The relocation of ambulances is a more challenging issue since it arises more frequently and requires immediate attention. In this instance, more robust problem-solving approaches are required. The dynamic double standard model (DDSM) proposed by Gendreau et al. [12] is used for resolving ambulance relocation problems. The constants M_{jl}^t associated with the relocation of an ambulance $l = (1, ..., p)$ from its current location at time t to the location site represent the dynamic aspect of the model. y_{jl} is a binary variable equal to 1 if and only if ambulance l is moved to site j. The objective function in DDSM is based on Equation (9), which corresponds to the demand covered twice within r_1 time units, minus the sum of penalties associated with vehicle moves at time t. Additionally, Equation (10) and Equation (11) express the single and double coverage requirements. Equation (12) states that the number of ambulances located within r_1 units should be at least one if $x_i^1 = 1$ or at least two if $x_i^2 = x_i^1 = 1$ and x_i^k is a binary variable equal to 1 if and only if the location i is covered at least k times.

Maximize

$$\sum_{i \in I} d_i x_i^2 - \sum_{j \in J} \sum_{i=1}^{p} M_{jl}^t y_{jl} \tag{9}$$

Subject to

$$\sum_{j \in J_i^2} \sum_{i=1}^{p} y_{jl} \geq 1, \forall i \tag{10}$$

$$\sum_{i\in I} d_i x_i^1 \geq \alpha \sum_{i\in I} d_i \tag{11}$$

$$\sum_{j\in J_i^2} \sum_{i=1}^{p} y_{jl} \geq x_i^2 + x_i^1 \tag{12}$$

$$x_i^2 \leq x_i^1 \tag{13}$$

$$\sum_{j\in J} y_{lj} = 1 \tag{14}$$

$$\sum_{l=1}^{p} y_{lj} \leq p_j \tag{15}$$

$$x_i^2, x_i^1 \in \{0,1\} \tag{16}$$

$$y_{lj} \in \{0,1\} \tag{17}$$

4 Static Ambulance Dispatching Approaches

Static ambulance location models involve predetermined ambulance locations and can be classified into various types, including single-coverage deterministic models, multiple-coverage deterministic models, and probabilistic and stochastic models. Over time, these models have advanced to incorporate realistic considerations like traffic congestion and the availability of vehicles.

4.1 Probabilistic Approaches

In the case of probabilistic models, Boujemaa et al. [7] introduced a location-allocation model for stochastic programming that operates in two stages. The model allows for the simultaneous determination of the demand regions served by each station, the number and types of ambulances required, and the location of ambulance stations. To handle realistic scenarios, the authors proposed a sample average approximation method to solve the problem. Nelas and Dias [22] established two EMS models, deterministic and stochastic, that took into account various types of ambulances, the potential for substituting ambulances, and the possibility of deploying multiple vehicles for a single emergency situation. The stochastic model introduced uncertainty by utilizing scenarios to simulate unpredictable emergency episodes. Several studies have explored the concept of emergency uncertainty by constructing fuzzy location models. Wan et al. [27] developed a bi-objective fuzzy emergency location model in which all parameters are represented by trapezoidal fuzzy numbers (TrFNs) by using the α-cut set and analyzed its desirable properties to balance the "urgency" and "cost" of emergency rescues and cope with the uncertain information of large-scale crises. The sensitivity and comparison studies are presented to support the suggested method's flexibility and superiority.

4.2 Metaheuristic Approaches

Intelligent optimization algorithms like the genetic algorithm (GA), ant colony algorithm (ACO), and particle swarm optimization algorithm (PSO) are commonly utilized to tackle complex ambulance dispatching problems, which are known to be NP-hard. Gao et al. [11] proposed a hybrid optimization algorithm that combined a genetic algorithm (GA) with a fuzzy C-means (FCM) clustering algorithm. The algorithm utilized Manhattan distance to determine the distance between an injured patient and an EMS center, with the aim of minimizing total travel time and the overall mortality risk for patients in a disaster scenario. To retain structures and other spatial information and to optimize the placements of EMS stations, Song et al. [24] employed GA with a spatial configuration of regional variables and developed several fundamental approaches to GA crossover and mutation operators. Attari et al. [4] aimed to minimize time and financial expenses by reducing hospital and transportation costs. For that purpose, a stochastic mathematical model with two meta-heuristic algorithms consisting of Non-dominated Sorting Genetic Algorithm II (NSGA-II) and PSO has been applied. The work of Talebi et al. [26] also used NSGA-II and the Multi-Objective Bees Algorithm with different types of vehicles. They proposed a new bi-objective ambulance routing problem to minimize total response time and EMS vehicle assignment costs. Zhang and Xiong [29] proposed an immune ACO (IACO) algorithm to maximize demand point satisfaction and minimize cost and response time. Giri et al. [13] compared Ant Colony Optimization (ACO), Adaptive ACO, and Firefly algorithms to minimize incident response time and the total travel time between the dispatch location and the destination. ACO produced the best results, but over a longer period of time.

4.3 Unsupervised Machine Learning Approaches

Unsupervised Machine learning, especially unsupervised clustering approaches, was used to cluster a sizeable geographic zone to contribute to solving ambulance dispatching by optimizing the transportation time and the coverage of all the calls [10]. In this context, Houacine et al. [16] proposed a novel DBSCAN-based approach called a Heterogeneous DBSCAN (HDBSCAN) approach. The authors studied the Global Positioning System (GPS) of static bases and dynamic incoming calls to group a finite number of emergency calls into clusters containing a minimum number of bases, thus delimiting the ambulance dispatch space. The work reported by Kerakos et al. [17] used the K-Means algorithm to divide Stockholm County into small clusters over which predictions of ambulance demand could be made within a specific time frame. These predictions were used to distribute ambulances and reduce the response time. Olivos et al. [23] proposed a multi-objective model solved using an iterative ϵ-constraint method to minimize the response time and maximize coverage, the ward algorithm for cluster analysis was used to reduce computational complexity.

5 Dynamic Ambulance Dispatching Approaches

The previous models discussed were static and unable to provide optimal solutions in real-life scenarios where an ambulance may become unavailable after being dispatched to a call. The issue of static ambulance placement involves selecting a set of stations where ambulances can wait in between emergency call assignments, assuming that they will return to their assigned home base after each mission. Sometimes it is beneficial to adjust the location of an ambulance base over time to better respond to EMS demands, for example, by relocating an ambulance from base A to base B. In the literature, there are two primary approaches to ambulance relocation: offline redeployment and real-time ambulance relocation.

5.1 Offline Redeployment Approaches

The offline method is used for various scenarios to precompute solutions to the ambulance relocation problem. When an emergency situation occurs in real-time, the appropriate relocation strategy is looked up and applied. Zhang and Zeng [30] presented the first two-stage robust optimization model (RO) that utilized mixed-integer recourse for relocation to address ambulance location problems. The model demonstrated the robustness of the two-stage RO approach in effectively capturing the EMS configuration and service requirements. Bertsimas and Ng [6] proposed stochastic and robust formulations for the ambulance deployment problem. The approach considered demand interactions across regions and improved upon probabilistic models with adaptive recourse functions that capture sparse demands and concurrent calls. They also compared MEXCLP with MALP and used cross-validation to pick the best performance. Sudtachat et al. [25] investigated the use of a Tabu search heuristic to solve the maximum realized covering relocation and districting problem (MRCRDP). The optimization process was based on the nested-compliance model, with the aim of maximizing the overall realized expected coverage.

5.2 Online Redeployment Approaches

In these approaches, deployment decisions are made in real time based on the current state of the system. The purpose is to move idle ambulances to provide the best possible coverage, defined as the proportion of future calls that are responded to within a set time frame. Drias et al. [10] proposed QOPTICS with a deep self-learning approach to simulate the improvement of the Artificial Orca Algorithm (AOA) and Elephant Herding Optimization (EHO) to manage the dispatching of emergency vehicles throughout a vast area in the context

Table 1. Some Recent Research Papers on Emergency transportation

Reference	Static/Dynamic model	Solution Approach	Objective (s)	Ambulance types
[6]	DM Off-line	MEXCLP/MALP	Minimize response times	Single type
[22]	SM	Two-stage stochastic programming	Maximize coverage	Two types
[27]	SM	Fuzzy logique	Balance the "urgency" and "cost" of the emergency rescues	Single type
[11]	SM	GA /FCM	Minimize travel time and the total morality risk	Single type
[24]	SM	NSGA-II	Maximizing expected coverage, minimization of the number of locations	Single type
[7]	SM	Stochastic model	Minimize the capacity cost, transportation cost and penalty cost	Two types
[4]	SM	NSGA-II/PSO	Minimize the expected time cost	Single type
[29]	SM	ACO	Maximize demand point satisfaction and response times cost	Single type
[26]	SM	NSGA-II /OBS	Minimize total response time	Two types
[13]	SM	ACO	Minimize total travel time	Single type
[23]	SM	ϵ-constraint /the ward algorithm	Minimize the response time and maximize the coverage	Single type
[16]	SM	HDBSCAN	Minimize reponse time	Single type
[17]	SM	K-Means algorithm	Minimize reponse time	Single type
[30]	DM-Offline	MILP-RO	Maximize coverage	Single type
[25]	DM-Offline	Tabu search heuristic	Maximize coverage	Single type
[15]	DM-Online	model-driven decision	Maximize coverage, Minimize travel time	Single type
[18]	DM-Online	two-stage stochastic programming model	Minimize response time, on-site treatment time, and transfer time	Single type
[5]	DM-Online	DSLAOA	Minimize travel time, waiting calls, unserved priorities	Single type
[10]	DM-Online	QOPTICS/ AOA and EHO	Minimize travel time, waiting calls, unserved priorities	Single type
[14]	DM-Online	MVO/GA	Maximize the expected coverage	Single type

of COVID-19. Bendimerad and Drias [5] presented a novel Deep Self-Learning approach applied to AOA based on Cauchy and Gaussian mutation operators. This approach was applied to a real case study of Saudi Arabia in Covid-19. Hajiali et al. [15] proposed a decision assistance system that used an online approach to tackle the ambulance relocation problem using a mathematical model. The first goal is to maximize demand coverage, and the second is to minimize travel time due to relocation. The number of demand points covered is determined in real-time and called into the model according to changes in the system state. Lee et al. [18] introduced a two-stage stochastic programming model with uncertainty to relocate ambulances to minimize the term Time to Arrive at Hospital (TAH). A truncated Poisson distribution was used for forecasting near-future EMS demands. A hypercube model for a queuing system was provided by Golabian et al. [14] in order to determine the optimal strategy for maximizing the predicted coverage based solely on the placements of idle ambulances on the stations. The best solution was then determined using the multi-verse optimizer and genetic algorithms with simulation-based decoding.

6 Conclusion and Future Directions

Over the past three decades, ambulance location and relocation models have seen significant progress. This study aims to provide a comprehensive review of the EMS problem, covering both static and dynamic versions as well as recent advancements and applications. Based on the papers studied, multiple solutions have been proposed to aid decision-makers with ambulance dispatching and allocation. Since 2017, metaheuristic methods have been the most commonly proposed strategies to tackle the complex ambulance location and relocation problem. Nonetheless, researchers are exploring ways to capture the uncertainty and dynamism inherent in these problems.

Despite significant efforts to address location and relocation issues, other research directions still require investigation. Firstly, most of the papers discussed in this study did not consider the type of ambulances (e.g., ALS, BLS) in their strategies. To offer patients adequate care, especially in extreme emergencies, it is crucial to include various types of ambulances in the model to make it as realistic as possible. Recent studies have focused on real-life or realistic cases. Additionally, models are emerging that consider more fuzzy factors, such as traffic conditions, economic level, coverage range, construction costs, and environmental protection. Finally, it is noteworthy that only three studies included geographic information systems (GIS) in the modeling, despite the fact that many issues require geographic information to estimate trip times or distances.

References

1. Al Amiry, A., Maguire, B.J.: Emergency medical services (ems) calls during covid-19: early lessons learned for systems planning (a narrative review). Open Access Emergency Med.: OAEM **13**, 407 (2021)
2. Amorim, M., Antunes, F., Ferreira, S., Couto, A.: An integrated approach for strategic and tactical decisions for the emergency medical service: exploring optimization and metamodel-based simulation for vehicle location. Comput. Ind. Eng. **137**, 106057 (2019)

3. Athey, S., Castillo, J.C., Chaudhuri, E., Kremer, M., Gomes, A.S., Snyder, C.: Expanding capacity for vaccines against covid-19 and future pandemics: a review of economic issues (2022)
4. Attari, M.Y.N., Ahmadi, M., Ala, A., Moghadamnia, E.: RSDM-AHSNET: designing a robust stochastic dynamic model to allocating health service network under disturbance situations with limited capacity using algorithm NSGA-ii and PSO. Comput. Biol. Med., 105649 (2022)
5. Bendimerad, L.S., Drias, H.: An efficient deep self-learning artificial orca algorithm for solving ambulance dispatching and calls covering problem. In: Abraham, A., Engelbrecht, A., Scotti, F., Gandhi, N., Manghirmalani Mishra, P., Fortino, G., Sakalauskas, V., Pllana, S. (eds.) SoCPaR 2021. LNNS, vol. 417, pp. 136–145. Springer, Cham (2022). https://doi.org/10.1007/978-3-030-96302-6_12
6. Bertsimas, D., Ng, Y.: Robust and stochastic formulations for ambulance deployment and dispatch. Eur. J. Oper. Res. **279**(2), 557–571 (2019)
7. Boujemaa, R., Jebali, A., Hammami, S., Ruiz, A., Bouchriha, H.: A stochastic approach for designing two-tiered emergency medical service systems. Flexible Serv. Manuf. J. **30**(1), 123–152 (2018)
8. Church, R., ReVelle, C.: The maximal covering location problem. In: Papers of the Regional Science Association, vol. 32, pp. 101–118. Springer-Verlag (1974). https://doi.org/10.1007/BF01942293
9. Current, J.R., Schilling, D.A.: Analysis of errors due to demand data aggregation in the set covering and maximal covering location problems. Geograph. Anal. **22**(2), 116–126 (1990)
10. Drias, H., Drias, Y., Houacine, N.A., Bendimerad, L.S., Zouache, D., Khennak, I.: Quantum optics and deep self-learning on swarm intelligence algorithms for covid-19 emergency transportation. Soft Comput., pp. 1–20 (2022)
11. Gao, X., Zhou, Y., Amir, M.I.H., Rosyidah, F.A., Lee, G.M.: A hybrid genetic algorithm for multi-emergency medical service center location-allocation problem in disaster response. Int. J. Ind. Eng. **24**(6) (2017)
12. Gendreau, M., Laporte, G., Semet, F.: A dynamic model and parallel tabu search heuristic for real-time ambulance relocation. Parallel Comput. **27**(12), 1641–1653 (2001)
13. Giri, A.R., Chen, T., Rajendran, V.P., Khamis, A.: A metaheuristic approach to emergency vehicle dispatch and routing. In: 2022 IEEE International Conference on Smart Mobility (SM), pp. 27–31. IEEE (2022)
14. Golabian, H., Arkat, J., Tavakkoli-Moghaddam, R., Faroughi, H.: A multi-verse optimizer algorithm for ambulance repositioning in emergency medical service systems. J. Ambient Intell. Hum. Comput. **13**(1), 549–570 (2022)
15. Hajiali, M., Teimoury, E., Rabiee, M., Delen, D.: An interactive decision support system for real-time ambulance relocation with priority guidelines. Decis. Supp. Syst. **155**, 113712 (2022)
16. Houacine, N.A., Bendimerad, L.S., Drias, H.: Heterogeneous DBSCAN for emergency call management: a case study of covid-19 calls based on hospitals distribution in Saudi Arabia. In: International Conference on Innovations in Bio-Inspired Computing and Applications, pp. 402–411. Springer (2021). https://doi.org/10.1007/978-3-030-96299-9_39
17. Kerakos, E., Lindgren, O., Tolstoy, V.: Machine learning for ambulance demand prediction in stockholm county: towards efficient and equitable dynamic deployment systems (2020)

18. Lee, Y.C., Chen, Y.S., Chen, A.Y.: Lagrangian dual decomposition for the ambulance relocation and routing considering stochastic demand with the truncated poisson. Transp. Res. Part B: Methodol. **157**, 1–23 (2022)
19. MacLachlan, J., Mei, Y., Zhang, F., Zhang, M.: Genetic programming for vehicle subset selection in ambulance dispatching. In: 2022 IEEE Congress on Evolutionary Computation (CEC), pp. 1–8. IEEE (2022)
20. Nasrollahzadeh, A.A., Khademi, A., Mayorga, M.E.: Real-time ambulance dispatching and relocation. Manuf. Serv. Oper. Manage. **20**(3), 467–480 (2018)
21. Neira-Rodado, D., Escobar-Velasquez, J.W., McClean, S.: Ambulances deployment problems: categorization, evolution and dynamic problems review. ISPRS Int. J. Geo-Inf. **11**(2), 109 (2022)
22. Nelas, J., Dias, J.: Optimal emergency vehicles location: an approach considering the hierarchy and substitutability of resources. Eur. J. Oper. Res. **287**(2), 583–599 (2020)
23. Olivos, C., Caceres, H.: Multi-objective optimization of ambulance location in antofagasta, chile. Transport **37**(3), 177–189 (2022)
24. Song, J., Li, X., Mango, J.: Location optimization of urban emergency medical service stations: a hierarchical multi-objective model with a new encoding method of genetic algorithm solution. In: Di Martino, S., Fang, Z., Li, K.-J. (eds.) W2GIS 2020. LNCS, vol. 12473, pp. 68–82. Springer, Cham (2020). https://doi.org/10.1007/978-3-030-60952-8_7
25. Sudtachat, K., Mayorga, M.E., Chanta, S., Albert, L.A.: Joint relocation and districting using a nested compliance model for ems systems. Comput. Ind. Eng. **142**, 106327 (2020)
26. Talebi, E., Shaabani, M., Rabbani, M.: Bi-objective model for ambulance routing for disaster response by considering priority of patients. Int. J. Supply Oper. Manage. **9**(1), 80–94 (2022)
27. Wan, S.P., Chen, Z.H., Dong, J.Y.: Bi-objective trapezoidal fuzzy mixed integer linear program-based distribution center location decision for large-scale emergencies. Appl. Soft Comput. **110**, 107757 (2021)
28. Yoon, S., Albert, L.A., White, V.M.: A stochastic programming approach for locating and dispatching two types of ambulances. Transp. Sci. **55**(2), 275–296 (2021)
29. Zhang, Q., Xiong, S.: Routing optimization of emergency grain distribution vehicles using the immune ant colony optimization algorithm. Appl. Soft Comput. **71**, 917–925 (2018)
30. Zhang, R., Zeng, B.: Ambulance deployment with relocation through robust optimization. IEEE Trans. Autom. Sci. Eng. **16**(1), 138–147 (2018)

Machine and Deep Learning

Sewer Systems Control Using Internet of Things and eXplainable Artificial Intelligence

Mohamed Zakaria Bourahla and Mustapha Bourahla(✉)

University of M'Sila, M'Sila 28000, Algeria
mustapha.bourahla@univ-msila.dz

Abstract. This paper presents a real-time control on sewer systems to prevent overflow using the Internet of Things and eXplainable Artificial Intelligence. The Internet of Things is used to offer continuous data to be used in two steps. In the first step, we use historical data to construct Artificial Intelligence-based prediction models to forecast future system states and then, in the second step, we use the real-time data for monitoring and control of sewer systems using the prediction models combined with eXplainable Artificial Intelligence (XAI) technique. The prediction model is used to predict the labels outputs of real-time inputs observed by sensors installed in different locations of the sewer system. These predictions will be analyzed by a technique of explainable artificial intelligence to diagnose the sewer system if an abnormal behavior is observed.

Keywords: Sewer System Control · Internet of Things · Artificial Intelligence · eXplainable Artificial Intelligence

1 Introduction

The sewer system is designed as an integral aspect of the infrastructure of cities to carry wastewater and storm water away from city centers in order to protect public health [1]. The polluted water should be treated before being discharged into the environment, with the sewage systems and treatment plants focusing not only on public health but also on the environment and resource recovery [2].

If the water flow in some sewage canals is measured to be not at the desired level, there will be problems when heavy rainstorms happened, causing infrastructure damage by causing floods and wastewater overflows due to sewer system surcharges in certain locations [3].

Sewer overflows are becoming more common as a result of increased urbanization and significant rainfall events, resulting in water pollution and negative environmental, health, and fiscal consequences. Chemical and microbiological contamination, dangerous compounds, and other micro-pollutants in sewer overflows can degrade the water quality [4].

The major goal of this work is to examine the application of real-time control on sewer systems to prevent overflow using the Internet of Things (IoT)

H. Drias et al. (Eds.): AID 2022, CCIS 1852, pp. 207–220, 2023.
https://doi.org/10.1007/978-981-99-4484-2_16

and eXplainable Artificial Intelligence (XAI). The Internet of Things [5] is used to offer continuous monitoring and control of wastewater systems in real time. The data acquired by the Internet of Things can also be used to construct and calibrate models that are useful for simulation and prediction.

Models that are suited for prediction [6] are frequently used to forecast future system states. They rely on system measurement data and must operate at a high computational speed. The model prediction can be explained using the XAI technique [7,8] to help diagnosis of the sewer system behavior.

A simulation of a case study was undertaken for this project in M'Sila, Algeria, to demonstrate how real-time control can be used to manage sewer systems. A hydraulic model was utilized in this study to examine the viability of various control systems. The study looked into the prospect of employing artificial intelligence as a model for prediction, given recent breakthroughs in artificial intelligence and the huge amount of data collected through the Internet of Things.

This paper is organized as follows. In Sect. 2, we present the method to collect the data using the simulation of a network model of Internet of Things placed on the map of the sewer system. Section 3 presents the construction of real-time control model, which will be used as predication model. From this predication, we build an associated explainer using the XAI method. In Sect. 4, experimental results are presented to show how we use this real-time prediction model combined with its explainer. Related works are presented in Sect. 5. Section 6 presents conclusions and perspectives.

2 Collecting Data Using the Internet of Things

To build a sewer model, we use the IoT technology to track process factors like water level and flow rate. Furthermore, the IoT not only connects items, but also generates massive amounts of data from those things. Sensors, wireless communication protocols, actuators, and web interfaces are among the technologies that enable things to interact and collaborate with one another to achieve common goals. A sensing layer, a network layer, and an application layer make up the IoT architecture.

Users can access all of the system's features through the application layer, which is located at the top of the architecture. The sensing layer is at the bottom of the IoT architecture, and it uses sensors to track the state of devices. The network layer sits between the sensing and application layers, transmitting data from sensors via wireless communication protocols and linking the physical and digital worlds.

To construct a city wide IoT, the sensor nodes can be placed across the city and the data can be kept in a centralized storage facility. Sensor nodes collect data on rainfall amount, and other variables of water and wastewater. Using the tool ArcMap of ArcGIS [9], a spatial database has been created from the sewer map of the city of M'Sila to manage the transferred data, making it easier to search, amend, and share real-time information in a user-friendly manner.

The sewer system is a completely detailed hydraulic model. The sensor network technique is based on using different sensors that send the data in real-time to this database where it is stored. The different sensors in the system could be water-level sensors in waste-water pipes, groundwater sensors, rain-level sensors, and water-level sensors in drainage systems.

The data from the water-level sensors in waste-water pipes could be used to calculate the flow rate, the data from the groundwater sensors could be used to calculate the movement of groundwater, the data collected from rain-level sensors could help track any correlation with rainfall and data collected from water-level sensors in drainage systems which help predict any potential future flooding.

As we don't have a sewer system equipped with a network of IoT, we have generated synthetic data using simulation with NetSim [10]. NetSim is a network simulator, which enables us to virtually create a network with devices, links, applications, etc. The simulation will be run using the discrete event simulation and the results can be visualized using the packet animator to view the flow of packets, where the results are analyzed to examine output performance metrics.

In NetSim, IoT is modeled as a Wireless Sensor Network (WSN), which is a group of spatially dispersed sensors that monitor and collect the physical conditions of the environment and transmit the data they collect to a central location via the gateway. WSN in NetSim is part of NetSim's IoT library that connects to the internet via a 6LowPAN Gateway.

We developed an ArcMap map for the sewer system of the city of M'Sila to identify locations for the placement of the different sensors. Thus, an equivalent IoT network scenario is designed in NetSim, consisting of 15 sensor nodes, a 6LoWPAN Gateway, a router, and a server. The sensors are connected to a server.

A C program is written using the NetSim libraries for each sensor to periodically generate data as packets and forward them to the server via its gateway named 6LoWPAN. The C program packet inter-arrival time has been set as the time stamps to index the data sent by the different sensors to be stored in geographical database.

Thus, we create a CSV file for each sensor node, which can be accessed from the results dash board after the simulation. The CSV files will show the readings of the sensors. The first column has the time stamps for the subsequent column having values from the different sensors measuring the groundwater level, the water consumption, the precipitation and the flow levels in the network.

Thus, in addition to the main table in the database containing information about sensors as their identifiers and locations, each sensor is associated with a table in the spatial database to record its measures sent to server. The structure of all the sensors tables is the same. There is a field to capture the time stamp of the received measure and its value.

3 Building Models for Real-Time Control

Models are required for real-time control, which are sets of equations that describe the evolution of state variables in space and time. Models in the domain of sewer systems are data-driven models (derived directly from data). The data collected by the IoT supports in model building and calibration to be used for predicting future system conditions, which provide us enough time to implement control measures.

An IoT-based sewage surveillance model has been built with NetSim as part of this project to simulate the water level and velocity of the sewer system's main pipes, as well as rainfall. The information gathered can be utilized to construct artificial intelligence models. In the real sewer system, the sensing layer will comprise of ultrasonic water level sensors, Doppler velocity sensors, and rain gauges. Wireless telemetry will be used to send the data collected by the sensors and rain gauges to a remote server.

The goal is to develop an effective and efficient technique to monitor sewage systems to increase their capacity. We intensively simulated the IoT-based model with NetSim, and we were able to acquire information on precipitation, groundwater levels, and sewage water volumetric flow using these sensors model. All of the sensors are connected to the database via a wireless network, which can be viewed on the NetSim's IoT design. Scripts can be used to get both historical and real-time data from the database.

There are 12 sensors (we call them flow sensors) installed within the sewage system model to measure how much in liters per hour the flow of wastewater through the pipes. Each flow sensor is identified by the name 'fsi', where $i = 1, \cdots, 12$ and each flow sensor 'fsi' is associated with a CSV file named 'ffi.csv' where its content is taken from the geographical database. The groundwater level is adjusted to a zero point and was calibrated to this point by the installation of the groundwater sensor within the NetSim model, which is identified by the name 'gws' and it is associated with a CSV file named 'gwf.csv'.

The area's precipitation is calculated using an automatic rain gauge that calculates how many millimeters of rain are gathered every ten minutes, and then we choose the maximum amount for that hour to fix the model parameter of its associated IoT sensor. It is associated with the CSV file 'pf.csv'. The municipality offers us the water consumption every hour in liters. This information is saved in a CSV file named 'wcf.csv'.

When running the simulation, the C programs associated with these model sensors will read their data into their appropriate CSV files. These filled files by the simulation execution will be used to construct the prediction model after their processing. The simulation is executed for different time stamps of 8760 periods representing number of hours over one year.

3.1 Processing the Training Data

We use Python, a high-level all-purpose programming language running on the Jupyter Notebook (a web-based interactive computing platform) to develop explainable prediction model. We import the Python library Pandas for data manipulation: to create and manipulate the sensor data into usable CSV files, to load the dataset as a data frame and arrange the raw data in the format of the desired array.

```
import pandas as pd
from warnings import simplefilter
import os
import sys
# Assign main directory to a variable
dir=os.path.dirname(sys.path[0])
# Ignore all future warnings
simplefilter(action='ignore', category=FutureWarning)
```

We used historical data to train our machine learning model. We had to first index all the values to the same time stamp intervals so that we had a matching index for all the variables when obtaining the data. We rounded all the time stamps to the nearest hour, where the hour is our index and chose the greatest value for each time stamp. After processing the data in this manner, we used append on the Pandas data frame to join all of the files together, yielding a CVS file with all values indexed in full rows.

```
def get_dataset():
    # Array to specify the csv files containing sensors data
    csvFiles = [dir+'/sewer/dataset/wuf.csv',dir+'/sewer/dataset/pf.csv',
     dir+'/sewer/dataset/gwf.csv', dir+'/sewer/dataset/ff1.csv',
     dir+'/sewer/dataset/ff2.csv', dir+'/sewer/dataset/ff3.csv',
     dir+'/sewer/dataset/ff4.csv', dir+'/sewer/dataset/ff5.csv',
     dir+'/sewer/dataset/ff6.csv', dir+'/sewer/dataset/ff7.csv',
     dir+'/sewer/dataset/ff8.csv', dir+'/sewer/dataset/ff9.csv',
     dir+'/sewer/dataset/ff10.csv', dir+'/sewer/dataset/ff11.csv',
     dir+'/sewer/dataset/ff12.csv']
    # Array to store the rounded files for combination
    l = []
    for f in csvFiles:
        # read the csv file,in this case they used the delimiter ','
        r = pd.read_csv(f, delimiter=",")
        # Round each time stamp to the nearest hour
        r['Time Stamp'] = pd.to_datetime(r['Time Stamp']).round('h')
        # Save this to a new csv file and set indexing to false
        r.to_csv(dir+'/sewer/dataset/r.csv', index=False)
        # read the file again but now set the index to column 0 (ST)
        fr = pd.read_csv(dir+'/sewer/dataset/r.csv', index_col=0)
        # pick the highest value for that index
        fr = fr[~fr.index.duplicated(keep='first')]
        # append to l to get stored
        l.append(fr)
    # Turn the array into a frame and save to file
    frame = pd.concat(l, axis = 1)
```

```
    frame = frame[~frame.index.duplicated(keep='first')]
    # Row that has missing data is filled with the past data if it exists
    frame.fillna(method='pad', inplace=True)
    # with the next data if the past doesnÃćâĆňâĎćt exist
    frame.fillna(method='bfill', inplace=True)
    frame.to_csv(dir+'/sewer/dataset/com.csv')
    df_features = pd.read_csv(dir+'/sewer/dataset/com.csv',
            index_col = 'Time Stamp', parse_dates=True)
    df_labels = pd.read_csv(dir+'/sewer/dataset/Labels.csv',
        index_col = 'Time Stamp', parse_dates=True)
    return df_features, df_labels

import plotly.figure_factory as ff
def save_frame(df):
    fig =  ff.create_table(df.round(2),index=True)
    fig.update_layout(autosize=False,width=1000,height=200)
    fig.write_image(dir+'/sewer/dataset/table_plotly.png', scale=2)
```

We begin by creating the dataset with the call "X, y = get_dataset()" to get the training input "X" and the training output "y" and then the definition of the prediction model. Figure 1, which is produced by the call "save_frame(X.iloc[:5, :)" depicts the first five lines of the training data after it has been processed.

The first column represents time stamps, the index for our experiment. The second column shows the water consumption over an hour period. The area's precipitation is shown in the third column, while the fourth column represents the groundwater level. The last twelve columns represent the different flows of wastewater through the pipes, which can measure how much wastewater flows through the pipes in liters per hour in different locations.

	Water Consumption	Precipitation	Ground Water Level	Flow 1	Flow 2	Flow 3	Flow 4	Flow 5
2021-01-01 00:00:00	462.54	0.16	4.2	341.25	304.12	329.13	330.12	272.95
2021-01-01 01:00:00	408.53	0.0	3.46	387.04	317.16	247.02	380.81	282.62
2021-01-01 02:00:00	483.12	0.0	3.9	270.67	363.98	328.71	244.54	367.29
2021-01-01 03:00:00	392.06	0.63	3.88	243.39	314.46	387.5	311.55	382.35
2021-01-01 04:00:00	416.18	0.0	3.88	359.0	233.58	409.62	271.56	392.15

Flow 6	Flow 7	Flow 8	Flow 9	Flow 10	Flow 11	Flow 12
289.12	325.38	287.02	298.69	249.25	288.35	222.81
313.51	264.85	258.93	340.66	281.51	293.53	237.18
359.11	262.75	376.86	409.99	314.99	282.19	267.16
318.92	378.72	279.88	293.57	400.94	293.23	348.14
330.17	253.22	243.49	353.37	356.3	307.68	313.21

Fig. 1. Data frame of proceeded data

3.2 Definition of the Prediction Model

The prediction model is a Keras sequential model composed of two dense layers. A dense layer is the regular deeply connected neural network. It returns the result of "activation(dot(input, kernel) + bias)" as its output. If the activation is none, then the output layer of the network is performing regression, which should be naturally linear.

```
from keras.models import Sequential
from keras.layers import Dense
def define_model(n_inputs, n_outputs):
    model = Sequential()
    model.add(Dense(32, input_dim=n_inputs,
              kernel_initializer='he_uniform', activation='relu'))
    model.add(Dense(n_outputs, kernel_initializer='he_uniform'))
    model.compile(loss='mae', optimizer='adam', metrics=['accuracy'])
    return model
```

The first dense layer has a number of inputs equals "n_inputs = 12 + 3 = 15" inputs and 32 outputs with weights initialized by heUniform() and activation function relu(). The second dense layer has 32 inputs, which are the outputs of the previous dense layer and 12 outputs (n_outputs = 12) and without activation function (linear regression model). The compilation uses the loss function mae() and the optimizer adam().

```
def create_model():
    # Get the number of inputs and outputs from the dataset
    n_inputs, n_outputs = X.shape[1], y.shape[1]
    model = define_model(n_inputs, n_outputs)
    history = model.fit(X, y, verbose=1, batch_size=10, epochs=100,
              validation_split=0.2)
    summarize_diagnostics(history)
    model.evaluate(x = X, y = y)
    return model
```

We create an object of our prediction model with the call "model = create_model()". Figure 2 shows its accuracy, which is more than 75%.

For prediction explanation, we use the package SHAP (SHapley Additive exPlanations), which is a game theoretic approach to explain the output of any machine learning model. It connects model prediction with local explanations using the classic Shapley values from game theory and their related extensions [11].

```
import shap
def create_explainer():
    # print the JS visualization code to the notebook
    shap.initjs()
    explainer = shap.KernelExplainer(model = model.predict,
                   data = X, link = "identity")
    return explainer
explainer = create_explainer()
```

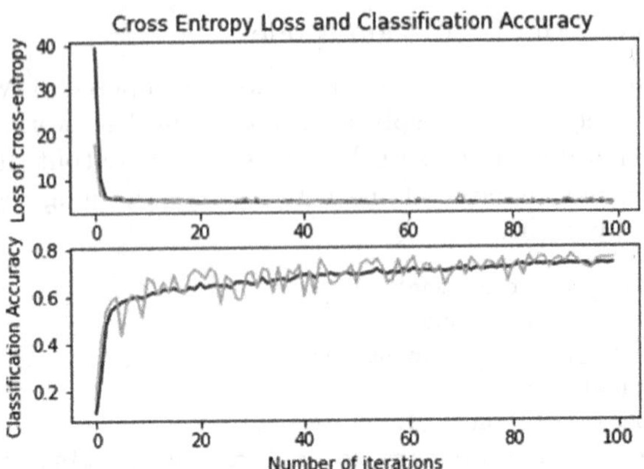

Fig. 2. Cross entropy and classification accuracy

The jupyter-widgets (ipywidgets) or simply widgets are interactive HTML widgets for Jupyter notebooks and the IPython kernel. Notebooks come alive when interactive widgets are used. Users gain control of their data and can visualize changes in the data. Widgets are eventful Python objects that have a representation in the browser, often as a control like a slider, textbox, etc. They can be used to build interactive GUIs for our notebooks. We can also use widgets to synchronize stateful and stateless information between Python and JavaScript.

```
# This import is for feature selection
import ipywidgets as widgets
def create_labels():
    # Create the list of all labels for the drop down list
    list_of_labels = y.columns.to_list()
    # Make a list of tuples such that it returns the label's index
    tuple_of_labels = list(zip(list_of_labels,
                                range(len(list_of_labels))))
    # Create a widget for the labels and then display the widget
    current_label = widgets.Dropdown(options=tuple_of_labels,
           value=0, description='Select Label:', disabled=False)
    return list_of_labels, current_label
list_of_labels, current_label = create_labels()
```

The call to the function create_labels() will create a list of labels (the model outputs) and a drop down to select the current label to be used for prediction explication to take decisions. To explain the model prediction on a data frame (df) representing the observation values of the flow level sensors, we call the function below and we specify the name of the current label selected by the drop down selection. The explanation can be saved as a "png" file. This GUI contains a button to generate explanation for the model predication, which is developed with the package SHAP.

```
def explain_model_prediction(df):
   shap_value_single=explainer.shap_values(X = df, nsamples = 100)
   return shap.force_plot(
      base_value = explainer.expected_value[current_label.value],
      shap_values = shap_value_single[current_label.value],features=df
   ), current_label.value

def save_plot(df):
    shap_value_single = explainer.shap_values(X = df, nsamples = 100)
    shap.force_plot(
      base_value = explainer.expected_value[current_label.value],
      shap_values = shap_value_single[current_label.value],
      features = df, matplotlib = True, show = False
    )
    pyplot.savefig(dir+'/sewer/dataset/'+
                        str(list_of_labels[current_label.value])+'.png')
    pyplot.close()
```

4 Experimental Results

To use this prediction model, which was built using data from a NetSim simulation of an IoT-based model of the sewage system in the city of M'Sila, we first generate a data frame from real-time information sent by sensors to predict the labels values.

The following is the code to define a data frame "df" containing the data sent by the different sensors, which is indexed by the information of the time stamp and it contains information sent by the different sensors for the water consumption, precipitation, ground water level and the twelve flow levels. Figure 3 shows more clearly the features values of this data frame.

```
df = pd.DataFrame({
  'Time Stamp' : ['2021-01-01 00:00:00'], 'Water Consumption' : [462.54],
  'Precipitation' : [0.16], 'Ground Water Level' : [4.20],
  'Flow 1' : [341.25], 'Flow 2' : [304.12], 'Flow 3' : [329.13],
  'Flow 4' : [330.12], 'Flow 5' : [272.95], 'Flow 6'  : [289.12],
  'Flow 7' : [325.38], 'Flow 8' : [287.02], 'Flow 9' : [298.69],
  'Flow 10' : [249.25], 'Flow 11' : [288.35], 'Flow 12' : [222.81]})
df = df.set_index('Time Stamp')
```

To predict the label (output) values, the data frame "df" is passed to the prediction function of the model. The code below is used to realize the prediction and displaying the prediction values of the labels. The results are shown in Fig. 4.

```
pr = model.predict(df)
# Display the prediction values of the labels
for i in range(len(list_of_labels)):
    print('Label '+str(i+1)+' output: ', pr[0,i], '%')
```

	Water Consumption	Precipitation	Ground Water Level	Flow 1	Flow 2	Flow 3	Flow 4
2021-01-01 00:00:00	462.54	0.16	4.2	341.25	304.12	329.13	330.12

Flow 5	Flow 6	Flow 7	Flow 8	Flow 9	Flow 10	Flow 11	Flow 12
272.95	289.12	325.38	287.02	298.69	249.25	288.35	222.81

Fig. 3. Data frame sent by the sewer sensors

```
Label 1 output:  44.55138 %
Label 2 output:  53.40689 %
Label 3 output:  52.180103 %
Label 4 output:  58.580154 %
Label 5 output:  50.863182 %
Label 6 output:  60.688377 %
Label 7 output:  51.26418 %
Label 8 output:  57.477436 %
Label 9 output:  51.55485 %
Label 10 output:  43.892826 %
Label 11 output:  53.034832 %
Label 12 output:  60.96122 %
```

Fig. 4. Prediction of outputs

Then, we select a label using the drop down to explain its prediction (the execution of the code below will display the dropdown list for selection of a label). In this case we have chosen the label number 8 to explain its prediction (Fig. 5).

```
# Display the dropdown list for selection of a label
current_label
```

Fig. 5. Selection of label number 8

After checking the labels values and if we need an explanation about one label value how it is affected by the model inputs, we can use the code below to generate an explanation diagram by running the model explainer on the data frame "df" that was used for predicting the labels values.

```
explain_result, current_label_value = explain_model_prediction(df)
# Display the name of the current label
print(f'Current label Shown: {list_of_labels[current_label_value]}')
# Display the diagram (schema), which explains the prediction
explain_result
```

The objective is to diagnose the sewer system if there is an abnormal behavior following this approach using the developed explainable prediction model. If we notice that there is abnormal operation in a pipe in the sewer system, for example, the observed level of flow in a pipe measured by a sensor is much more different from the predicted flow level, in this case we select the appropriate label and we generate the explanation diagram.

For example, the data frame "df" represents information observed on all the sensors of the sewage network at a specific time and after analysis of the predicted values of the model labels using the model prediction of this data frame, it will be possible that a model label shows an abnormal behavior as the predicted value is much different from the expected value. In this case, we use the explanation model to diagnose our sewage system.

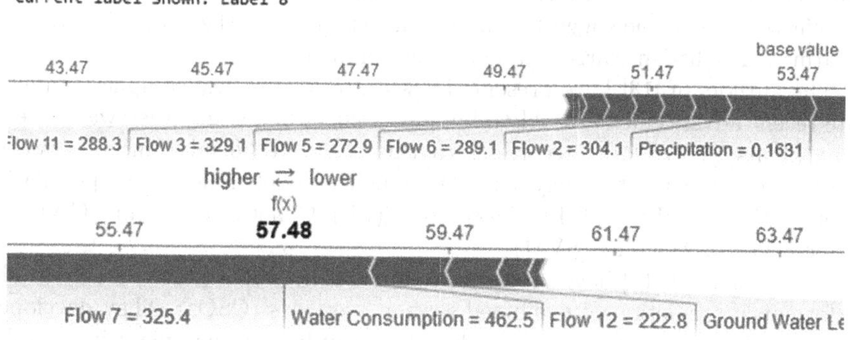

Fig. 6. Prediction explanation

Figure 6 contains the diagram generated by the given code. This diagram shows the model prediction of label number 8 regarding the feature values in Fig. 3, where the predicted value is 57.477436 and is verified to be different from expected.

The explanation shows how the feedback provided by the sewer sensors affected the value of Label 8, from the highest effect on the left to the lowest effect on the right. This result of explanation helps us to diagnose our sewage network in the following way.

We start by checking the location associated with the leftmost feature in the explanation diagram, in this case it is the flow level sensor located in position number 11 (the feature value its sensor is observing is 288.3). If the associated pipe is checked to be normal, we move on to the next pipe until we have a diagnosis of the problem. If the pipe is checked to be defective, we repair it and then we redo the work until we have a sewage system that works without problems.

To annotate the prediction on another label's output, simply select that label and run the above code again to get an explanation of the prediction on the new selection. This way we can use this application to control the sewage system.

5 Related Works

To our knowledge, no work in the literature uses eXplainable Artificial Intelligence to diagnose sewer networks and prevent them from overflowing, however there are works using the technique of artificial intelligence to predict their overflow.

Zhang et al. [12] have developed models for forecasting wastewater input, which are based on a multilayer perceptron neural network (MLPNN) and an autoregressive integrated moving average (ARIMA) time series analysis. To show the effectiveness of the suggested models, a case study of the Barrie Wastewater Treatment Facility in Barrie, Canada, was conducted.

The authors of [13] have presented a work to investigate, compile, and evaluate recent advancements in AI techniques used for modeling wastewater treatment plants (WWTPs). According to this work, Artificial Neural Networks (ANN) were the most widely used standalone model, followed in popularity order by Decision Trees (DT), Fuzzy Logic (FL), Genetic Algorithm (GA), and Support Vector Machine (SVM).

The authors of [14] have used artificial neural networks (ANN) for hydraulic performance prediction of combined sewage overflows (CSOs). They developed their model using rainfall intensity data that can be obtained via rainfall radar equipment. Real data from a CSO for a catchment in the North of England, UK, is used to present the results. They claimed that for forecasts more than an hour in advance for unknown data, an ANN model trained with the pseudo-inverse rule was demonstrated to be capable of forecasting CSO depth with less than 5% inaccuracy, and the management of combined sewer systems in the future will benefit from such predictive methods.

In [15], a comparison is presented on models for wastewater treatment systems (WWTs) developed on available data. Artificial neural network (ANN), fuzzy logic (FL), random forest (RF), and long short-term memory (LSTM) algorithms were utilized applied models in WWTs. The effluent parameters biological oxygen demand (BOD), chemical oxygen demand (COD), nutritional parameters, solids, and metallic compounds are used to test these models through predictive control. The accuracy analysis was primarily conducted using the following model performance indicators: root mean square error (RMSE), mean square error (MSE), and determination coefficient (DC).

In [16], a reverse osmosis desalination process' performance was predicted using an artificial neural network (ANN), which was applied to provide water temperature modeling. Water is produced through desalination for domestic consumption, the food industry, water supply, and other uses. The model of an artificial neural network (ANN) was created to optimize the results of water treatment and desalination experiments.

6 Conclusions and Perspectives

In this paper, a Python program running on the notebook of jupyter-lab is developed to create data-driven prediction model. This model is trained with data collected using the Internet of Things. After data processing and model training, the result model will be used to predict outputs of the real-time inputs. A corresponding explainer is developed with Shap to explain the prediction, which will help us to diagnose the behavior of our sewer system.

Our perspective is to realise this virtual sewer system in the region of M'Sila, which will help us to construct a prediction model on real data, then we integrate this work with the simulator based on ArcGIS system to be used in the municipality of M'Sila for monitoring its sewage system.

References

1. Ferriman, A.: BMJ readers choose the sanitary revolution as greatest medical advance since 1840. In: BMJ 2007, pp. 334–111 (2007)
2. Mollerup, A.L., Mikkelsen, P.S., Sin, G.: A methodological approach to the design of optimising control strategies for sewer systems. Environ. Model. Softw. **83**, 103–115 (2016)
3. Lund, N., Morten, B., Henrik, M., Ole, M., Peter, M.: CSO Reduction by integrated model predictive control of stormwater inflows: a simulated proof of concept using linear surrogate models. Water Resources Res. vol. 56, (2020). https://doi.org/10.1029/2019WR026272
4. Sola, J. K., Bjerkholt, J.T., Lindholm, O.G., Ratnaweera, H.: Infiltration and Inflow (I/I) to wastewater systems in Norway, Sweden, Denmark, and Finland. In: Water , vol. 10, p. 1696 (2018). https://doi.org/10.3390/w10111696
5. Li, S., Xu, L.D., Zhao, S.: The internet of things: a survey. Inf. Syst. Front. **17**(2), 243–259 (2015)
6. Russell, S., Norvig, P.: Artificial Intelligence: A Modern Approach, 4th edn. Pearson, London (2020)
7. Razavian, N., Knoll, F., Geras, K.J.: Artificial intelligence explained for nonexperts. In: Seminars in Musculoskeletal Radiology **24**(1), pp. 003–011, Thieme Medical Publishers, (2020)

8. Collier, Z. K., Zhang, H., Liu, L.: Explained: artificial intelligence for propensity score estimation in multilevel educational settings. Pract. Assess. Res. Eval. **27**(1) (2022)
9. ESRI: ArcGIS Desktop: Release 10. Redlands, CA: Environmental Systems Research Institute (2011)
10. Akanda, W., Marcin, B., Katarzyna, M.: NetSim - The framework for complex network generator. Procedia Comput. Sci. **126**, 547–556 (2018)
11. Lundberg, S. M., Lee, S.-I.: A unified approach to interpreting model predictions. In: Bengio, I.G., Wallach, H., Fergus, R., Vishwanathan, S., Garnett, R., Advances in Neural Information Processing Systems, vol. 30 (pp. 4765–4774). Curran Associates Inc, (2017)
12. Zhang, Q., Li, Z., Snowling, S., et al.: Predictive models for wastewater flow forecasting based on time series analysis and artificial neural network. Water Sci. Technol. **80**(2), 243–253 (2019)
13. Bahramian, M., Dereli, R.K., Zhao, W., Giberti, M., Casey, E.: Data to intelligence: the role of data-driven models in wastewater treatment. Expert Syst. Appl. vol. 217, (2023)
14. Mounce, S.R., Shepherd, W., Sailor, G., Shucksmith, J., Saul, A.J.: Predicting combined sewer overflows chamber depth using artificial neural networks with rainfall radar data. Water Sci. Technol. **69**(6), 1326–1333 (2014)
15. Singh, N.K., et al.: Artificial intelligence and machine learning-based monitoring and design of biological wastewater treatment systems, Bioresource Technology, vol. 369, (2023)
16. Ahmed, I.: Taloba an artificial neural network mechanism for optimizing the water treatment process and desalination process. Alexandria Eng. J. **61**(12), 9287–9295 (2022)

Road Accident Occurrence Prediction: A Machine Learning Based Approach

Aymene Krioudj(✉), Zakaria Abdelmoumen Kermouche, and Amina Selma Haichour

Higher National School of Computer Science (ESI ex INI), Algiers, Algeria
{ha_krioudj,hz_kermouche,a_haichour}@esi.dz

Abstract. Road accidents are highly regarded as one of the most critical issues the world has to deal with, causing many deaths, injuries and economic losses every year. Consequently, road safety is a major concern worldwide, and everyone has been trying to improve it for years. Many road accidents occur due to several factors that are human, environmental or material. Understanding these factors can help to combat the occurrence of this scourge by building predictive models to forecast future road accidents. The work exposed in this paper presents a modeling approach that builds an efficient Machine Learning model to predict the occurrence of road accidents. The built model predicts where and when road accidents will occur and is based on the XGBoost method achieving an accuracy up to 94.31%. It also has the ability to be integrated into road safety systems to predict future accidents using as input historical data of accidents that have already occurred in any area of interest.

Keywords: XGBoost · Machine Learning · Road Accident Prediction · Road Safety

1 Introduction

Road accidents are one of the most important issues worldwide. The World Health Organization (WHO) has published in June 2022 that about 1.3 million people die each year from road accidents and between 20 and 50 million more people suffer non-fatal injuries. Furthermore, this type of accidents cause considerable economic losses to individuals, their families, and to nations as a whole. The WHO has reported that road accidents cost most countries 3% of their gross domestic product.

To reduce the number of accidents, methods and rules are used to prevent road users from being killed or seriously injured, this is called road safety. In fact, rules such as respecting speed limits, crossing the road on a pedestrian crossing and others can help prevent accidents. These rules are imposed and controlled by the road safety authorities, in order to ensure the protection of human life.

H. Drias et al. (Eds.): AID 2022, CCIS 1852, pp. 221–232, 2023.
https://doi.org/10.1007/978-981-99-4484-2_17

However, road accidents still occur and cause a large number of deaths, injuries and also large-scale economic losses. This is why efforts are being deployed by the scientific community to help road safety authorities decrease the number of road accidents and their negative consequences. Indeed, scientists focus on analyzing accident data and try to predict future ones using artificial intelligence methods. The concerned authorities can thus carry out targeted prevention actions. For instance, allocating police forces in advance of road accidents.

The work exposed in this paper fits into this context and presents a modeling approach allowing the construction of an efficient Machine Learning model for road accident occurrence prediction. This model can predict where and when accidents may occur. It also has the ability to be integrated into road safety systems to predict future accidents using as input historical data of accidents that have already occurred in any area of interest.

The rest of the paper is organized as follows: Sect. 2 introduces some previous works that are related with the present one. Section 3 describes the proposed modeling approach followed to obtain the efficient road accident predictive model. Section 4 presents and discusses the experimental results. Section 5 gives conclusions and some future works.

2 Related Work

Road accident prediction is a growing research topic. This field is highly relevant because of its impact on the reduction of the number and severity of accidents. In order to predict and prevent the occurrence of road accidents, an in-depth analysis of the huge flow of data concerning them is necessary. Such analysis can highlight key factors that are closely related to road accidents, thus enabling their anticipation. The analysis of road accident data has benefited from Machine Learning techniques. These techniques allow the selection of appropriate variables for prediction and the generation of accurate predictive models [3,6,8]. Kumar and Toshniwal [3] found that the accident severity, the road type, the lighting present on the latter and the type of area around it are the major variables in the occurrence of accidents. Taamneh et al. [6] concluded that the variables that have the most effect on the number of deaths by accident are age, sex, nationality, year of the accident and type of accident. Therefore, it is apparent that the analysis of the causal factors of accident occurrence contributes to more models and knowledge that can be used in the prevention of accidents.

Some of these predictive models are limited to indicating where accidents will occur and omit specifying when they may occur [8]. This information can be very important, as the possibility of knowing the time of occurrence of road accidents, allows to act and prevent their occurrence in time. Other models are built from limited datasets with a restricted number of data rows and features chosen as model inputs. This leads to models with low accuracy results. As an example, Sun et al. [5] achieved an accuracy of 29.4% with their model based on RNN using only 90 rows of recorded crash data. Moreover, most of the existing models have a limited scope. In fact, many models give unsatisfactory results when applied to a location other than the one on which they were trained. Take the example of Theofilatos et al. [7], their model considers only traffic data as predictor variables and has a limited scope (the built model only performs on the Athens city highway).

AlMamlook et al. [1] based on the main factors causing road accidents (human, environmental, and material factors) to predict their severity (minor or fatal accidents). For this purpose, they applied several Machine Learning techniques and compared their performance results. The authors built the classification rules for the best performing prediction models : AdaBoost, Random Forest (RF), Naïve Bayes (NB) and Logistic Regression (LR). They showed that Machine Learning algorithms can predict road accidents with an accuracy up to 75.50%. According to the authors, the best model for predicting road accidents is the Random Forest model. Indeed, the latter has demonstrated its resistance to noisy and changing data by presenting the best recall. Yassin and Pooja [9], also worked on predicting road accident severity and demonstrated that hybridization between several Machine Learning methods achieves fine results in terms of precision and accuracy. Specifically, they used a data clustering method (K-means clustering) and a classification method (Random Forest, Logistic Regression, etc.). As a matter of fact, the use of clustering minimizes the complexity of the input dataset of the prediction model, improving its efficiency. According to this study, the most promising hybridization remains that of K-means clustering and Random Forest. It gives the best performances in terms of precision, recall, F1-score and accuracy. For the same experimentation, the precision, recall and F1-score reached 100% and the accuracy was 99.86%. This proves the strength of this hybrid method, giving it a significant advantage in predicting road accident severity and the factors that lead to these disasters.

3 Methodology

In this paper, an efficient Machine Learning model is built for predicting where and when road accidents will occur and Fig. 1 illustrates the proposed modeling approach followed for this purpose. In the proposed modeling approach, a supervised classification, more precisely, a "binary classification" is opted for. Besides, in this approach, the selected dataset undergoes pre-processing in order to select characteristics and target variables suitable for road accident occurrence prediction. Once the pre-processing is completed, the dataset is divided into three sets for training, validation and test. The first set is used to build different prediction models and the second one is dedicated for validating them. The last set is used to compare these built models in order to choose the best performing model for road accident occurrence prediction. More details about the data source, data manipulation and pre-processing, data splitting, building the classification models, and their evaluation, are exposed in this section.

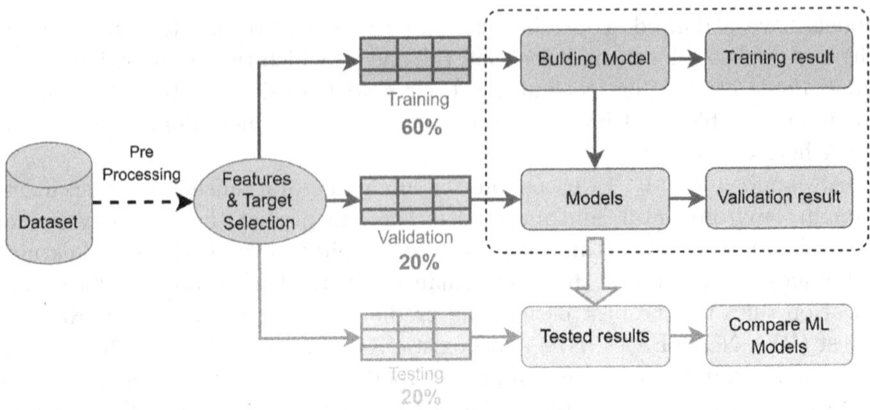

Fig. 1. Proposed modeling approach for road accident occurrence prediction.

3.1 Data Source

The selected dataset comes from the UK transport department which collected traffic data from 2004 to 2017, recording over 2 million road accidents. It includes information about dates, times and geographical locations of accident occurrences. It also contains information about vehicles, drivers, weather conditions, etc. The dataset covers a very wide range of event dates that most of the coded data variables have been transformed into text strings, allowing for a more efficient analysis. In addition, the dataset provides a large number of variables related to accidents and vehicles involved in those accidents, that comes in two separate "csv" files.

To set up the dataset for the proposed modeling approach, the two files are linked by the unique traffic accident identifier (Accident_Index column) into one "csv" file. Besides, the most relevant and common variables across countries are chosen. Indeed, the chosen variables may be available for any study area, not just the UK. These variables are: *Accident Index, Date, Time, Year, Longitude, Latitude, City, Road Type, Area Type, Driver Age, Driver Gender, Vehicle Age, Vehicle Type* (as shown in the following figure).

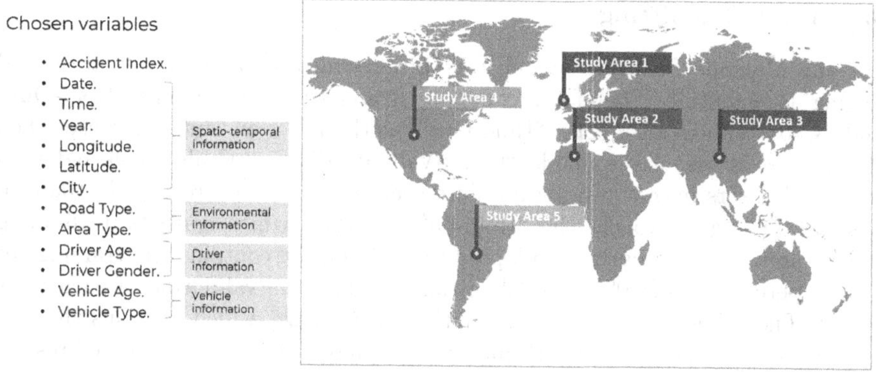

Fig. 2. Widely available variables involved in road accidents (Easily obtainable for any area of Interest).

3.2 Data Pre-Processing

In the proposed modeling approach, the pre-processing step prepares the target dataset for use, through a series of consciously chosen tasks. These include filling the NaN values with the corresponding Mode or Average values depending on the situation, checking for the presence of null objects, renaming certain columns for a better handling, and converting string values into numerical values.

Regarding the output, and as the prediction of the occurrence of accidents is considered in the proposed modeling approach, the column "Accident" is added to the dataset. It is a binary variable, with the value "0" to indicate the case of non-accident, and the value "1" for the presence of accident.

By adopting a binary classification, and having a dataset with only samples of accidents that have already occurred, considered as positive samples, the classification cannot be correctly done. The absence of samples representing non-accidents creates an imbalance between the two classes, i.e. the accident class and the non-accident class. In order to solve this class imbalance, the "Negative Sampling" method [10] is adopted. This method consists of generating other observations from the positive ones by changing some characteristics. Actually, in the proposed modeling approach, the observations whose schedules did not experience the occurrence of accidents at a given location, are considered as a non-accident, by changing other features by random values in the range of values in each column. In fact, accidents do not occur throughout the day. This led to the choice of generating for each accident sample three negative (non-accident) observations, by assigning random values to the columns of accident time of occurrence, driver age, driver gender, vehicle age, and vehicle type. Thus, a balance between the two classes mentioned above, is being achieved.

3.3 Dataset Splitting

For any Machine Learning model, a step allowing its training, validation and testing is essential. Therefore, common strategies exist namely "Hold-Out" and "Cross-Validation". The "Hold-Out" method is well suited for use when the dataset is very large, while "Cross-Validation" is generally preferred with smaller datasets in order to obtain more accurate validation results. In the proposed modeling approach, the "Hold-Out" method which consists in dividing the dataset into two parts, is adopted. The first part contains the training set with a percentage of 60% and 20% is allocated to the validation of each built model. The other 20% is reserved for the second part, which contains the test set. Hence, once each model is trained and validated, it can give unbiased results on an unknown set. This division has the advantage of building robust and more accurate prediction models, thus avoiding model overfitting.

3.4 Model Building

Machine Learning methods based on Decision Trees have shown their performance in the field of road accident prediction. Furthermore, the hybridization of clustering and classification methods based on Decision Trees in the same area, has proven its effectiveness by leading to promising results. It can be achieved by preparing the data in clusters and then applying a classification method to each cluster independently.

However, Decision Trees can suffer from overfitting, where the model becomes too complex and captures noise in the training data, leading to poor generalization performance on new data. To overcome this issue, two main concepts are used in Decision Tree algorithms: bagging and boosting [4]. Bagging involves creating multiple subsets of the training data by sampling with replacement and training a decision tree on each subset. The final prediction is then made by combining the predictions of all the trees, either by taking a majority vote for classification or an average for regression. The most widely used for this technique is the Random Forest [2]. Boosting, on the other hand, involves creating an ensemble of decision trees sequentially, where each subsequent tree is trained to correct the errors of the previous tree. Among the boosting techniques, there are: XGBoost and AdaBoost. XGBoost is preferred over AdaBoost because of the sensitivity of the latter to noisy data, which can lead to overlearning of the model [2]. Moreover, XGBoost has proven to be more effective on a wide range of datasets and can efficiently handle large-scale problems [2].

Therefore, the selected Machine Learning methods in the proposed modeling approach for road accident occurrence prediction, are mentioned below. Using these methods, four prediction models are performed as follows: *Random Forest, XGBoost, k-means + Random Forest, k-means + XGBoost.*

- **Random Forest (RF):**
  Random Forest is a supervised Machine Learning algorithm widely used for

classification and regression problems. It constructs Decision Trees on different samples and takes their majority vote for classification and the mean in the case of regression.

- **Extreme Gradient Boosting (XGBoost):**
  XGBoost is an implementation of Gradient Boosted Decision Trees. The idea behind XGBoost is that each predictor corrects the residual error of its predecessor. It is based on the intuition of combining the next model, which must be the best possible, with the previous models, in order to minimize the global prediction error.
- **k-means Clustering:**
  k-means is an unsupervised learning algorithm that is used to solve clustering problems in Machine Learning or Data Science. The algorithm takes the unlabeled dataset as input, divides the dataset into a number of "k" clusters, and repeats the process until it does not find the best clusters. The value of "k" must be predetermined in this algorithm. The simplicity and efficiency of k-means make it suitable for analyzing large datasets with many features.

3.5 Model Evaluation

Four measures are used to compare the performances of the four Machine Learning models for road accident occurrence prediction, namely : accuracy, precision, recall, and F1-Score. A confusion matrix must be used to calculate these metrics which involves a comparison between the original and predicted values of the target variable.

$$Accuracy = \frac{TN + TP}{TN + FP + TP + FN} \tag{1}$$

$$Precision = \frac{TP}{TP + FP} \tag{2}$$

$$Recall = \frac{TP}{TP + FN} \tag{3}$$

$$F1Score = 2 \times \frac{Precision \times Recall}{Precision + Recall} \tag{4}$$

where:

- TP (True Positive) indicates correctly the presence of a condition or a characteristic.
- TN (True Negative) indicates correctly the absence of a condition or a characteristic.
- FP (False Positive) indicates falsely that a particular condition or attribute is present.
- FN (False Negative) indicates falsely that a particular condition or attribute is absent.

4 Results and Discussion

The obtained results when training and validating the four performed models for road accident occurrence prediction, are very satisfying in terms of the metrics previously proposed. As already mentioned, an untrained part (20% of the dataset) is left to test the four prediction models. These tests confirm the training results, with promising ones as shown in Table 1. Meanwhile, Table 2 displays the testing computation time for each of the 4 models.

Table 1. Performance Measurements of the deployed models for road accident occurrence prediction.

Classifier	Accuarcy	Precision	Recall	F1-Score
Random Forest	94.42%	93.95%	90.92%	92.30%
XGBoost	94.13%	93.56%	90.52%	91.91%
K-*means*+Random Forest	93.80%	93.69%	89.49%	91.33%
K-*means*+XGBoost	93.98%	93.38%	90.27%	91.60%

From Table 1, a convergence between the values of the different metrics is noticed for the four deployed models, with a slight increase for the Random Forest and the XGBoost models. As it can be seen from Table 2, the results in terms of computation time differ from one model to another. Moreover, the XGBoost model takes much less time than the Random Forest model. The XGBoost model allows more performance in terms of metrics and computation time. Thus, XGBoost can be considered as the best performing model for road accident occurrence prediction.

Table 2. Computation Time of the deployed models for road accident occurrence prediction.

Deployed Model	Computation Time
Random Forest	67 s
XGBoost	6 s
K-*means*+Random Forest	78 s
K-*means*+XGBoost	40 s

The built XGBoost model allows to identify the variables most involved in the occurrence of accidents. These variables are shown in the bar chart exposed in Fig. 3. This new knowledge extracted through the built XGBoost model can serve the road safety field.

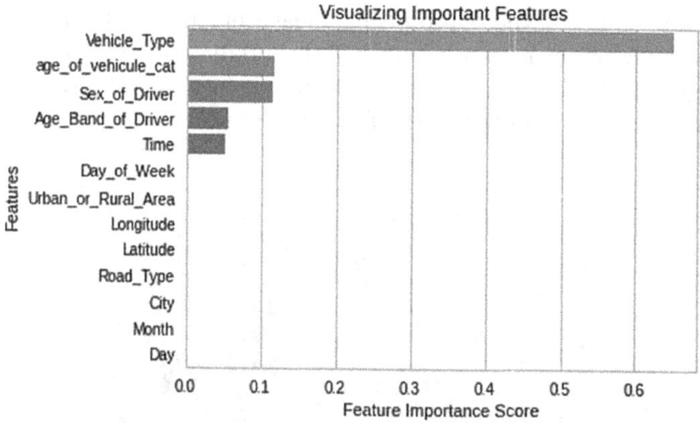

Fig. 3. The variables most involved in road accidents reported by the XGBoost model.

The proposed modeling approach has allowed the building of an efficient model, the XGBoost model, for road accident occurrence prediction. Moreover, the prediction can easily cover a wide range of road segments corresponding to the accident hotspots distributed over the territory in question. This is due to the use of historical data of accidents that have already occurred on the whole territory. In fact, after choosing variables common to any study area, the built XGBoost model can be integrated to road safety systems in order to predict future accidents by using as input the historical data of accidents that have already occurred in the area of interest. For instance, this model is used in a proposed decision support system for road safety in Algeria. The system allows the analysis and prediction of future accidents by identifying the hotspots of upcoming accidents in a region of interest over a given period of time. Regarding the predictive aspect of the said system, the results obtained have been very promising despite the fact that the input data concerns the Algerian territory and not the United Kingdom for which the model is trained (this is due to the use of variables common to any study area, as mentioned before). Table 3 reveals the performance of XGBoost in the Algeria area.

Table 3. Performance Measurements of the XGBoost model in the Algerian territory.

Measurements	XGBoost performances
Accuracy	95.99%
Precision	94.73%
Recall	94.60%
F1-score	94.86%

In order to confirm these promising measurement results in the Algerian territory, a comparison is made between the predicted accidents and the real accidents recorded during the same period in the last week of March 2022. The comparison result is presented in the following figure.

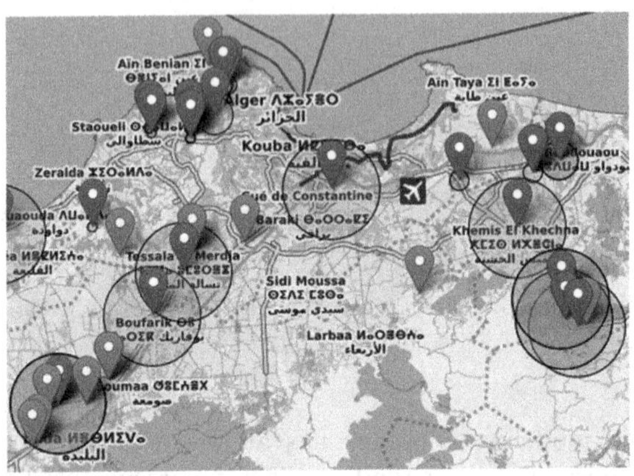

Fig. 4. Comparison of real and predicted accidents in Algeria.

As shown in the Fig. 4, the built XGBoost model is successful in identifying the correct area of future accidents. The predicted accident spots (shown in red) are very close to the real accident spots (shown in green) produced for the said period.

5 Conclusion

A modeling approach to build an efficient Machine Learning model to predict where and when road accidents will occur, is presented using the UK traffic data from 2004 to 2017. Preprocessing tasks were performed on these data and variables that are common in each study area were chosen to have a prediction model that can be used everywhere. Various Machine Learning methods have been used to establish the best performing model for road accident occurrence prediction. Results show that Machine Learning algorithms based on Decision Trees as well as when they are combined with k-means clustering methods can predict accidents with high accuracy by over 90%. The XGBoost model attains the best performance metrics by obtaining an accuracy of 94.31%, as well as the shortest computation time, making it the most efficient and recommended model for road accident occurrence prediction.

The achieved XGBoost model can be implemented in road safety decision support systems worldwide simply by generating and randomizing the input spatial variable, vehicle and driver characteristics from recent historical data of an area of interest. Indeed, this has been the case for the Algerian territory, for which the model performed well.

However, future work will seek to collect related information and investigate other traffic accident factors that were not considered due to the lack of suitable data available in all study areas worldwide. In fact, other variables can be considered in order to get more precise prediction results close to reality, such as weather conditions, road conditions, turning intensity, road gradient, traffic volume, presence of road works, traffic direction, etc. Also, more refined and accurate prediction results can be achieved by using the Reinforcement Learning approach. Indeed, the prediction can be based on the comparison between the accidents actually produced, and those predicted during the same period.

Acknowledgments. We would like to express our heartfelt gratitude to A. KRIOUDJ, Z. A. KERMOUCHE, and A. S. HAICHOUR for their invaluable contributions to this research project.

We would also like to express our appreciation for the opportunity to conduct this research and share our findings with the scientific community. We hope that our work will contribute to ongoing efforts to improve road safety, to prevent accidents and thus to save human lives.

References

1. AlMamlook, R.E., Kwayu, K.M., Alkasisbeh, M.R., Frefer, A.A.: Comparison of machine learning algorithms for predicting traffic accident severity. In: IEEE Jordan International Joint Conference on Electrical Engineering and Information Technology (JEEIT), vol. 2019, pp. 272–276 (2019)
2. Jafarzadeh, H., Mahdianpari, M., Gill, E., Mohammadimanesh, F., Homayouni, S.: Bagging and boosting ensemble classifiers for classification of multispectral, hyperspectral and PolSAR data: a comparative evaluation. Remote Sens. **13**(21), 4405 (2021)
3. Kumar, S., Toshniwal, D.: Analysis of hourly road accident counts using hierarchical clustering and cophenetic correlation coefficient (CPCC). J. Big Data **3**(1), 1–11 (2016). https://doi.org/10.1186/s40537-016-0046-3
4. Plaia, A., Buscemi, S., Fürnkranz, J., et al.: Comparing boosting and bagging for decision trees of rankings. J. Classif. **39**, 78–99 (2022)
5. Sun, J., Sun, J., Chen, P.: Use of support vector machine models for realtime prediction of crash risk on urban expressways. Transp. Res. Record **2432**(1), 91–98 (2014)
6. Taamneh, M., Alkheder, S., Taamneh, S.: Data-mining techniques for traffic accident modeling and prediction in the United Arab Emirates. J. Transp. Safety Secur. **9**(2), 146–166 (2017)
7. Theofilatos, A., Yannis, G., Kopelias, P., Papadimitriou, F.: Predicting road accidents: a rare-events modeling approach [Transport Research Arena TRA2016]. Transp. Res. Procedia **14**, 3399–3405 (2016)
8. Wang, C., Quddus, M.A., Ison, S.G.: Predicting accident frequency at their severity levels and its application in site ranking using a two-stage mixed multivariate model. Accid. Anal. Prev. **43**(6), 1979–1990 (2011)

9. Yassin, S.S., Pooja.: Road accident prediction and model interpretation using a hybrid K-means and random forest algorithm approach. SN Appl. Sci. **2**(9), 1576 (2020)
10. Yuan, Z., Zhou, X., Yang, T., Tamerius, J., Mantilla, R.: Predicting traffic accidents through heterogeneous urban data: a case study (2017)

Extreme Learning Machines Based on Convolutional Neural Network and Convolutional Autoencoder for Image Classification: Comparative Study

Selma Kali Ali(✉) and Dalila Boughaci

Faculty of Computer Science, LRIA-USTHB, Algiers, Algeria
{skaliali,dboughaci}@usthb.dz, kali.ali.selma@gmail.com,
dalila_info@yahoo.fr

Abstract. Feature extraction is a critical process for any machine learning model. It provides a representation that contains the most relevant data. Convolutional Neural Network (CNN) and Convolutional Autoencoder (CAE) models have recently successfully been applied as feature extraction techniques. In this work, we combine them with the Extreme Learning Machine (ELM) classifier to study the performance of CNN-ELM and CAE-ELM models. The image classification task is used to evaluate the studied methods. The tests are performed on three benchmark datasets: MNIST, CIFAR10, and CIFAR-100. According to the experimental results, although the CNN-ELM outperforms the CAE-ELM in terms of accuracy, it still suffers from the overfitting problem.

Keywords: Extreme Learning Machine · Convolutional Neural Network · Convolutional Autoencoder · Feature Extraction · Image Classification

1 Introduction

The Extreme Learning Machine [6] (ELM) is a relatively simple machine learning method. Its advantages over other conventional methods, such as backpropagation (BP) are its ease of implementation and speed of training. ELM has been successfully applied to supervised [5,24] and unsupervised [7,12] learning problems in various application areas such as medicine [4,16], chemistry [8], transportation [21], economics [14], and robotics [23].

The fundamental ELM method can handle a wide range of problems, but it sometimes suffers from low accuracy and overfitting. Several solutions have been proposed to address these issues. These contributions include optimizing the initial weights and biases [15,23,25] and preprocessing the input data by extracting a high-level feature representation [2,18,20].

In classification problems, the features chosen as inputs are crucial. For complex visual tasks, the performance is greatly reduced when the ELM model is fed directly with the original image data. To solve this problem, the ELM has

H. Drias et al. (Eds.): AID 2022, CCIS 1852, pp. 233–244, 2023.
https://doi.org/10.1007/978-981-99-4484-2_18

been combined with deep learning (DL) models, which provide a reliable feature extraction process. Convolutional Neural Networks [3] (CNNs) represent one of the most popular methods to address this problem. Therefore, the CNN-ELM training model was introduced in [2,20]. With the help of a CNN, only the most important details are captured in a stable and robust visual representation. The Convolutional Autoencoder [13] (CAE) is another powerful model applied in this situation. The main area in which CAE-ELM techniques have been used is 3D shape classification, where the CAE learned 3D features as in [1,22]. However, CAE was also used in [17] as a feature extractor for 2D images, where the output of CAE is fed to a CNN model that handles the classification.

In this study, we investigate the image classification tasks using both CNN-ELM and CAE-ELM approaches. Our main contribution is an experimental comparison of these two methods to examine the feature extraction of 2D images by the CNN and CAE models. In order to perform a robust comparative analysis, the evaluation is performed on three benchmark datasets, MNIST, CIFAR-10 and CIFAR-100, with different hidden node sizes of the ELM model. To understand how input features influence classification, our analysis focuses on the accuracy rate as well as the difference between training accuracy and test accuracy.

The rest of this article is structured as follows: Sect. 2 presents a summary of the theoretical aspects used in this work. Section 3 describes our two approaches, CNN-ELM and CAE-ELM. Section 4 reports the achieved results. Finally, Sect. 5 provides a brief conclusion.

2 Background

In this section, we give a brief theoretical overview of ELM, CNN, and CAE models to better understand this work.

2.1 Extreme Learning Machine

Extreme Learning Machine (ELM) was first proposed in 2004 by Huang et al [6]. ELM belongs to the family of single hidden-layer feedforward networks (SLFN). Unlike conventional neural networks based on the backpropagation (BP) algorithm, ELM uses the Moore Penrose (MP) generalized inverse to estimate the target outputs. This significantly reduces the training time.

For a training set $\{(x_i, t_i)\}_{i=1}^{N}$ with N distinct instances, where $x_i = [x_{i,1}, x_{i,2}, ..., x_{i,n}]^T$ is the vector of input attributes and $t_i = [t_{i,1}, t_{i,2}, ..., t_{i,m}]^T$ is the vector of output training values of m classes, a basic SLFN with N hidden nodes and a single hidden layer can be modeled mathematically as follows:

$$\sum_{i=1}^{\check{N}} \beta_i f_i(x_j) = \sum_{i=1}^{\check{N}} \beta_i f_i(a_i \cdot x_j + b_i) \tag{1}$$

where $a_i = [a_{i,1}, a_{i,2}, ..., a_{i,n}]^T$ is the weight vector connecting the ith hidden node with the input nodes, and $\beta_i = [\beta_{i,1}, \beta_{i,2}, ..., \beta_{i,m}]^T$ is the weight vector connecting the ith hidden node with the output nodes. b_i represents the bias of the ith hidden node and f is an activation function. $\cdot$ Represents the scalar product.

We can reduce the equation and write it in the form:

$$H \cdot \beta = T \tag{2}$$

H represents the hidden layer output matrix of the neural network. In ELM algorithm, the input weights and hidden layer biases are randomly initialized, and then the hidden layer output matrix H is determined. Thus, feedforward training can be transformed by computing the output weights matrix by the least squares principle of the following linear system:

$$\check{\beta} = H^{+} \cdot T \tag{3}$$

where H^{+} is the Moore-Penrose generalized inverse of matrix H.

The steps of ELM learning are described in Algorithm 1.

Algorithm 1. ELM learning algorithm

Input

Training Set, Test Set, Activation Function, Hidden Node Number

Steps

1. Randomly initialize the input weights and biases
2. Calculate hidden layer output H
3. Calculate output weight matrix $\check{\beta}$
4. Use $\check{\beta}$ to make predictions on test set

2.2 Convolutional Neural Network

Convolutional Neural Network [3] (CNN) is a category of deep learning models suitable for complex data representations, including images. A CNN model consists of two parts: feature extraction and classification, as shown in Fig. 1. The first part extracts substantive features from images, while the second part combines the extracted features to classify the images.

The feature extraction part is mainly composed of two elements, the convolution layer and the pooling layer. The convolution layer consists of a set of filters (kernels). The output of a convolution layer is calculated by a dot product between the input matrix and the kernel. This is called the convolution operation. This operation can be represented mathematically as follows:

$$z_{i,j,k}^{[l]} = w_k^{[l]} x_{i,j}^{[l]} + b_k^{[l])} \tag{4}$$

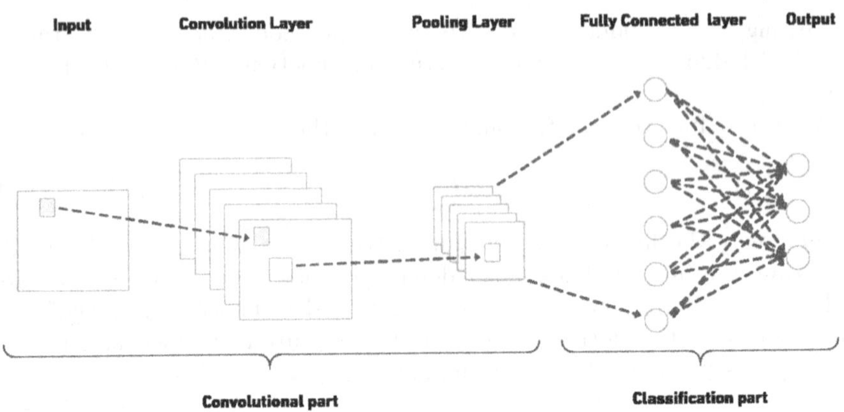

Fig. 1. Standard CNN architecture adapted from [19].

where for a layer l, $x_{i,j}$ is the input and $z_{i,j,k}$ is the output value of the kth kernel at location i, j. The filter weights are denoted by w, and b is the bias. Next, we apply an activation function to $z^{[l]}_{i,j,k}$.

$$g^{[l]}_{i,j,k} = g(z^{[l]}_{i,j,k}) \tag{5}$$

Typically, convolutional layers are followed by a pooling layer that applies a statistical measure such as maximum, mean, and median to reduce the resolution of the output of the convolutional layers.

$$y^{[l]}_{i,j,k} = pooling(g^{[l]}_{i,j,k}) \tag{6}$$

The classification part involves one or more fully connected layers (FC), and a softmax output layer used for classification. This second part combines the results of the first part to define the output label.

2.3 Convolutional Autoencoder

Convolutional Autoencoder [13] (CAE) represents a version of the autoencoder (AE) network suitable for the 2D image structure, since it is based on convolutional layers. CAEs are mainly used to reconstruct input images by compressing them and removing noise while retaining the most significant features. The CAE training procedure can be considered as an unsupervised method.

ACEs are composed of two parts based on convolutional layers, the encoder and the decoder. The encoder extracts the features of the input image into a lower dimensional representation. While the decoder reconstructs this compressed representation by generating an output image similar to the input image. Fig. 2 illustrates CAE model pipeline.

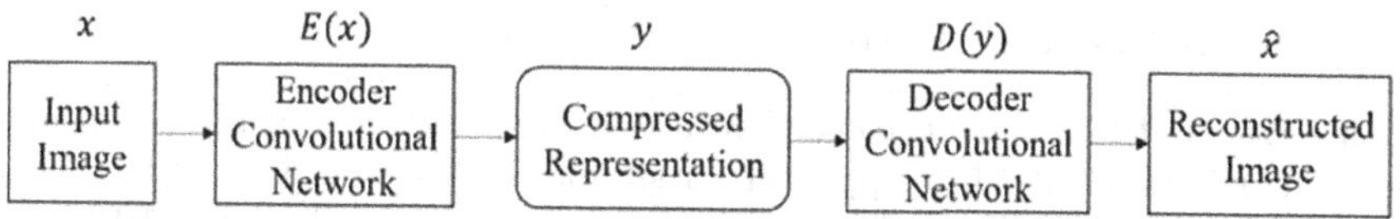

Fig. 2. Standard CAE architecture from [17].

A standard CAE network contains four types of layers: convolutional, pooling, deconvolutional and unpooling layers. The deconvolution and unpooling layers allow the reconstruction of the original image at the decoder level, as they represent the inverse operations of the convolutional and pooling layers, respectively. We note that the deconvolution operation is in fact the transposition operation.

3 Methodology

In this work, we propose two hybrid architectures with ELM based on feature extraction. The first architecture extracts features from CNN model and the second one from CAE model.

3.1 CNN for Feature Extraction

As mentioned earlier, CNN includes a feature extraction component that has the ability to compress the input image. Therefore, ELM is associated with a CNN model to get invariant and stable input features. Initially, a basic CNN model is trained on the training data set. The output of the CNN feature extraction process is fed to the ELM model, which will be trained to perform the final prediction. To ensure an optimal ELM training time the chosen CNN architecture must provide input size reduction. This approach is detailed in Fig. 3.

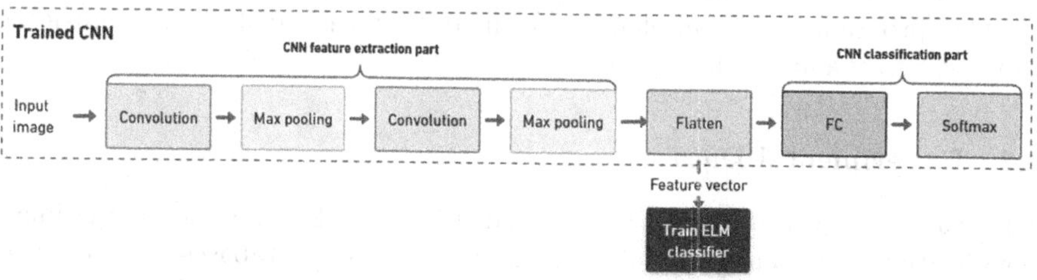

Fig. 3. Structure of the proposed CNN-ELM method.

3.2 CAE for Feature Extraction

With CAE, features can be learned in a way that can be considered as unsupervised. In the CAE-ELM approach, a simple CAE model is first trained on the training data set. Once the training procedure is complete, the ELM classifier is fed with the encoder output vector. Here again, the CAE architecture must ensure that the input dimensionality is reduced while keeping the most important features. Finally, the ELM classifier will be trained to make the final prediction. Figure 4 illustrates this approach.

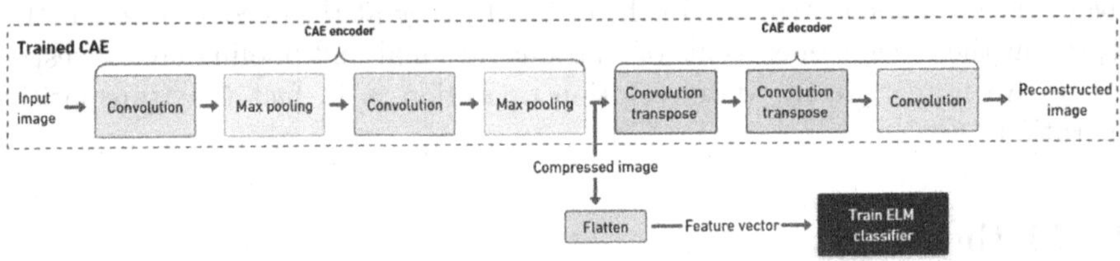

Fig. 4. Structure of the proposed CAE-ELM method.

4 Experiments

This section first describes our test environment. Then, it presents the datasets used. And finally, it reports the different obtained results.

4.1 Software and Hardware Setup

All our tests were performed on a desktop computer with the following characteristics: an AMD RYZEN 7 3700X CPU with 16 GB of RAM, a single GPU (RTX 2060 super) and an Ubuntu 18.04 operating system.

The programs were implemented in Python using: Keras, scikit-learn, NumPy, SciPy and pandas.

4.2 Experimental Data

The evaluation of the approaches studied in this work was done on the image classification task. Three popular image classification databases were used for this purpose:

- MNIST dataset [11]: this dataset contains a total number of 70,000 grayscale images of size 28×28, divided into training and test data. It includes handwritten numbers between 0 and 9. This dataset is slightly unbalanced.

- CIFAR-10 dataset [10]: it contains a total number of 60 000 colored images of size 32 × 32, with 10 classes. This dataset is also divided into two parts: the training set and the test set. It is completely balanced, as the number of instances in each set is the same.
- CIFAR-100 dataset [9]: is a similar database to CIFAR-10, except that it has 100 classes.

Table 1 gives a summary of the datasets used.

Table 1. Dataset description.

Dataset	#Training set	#Testing test	Image size	Color	#Classes
MNIST	60,000	10,000	28 × 28	Gray	10
CIFAR-10	50,000	10,000	32 × 32	RGB	10
CIFAR-100	50,000	10,000	32 × 32	RGB	100

4.3 Experimental Setup

In this comparative study, we implemented all three methods: ELM, CNN-ELM, and CAE-ELM.

Two CNN architectures were used, one adapted for MNIST and the other for CIFAR-10 and CIFAR-100. Table 2 details the CNN architectures used. For the other parameters, we used the Adam optimizer with a learning rate equal to 0.001, a batch size of 64, and a total number of training epochs equal to 200.

Similarly for CAE, we implemented two architectures. One for MNIST and the other for CIFAR-10 and CIFAR-100. Table 3 gives a detailed description of the CAE architecture used. We also used the Adam optimizer, a learning rate equal to 0.001, a batch size equal to 64, and a total number of training epochs of 200.

For ELM, we used only the relu activation function. All methods were evaluated on different numbers of hidden nodes: 5, 10, 50, 100, 200, 300, 400, 500, 1000 and 1500.

We note that the choice of the CNN and CAE architecture was based on the complexity of the dataset while ensuring that the size of the input features was reduced in order to optimize the training time of ELM.

4.4 Evaluation Measure

The ELM model, which is fed directly with the original image data without any feature extraction process, is used as our baseline model. We performed 30 separate iterations for each approach because the weights and biases are initialized randomly. Since there is no substantial class imbalance problem in any dataset, the accuracy score is used to evaluate the performance of the three classifiers (ELM, CNN-ELM and CAE-ELM).

Table 2. CNN architecture.

CNN architecture for MNIST dataset				
Layer	Type	Output shape	Kernel size	Activation function
1	Convolution	24 × 24 × 2	5	tanh
2	Max pooling	12 × 12 × 2	2	–
3	Convolution	8 × 8 × 16	5	tanh
4	Max pooling	4 × 4 × 16	2	–
5	Flatten	256	–	–
6	Dense	128	–	tanh
7	Softmax	10	–	Softmax
CNN architecture for CIFAR-10 and CIFAR-100 datasets				
Layer	Type	Output shape	Kernel size	Activation function
1	Convolution	29 × 29 × 32	4	relu
2	Max pooling	14 × 14 × 32	2	–
3	Convolution	11 × 11 × 32	4	relu
4	Max pooling	5 × 5 × 32	2	–
5	Flatten	800	–	–
6	Dense	128	–	relu
7	Softmax	10	–	Softmax

Table 3. CAE architecture.

CAE architecture for MNIST dataset					
Layer type		Output shape	Kernel size	Stride	Activation function
Encoder	Convolution	28 × 28 × 2	5	1	relu
	Max pooling	14 × 14 × 2	2	2	–
	Convolution	14 × 14 × 16	5	1	relu
	Max pooling	7 × 7 × 16	2	2	–
Decoder	Conv transpose	14 × 14 × 2	5	2	relu
	Conv transpose	28 × 28 × 16	5	2	relu
	Convolution	28 × 28 × 1	5	–	sigmoid
CAE architecture for CIFAR-10 and CIFAR-100 datasets					
Layer type		Output shape	Kernel size	Stride	Activation function
Encoder	Convolution	32 × 32 × 32	5	1	relu
	Max pooling	16 × 16 × 32	2	2	–
	Convolution	16 × 16 × 32	5	1	relu
	Max pooling	8 × 8 × 32	2	2	–
Decoder	Conv transpose	16 × 16 × 7	5	2	relu
	Conv transpose	32 × 32 × 32	5	2	relu
	Convolution	32 × 32 × 3	5	–	sigmoid

4.5 Results and Discussion

Figure 5 shows the average accuracy obtained on the test set by the three approaches according to the number of hidden nodes on MNIST, CIFAR-10, and CIFAR-100 datasets.

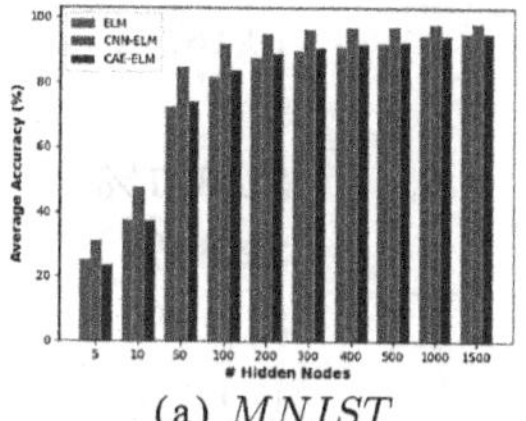

(a) *MNIST*

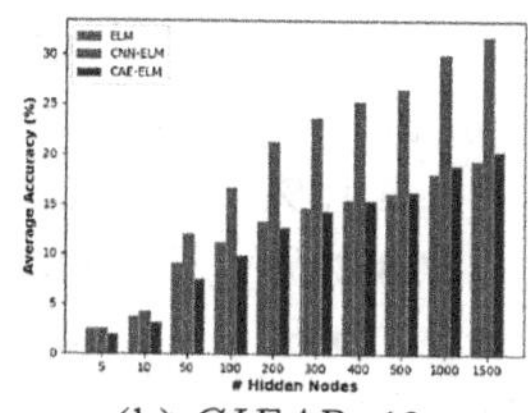

(b) *CIFAR*−10

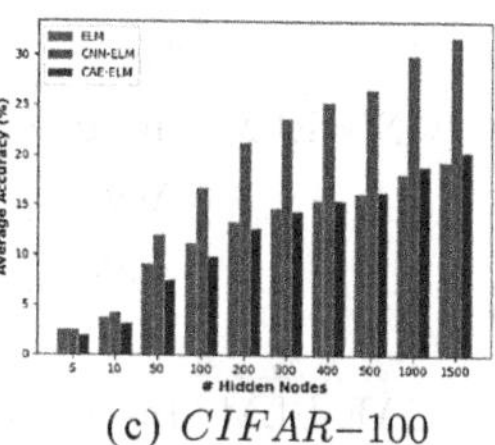

(c) *CIFAR*−100

Fig. 5. Average accuracy of the three approaches: ELM, CNN-ELM, and CAE-ELM.

Comparing these approaches on the MNIST dataset, we first notice that the accuracy of all three methods improves as the number of hidden nodes increases. However, the improvement rate decreases significantly as the number of nodes increases. On the other hand, it is obvious that CNN-ELM outperforms both ELM and CAE-ELM, no matter the number of nodes. On the other hand, CAE-ELM obtains the worst average accuracies. Nevertheless, the performance of the three approaches becomes closer as the number of nodes increases.

For the two datasets CIFAR-10 and CIFAR-100, which are more complex than MNIST dataset, the observations are almost the same, except that the difference between the performances of the three approaches is more significant here, especially with a large size of nodes.

As observed earlier, the best average accuracy achieved by the three models is obtained with a number of nodes equal to 1500. Therefore, we report in Table 4 the average (Avg), worst (Min), and best (Max) classification accuracy obtained on the test set by each method with 1500 hidden nodes. The best results are in bold. These results once again confirm the high performance of CNN-ELM over ELM and CAE-ELM on all datasets in terms of average, minimum, and maximum accuracy. As indicated in the table, the best accuracies obtained for CNN-ELM model are 98.29%, 64.35%, and 32,31% on MNIST, CIFAR-10, and CIFAR-100 datasets, respectively.

Overfitting is a common problem in deep learning models. It causes very high performance on the training set compared to the test set. Figure 6 shows the generalization gap, i.e., the difference between the learning accuracy and the test accuracy, of the three approaches on the three datasets. As we note, despite the good performance of CNN-ELM model, it can suffer from the overfitting problem, especially with a high number of hidden nodes on complex datasets (CIFAR-10 and CIFAR-100). Furthermore, although CAE-ELM obtained the worst accuracies, it is more stable than CNN-ELM when the number of nodes is high.

Table 4. Results obtained with 1500 hidden nodes.

Method	Metric	MNIST	CIFAR-10	CIFAR-100
ELM	Input feature size	$28 \times 28 = 784$	$32 \times 32 \times 3 = 3072$	3072
	Avg	95.34%	45.59%	19,44%
	Max	95.67%	46.3%	19,63%
	Min	95.11%	44.53	19,18%%
CNN-ELM	Input feature size	256	800	800
	Avg	**98.13%**	**63.75%**	**31,821%**
	Max	**98.29%**	**64.35%**	**32,31%**
	Min	**97.96%**	**63.18%**	**31,15%**
CAE-ELM	Input feature size	512	1792	1792
	Avg	95.28%	48.24%	20,35%
	Max	95.79%	49.05%	20,95%
	Min	95.01%	47.55%	19,9%

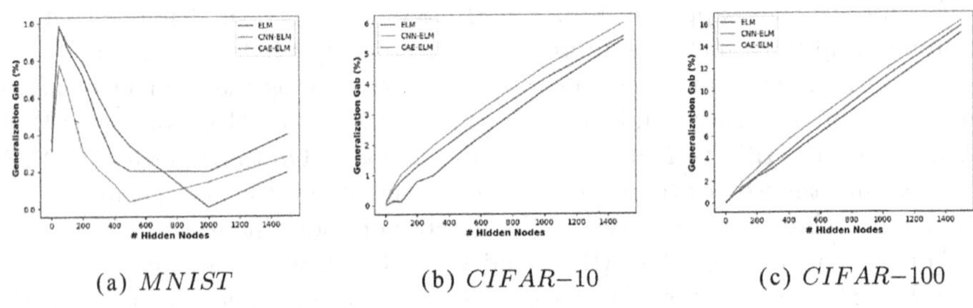

(a) *MNIST* (b) *CIFAR*−10 (c) *CIFAR*−100

Fig. 6. Generalization gap of the three approaches: ELM, CNN-ELM, and CAE-ELM.

A comparison of the two models, CNN-ELM and CAE-ELM, reveals the effectiveness of CNN in extracting important features from 2D images compared to CAE. However, CNN is more exposed to the overfitting problem since the training procedure is supervised, unlike CAE. This means that the extracted features are more suitable for the training set than for the test set. In addition, the unsupervised training of CAE makes the choice of the model architecture more complicated compared to CNN.

5 Conclusion

This paper compared a number of ELM-based approaches on an image classification task. The basic ELM model was combined by CNN as well as CAE to extract the most important and robust features. We conducted our tests on MNIST, CIFAR-10, and CIFAR-100 datasets. The experimental results show that CNN-ELM outperforms both ELM and CAE-ELM models in terms of classification accuracy. However, CNN-ELM can be exposed to the overfitting problem. We also find that CAE is more difficult to train than CNN because the training is unsupervised and selecting the correct architecture is a complex task.

To enrich this work, we need to perform further tests on complex datasets in the future. It is also necessary to study the different architectures of CNN and CAE. We later aim to provide improvements on both CNN-ELM and CAE-ELM models in order to solve frequent problems in conventional ELM.

References

1. Chen, J., Zeng, Y., Wang, S., Min, S.L., Huang, G.B.: Octree-based convolutional autoencoder extreme learning machine for 3D shape classification. In: 2018 International Joint Conference on Neural Networks (IJCNN), pp. 1–7. IEEE (2018)
2. Dos Santos, M.M., da Silva Filho, A.G., dos Santos, W.P.: Deep convolutional extreme learning machines: filters combination and error model validation. Neurocomputing **329**, 359–369 (2019)
3. Fukushima, K., Miyake, S.: Neocognitron: a self-organizing neural network model for a mechanism of visual pattern recognition. In: Amari, Si., Arbib, M.A. (eds) Competition and Cooperation in Neural Nets. LNB, vol. 45, pp. 267–285. Springer, Heidelberg (1982). https://doi.org/10.1007/978-3-642-46466-9_18
4. Hu, T., Khishe, M., Mohammadi, M., Parvizi, G.R., Karim, S.H.T., Rashid, T.A.: Real-time COVID-19 diagnosis from x-ray images using deep CNN and extreme learning machines stabilized by chimp optimization algorithm. Biomed. Sig. Process. Control **68**, 102764 (2021)
5. Huang, G.B., Zhou, H., Ding, X., Zhang, R.: Extreme learning machine for regression and multiclass classification. IEEE Trans. Syst. Man Cybern. Part B (Cybernetics) **42**(2), 513–529 (2012). https://doi.org/10.1109/TSMCB.2011.2168604
6. Huang, G.B., Zhu, Q.Y., Siew, C.K.: Extreme learning machine: a new learning scheme of feedforward neural networks. In: 2004 IEEE International Joint Conference on Neural Networks (IEEE Cat. No.04CH37541), vol. 2, pp. 985–990 (2004). https://doi.org/10.1109/IJCNN.2004.1380068
7. Huang, J., Yu, Z.L., Gu, Z.: A clustering method based on extreme learning machine. Neurocomputing **277**, 108–119 (2018). https://doi.org/10.1016/j.neucom.2017.02.100, https://www.sciencedirect.com/science/article/pii/S0925231217313930, hierarchical Extreme Learning Machines
8. Kang, X., Zhao, Y., Li, J.: Predicting refractive index of ionic liquids based on the extreme learning machine (elm) intelligence algorithm. J. Mol. Liq. **250**, 44–49 (2018)
9. Krizhevsky, A., Nair, V.: Cifar-100 (Canadian institute for advanced research). 30 [65] alex krizhevsky, ilya sutskever, and geoffrey e hinton. imagenet classification with deep convolutional neural networks. In: Advances in Neural Information Processing Systems, vol. 25, pp. 1097–1105, 26 (2012)
10. Krizhevsky, A., Nair, V., Hinton, G.: Cifar-10 (Canadian institute for advanced research). http://www.cs.toronto.edu/kriz/cifar.html
11. LeCun, Y., Cortes, C., Burges, C.: Mnist handwritten digit database. ATT Labs, February 2010 [Online]. http://yann.lecun.com/exdb/mnist

12. Liu, T., Liyanaarachchi Lekamalage, C.K., Huang, G.B., Lin, Z.: Extreme learning machine for joint embedding and clustering. Neurocomputing **277**, 78–88 (2018). https://doi.org/10.1016/j.neucom.2017.01.115, https://www.sciencedirect.com/science/article/pii/S0925231217314078, hierarchical Extreme Learning Machines
13. Masci, J., Meier, U., Cireşan, D., Schmidhuber, J.: Stacked convolutional auto-encoders for hierarchical feature extraction. In: Honkela, T., Duch, W., Girolami, M., Kaski, S. (eds.) ICANN 2011. LNCS, vol. 6791, pp. 52–59. Springer, Heidelberg (2011). https://doi.org/10.1007/978-3-642-21735-7_7
14. Milačić, L., Jović, S., Vujović, T., Miljković, J.: Application of artificial neural network with extreme learning machine for economic growth estimation. Physica A **465**, 285–288 (2017)
15. Nayak, D.R., Dash, R., Majhi, B.: Pathological brain detection using extreme learning machine trained with improved whale optimization algorithm. In: 2017 Ninth International Conference on Advances in Pattern Recognition (ICAPR), pp. 1–6. IEEE (2017)
16. Pan, H., Lü, Z., Wang, H., Wei, H., Chen, L.: Novel battery state-of-health online estimation method using multiple health indicators and an extreme learning machine. Energy **160**, 466–477 (2018)
17. Pintelas, E., Livieris, I.E., Pintelas, P.E.: A convolutional autoencoder topology for classification in high-dimensional noisy image datasets. Sensors **21**(22), 7731 (2021)
18. Qing, Y., Zeng, Y., Li, Y., Huang, G.B.: Deep and wide feature based extreme learning machine for image classification. Neurocomputing **412**, 426–436 (2020)
19. Tupe, P.R., Vibhute, P., Sayyad, M.: An architecture combining convolutional neural network (CNN) with batch normalization for apparel image classification. In: 2020 IEEE International Symposium on Sustainable Energy, Signal Processing and Cyber Security (iSSSC), pp. 1–6. IEEE (2020)
20. Wang, P., Zhang, X., Hao, Y.: A method combining CNN and elm for feature extraction and classification of SAR image. J. Sens. **2019** (2019)
21. Wang, W., Wang, J.: Determinants investigation and peak prediction of CO2 emissions in China's transport sector utilizing bio-inspired extreme learning machine. Environ. Sci. Pollut. Res. **28**(39), 55535–55553 (2021)
22. Wang, Y., Xie, Z., Xu, K., Dou, Y., Lei, Y.: An efficient and effective convolutional auto-encoder extreme learning machine network for 3D feature learning. Neurocomputing **174**, 988–998 (2016)
23. Yuan, P., Chen, D., Wang, T., Cao, S., Cai, Y., Xue, L.: A compensation method based on extreme learning machine to enhance absolute position accuracy for aviation drilling robot. Adv. Mech. Eng. **10**(3), 1687814018763411 (2018)
24. Zhang, J., Xiao, W., Li, Y., Zhang, S.: Residual compensation extreme learning machine for regression. Neurocomputing **311**, 126–136 (2018). https://doi.org/10.1016/j.neucom.2018.05.057, https://www.sciencedirect.com/science/article/pii/S0925231218306428
25. Zheng, L., Wang, Z., Zhao, Z., Wang, J., Du, W.: Research of bearing fault diagnosis method based on multi-layer extreme learning machine optimized by novel ant lion algorithm. IEEE Access **7**, 89845–89856 (2019)

Machine Learning Assisted Resonant Inverter Control for Temperature Regulation in Rubber Manufacturing

Abdelkader Yahi(✉) and Houcine Zeroug

Laboratory of Characterization and Diagnostics of Electrical Systems, University of Sciences and Technologies Houari Boumediene Algiers, Bab Ezzouar, Algeria
yahiabdou96@gmail.com, hzeroug@usthb.dz

Abstract. This paper proposes a new approach for temperature regulation in rubber product manufacturing using a deep neural network-based controller. Traditionally, a PI temperature regulator is used to control the temperature during the heating process using high frequency resonant power converters. However, this method often leads to unsatisfactory results when operating conditions are altered under various disturbances, even with tuned PI coefficients. The proposed approach uses machine learning to construct a controller based on PI results as datasets. The obtained predicted model for the controller is very consistent and capable of offsetting all the drawbacks encountered in a classic PI regulator. The model is simulated using MATLAB, and the results show higher performance when exposed to various disturbances. This approach has the potential to be implemented in an embedded hardware for validation.

Keywords: Resonant inverter · PI control · Machine Learning · Induction Heating

1 Introduction

In many manufacturing processes that require heat, there is a strong incentive to maximize efficiency, enhance quality, and increase production while minimizing costs and environmental impact [2]. The rubber products platform is generally made through hot metal plates that consist of two parts, the fixed lower part and the mobile upper part in which the rubber paste is placed at the temperature up to 150 °C before undergoing a pressure of 150 bars to achieve the required transformation. In the existing equipment, each heating in the lower and higher parts are equipped with 3 pair of resistors of 2 kW each, supplied by 50 Hz electrical network allowing the heat transfer by conduction to the mold in which the rubber is embedded. Figure 1(a) shows the layout of the industrial platform and its components.

H. Drias et al. (Eds.): AID 2022, CCIS 1852, pp. 245–259, 2023.
https://doi.org/10.1007/978-981-99-4484-2_19

The plates (30 * 30 cm) used for heating and pressing with heating resistance elements are shown in Fig. 1 (b). Here, the heat is transferred from the resistors to the rubber, mold, and support elements, with energy loss occurring through convection, conduction, and radiation. Achieving a homogeneous temperature distribution requires longer heating times and higher energy consumption [3]. Therefore, there is a need to explore alternative heating methods that can achieve faster heating rates and more homogeneous temperature distributions while reducing and energy consumption. One promising alternative is the use of high-frequency series inverters as generators for induction heating, which can offer higher efficiency, more precise temperature control, and lower environmental impact. Generally, this is performed under proportional-integral (PI) temperature regulator before rubber transformation. However, this is accompanied by unsatisfactory results when operation conditions are altered under various disturbances even with tuned PI coefficients. This is well reflected through longer settling times and recurrent overshoots, which ultimately leads to non-even temperature distribution, subsequently affecting the product processing.

One alternative technique for temperature regulation is to use predefined PI profiles that describe well-regulated temperature responses for various PI coefficient values [1, 2, 8]. In this study, the approach was investigated to evaluate its performance under various operating conditions [4–6]. This approach involves finding appropriate function approximations that can fit well with the desired output responses. While combining several non-linear functions for approximation may be effective, it can be computationally intensive and require complicated coefficient calculations [2, 9–11]. Therefore, the use of modern and intelligent techniques for accurate identification of load temperature responses seems appropriate. In fact, the heating process can be readily customized to embody these advanced techniques as long as the PI temperatures profiles are well identified.

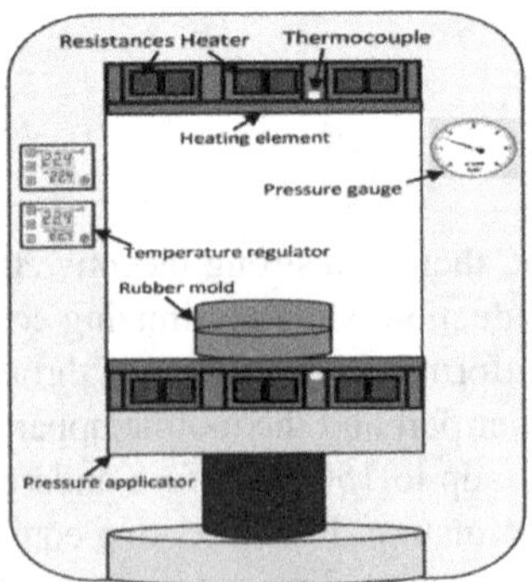

Fig. 1. (**a**) Schematic of rubber molding platform. (**b**)Industrial platform.

In this context, a deep neural network (DNN) model is developed using a supervised machine learning approach. The DNN model is created using MATLAB deep learning libraries and is based on an experimental dataset obtained from a simulation model with a classic PI regulator. The dataset contains temperature response profiles under various PI coefficients when subjected to various disturbances. The present approach proposes a deep neural network based on multilayer perception (MLP) to learn the temperature response profiles and estimate the power density required for an effective and robust temperature regulation without the aforementioned drawbacks. To achieve a consistent machine learning approach for obtaining a predicted model, an identification of the system was conducted through an open loop response to obtain the transfer function of the inverter system for power generation with respect to the control parameter based on power density modulation (PDM) control. Additionally, prior to temperature regulation, the load consisting of the coil and mold was identified as a resistive thermal network [3]. To generate the dataset for training the neural network, temperature regulation was carried out using a conventional PI controller in a closed loop under various operating conditions. A high frequency resonant inverter was used to supply power to a coil, upon which a metallic recipient containing the mold was placed. Heat was generated through induction heating (IH) and transferred to the rubber through conduction, resulting in higher efficiency as shown in Fig. 3. Finally, the system model was trained using a neural network approach, with careful configuration of the parameters to obtain accurate predictions in a simulation model. A part of the dataset was utilized for approach validation. The paper first presents the modeling of the system in open loop control, which includes the inverter with power density modulation control (PDM) and an identified load using a thermal network that represents the coil and the recipient of the rubber. This approach allowed the transfer function of the system to be determined. Data was then generated, producing temperature response profiles under the classic PI controller with various disturbances. Finally, the machine learning approach was implemented and presented to overcome the drawbacks encountered. The NN predicted model simulation results were then compared to those of the classic PI controller in terms of performances.

2 System Modeling

2.1 System Performance Assessment in Open Loop

To investigate the system, the performance assessment of the power supply was carried out in order to generate the required power at the desired frequency based on the workpiece's temperature gradient. After analyzing the testing bed parameters, a series resonant inverter configuration capable of providing up to 1 kW of power was selected. The simulation of the model in Fig. 1(a) was carried out using the PSIM environment, accounting for power device losses. The simulation model is presented in Fig. 2.

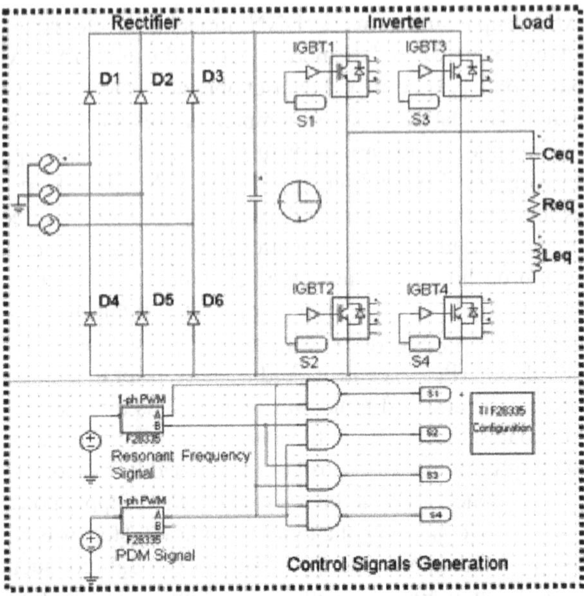

Fig. 2. Simulation modeling diagram of IH system with PDM control.

2.2 Thermal Model

The thermal model of the induction heating system is described in this section. It should be noted that while the paper focuses on modeling an induction heating system for molds used in the soles foaming process, the proposed approach can be applied to any similar induction heating system. In fact, induction heating has been used for various purposes, including heating metal parts for processes like injection molding, hardening, tempering, and annealing. In the context of molding and foaming, induction heating is commonly used to heat the metallic recipient of a mold more efficiently through conduction. This is depicted in Fig. 3.

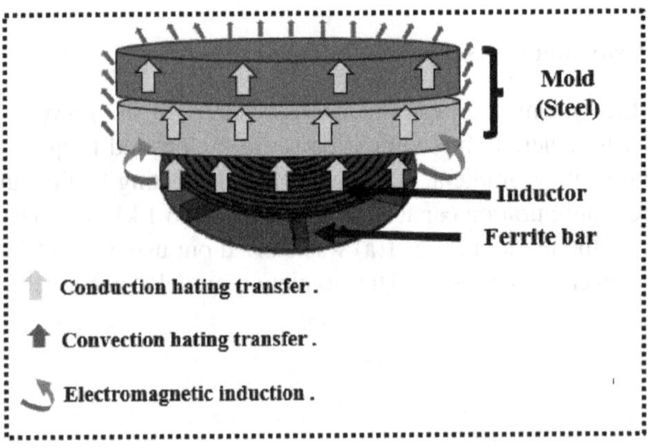

Fig. 3. Induction heating system.

Figure 3 describes the proposed induction heating system for molds. The system consists of an inductor that generates an electromagnetic field and a mold to be heated. The figure is composed of two parts: the inductor and the steel part representing the mold.

2.2.1 Simulink Thermal Model

The proposed thermal model is based on a thermal resistive network implemented in MATLAB/SIMULINK environment. Figure 5 shows the mold heating modeled as an equivalent thermal circuit. The approach based on heat transfer principles leads to two equivalent resistances representing the heat transfer inside the steel plate, and the heat exchange between the mold and the ambient temperature of 25 °C, and a thermal resistance simulating the heat transfer during the induction mold heating. The temperature level is monitored by the T1 sensor. The heating system parameters have been predetermined experimentally with a minor error of 5%, so that the expected temperature from the thermal network agrees with the experimental results. The model is considered as a subsystem in the electromagnetic simulation presented in the following sections. The model input is the thermal power profile generated by the induction system, with the induction system described in Fig. 3 as an input highlighted as a power step function. The final system for simulation as depicted in Sect. 3, embodies the induction equations. Their resolution leads to determine the thermal power transferred to the recipient (Fig. 4).

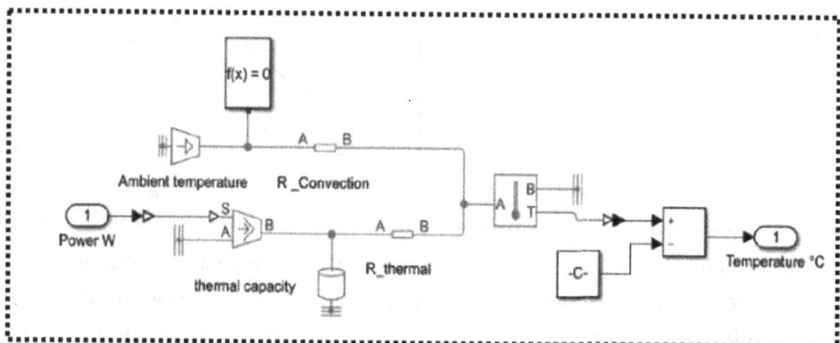

Fig. 4. Simulink thermal model.

2.2.2 Transfer Function of Power System for Temperature Control

In order to develop a control strategy, it is necessary to define an approximate model of the present system. Since the Simulink model of the mold is a system with the thermal power as input, and the temperature output, the circuit can be described in Fig. 5, using the MATLAB System Identification toolbox.

The system identification toolbox allows us to estimate mathematical models of dynamic systems using measured data. This involves collecting and pre-processing data, estimating a model structure, validating the model, and analyzing its behavior. The toolbox provides various model structures and analysis functions to facilitate this process and can be used in various applications, including control engineering and signal processing.

We note that in order to identify the model parameters, the latter are obtained using an adequate fitting of the data derived from the experimental system temperature response to those used for the identification toolbox. In fact, experiment was carried out under certain operating conditions. In this case, the load which includes the induction coil with working piece on the top was fed with the high frequency resonant inverter. The temperature was monitored during the heating cycle. The data collected from this temperature response was introduced in the identification tool box [10]. After several trials, an adequate fitting was obtained corresponding to this response characteristic, leading an appropriate transfer function.

Here the system can be represented as a third order transfer function in Laplace domain as follows:

$$H(s) = \frac{1.749s^2 + 0.0002672s + 4.823 \times 10^{-8}}{s^3 + 14.77s^2 + 0.006323s + 1.008 \times 10^{-6}} \tag{1}$$

Further, to support this identification process, other criteria related to asymptotic stability have been taken into account. As a result, the response of the system is shown in Fig. 6.

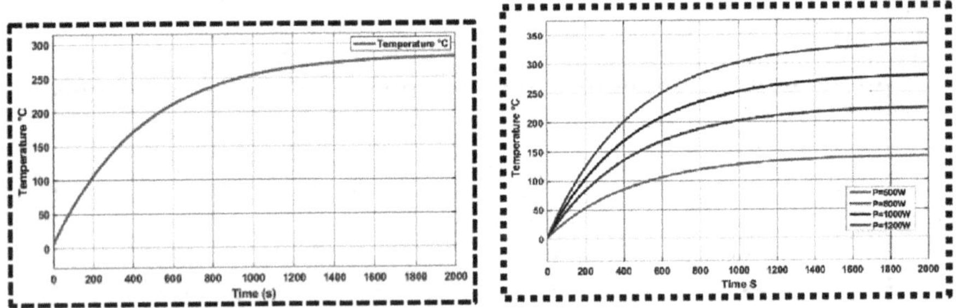

Fig. 5. Step response of the linearized system. **Fig. 6.** Temperature variation with time.

Figure 5 shows the temperature variation as a function of time with different power values in open loop operating mode. Figure 6 illustrates the evolution of the temperature with respect to the input power.

2.3 System Performance Assessment in Closed Loop

In this section, the aim is to maintain the temperature in the mold at 150 °C. To satisfy this condition, we use a proportional integral (PI) controller Fig. 7 represents the global system in closed loop, comprising a PI controller used for the process.

Following this identification, the system parameters values are depicted in Table 1.

2.3.1 Simulation Results Without Disturbances

After applying a step power input, the temperature response shows that the desired temperature of 150 °C is reached quickly with a response time of 18 s and remains

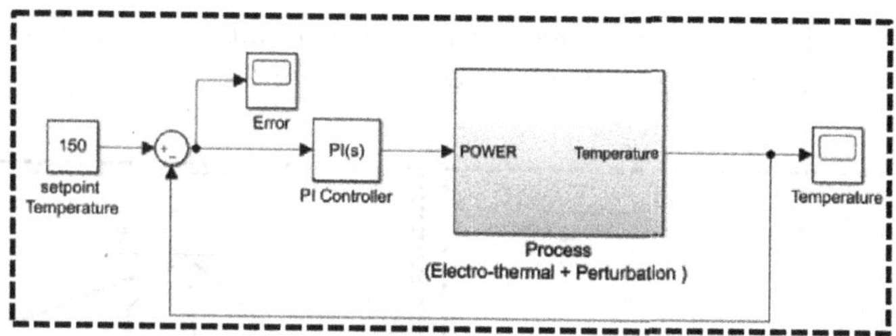

Fig. 7. Bloc diagram of the entire system.

Table 1. Parameters values for simulation.

Symbol	Component	Value
K_p	Proportional constant	1
K_i	Proportional constant	3.5
F_r	Resonance Frequency	17 kHz
C_{eq}	Tank Capacitor	4 uF
L_{eq}	Equivalent Inductance	21.91 uH
R_{eq}	Equivalent Resistor	0.5 Ω

constant at 150 °C with a slight overshoot of up to 200 °C. This can be seen clearly in Fig. 8.

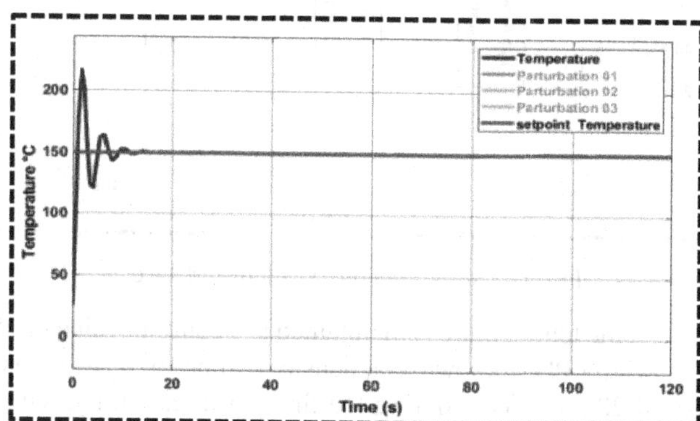

Fig. 8. Temperature maintains without disturbance.

2.3.2 Simulation Results with Disturbances

In this part, a PI controller is used for temperature regulation with well-tuned PI coefficients. The temperature response remains almost constant at 150 °C, which is clearly shown in Fig. 9. However, there is a persistent minimum overshoot due to this disturbance, which was found difficult to reduce even further.

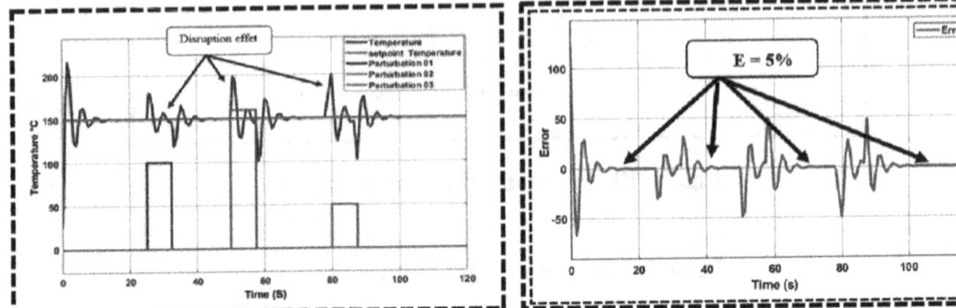

Fig. 9. Maintain the temperature with disturbance

Fig. 10. Error static variation

The error is quantified and its variation are illustrated in Fig. 10. Concerning the static error shown in Fig. 10, it appears to be low and exhibits minimal values without a major effect on the system (Fig. 11).

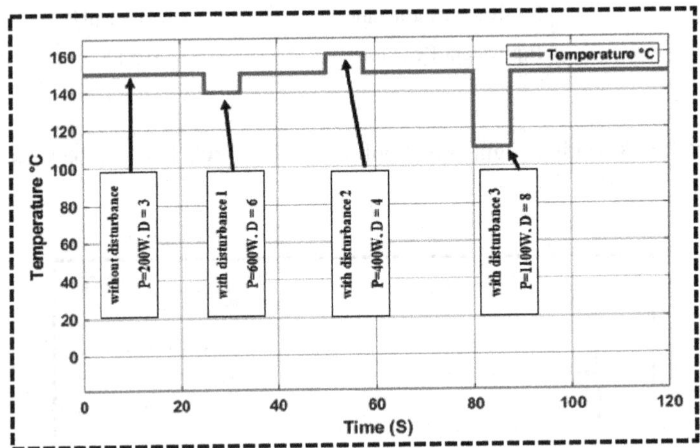

Fig. 11. Variation Power with disturbance.

In the first stage, the temperature is maintained at a constant value of 150 °C without any perturbation, with a PDM known as a density number of 3, which is equivalent to an output power of 200 W. Then, during the first perturbation, the temperature drops to 140 °C, and in response, the input power is increased to 500 W with a PDM of 6. Similarly, the temperature is brought back to 150 °C without any perturbation. During the next perturbation, the temperature increases to 160 °C with an input power of 400 W and a PDM of 4. Afterward, the system settles back to the desired temperature of 150 °C as in the first stage. Overall, the system responds to each perturbation by adjusting the PDM to either increase or decrease the temperature, ultimately bringing the temperature back to 150 °C. However, it was noticed that each perturbation resulted in an overshoot, which required the adjustment of the PI coefficients to minimize it. Later on, it will be demonstrated that this overshoot can be reduced even further to an acceptable level using an advanced control strategy based on artificial intelligence neural network techniques.

3 Application of Machine Learning for Temperature Adaptation: Predict Model Elaboration

As it appears from the characteristics determined in the previous section, the trend shows that model-based machine learning can be appropriate with a careful neural network (NN) design. Theoretical advances and practical success have shown that using NN offers solutions with greater flexibility, leading to a better capacity for approximating functions and learning data representations [12, 13]. The NN used in this study involves a standard feedforward net with β activations composed of a sequence of layers. These layers perform non-linear transformations, which can be represented as follows:

$$F(x) = A_{L+1} \circ \beta_L \circ A_L \circ \ldots \circ \beta_1 \circ A_1(x) \tag{2}$$

where x is the input of the NN, L is the number of layers, A is affine transformation expressed in Eq. (3) and β is nonlinear function called activation function.

$$A_l(\zeta_{l-1}) W_l \zeta_{l-1} b_l \tag{3}$$

where: ζ_{l-1} is the output of the previous layer and the W_l and bl are called the weights and biases at layer l and their value is determined by training the NN with known input-output pairs.

In the artificial network, the MLP is well suited for fitting non-linear systems to data. The architecture of the MLP can have a direct impact on the convergence and performance of the network. In this work, we chose a network composed of 6 layers. The first layer consists of input neurons for the power, followed by 4 hidden layers, and one output neuron for the temperature. The architecture of the NN is shown in Fig. 12.

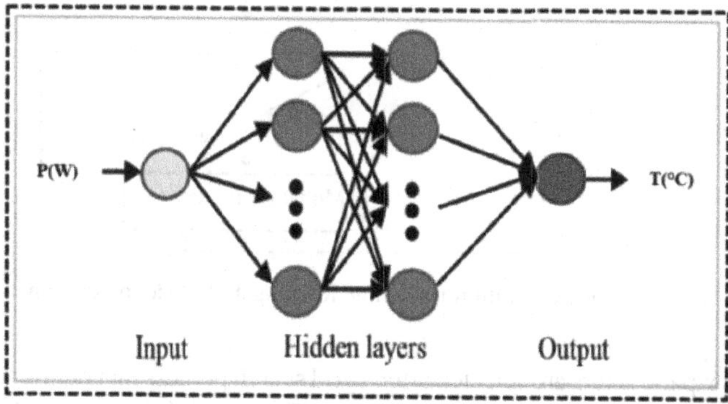

Fig. 12. Representation of NN architecture.

The block diagram in Fig. 13 outlines the steps taken in the design of our NN. The dataset used for training and testing is split into 80% and 20% respectively. Hyperparameters are selected, and the training process is aimed at minimizing the error between the predicted and actual experimental values at each iteration.

The proposed NN model is designed and trained using MATLAB code and the neural network library. A dataset of 2001 samples was collected through Simulink simulation and then normalized to a range between (−1,1). The appropriate activation functions were selected for the network. ReLU activation function was used for the hidden layers, while Hyperbolic Tangent (Tanh) function was used for the output layer. These functions are defined by Eqs. (4) and (5).

$$ReLU : \beta = max\{0, x\} \quad (4)$$

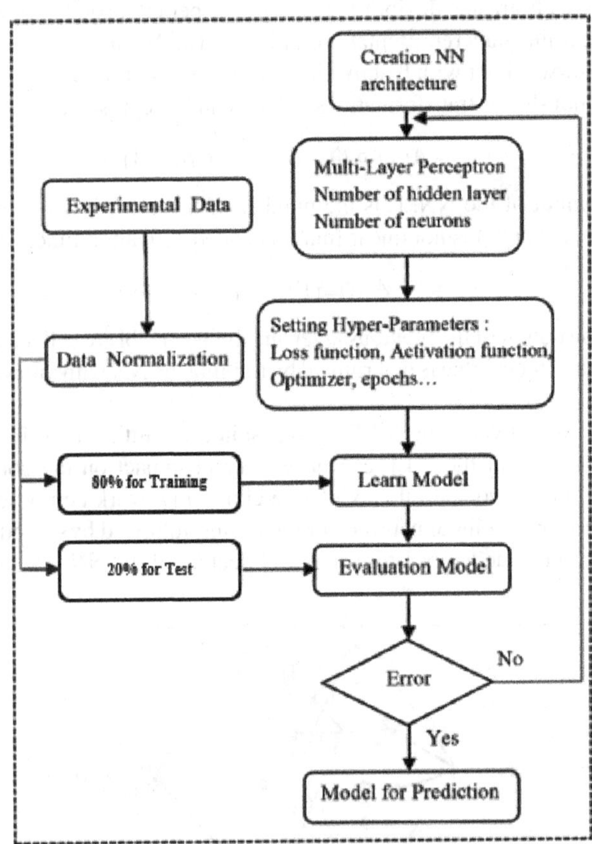

Fig. 13. Bloc diagram for machine learning and model prediction.

The hyper-parameters are selected after a grid search process that builds and evaluates the model for each combination of parameters. The search is performed by defining a subset of values for each hyper-parameter and then using all possible combinations of elements from the subsets. The resulting model has the configuration shown in Table 2.

The proposed neural network model is designed and trained using a function with routines defined as DL mathematical libraries programmed in MATLAB code. This library is aimed to define, adjust, and evaluate the standard DL models. In particular

Table 2. Hyper-parameters used for training the RN

Hyper parameters	Values
Optimizer	**RMSProp**
Activation function Hidden layer	**RELU**
Output layer	**Tanh**
Layer type	**Fully connected**
Hidden layers	**4**
Number HL neurons	**2,5,8,8**
Weight initialization	**Uniform**
Batch size	**32**
Number of epochs	**202**

the function known as "newff" library has become commonly used for solving machine learning applications [10].

$$Tanh : \beta = \frac{e^x - e^{-x}}{e^x + e^{-x}} \tag{5}$$

With x is the input of neuron.

The training is based on the RMSprop algorithm optimizer [12], which is used to test and train the dataset. The difference between the target and the data output is calculated using the root mean squared error (RMSE), as given by Eq. (6). The weights W(l) and biases b(l) of the network are adjusted in each iteration to minimize this difference and achieve convergence.

$$RMSE\left(\hat{\theta}\right) = \sqrt{\frac{\sum_{n=1}^{N} (\hat{y}_n - y_n)^2}{N}} \tag{6}$$

where N is the total number of training samples, $\hat{y}_n$ is the predicted value and y_n is known output value for each input $\hat{\theta}$.

3.1 Model Simulation Results

Based on the results of the simulations with conventional PI presented earlier, we used these points as the dataset for our RN. We subjected the dataset to several learning runs until we reached a highly acceptable level of accuracy. The results of several attempts that we followed for creating and training our network are illustrated in Table 3:

Simulation was performed to produce a model for each sample. Figure 14. Shows the curve reflecting the model for prediction, which agrees well with the simulation dataset trend. This comparison is supported by the error found at the end of the training stage, which implies that the model has been well trained to learn the power-temperature profile of the system. For model accuracy evaluation, the value of RMSE produced was found to equal to 4.9417e-14 with trained parameter number up to 2001.

Table 3. Result of multiple attempts

DATASET	H-L	Neurons in H-L	EPOCHS	Accuracy
30	2	2,4	50	**6.07 e – 5**
120	3	2,3,4	100	**6.07 e – 7**
2001	4	2,5,8,8	202	**4.941e-14**

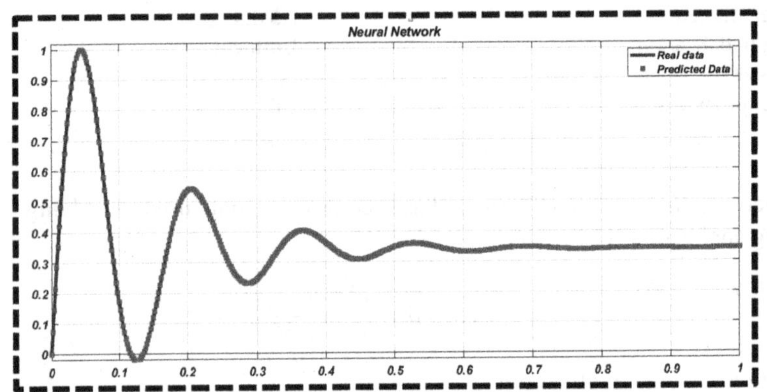

Fig. 14. PI profile: simulation and predicted NN.

It is clear that the simulation and the predicted profiles agree well, indicating that the system was subjected to consistent training with a well-accepted accuracy. Figure 15(a) and (b) illustrate the performance of the NN produced.

Here, in order to outline the merits of NN controller approach, the temperature controller for the power system was subject to performance assessment using the conventional PI and PI neural network in the presence and absence of perturbation as shown in Fig. 16. Here the top part represents the classic PI controller whereas the one in bottom is dedicated to PI NN predicted model based.

In the presence of disturbances as illustrated in Fig. 17 the conventional PI controller and the PI neural network controller are able to regulate the system temperature and bring the system back to stability, with a settling temperature of 150 °C.

The results in Figs. 17 and 18 respectively show that the PI neural network outperforms the conventional PI controller in terms of response time and eliminates the overshoot caused by disturbances. The error between the settling temperature and the reference demand of 150 °C is also minimal for the PI neural network based.

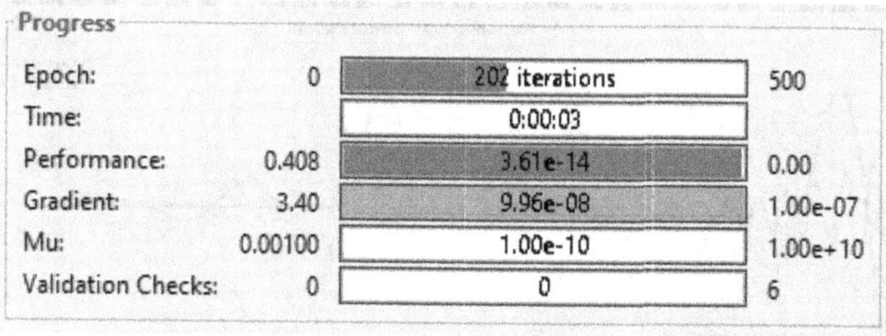

(a)

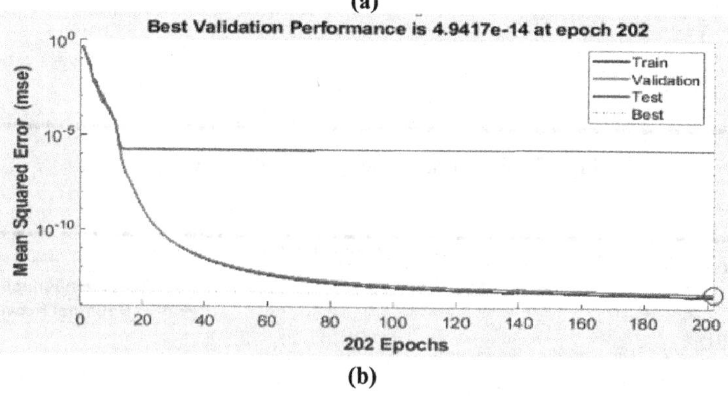

(b)

Fig. 15. NN performance evolution.

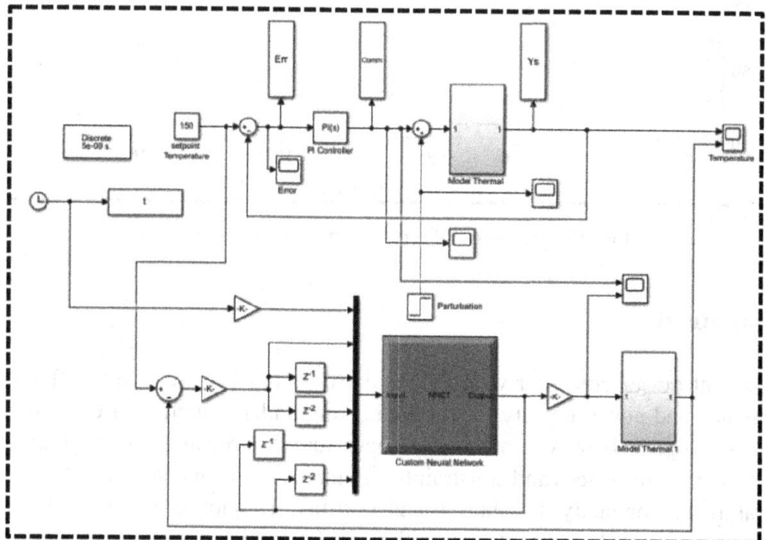

Fig. 16. System modeling with two temperature regulation schemes for comparison.

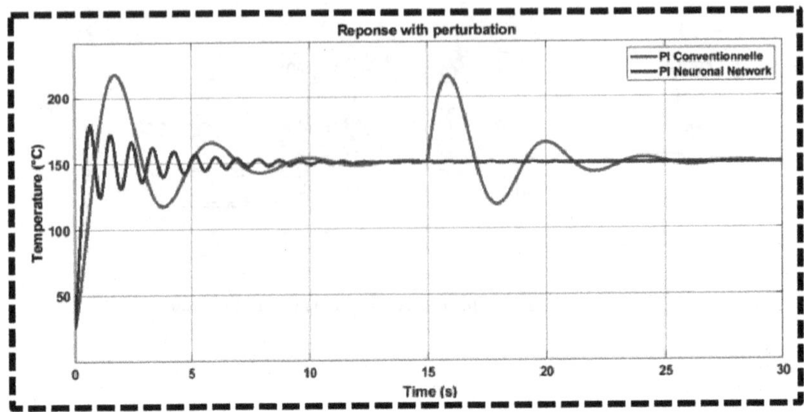

Fig. 17. Response of the system with disturbance

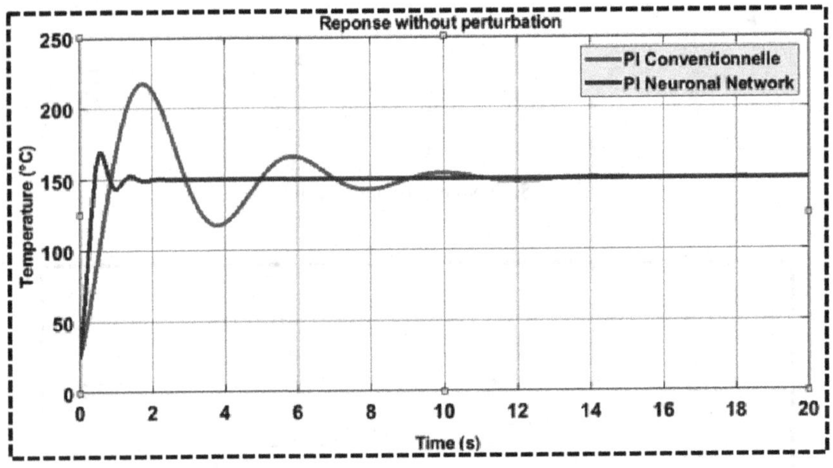

Fig. 18. Response of the system without disturbance.

4 Conclusion

The resonant power converter with PDM controller has been shown to offer superior performance and power density for rubber heating under induction effect compared to other technologies. However, accurate temperature control under PI regulation for a wide range of disturbances and constraints remains a significant challenge for achieving temperature homogeneity distribution and stability. To address these challenges, this paper proposes a ML-based controller with a regulator to improve dynamic performance and settling times. The approach involves selecting appropriate activation functions and neural network parameters to achieve good accuracy when comparing predicted and experimental datasets using a classical PI regulator. The use of machine learning appears promising for future implementation through an embedded system and offers good prospects for the rubber manufacturing industry.

References

1. Vishnuram, P., Ramachandiran, G., Ramasamy, S., Dayalan, S.: A comprehensive overview of power converter topologies for induction heating applications. Int. Trans. Electr. Energ. Syst. **30**(10), 12554 (2020)
2. Hammouma, C., Zeroug, H., Attab, A.: Combined PDM with frequency temperature profile adaptation control for induction metal hardening.In: IECON 44th Annual Conference of the IEEE Industrial Electronics Society (2018)
3. Wei Han, K.T., Chau, W.H.L.: All-utensil domestic induction heating system. Energy Convers. Manage. **195**, 1035–1043 (2019)
4. Ishizawa, H., Tanabe, T., Daiki Yoshida, S., Hosseini, H.R., Katsuki, S., Akiyama, H.: Focusing system of burst electromagnetic waves for medical applications. IEEE Trans. Dielectr. Electr. Insul. **20**(4), 1321–1326 (2013)
5. Ye, L., Liang, C., Liu, Y., Li, D., Liu, Z.: Performance analysis and test of novel eddy-current braking & heating system for electric bus. Energy Convers. Manage. **183**, 440–449 (2019)
6. Candeo, A., Ducassy, C., Bocher, P., Dughiero, F.: Multiphysics modeling of induction hardening of ring gears for the aerospace industry. IEEE Trans. Magn. **47**(5), 918–921 (2011)
7. Rudnev, V., et al.: Handbook of induction heating. Inductoheat Inc, Madison Heights (2003)
8. Barragan, L.A., Navarro, D., Acero, J., Urriza, I., Burdio, J.M.: FPGA implementation of a switching frequency modulation circuit for emi reduction in resonant inverters for induction heating appliances. IEEE Trans. Industr. Electron. **55**(1), 11–20 (2008)
9. Chen, M.-P., Jan-Ku Chen, K., Murata, M., Nakahara, K.H.: Surge analysis of induction heating power supply with PLL. IEEE Trans. Power Electron. **16**(5), 702–709 (2001)
10. Matlab-Simulink Tool box, identification libraries. MathWorks Manual (2016)
11. Lucia, O., Navarro, D., Guillen, P., Sarnago, H., Lucia, S.: Deep learning-based magnetic coupling detection for advanced induction heating appliances. IEEE Access **7**, 181668–181677 (2019)
12. Lucia, S., Navarro, D., Karg, B., Sarnago, H., Lucia, O.: Deep Learning-based Model Predictive Control for Resonant Power Converters. IEEE Trans. Industr. Inf. **17**(1), 409–420 (2020)
13. Hanin, B.: Universal Function Approximation by Deep Neural Nets with Bounded Width and ReLU Activations. Mathematics **7**, 992 (2019)

NLP and Text Mining

Mitigating Emotional Harm on Social Media: A Filtering Approach Using Synesketch and Euclidean Distance

Ferdaous Benrouba(✉) and Rachid Boudour

Embedded Systems Laboratory, Department of Computer Science, Badji Mokhtar Annaba-University, BO 12, Annaba, Algeria
benrouba.ferdaous@gmail.com

Abstract. Social media has become a prevalent issue that has attracted the attention of both society and researchers. Social media platforms have undergone tremendous expansion over the past ten years, offering users the ability to share personal messages, information, pictures, videos and ideas at an unprecedented pace. The negative impacts of social media usage are especially concerning for the younger generation, who spend a significant amount of time engaging in online social interactions and are thus more susceptible to harm. To address these concerns, we propose a solution that uses Synesketch and the Euclidean distance measure to filter emotionally harmful content in social media. We demonstrated the practical application of our approach on a dataset of tweets obtained through the Twitter API and achieved promising results. Our proposed approach can be valuable in various natural language processing applications, such as sentiment analysis, opinion mining, and social media monitoring.

Keywords: Synesketch · Artificial Intelligence · Sentiment analysis · Natural Language Processing · Twitter API

1 Introduction

Social media has had a significant impact on society and has become a major topic of concern for scientists and the general public. Social media platforms, which include chat platforms like Instagram and Facebook, as well as online gaming and virtual worlds like Reddit and Youtube, have grown exponentially over the past decade. These platforms provide accessible gateways for communication and entertainment for people of all ages, but especially for younger generations who spend a significant amount of time socializing online. As social media continues to gain popularity, it has become an integral element of daily life. Facebook alone has had an estimated 1 billion active members since 2015. It has also had a significant impact on various aspects of modern digital life, including marketing, politics, education, health, and human connection. Despite its relative youth, some studies have already analyzed the impact of frequent social

H. Drias et al. (Eds.): AID 2022, CCIS 1852, pp. 263–277, 2023.
https://doi.org/10.1007/978-981-99-4484-2_20

media usage on mental health and overall well-being [47]. The overuse of social media, especially among young people, has become a growing concern. Studies have shown a correlation between social media use and negative effects such as stress, increased anxiety, depression, loneliness, and eating disorders [49]. The lack of awareness regarding these negative consequences is particularly alarming for the younger generation, who spend a significant amount of time socializing online and are therefore at a higher risk of harm. To address these concerns, we propose filtering emotionally harmful social media content using Synesketch and the Euclidean distance measure. Our approach involves extracting user posts from Twitter using the Twitter API and using Synesketch software to classify emotions into six categories: happiness, sadness, anger, fear, disgust, and surprise. Afterwards, we create a collection of emotions in a file called JSON. We also define a perfect set of emotions where joy and happiness have a value of 1, while all other emotions have a value of 0. By comparing the emotions in each tweet to this ideal set, we measure the similarity using a method called Euclidean distance. To determine if the content is suitable for display, we set a limit of 0.4. If the distance between the two sets is equal to or lower than this limit, it is considered safe. However, if the distance exceeds the limit, a warning message is shown to indicate that the content could be emotionally harmful. In this paper, we organize the information into several sections. We provide a review of related works and previous research in Sect. 2. In Section 3, we present an overview of our proposed approach. We discuss the results obtained from our approach in Sect. 4. Finally, in Sect. 5, we conclude the paper and outline future work.

2 Literature Review

In this section, we will explore how artificial intelligence (AI) filters can be used for emotion detection in text-based content. Emotion detection involves using AI models to understand the emotions and expressions conveyed in text, which is essential for analyzing social media content.

Over the past ten years, various approaches have been developed for text-based emotion detection. One such method, described by J. Tao in [1], is the keyword-based emotion recognition approach. This method involves analyzing each sentence as a combination of content words or Emotional Function words (EFW), which can be emotional keywords, modifiers, or metaphors. Emotion keywords are assigned specific weights based on six emotion labels from Ekman's emotion model.

Bruyne et al. (2018) created a system to classify emotions in English tweets, as described in [2]. Their approach involved several techniques for preprocessing the text, including tokenization, stemming, lowercasing, and POS-tagging. They then extracted a range of features such as n-grams, lexicon features, and semantic and syntactic features. To address the multi-class multi-label problem, they developed a set of eleven binary classifiers, one for each possible emotion class. The models used the predictions from the previous models as additional features, allowing them to create a multi-label representation of the predictions.

In [3–6], researchers explored a deep learning technique, which is a type of machine learning that uses artificial neural networks to learn complex concepts by breaking them down into simpler ones. To apply this approach, the researchers first preprocessed the dataset and then created an embedding layer where the text data is converted into numerical representations. These numerical representations were then fed into one or more deep neural network layers, depending on the number of emotion labels. The model learned patterns from the data and predicted the labels using classification.

In their work presented in reference [7], Rathnayaka and colleagues introduced a deep learning framework aimed at tackling the challenge of multi-label emotion identification in microblogging. They utilized the Ekphrasis tool for data preprocessing, which performed tasks such as word normalization, tokenization, spell correction, and segmentation. The authors also used GloVe, a pre-trained word embedding algorithm, to extract features from the data. These features were then input into two Bidirectional-Gated recurrent unit layers, and the output of the first Bi-GRU layer was fed to the first attention layer. The two attention layers were then combined and fed to a DNN with a sigmoid activation function for classification. The study used 11 emotion categories to classify emotions. The use of neural network models is being considered as a solution to filter out negative emotions on social media platforms. These models use unique words as input in parse trees to generate synthetic and semantic data, which helps in deriving the composition of emotions. Recurrent neural networks and convolution neural networks are gaining popularity and do not require parse trees to extract features from sentences. Instead, they use word embeddings that already include semantic and synthetic data as inputs.

In reference [9], the authors employed a semi-supervised model for sentence-level sentiment analysis using the recursive automatic coding network (RAN). The RAN generated a vector representation with low dimensions. Reference [9] describes the new matrix-vector recursive neural network (MVRNN) which associates a tree representation of the matrix with each context. Reference [10] describes a collaboration between Recurrent Neural Network (RNN) and Convolutional Neural Network (CNN) architecture for sentiment classification of short contexts. The tree structure is derived from an external parser, and coarse-grained features generated by CNN are utilized in this collaboration. Authors in [12] propose an approach for effective sentiment prediction based on Linguistic Long Short-Term Memory (LSTM) models that incorporates a sentiment lexicon as both highly intensive and negative context, article by Abualigah et al. [12]. (2021) is a comprehensive survey on the use of meta-heuristic optimization algorithms in big data text clustering. It examines the challenges associated with clustering large volumes of textual data and explores the potential of meta-heuristic algorithms, such as genetic algorithms and ant colony optimization, in addressing these challenges. The article reviews recent advancements in the field, discusses the integration of different algorithms, and presents case studies showcasing improved clustering accuracy and efficiency.

Other researchers have explored the use of biometric data to detect emotional states of social media users, as an initial step towards early anxiety detection and developing intervention strategies to counter anxiety. Reference [47] presents a study where biometric data was used to detect emotional states of social media users. Souri et al. [13] developed a personality classification model using machine learning that analyzes user activities on Facebook. They collected data from 100 users via the Facebook API and demonstrated that their method can also recommend friends in Facebook groups.

In addition to sentiment analysis and emotional state detection, some researchers have studied the use of sentiment analysis techniques in group decision-making using social media. Morente-Molinera et al. [18] proposed a method to generate preference relations that can be utilized for group decision-making using sentiment analysis techniques.

Another area of study in sentiment analysis is identifying and categorizing user-generated content in social media. Risch and Krestel [9] proposed a deep learning-based model to identify the aggregation of user-generated content in social media. Their proposed method utilizes a recurrent neural network based on a bidirectional gated recurrent unit, and they augmented the dataset used for model training by using machine translation.

Subramani et al. [11] presented a domestic violence identification system that utilizes deep learning. The dataset used for the proposed system was collected from Facebook, and they used a binary text classification approach to detect whether the content created by a user is critical or uncritical. A domestic violence identification system based on deep learning was introduced in [21], which can categorize multi-class posts into five categories: general, empathy, awareness, personal story, and fundraising. The evaluation of the system was performed using a dataset comprised of user-generated content from Facebook and resulted in a high accuracy rate. Other researchers have utilized sentiment analysis for various applications, such as predicting the outcome of political elections, measuring happiness in a specific region, and analyzing sentiment towards teaching in a classroom setting. Budiharto and Meiliana [19] utilized sentiment analysis to predict the outcome of the Indonesian presidential election, and their method's prediction turned out to be correct. Al Shehhi et al. [22] conducted a study to measure happiness in the United Arab Emirates (UAE) using sentiment analysis techniques on tweets collected from Twitter users in both English and Arabic. Ibrahim et al. [26] presented a model for detecting toxic content using a combination of convolutional neural networks (CNN), bidirectional gated recurrent units (GRU), and bidirectional long short-term memory (LSTM). The model was evaluated using the Wikipedia dataset, and achieved high accuracy rates for predicting toxicity types and classifying content as toxic or non-toxic.

Overall, sentiment analysis has many potential applications in various fields, and researchers continue to explore and develop new techniques and approaches to better understand and analyze user-generated content on social media. In the next section of the article, we will delve into our proposed solution for filtering emotionally harmful content on social media platforms. Our approach is based on the use of Synesketch, a powerful natural language processing tool, and the Euclidean distance measure, which enables us to identify and classify potentially harmful content. We will provide a detailed explanation of how our method works and demonstrate its effectiveness on a dataset of tweets obtained through the Twitter API. This approach has significant potential for a wide range of applications, including sentiment analysis, opinion mining, and social media monitoring. With its ability to identify emotionally charged content and filter out harmful posts, our approach has the potential to make social media a safer and more positive environment for users of all ages.

3 Proposed Approach

Our proposed solution focuses on enhancing the emotional experience of social media users, specifically on Twitter. We utilized the Twitter API to extract user-generated content, which was then analyzed and classified based on six fundamental emotional categories. These categories were defined by Ekman and are illustrated in Fig. 1.

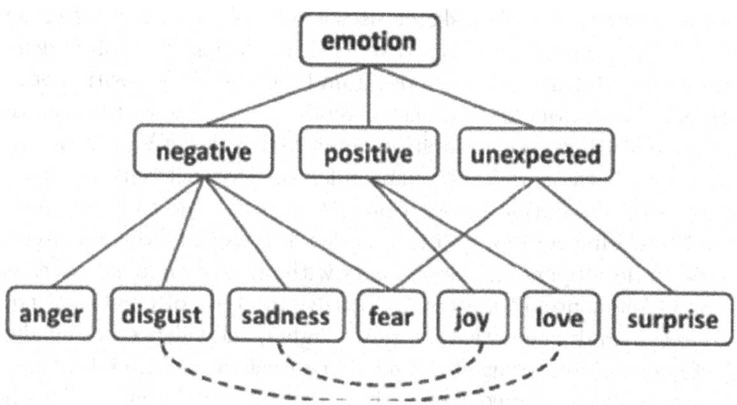

Fig. 1. The schema used in the figure has been obtained from the ontology suggested by Kirk et al. for categorizing the six basic emotions defined by Ekman, as referenced in [44].

To perform the emotion analysis, we used Synesktech software, an open-source tool for textual emotion recognition. After analyzing each post, we output the resulting emotional category data into a JSON file array of emotions. Next, we defined a perfect emotion array with the values of joy and happiness equaling 1 and all other emotions equaling 0. We then calculated the Euclidean distance (a similarity metric) between the emotion array of each tweet content and the perfect emotions array. We then defined a threshold value of 0.4. If the calculated distance was equal to or less than the threshold, we assumed that the content was emotionally safe. However, if the calculated distance exceeded the threshold, we displayed a warning message to the user that the content may be emotionally harmful.

3.1 Data Preprocessing

To start developing our application, we needed to obtain data from social media. We opted to use the Twitter API to obtain the necessary data for our analysis, as it provides access to a vast amount of data from millions of users, making it an ideal source of social media content for analysis. The API offers developers a range of data, including user profiles, tweets, and other metadata, allowing for various analyses such as sentiment analysis, topic modeling, and network analysis. With this data, developers can gain insights into user behavior and trends on the platform.

3.2 Synesketch Tool

According to [44], Synesketch is a software that is freely available on the web, and it is open-source. It is designed to recognize emotions in textual content and visualize them artistically. Synesketch uses algorithms to analyze text sentences for their emotional content in terms of six basic emotions. The software also takes into account the intensity of the emotion and whether it is positive or negative. The recognition technique of Synesketch relies on a sophisticated keyword spotting method that utilizes a combination of heuristic rules, a WordNet-based word lexicon, and an emoticon and abbreviation lexicon. Synesketch was chosen as the software for textual emotion recognition in this study due to its unique features and capabilities. First and foremost, Synesketch is free and open-source, making it accessible to developers and researchers without any financial barriers. Additionally, Synesketch provides a comprehensive analysis of emotional content in text sentences, including emotional types, weights, and valence, which aligns with the project's goal of analyzing social media content for emotional safety. Finally, Synesketch employs a refined keyword spotting method that utilizes heuristic rules, WordNet-based word lexicons, and emoticons and common abbreviations, ensuring accurate and nuanced emotion recognition in a wide range of texts.

3.3 Tweet Content and Sentiment Analysis

To analyze the emotional content of the tweets we collected from the Twitter API, we used Synesketch software, which is a free and open-source tool for textual emotion recognition. The software's algorithms analyze the emotional content of text sentences in terms of emotional types, weights, and valence. Specifically, we focused on the aspect-based classifier of Synesketch, as well as its packages such as WordNet and Lexicon. The software provides us with an emotion array $X[i, j]$ for each tweet, with each entry associated with six emotional weights corresponding to the six basic emotional categories defined by

Ekman. We chose to use Ekman's model as it is widely used in the field of emotion classification. After obtaining the JSON array of emotions for each tweet from Synesketch, we proceeded to analyze the emotional safety of the content in the next step.

3.4 Tweet Content and Emotion Analysis

We have created a perfect emotion array for all tweets in this step, where the values for joy and happiness are set to 1, and all other emotions are set to 0. This perfect emotion array is a 2-dimensional matrix represented as Y, with each row representing a sample and each column representing joy, happiness, and other emotions respectively. The value of $Y[i, j]$ represents the presence of joy and happiness (j) and the absence of other emotions (i), with a value of 1 indicating the presence and 0 indicating the absence.

Emotions Evaluation. To classify the emotion array obtained from the given tweet in the dataset, we will calculate the Euclidean distance between the tweet's emotion array in the JSON output $X[i, j]$ and the perfect emotion array $Y[i, j]$ for all tweets in the dataset. The Euclidean distance is a measure of the distance between two points in a multi-dimensional space, where each emotion category represents a dimension. This will allow us to quantify how close or far each tweet's emotion array is from the perfect emotion array. We will then use the distance value to classify each tweet as either having a positive or negative sentiment, based on which emotion category it is closest to.

Euclidean Distance. The Euclidean distance is a widely used measure of similarity or dissimilarity between two vectors in a multi-dimensional space. It calculates the distance between two points X,Y by computing the square root of the sum of the squared differences between their corresponding coordinates. In other words, it measures the straight-line distance between two points in space (The entirety of this information can be condensed into a single equation, which can be found by referring to Eq. 1).

$$\text{Euclidean distance}(x, y) = \sqrt{\sum_{i=1}^{d}(x_i - y_i)^2 + \sum_{j=1}^{d}(x_j - y_j)^2} \tag{1}$$

In the context of text classification and clustering, the Euclidean distance is used to calculate the similarity or dissimilarity between text documents based on the frequency of their words or the distribution of their features (please refer to the citation [45] for comprehensive information on the subject). It has been found to be effective in this context, as it can capture the geometric relationship between text documents in a multi-dimensional space. Additionally, it is a commonly used distance metric in various fields, and its inverse form can be used as a similarity function. We have set a threshold of 0.4 to classify tweets as emotionally safe or harmful. This threshold value was chosen based on two reasons. Firstly, the smaller the Euclidean distance between the tweet's emotion array and the perfect emotion array, the greater the similarity between them. Secondly, after conducting experiments and observing a focus group, we found that 0.4 was the most appropriate threshold value for our analysis.

- In addition to the reasons mentioned, setting a threshold of 0.4 can also help reduce the risk of false positives and false negatives. False positives occur when a tweet is classified as harmful when it is actually safe, while false negatives occur when a tweet is classified as safe when it is actually harmful. By setting a threshold, we can reduce the likelihood of these errors and increase the accuracy of our classification.
- It's worth noting that the choice of threshold value can vary depending on the specific dataset and context of the analysis. In some cases, a higher or lower threshold value may be more appropriate for the task at hand. It's important to carefully consider the trade-offs between precision and recall when choosing a threshold, as well as any ethical or legal implications of the classification.
- When setting a threshold, it's also important to keep in mind the distribution of the data. For example, if the dataset contains a disproportionate number of tweets with a certain emotional content, this can skew the results and affect the optimal threshold value. In such cases, techniques such as resampling or adjusting the threshold based on the prevalence of different emotional categories may be necessary.
- Another factor to consider when setting a threshold is the consequences of misclassification. For example, if the task is to identify harmful tweets that could potentially cause harm to individuals or communities, setting a higher threshold may be more appropriate to reduce the risk of missing such tweets. On the other hand, if the task is to identify tweets with low emotional content that are unlikely to have any impact, setting a lower threshold may be more appropriate to avoid false positives.

Once we compute the Euclidean distance between each tweet in the dataset and the perfect emotion array, we can compare it with the threshold value of 0.4. If the distance is less than or equal to 0.4, we can classify the tweet as emotionally safe, meaning it has a positive or neutral emotional content. On the other hand, if the distance is greater than 0.4, we assume that the tweet has a negative emotional content and could be emotionally harmful to the user.

By setting this threshold value of 0.4, we can effectively differentiate between emotionally safe and harmful content. If the threshold value is set too low, we may mistakenly classify emotionally harmful tweets as safe, leading to potential harm to the user. On the other hand, if the threshold value is set too high, we may unnecessarily classify emotionally safe tweets as harmful, leading to inaccurate results and unnecessary warnings.

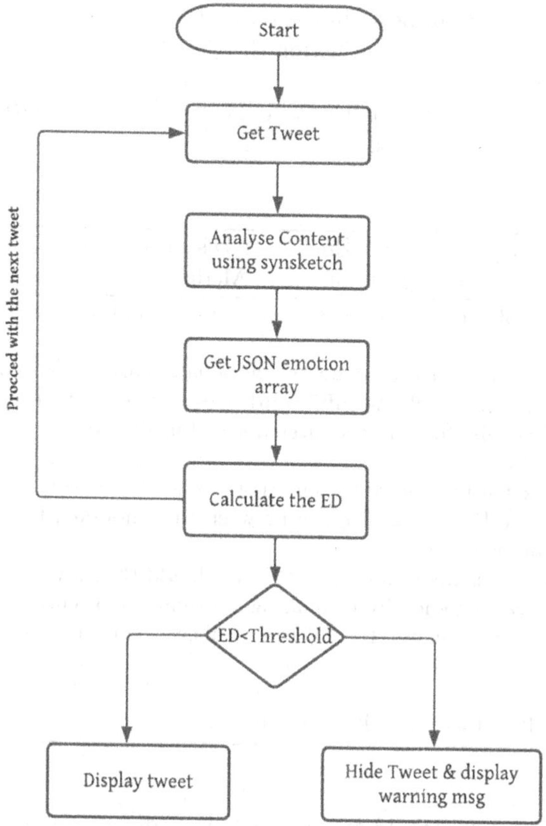

Fig. 2. A diagram outlining the suggested methodology.

Figure 2 provides a detailed overview of our proposed approach. We developed the application by utilizing the Nodejs and Angular framework and made it open-source by uploading the source code and installation instructions on Github. More information can be found in reference [48].

The proposed method comprises the following steps: (These steps are typically explained in Algorithm 1):

1. Collect the dataset of social media content, such as tweets, through the Twitter API.
2. Preprocess the data by removing stop words, punctuation, and other unnecessary characters.
3. Use the Synesketch library to extract emotion-related features, such as valence, arousal, and dominance, from the preprocessed text.
4. Calculate the Euclidean distance between the extracted features of each post and a set of predefined thresholds for harmful emotions.
5. If the distance is above a certain threshold, label the post as emotionally harmful and filter it out.

6. Repeat steps 3-5 for all posts in the dataset.
7. Fine-tune the approach by adjusting the threshold values based on the evaluation results.
8. Apply the approach to monitor and filter emotionally harmful content in real-time social media feeds.

Algorithm 1. Synesketch and Euclidean Distance-Based Filtering Algorithm for Mitigating Negative Impacts of Social Media

---

Input: A dataset of social media posts (e.g., tweets) obtained through the Twitter API
Output: A filtered dataset that removes emotionally harmful content

```
Define a list of emotionally harmful words and phrases to be used as a filter.
Create an empty list to store the filtered social media posts.
while L ≠ ∅ do
    Use Synesketch to analyze the emotional tone of the post.
    Calculate the Euclidean distance between the emotional tone of the post and
  the perfect emotions array.
    If the distance is above a certain threshold, add the post to the filtered list.
    Check for convergence by comparing the number of clusters in the previous
  iteration to the current iteration. If the number of clusters has not changed, stop
  the algorithm.
end while
Output the filtered list of social media posts.
```

Note that the exact threshold for the Euclidean distance may vary depending on the specific dataset and context. Additionally, this algorithm can be further optimized and customized with additional features and techniques, such as using machine learning algorithms for emotion detection and classification.

4 Results and Discussion

The results presented in Table 1 demonstrate that the proposed approach is effective in accurately detecting the primary emotions associated with the tweets. The first example showed the tool's ability to detect disgust with a score of 0.15 and classify it as harmful. In the second example, the tool identified joy with a score of 0.8, and the tweet was classified as safe. The third example further confirmed the tool's ability to detect fear, with a score of 1.1, and classify the tweet as safe. Overall, these results suggest that the proposed technique is a valuable resource for identifying emotions in social media content and can contribute to improving the emotional quality of social media platforms.

However, while building the application, we encountered several limitations that made the task even more challenging. One such limitation is related to the language and intentions of the tweets. The meaning of a tweet can vary depending on the language used and the intention of the author. This variation in meaning makes it difficult to accurately classify the emotional content of the tweet. Additionally, social media platforms are not limited to text-based content only. There are various forms of media such as photos and videos that can also contain emotionally harmful content. This means that our approach needs to be expanded beyond text-based analysis to incorporate other forms of media. Moreover, there are some threats to the validity of our approach, primarily due to inherent differences between the compared tools. For instance, calculating the Euclidean distance could have resulted in inconsistencies, and Synesketch does not treat neutral as a special type, which required us to determine a threshold of 0.4. Similarly, the emotional model used by Neviarouskaya et al. had certain inconsistencies. In our experiments, we found that Synesketch made errors when additional context was required to interpret the emotional content accurately. This highlights the need to include word sense disambiguation in future research. We also found errors in cases where the correct emotion was present in Synesketch's output JSON file but was not the dominant one based on its weight. Further research is required to determine the extent to which the difference between the dataset and the second dataset's emotion affects Synesketch's final accuracy. The vocabulary and style used in fairy tales were significantly different from contemporary language use, resulting in errors. Although expanding our lexicon might help reduce these errors, it is uncertain whether this approach will be effective in contexts other than fairy tales. Table 1 below provides an example of our classification based on the Euclidean distance.

Table 1. Examples of Emotional classification based on ED.

Tweet	Emotion	Synesketch's Score	ED	Classification
FRT @NerdyWonka: Hilary is calm, measured, has the facts on her side. Trump is turning red and frothing at the mouth like a twitter troll	disgust	0.15	0.85	harmful
RT @HillaryClinton: RT this if you're proud to be standing with Hillary tonight. #debatenight https://t.co/91tBmKxVMs	joy	0.8	0.2	safe
@realDonaldTrump shut up and let her speak you 3 year old brat	anger	0.1	0.9	Harmful
RT @NubianAwakening: Hillary invited Marc Cuban to the debates as we all know; unfortunately, not everyone could make it. RIP #SethRich #deb	sadness	0.25	0.75	Harmful
RT @KellyannePolls:#Polls showing @realDonaldTrump surging, @hillaryclinton #slipping, have HER camp on defense/lowering expectations,	surprise	-0.1	1.1	Harmful
RT @HeidiL_RN: Hillary Clinton policy created ISIS. She is dangerous AF. Plus she is a huge LIAR #debatenight https://t.co/NdYJgBL8R4,	fear	-0.1	1.1	safe

5 Conclusion

In conclusion, we presented an approach for text emotion detection using Synesketch and the Euclidean distance measure. We demonstrated the application of our approach on a dataset of fairy tale texts and achieved promising results. Our approach showed that Synesketch is a reliable tool for emotion detection, although there are some limitations and potential sources of error that need to be addressed. Additionally, our approach can be further extended to other domains beyond fairy tales, provided that additional lexicons are included to handle the diversity of language and contexts. Overall, our approach can be useful for various applications in natural language processing, such as sentiment analysis, opinion mining, and social media monitoring. We hope that our work will contribute to advancing the field of text emotion detection and inspire further research in this area.

In terms of future works, several avenues can be explored to further enhance the proposed approach for filtering emotionally harmful content in social media. Firstly, expanding the lexicons used in Synesketch to cover a wider range of emotions and linguistic nuances would improve the accuracy and comprehensiveness of emotion detection. Additionally, incorporating machine learning techniques, such as deep learning models, could enhance the performance of the emotion detection system by leveraging the power of neural networks to capture complex patterns in textual data. Moreover, conducting extensive evaluations and comparisons with existing approaches on diverse datasets from different social media platforms would provide a more comprehensive understanding of the effectiveness and generalizability of the proposed solution. Furthermore, considering the evolving nature of social media and the emergence of new platforms, it would be valuable to adapt and optimize the approach to handle novel challenges and variations in user-generated content. Lastly, investigating the ethical implications and potential biases in content filtering algorithms is crucial to ensure fair and responsible use of such systems. By addressing these directions, future research can contribute to the continued development and improvement of emotion detection techniques in the context of social media.

References

1. Tao, J.: Context-based emotion detection from text input. In: Proceedings of the 8th International Conference on Spoken Language Processing (ICSLP), pp. 1337–1340 (2004). Jeju Island, Korea, 4–8 October 2004
2. Bruyne, L., de clercq, O., Hoste, V.: LT3 at SemEval-2018 Task 1: a classifier chain to detect emotions in tweets, pp. 123–127 (2018). https://doi.org/10.18653/v1/S18-1016
3. Santamaria-Granados, L., Munoz-Organero, M., Ramirez-Gonzalez, G., Abdulhay, E., Arunkumar, N.J.I.A.: Using deep convolutional neural network for emotion detection on a physiological signals dataset (AMIGOS). IEEE Access **7**, 57–67 (2018)
4. Gjoreski, M., Gjoreski, H., Lustrek, M., Gams, M.: Deep affect recognition from R-R intervals, pp. 754–762 (2017). https://doi.org/10.1145/3123024.3125608

5. Tripathi, S., Acharya, S., Sharma, R., Mittal, S., Bhattacharya, S.: Using deep and convolutional neural networks for accurate emotion classification on DEAP data. In: Proceedings of the AAAI Conference on Artificial Intelligence, vol. 31, no. 2, pp. 4746–4752 (2017)
6. Drouin, M., Kaiser, D.H., Miller, D.A.: Phantom vibrations among undergraduates: prevalence and associated psychological characteristics. Comput. Hum. Behav. **28**, 1490–1496 (2012)
7. Rathnayaka, P., et al.: Gated recurrent neural network approach for multilabel emotion detection in microblogs (2019). arXiv preprint arXiv:1907.07653
8. Morente-Molinera, J.A., Kou, G., Samuylov, K., Ureña, R., Herrera-Viedma, E.: Carrying out consensual group decision making processes under social networks using sentiment analysis over comparative expressions. Knowl. Based Syst. **165**, 335–345 (2019)
9. Risch, J., Krestel, R.: Aggression identification using deep learning and data augmentation. In: Proceedings of the First Workshop on Trolling, Aggression and Cyberbullying (TRAC-2018), Santa Fe, NM, USA, pp. 150–158 (2018)
10. Subramani, S., Wang, H., Vu, H.Q., Li, G.: Domestic violence crisis identification from Facebook posts based on deep learning. IEEE Access **6**, 54075–54085 (2018)
11. Subramani, S., Michalska, S., Wang, H., Du, J., Zhang, Y., Shakeel, H.: Deep learning for multi-class identification from domestic violence online posts. IEEE Access **7**, 46210–46224 (2019)
12. Abualigah, L., et al.: Advances in meta-heuristic optimization algorithms in big data text clustering. Electronics **10**, 101 (2021)
13. Abualigah, L.M.Q.: Feature Selection and Enhanced Krill Herd Algorithm for Text Document Clustering. SCI, vol. 816. Springer, Cham (2019). https://doi.org/10.1007/978-3-030-10674-4
14. Mazari, A.C., Djeffal, A.: Sentiment analysis of Algerian dialect using machine learning and deep learning with word2vec. Informatica **46**, 67–78 (2022). https://doi.org/10.31449/inf.v46i6.3340
15. Shaha, A.-O., Amal, A.-R.: A review and comparative analysis of sentiment analysis techniques. Informatica **46**, 33–44 (2022). https://doi.org/10.31449/inf.v46i6.3991
16. Mountaga, D., Chayma, F., Hatem, H.: Bambara language dataset for sentiment analysis. Conference paper ICLR (2021)
17. Leung, C.W.K.: Sentiment analysis of product reviews. In: Encyclopedia of Data Warehousing and Mining, pp. 1794–1799, Second Edition. IGI Global (2009)
18. Ahmad, S., Asghar, M.Z., Alotaibi, F.M., Awan, I.: Detection and classification of social media-based extremist affiliations using sentiment analysis techniques. Hum. Centric Comput. Inf. Sci. **9**, 24 (2019)
19. Budiharto, W., Meiliana, M.: Prediction and analysis of Indonesia Presidential election from Twitter using sentiment analysis. J. Big Data **5**, 51 (2018)
20. Aniruddha Prabhu, B.P., Ashwini, B.P., Anwar Khan, T., Das, A.: Predicting election result with sentimental analysis using twitter data for candidate selection. In: Saini, H.S., Sayal, R., Govardhan, A., Buyya, R. (eds.) Innovations in Computer Science and Engineering. LNNS, vol. 74, pp. 49–55. Springer, Singapore (2019). https://doi.org/10.1007/978-981-13-7082-3_7
21. Cury, R.M.: Oscillation of tweet sentiments in the election of João Doria Jr. for Mayor. J. Big Data **6**, 42 (2019)
22. Al Shehhi, A., Thomas, J., Welsch, R., Grey, I., Aung, Z.: Arabia Felix 2.0: a cross-linguistic Twitter analysis of happiness patterns in the United Arab Emirates. J. Big Data **6**, 33 (2019)

23. Pong-inwong, C., Songpan, W.: Sentiment analysis in teaching evaluations using sentiment phrase pattern matching (SPPM) based on association mining. Int. J. Mach. Learn. Cybern. **10**, 2177–2186 (2018)
24. Aloufi, S., El Saddik, A.: Sentiment identification in football-specific tweets. IEEE Access **6**, 78609–78621 (2018)
25. Arias, M., Arratia, A., Xuriguera, R.: Forecasting with Twitter data. ACM Trans. Intell. Syst. Technol. (TIST) **5**, 8 (2013)
26. Ibrahim, M., Torki, M., El-Makky, N.: Imbalanced toxic comments classification using data augmentation and deep learning. In: 2018 17th IEEE International Conference on Machine Learning and Applications (ICMLA), pp. 875–878. IEEE (2018)
27. Abualigah, L., Diabat, A., Mirjalili, S., Abd Elaziz, M., Gandomi, A.H.: The arithmetic optimization algorithm. Comput. Methods Appl. Mech. Eng. **376**, 113609 (2021)
28. Abualigah, L., Yousri, D., Abd Elaziz, M., Ewees, A.A., Al-qaness, M., Gandomi, A.H.: Aquila Optimizer: a novel meta-heuristic optimization Algorithm. Comput. Ind. Eng. **157**, 107250 (2021)
29. Ringsquandl, M., Petkovic, D.: Analyzing political sentiment on Twitter. In: Proceedings of the 2013 AAAI Spring Symposium Series, pp. 25–27. Stanford, CA, USA, (2013)
30. Kušen, E., Strembeck, M.: Politics, sentiments, and misinformation: an analysis of the Twitter discussion on the 2016 Austrian presidential elections. Online Soc. Netw. Media **5**, 37–50 (2018)
31. Haselmayer, M., Jenny, M.: Sentiment analysis of political communication: combining a dictionary approach with Crowdcoding. Qual. Quant. **51**, 2623–2646 (2017)
32. Rathan, M., Hulipalled, V.R., Venugopal, K., Patnaik, L.: Consumer insight mining: aspect based Twitter opinion mining of mobile phone reviews. Appl. Soft Comput. **68**, 765–773 (2018)
33. Anastasia, S., Budi, I.: Twitter sentiment analysis of online transportation service providers. In: Proceedings of the 2016 International Conference on Advanced Computer Science and Information Systems (ICACSIS), pp. 359–365, 15–16 October 2016. Malang, Indonesia (2016)
34. Pagolu, V.S., Reddy, K.N., Panda, G., Majhi, B.: Sentiment analysis of Twitter data for predicting stock market movements. In: Proceedings of the 2016 International Conference on Signal Processing, Communication, Power and Embedded System (SCOPES), pp. 1345–1350, 3–5 October 2016. Paralakhemundi, India (2016)
35. Alomari, E., Mehmood, R.: Analysis of tweets in Arabic language for detection of road traffic conditions. In: Mehmood, R., Bhaduri, B., Katib, I., Chlamtac, I. (eds.) SCITA 2017. LNICST, vol. 224, pp. 98–110. Springer, Cham (2018). https://doi.org/10.1007/978-3-319-94180-6_12
36. Al-qaness, M.A., Abd Elaziz, M., Hawbani, A., Abbasi, A.A., Zhao, L., Kim, S.: Real-time traffic congestion analysis based on collected tweets. In: Proceedings of the 2019 IEEE International Conferences on Ubiquitous Computing & Communications (IUCC) and Data Science and Computational Intelligence (DSCI) and Smart Computing, Networking and Services (SmartCNS), pp. 1–8, 21–23 October 2019. Shenyang, China (2019)
37. Frank, M.R., Mitchell, L., Dodds, P.S., Danforth, C.M.: Happiness and the patterns of life: a study of geolocated tweets. Sci. Rep. **3**, 2625 (2013)
38. Giachanou, A., Crestani, F.: Like it or not: a survey of twitter sentiment analysis methods. ACM Comput. Surv. (CSUR) **49**, 1–41 (2016)

39. Devlin, J., Chang, M.W., Lee, K., Toutanova, K.: Bert: pre-training of deep bidirectional transformers for language understanding. arXiv:1810.04805 (2018)
40. Wulczyn, E., Thain, N., Dixon, L.: Ex machina: personal attacks seen at scale. In: Proceedings of the 26th International Conference on World Wide Web. International World Wide Web Conferences Steering Committee, pp. 1391–1399, 3–7 May 2017. Perth, Australia (2017)
41. Saeed, H.H., Shahzad, K., Kamiran, F.: Overlapping toxic sentiment classification using deep neural architectures. IEEE Int. Conf. Data Min. Workshops (ICDMW) **2018**, 1361–1366 (2018). https://doi.org/10.1109/ICDMW.2018.00193
42. Ekman, P.: Facial expression and emotion. Am. Psychologist **48**, 384–392 (1993)
43. Krcadinac, U., Pasquier, P., Jovanovic, J., Devedzic, V.: Synesketch: an open source library for sentence-based emotion recognition. IEEE Trans. Affect. Comput. **4**, 312–325 (2013). https://doi.org/10.1109/T-AFFC.2013.18
44. Roberts, K., Roach, M., Johnson, J., Guthrie, J., Harabagiu, S.: EmpaTweet: annotating and detecting emotions on Twitter. In: Proceedings Language Resources and Evaluation Conference (2012)
45. Maher, K., Joshi, M.S.: Effectiveness of different similarity measures for text classification and clustering. Int. J. Comput. Sci. Inf. Technol. **7**, 1715–1720 (2016)
46. Thomas, B., Vinod, P., Dhanya, K.A.: Multiclass emotion extraction from sentences. Int. J. Sci. Eng. Res. **5**(2), 12 (2014)
47. Sam, E., Mo, Z.: Using biometric data to detect the emotional state of social media user as a first step towards early anxiety detection and intervention. J. Student Acad. Res. **2**(1) 2021
48. https://github.com/benrouba/Emotional-Sentiment-Analysis-of-Social-Media-content-for-Mental-Health-Safety
49. Pantic, I.: Online social networking and mental health. Cyberpsychol. Behav. Soc. Netw. **17**(10), 652–657 (2014). https://doi.org/10.1089/cyber.2014.0070

SocialNER: A Training Dataset for Named Entity Recognition in Short Social Media Texts

Adel Belbekri(✉) and Fouzia Benchikha

LIRE Laboratory, Abdelhamid Mehri Constantine 2 University, Constantine, Algeria
{adel.belbekri,fouzia.benchikha}@univ-constantine2.dz

Abstract. Named entity recognition (NER) is one of the many natural language processing tasks in which deep learning has demonstrated superior performance. The effectiveness of deep learning models strongly depends on the quality of the training data. However, the training phase requires large amounts of labeled data. This paper presents SocialNer, a training dataset for deep learning models intended for the detection of named entities in short texts of social networks. SocialNer is constructed by merging information extracted from different challenge datasets of other natural language processing tasks (entity linking, question answering, information retrieval, etc.); and enriched with entity type, part of speech tag, and chunk tag. A well-tailored annotation procedure is adopted to ensure the quality of the dataset and an analysis of the constructed dataset is presented.

Keywords: Text analysis · NER · deep leaning · big data · social network

1 Introduction

Access to digital information and expressing ourselves through a blog or sharing videos on a social network have become common activities. This is made possible by the continuous development of information technologies and networks which provide ever easier and faster access to information. As a result, the huge stored information grows exponentially [1], this is Big Data. The latter refers to a massive amount of data that can't be managed by conventional database management or information management software. Every day, approximately 2.5 trillion bytes of data are created[1]. Various formats are utilized to impart this information. This includes, for example, video, speech, and writing. In this heterogeneous environment, the challenge is therefore to facilitate rapid and relevant access to the desired information.

On the other hand, one of the most popular tasks in data science[2] today is the processing of information presented in text form. Precisely, representing

[1] https://www.lebigdata.fr/definition-big-data.

[2] Combining knowledge of programming, mathematics, and statistics to extract meaningful insights from data.

H. Drias et al. (Eds.): AID 2022, CCIS 1852, pp. 278–289, 2023.
https://doi.org/10.1007/978-981-99-4484-2_21

text in the form of mathematical equations, formulas, paradigms, and models to understand the semantics (content) of the text for its ulterior processing: classification, fragmentation, etc. In general, all of these practices are brought together in the field of natural language processing (NLP). Several NLP applications are interested in developing methods and tools to meet this challenge, such as information extraction, information retrieval, indexing, automatic translation, spelling or grammar checking, text classification, summary production, etc. In these different domains, the task of Named Entity Recognition (NER) plays a transversal role.

The named entity concept appeared in the mid-1990s as a sub-task of information retrieval. It consists of identifying textual objects such as the names of people, organizations, and places. Over the years, research has focused on increasingly complex issues such as disambiguation and enriched annotation, but also their recognition in different contexts. The deployment of the Internet has led to a deep change in information sources. Messages published on social networks such as Twitter and Facebook as well as video and audio are gaining more and more ground over traditional sources of information such as journalistic articles published by news agencies. The processing of named entities now comes up against new difficulties inherent in the characteristics of the modality or the type of text to be processed [1].

One reason for the success of deep learning can be attributed to the availability of large-scale labeled data [19]. However, the available datasets suffer either in data quality or data quantity. Few datasets are available that satisfy the studied criteria, i.e. (1) datasets for short texts, indeed, the majority of available datasets deal with long texts. (2) datasets correctly annotated with named entities and their types (quality). (3) datasets that are rich enough (quantity) to satisfy the requirements of large-scale models.

The present study concerns the creation of a training dataset, named SocialNer, that satisfies both the quantity and quality of data. Multiple challenge datasets from other NLP tasks (entity linking, question answering, information retrieval, etc.) are merged and the annotation is enriched by adding automatically extracted information about words i.e. part of speech tag (pos-tag) and types retrieved from DBpedia. The latter is a knowledge graph that extracts structured information represented in Resource Description Framework (RDF) from Wikipedia. The aim is to construct a large-scale labeled training dataset for named entity recognition in short texts. The utilization of Deep Learning based models for analyzing social media texts can be enhanced through the implementation of this training dataset.

This paper is structured as follows: Sect. 2 presents the fundamental concepts. Existing studies are reviewed and analyzed in Sect. 3. Section 4 presents the dataset construction procedure. Finally, Sect. 5 concludes the paper and shows some perspectives.

2 Background

2.1 Deep Learning

Deep Learning Tools for discovering complex motifs from large sequence data sets. A powerful type of machine learning that enables computers to solve perceptual problems, such as speech and image recognition. Deep learning methods, such as deep artificial neural networks, use multiple processing layers to discover patterns and structures in extremely large data sets. The higher the level, the more abstract the taught concepts [5].

2.2 Dataset

In deep learning, a dataset is a collection of data pieces that can be treated by a computer as a single unit for analytic and prediction purposes. The collected data should be made uniform and understandable for a machine. Therefore, after collecting the data, it's important to preprocess it by cleaning and completing it, as well as annotating the data by adding meaningful tags readable by a computer.

2.3 Named Entity Recognition

A named entity is a word or phrase that identifies an entity, a real-world object, such as a person, location, organization, etc. that can be identified by a proper name. NER is the identification and categorization of named entities into predefined categories [6]. Formally, given a sequence of tokens $s = (w_1, w_2, ..., w_N)$, NER identifies a list of tuples (I_s, I_e, t), the named entities mentioned in s. $I_s \in [1, N]$ is the start index and $I_e \in [1, N]$ is the end index of a named entity mention; t is the entity type from a predefined category set.

2.4 Part of Speech Tag

Part-of-speech (POS) According to the definition of the word and its context, tagging is a common NLP method that involves categorizing words in a text in accordance with a certain part of speech (nouns, verbs, adjectives, adverbs, etc.). The lexical terms' distinctive grammatical arrangements inside a phrase or text are described by part-of-speech tags [17].

2.5 Chunk Tag

Chunk tag In natural language, chunks are groups of higher-order units with distinct grammatical meanings (noun or phrase groups, verb groups, etc.). Extracting phrases (chunks) from unstructured text is the procedure of chunking. Instead of using a single word that may not accurately convey the meaning of the text, a phrase or chunk is employed [18].

3 Related Work

The importance of datasets for machine learning[3] research has been largely proven [4]. According to Halevy et al. [2], datasets are the limiting factor for algorithmic development and scientific progress. The lack of a substantial, diverse, and high-quality annotated corpus is one of the primary obstacles impeding the development of methods and comparative evaluation of named entity recognition in social media.

Derczynski et al. [3] introduce the Broad Twitter Corpus (BTC), a sample of Twitter users from various regions, time periods, and user profiles. The gold-standard named entity annotations are created by a combination of NLP specialists and crowd employees, allowing them to leverage crowd recall without sacrificing quality. They also measure the entity drift observed in their dataset or the variation in entity representation over time. The corpus is made publicly available, including the original text and intermediate annotations.

Singh et al. [7] provide a corpus for NER in CodeMixed Hindi-English. The created corpus of code-mixed tweets contains tweets from the last eight years on topics such as Indian subcontinent politics, social events, and sports. The messages were extracted from Twitter using the Twitter Python API3, which utilizes Twitter's advanced search function. Using specified hashtags, tweets are mined into a JSON format containing all tweet-related information, including timestamps, URLs, text, users, replies, etc. The annotation of the Dataset for NE keywords in tweets was performed by two human annotators with linguistic backgrounds and Hindi and English proficiency.

Jiang et al. [8] Tweebank-NER is a NER corpus based on Tweebank V2 (TB2)[4]. The authors first annotate named entities in TB2 using Amazon Mechanical Turk and measure the quality of their annotations[5]. They release the dataset and make the models available for use "off-the-shelf" in future Tweet NLP research.

The same problem is observed. These datasets suffer from the low quantity of data due to manual human annotation that guarantees the quality of the annotation. However, when this quantity begins to be important, the huge and colossal work of annotation becomes more and more difficult to accomplish. In response, a training dataset is constructed for named entity recognition in short social media text in an automated manner. Annotated datasets, intended to evaluate other NLP challenges, are exploited and enriched to be suitable for named entity recognition.

4 Dataset Construction

Named entity recognition seeks to identify named entities mentioned in unstructured text. In addition, to identifying the mentioned entity, it must also be classified into pre-defined categories such as person names, organizations, locations, etc.

[3] (ML) is seen as a part of artificial intelligence algorithms to build a model based on sample data.

[4] https://paperswithcode.com/dataset/tweebank.

[5] https://www.clips.uantwerpen.be/conll2003/ner/.

Figure 1 explains the process of the creation of the dataset. The above steps are followed:

- Existing datasets are exploited to extract relevant information for the NER task.
- The extracted information is enriched so that it corresponds to a NER dataset, i.e. it contains the named entity but also its type, chunk-tag, and pos-tag.
- The datasets are merged and organized in the CoNLL-2003 format.

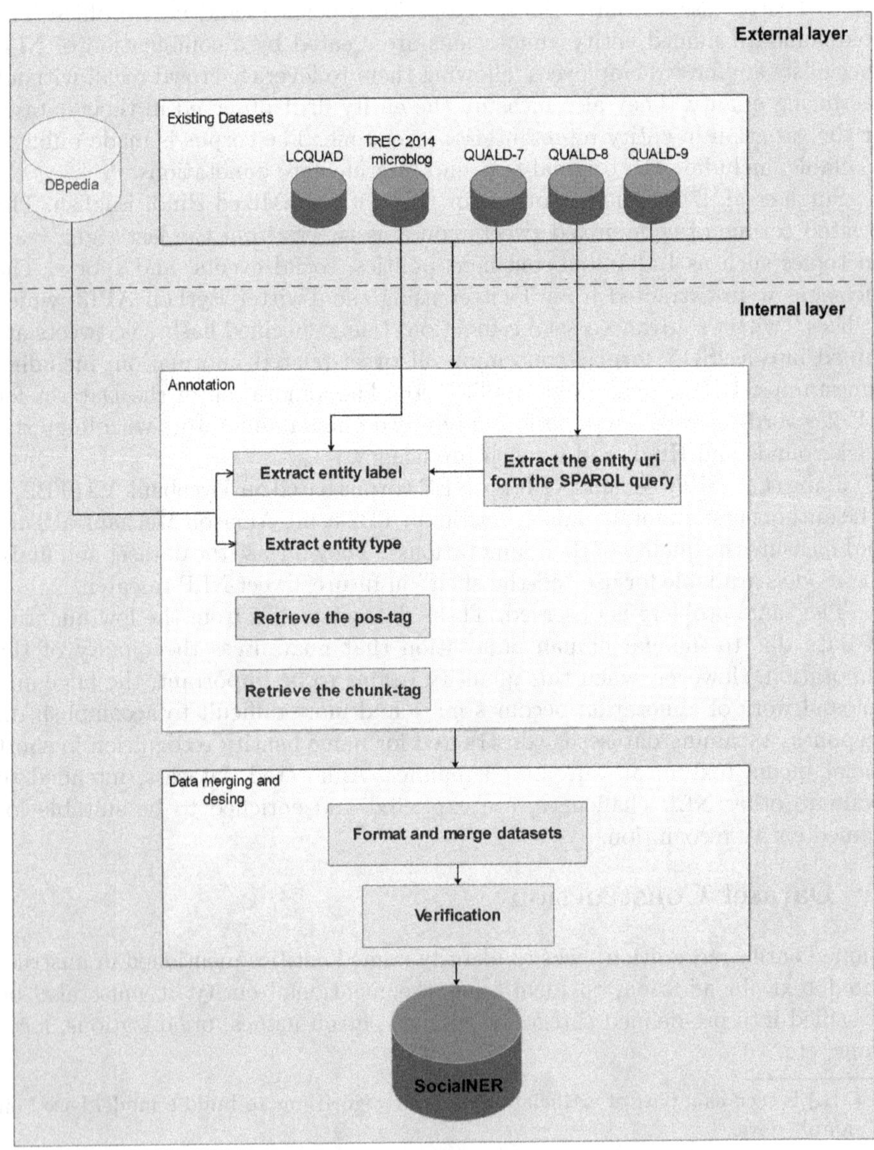

Fig. 1. The data set creation process

4.1 Data Extraction

A training dataset is generated by extracting interesting information for the NER task from several well-known datasets. The selected datasets are specifically designed to evaluate NLP challenge tasks, with NER being a critical sub-task that strongly influences the results. The datasets utilized in this study include LC-QuAD, QALD-7, QALD-8, QALD-9, and TREC 2014 microblog. Although these datasets are annotated with information for evaluating NLP tasks such as question-answering systems and information retrieval, they also contain pertinent information that can be leveraged for the NER task. Notably, the texts in these datasets are short and informal.

Data Sources

- LC-QUAD LC-QuAD is a large question-answering dataset with 5000 questions and its corresponding SPARQL query. The target knowledge base is DBpedia [13]. The SPARQL query is a formal translation of the natural language that retrieves the answer from DBpedia.
  The dataset is in JSON format, each record contains the following information:
  - Question: The text corresponding to the question
  - SerialNumber: the question number in the dataset
  - Sparql_query: The SPARQL query that retrieves the answer to the question
  - Id: the question identifier
  - Entity mapping: information about the named entity
    * "label": the token referring to the named entity
    * "uri": the URI[6] of the named entity on DBpedia
  - Predicate mapping
    * "label": the token referring to predicates
    * "uri": the corresponding predicates in DBpedia

  In this dataset, the question, the label, and the URI of the named entity are extracted.
- QALD-7 Task 3 Large-Scale Question Answering over RDF The QALD-7 is a large-scale test dataset. The training set consists of 100 questions. The test set of 2M questions is generated by an algorithm deriving new questions from the training set by varying both the query desire and the form of the natural language expression. Questions are annotated with SPARQL queries and answers [9]. This dataset is in CSV format. The question and the SPARQL query (to retrieve the named entity URI) are exploited.
- QALD-8 and QALD-9 The core task of QALD is to retrieve answers from an RDF data repository of a natural language question. The training data consists of 219 questions for QALD-8 and 408 for QALD-9 and the testing dataset contains 42 questions for QALD-8 and 150 questions for QALD-9. The questions are available in eight different languages. For our goal, only questions

[6] Uniform Resource Identifier.

in English are extracted. Each question is annotated with a SPARQL query and answers [12]. These datasets are formatted as shown in Listing 1.1. As for the QALD-7 dataset, the question and the named entity (extracted from the SPARQL query) are exploited.

```
{
    "id" : "2",
    "answertype" : "resource",
    "aggregation" : false,
    "onlydbo" : true,
    "hybrid" : false,
    {
      "language" : "en",
      "string" : "Who developed Skype?",
      "keywords" : "develop, Skype"
    } ],
    "query" : {
      "sparql" : "PREFIX dbo: <http://dbpedia.org/
   ontology/> PREFIX res: <http://dbpedia.org/
   resource/> PREFIX rdfs: <http://www.w3.org/2000/0
   1/rdf-schema#> SELECT DISTINCT ?uri WHERE { res:
   Skype dbo:developer ?uri. }"
    }
}
```

Listing 1.1. QALD-8 and QALD-9 examples

– TREC 2014 Microblog: The Text REtrieval Conference (TREC) is a test collection designed to evaluate text retrieval. The TREC 2014 Microblog[7] annotated by BOUARROUDJ et al. in [14] consists of 55 tweet texts. Listing 1.2 illustrates the dataset. The short text in "query" and the URI of the named entity in "query_annotation" are exploited.

```
{
  "num": "Number: MB171",
  "query": "Ron Weasley birthday",
  "querytime": "Sat Mar 02 10:43:45 EST 2013",
  "querytweettime": 307878904759201800,
  "query_annotation": ["http://dbpedia.org/resource/
   Ron_Weasley"]
}
```

Listing 1.2. TREC 2014 Microblog example

[7] https://trec.nist.gov/data/microblog2014.html.

4.2 Annotation

Entity Extraction from SPARQL Queries. The source code published by [16] is used. This code processes the SPARQL query to retrieve the URI of the named entity. This step is used with QALD datasets which are annotated with SPARQL queries corresponding to the questions.

Entity Label Extraction. Listing 1.3 details the SPARQL query used to retrieve the entity label.

```
PREFIX rdfs : <http://www.w3.org/2000/01/rdf-schema#>

SELECT * WHERE
{
    <http://dbpedia.org/resource/Algeria> rdfs:label ?y
   FILTER (lang(?y) = "en")
}
```

Listing 1.3. SPARQL query to retrieve the label of the entity

Entity Type Extraction. The SPARQL code in Listing 1.4 is used to retrieving the named entity type using the URI. The types retrieved from DBpedia are used to enrich the dataset. The types will be grouped into superclasses (coarse-grained categories), to improve the precision of the deep learning model.

```
PREFIX rdf  : <http://www.w3.org/1999/02/22-rdf-syntax-ns#>
PREFIX rdfs : <http://www.w3.org/2000/01/rdf-schema#>
PREFIX dbo :  <http://dbpedia.org/ontology/>

SELECT * WHERE
{
    <http://dbpedia.org/resource/Algeria> rdf:type ?y.
    ?y rdfs:label ?x FILTER (lang(?x) = "en")
 }
```

Listing 1.4. Example of the entity type extraction using the URI of the resource "Algeria"

Chunk-Tag and Pos-Tag Extraction. Information concerning the pos-tag [17] and chunk-tag [18] are added using the nltk python library [15] in order to make the model more relevant.

4.3 Data Merging and Design

Annotation Design. The data are formatted to feed a neural network. The data format described in CoNLL-2003 [10] as follows:

- One word per line with empty lines representing sentence boundaries.
- At the end of each line is a tag that states whether the current word is inside a named entity. The tag also encodes the type of named entity.
- Each line contains four fields: the word, its pos tag, its chunk tag, and its named entity tag.
- Words tagged with O are outside of named entities and the I-XXX tag is used for words inside a named entity of type XXX.
- Whenever two entities of type XXX are immediately next to each other, the first word of the second entity will be tagged B-XXX to show that it starts with another entity.
- The data contains entities of four types: persons (PER), organizations (ORG), locations (LOC), and miscellaneous names (MISC).

This tagging scheme is the IOB[8] scheme originally put forward by Ramshaw et al. [11]. As given in the CoNLL-2003, we assume that named entities are non-recursive and non-overlapping. When a named entity is embedded in another named entity, only the top-level entity is usually annotated.

4.4 Analysis of the Constructed Dataset

The constructed dataset, named SocialNER, contains **2 005 919 records** with short texts mainly search engine queries, questions used in question-answering systems, or tweets. These short texts contain around **2 005 900 annotated named entities**. The dataset contains on average **8.72 words** per sentence with **4** words minimum length and **13** words maximum length. In addition, some texts do not contain any named entities and others contain several ones. The objective is that the model that will use the dataset can learn the different possible phrases found in social networks. Regarding types, SocialNer contains in average **20%** persons, **6.6%** organizations, **38%** locations and **35,4%** miscellaneous names. The table 1 shows the number of types in SocialNer.

Table 1. Number of entity types in SocialNer

Entity type	PERSON	ORG	LOC	MISC
Total	401180	133727	757784	713209

The Listing 1.5 illustrates a few instances of the obtained dataset. The example extracted from the TREC microblog dataset "Ron Weasley birthday" can be explained as follows:

- "Ron NNP B-NP B-PER" - The word "Ron" is tagged as a proper noun (NNP) and belongs to the chunk category "B-NP" (beginning of a noun phrase) and "B-PER" (beginning of a person entity).

[8] Inside-outside-beginning (tagging).

- "Weasley NNP I-NP I-PER" - The word "Weasley" is tagged as a proper noun (NNP) and belongs to the chunk category "I-NP" (inside a noun phrase) and "I-PER" (inside a person entity).
- "birthday NN I-NP O" - The word "birthday" is tagged as a noun (NN) and belongs to the chunk category "I-NP" (inside a noun phrase). The "O" tag indicates that it is not part of a named entity.

In summary, the text mentions the actor "Ron Weasley" and his birthday. The "B-NP" and "I-NP" tags indicate that the words belong to a noun phrase, while the "B-PER" and "I-PER" tags indicate that they are part of a specific named entity.

```
Which          JJ   B-NP     O
comic          JJ   I-NP     O
characters     NNS  I-NP     O
are            VBP  B-VP     O
painted        VBN  B-VP     O
by             IN   B-PP     O
Bill           NNP  B-NP     B-PER
Finger         NNP  I-NP     I-PER
?              .    O        O

Ron            NNP  B-NP     B-PER
Weasley        NNP  I-NP     I-PER
##st_birthday    NN   I-NP    O

Splitting      NN   B-NP     O
of             IN   B-PP     O
US.            NNP  B-NP     B-ORG
Flight         NNP  I-NP     I-ORG
and            CC   O        O
Americans      NNP  B-NP     O

calf           NN   B-NP     O
muscles        NN   I-NP     O
discomfort     NN   I-NP     O
from           IN   B-PP     O
statin         NNS  B-NP     O
therapy        NNS  I-NP     O
How            WRB  O        O
tall           JJ   B-NP     O
is             VBZ  B-VP     O
Amazon         NNP  B-NP     B-PER
Eve            NNP  I-NP     I-PER
?              .    O        O
```

Listing 1.5. Example of a few instances of the obtained dataset

Table 2 shows the comparison of the SocialNer dataset with the state_of_art datasets, including their respective datasets, publication years, annotation methods (manual, expert, automatic), and the number of entities in each dataset.

Table 2. Information about different datasets related to named entity recognition

Work	Year	Annotation method	Number of Entity
Derczynski et al. : Broad Twitter Corpus (BTC)	2016	Manual Expert	12 117
Singh et al. : a corpus for NER in Hindi-English CodeMixed	2018	Manual Expert	5,007
Jiang et al.. :Tweebank V2 (TB2)	2022	Manual Amazon Mechanical Turk	2,154
Belbekri & Benchikha: SocialNer	**2022**	**Automatic** **DBpedia**	**2,005,900**

5 Conclusion

The results of the named entity recognition task have significantly improved since the use of deep learning approaches. One reason for this success is attributed to the availability of large-scale labeled data. However, the available datasets suffer either in data quality or data quantity.

This paper describes the development of SocialNer, a high-quality training dataset for deep learning models that perform named entity recognition in social network texts. The dataset is designed to meet the needs of both quantity and quality and is based on annotated data from previous challenge tasks. Additionally, the dataset has been enriched with information about pos-tag, chunk-tag, and named entity type, and is formatted in the CoNLL-2003 format

In the future, we plan to construct a neural network and train it with the created dataset. The results will be compared with other models trained by traditional datasets like OntoNotes 5.0 and CoNLL-2003 to evaluate the model.

References

1. Hatmi, M.: Reconnaissance des entités nommées dans des documents multimodaux. Université de Nantes, Diss (2014)
2. Halevy, A., Norvig, P., Pereira, F.: The unreasonable effectiveness of data. IEEE Intell. Syst. **24**(2), 8–12 (2009)
3. Derczynski, L., Bontcheva, K., Roberts, I.: Broad twitter corpus: a diverse named entity recognition resource. In: Proceedings of COLING 2016, the 26th International Conference on Computational Linguistics: technical Papers (2016)
4. Fu, J., Liu, P., Neubig, G.: Interpretable multi-dataset evaluation for named entity recognition. arXiv preprint arXiv:2011.06854 (2020)
5. LeCun, Y., Bengio, Y., Hinton, G.: Deep learning. Nature **521**(7553), 436–444 (2015). https://doi.org/10.1038/nature14539
6. Li, Ji., et al.: A survey on deep learning for named entity recognition. IEEE Trans. Knowl. Data Eng. **34**(1), 50–70 (2020)
7. Singh, V., et al.: Named entity recognition for Hindi-English code-mixed social media text. In: Proceedings of the Seventh Named Entities Workshop (2018)
8. Jiang, H., et al.: Annotating the Tweebank corpus on named entity recognition and building NLP models for social media analysis. arXiv preprint arXiv:2201.07281 (2022)

9. Usbeck, R., Ngomo, A.-C.N., Haarmann, B., Krithara, A., Röder, M., Napolitano, G.: 7th Open challenge on question answering over linked data (QALD-7). In: Dragoni, M., Solanki, M., Blomqvist, E. (eds.) SemWebEval 2017. CCIS, vol. 769, pp. 59–69. Springer, Cham (2017). https://doi.org/10.1007/978-3-319-69146-6_6
10. Sang, E.F., de Meulder, F.: Introduction to the CoNLL-2003 shared task: language-independent named entity recognition. arXiv preprint cs/0306050 (2003)
11. Ramshaw, L.A., Marcus, M.P.: Text chunking using transformation-based learning. In: Armstrong, S., Church, K., Isabelle, P., Manzi, S., Tzoukermann, E., Yarowsky, D. (eds.) Natural Language Processing Using Very Large Corpora. Text, Speech and Language Technology, vol. 11, pp. 157–176. Springer, Dordrecht (1999). https://doi.org/10.1007/978-94-017-2390-9_10
12. Usbeck, R., et al.: 8th challenge on question answering over linked data (QALD-8). Language **7**(1), 51–57 (2018)
13. Trivedi, P., Maheshwari, G., Dubey, M., Lehmann, J.: LC-QuAD: a corpus for complex question answering over knowledge graphs. In: d'Amato, C., et al. (eds.) ISWC 2017. LNCS, vol. 10588, pp. 210–218. Springer, Cham (2017). https://doi.org/10.1007/978-3-319-68204-4_22
14. Bouarroudj, W., Boufaida, Z., Bellatreche, L.: Named entity disambiguation in short texts over knowledge graphs. Knowl. Inf. Syst. **64**(2), 325-351 (2022)
15. Hardeniya, N.: NLTK essentials. Packt Publishing (2015)
16. Sakor, A., et al.: Old is gold: linguistic driven approach for entity and relation linking of short text. In: Proceedings of the 2019 Conference of the North American Chapter of the Association for Computational Linguistics: Human Language Technologies, Volume 1 (Long and Short Papers) (2019)
17. Heeman, P.A.: POS tags and decision trees for language modeling. In: 1999 Joint SIGDAT Conference on Empirical Methods in Natural Language Processing and Very Large Corpora (1999)
18. Skut, W., et al.: A linguistically interpreted corpus of German newspaper text. arXiv preprint cmp-lg/9807008 (1998)
19. Sun, C., et al.: Revisiting unreasonable effectiveness of data in deep learning era. In: Proceedings of the IEEE International Conference on Computer Vision (2017)

Hybrid Evidential System for Fake News Detection on Twitter

Hamza Tarik Sadouk(✉), Faouzi Sebbak, Walid Cherifi, Hichem Abdallah Ouldmessaoud, and Mohamed Amine Chouarfia

Ecole Militaire Polytechnique, PO Box 17, 16111 Bordj El Bahri, Algiers, Algeria
sadouk.hamza.tarik@gmail.com

Abstract. Fake news is a severe problem in today's society. It is becoming more widespread and more difficult to detect. The use of social media has created new trends in how most people access and consume news. On one side, consumers seek out and consume news via social media because it is cheap, easy to access, and transmits information faster than traditional media. On the other side, it allows the dissemination of fake news, that is, falsified news that deliberately contains fake information. One of the most challenging aspects of detecting false news is early detection. In this context, we designed a news authenticity verification system on Twitter based on the evidential fusion of machine learning models exploiting both content-based characteristics and social context-based characteristics. Our system is equipped with a chrome extension that allows users to check, in real-time, any tweet that might be fraudulent and filter the news feed based on the reputation of the profiles. Experiments were conducted to determine whether the theory of evidence could be applied in the context of social networks. These investigations revealed that the overall duration to combine various pieces of evidence from various sources does not exceed one second. Experimental assessments demonstrate the prevalence of evidential fusion rules for the real-time detection of false information.

Keywords: Fake news detection · Social media · Machine learning · Evidence theory · Chrome extension

1 Introduction

The human desire to communicate, along with advances in digital technology, has fueled the evolution of social media (such as Facebook and Twitter) and paved the way for the enormous dissemination of information. According to the most recent figures, more than half of the world's population (58.7%) now uses social media. Additionally, 196 million additional users joined the Internet in the previous year. These users spend an average of 2 h and 29 min per day on social media [1]. This expansion of social networks has given rise to a significant problem: the spread of fake news. The latter is considered a kind of propaganda aimed at influencing people's perception of the facts [7]. This material is presented as

H. Drias et al. (Eds.): AID 2022, CCIS 1852, pp. 290–301, 2023.
https://doi.org/10.1007/978-981-99-4484-2_22

a news product that the promoter is aware is fake. Fake news has hurt global society, including the economy and politics. Due to the vast spread of fake news and its negative impacts, identifying such content online has become a primary necessity. Generally, these strategies use fact-checking websites such as "PolitiFact" and "Snopes". The problem with this technique is that human experience is required, which costs time and money. More importantly, web-based fact-checking services only feature stories from specific areas, often politics, making detection in other areas tricky [5].

Fortunately, using machine learning algorithms based on the textual content of these posts and other characteristics made things easier [3]. These techniques can potentially play the role of an expert while reducing the verification time and cost. Thanks to these methods, we have been able to design a system for verifying the authenticity of information on "Twitter." Our solution uses the verification of *style content* on the one hand and, on the other hand, the *stance detection* of commentators concerning the target tweet. The use of two models to infer the correctness of news content is motivated by the inherent limits of each one. Models trained on fake news datasets are more likely to produce results based solely on the tweet's content, leaving valuable information in the surrounding context, such as users' opinions, in the case of social media platforms. However, inferring a tweet's trustworthiness based on users' opinions is challenging. The stance detection model may provide information on the opinion of users, but combining those positions to achieve a consensus in a noisy environment requires suitable mathematical tools.

Dempster Shafer Theory (DST), also identified as evidence theory [12], is a flexible mathematical framework that extends Bayesian theory by allowing each data source to include information at varying degrees of detail for addressing uncertainty [4]. It offers a powerful mechanism for consensus decision-making and has been extensively applied in many fields, especially in machine learning [14,15]. In our study, we investigate the use of evidence theory in categorizing fake content. It is the first work to introduce an evidence-based methodology to address data uncertainty in false content classification. This study proposes an approach based on the fusion of heterogeneous information sources, highlighting their ability to distinguish between normal and abnormal behaviour. As a result, we present a unified strategy for the automated identification of fraudulent material that employs content and social context characteristics.

The remaining paper is structured as follows: the second section presents some general information about the automatic detection of fake news. Section 3 recalls the theoretical tools used in the proposed approach. Section 4 discusses the general architecture and design of our automatic fake news detection system. Section 5 discusses the efficiency of the evidential fusion in the context of real-time fake news detection on social media. Section 6 concludes the paper by summarizing our work and suggesting potential future work.

2 Theoretical Background

2.1 Fake News Detection

"Fake news" is made-up information that resembles news media content in appearance but differs in terms of organizational method and goal. *Misinformation* (false or misleading information) and *disinformation* (false information that is purposely spread to deceive people) are two types of information disorders that overlap with fake news [7]. In our work, we use the term "fake news" to address both "disinformation" and "misinformation," the commonality of those two phenomena is that they share false information that can be detected using characteristics described in the following points.

Fake news detection in traditional media mainly relies on news content, while in social media, auxiliary information from social contexts can be used as additional data to help detect fake news. *K. Shu et al.* [13] defines a taxonomy of these characteristics to help detect false information.

Content-Based Approaches. Content-based approaches leverage multiple types of information from the news, such as article content, news source, headline, image, or videos. Specifically, existing approaches can be categorized as *Knowledge-based* and *Style-based* [3].

- *Knowledge-based:* Fake news tries to promote misleading claims in news material; the simplest way to spot it is to check the truthfulness of the claims in a news story to determine the news' reliability. External sources are used to fact-check the proposed material in this technique.
- *Style-based:* Fake news publishers frequently aim to propagate distorted information, necessitating specific writing styles that are not evident in actual news items to appeal to and persuade a wide range of consumers.

Social Context-Based Approaches. Because of the nature of social media, researchers have more resources to augment and improve *content-based models.* Existing approaches to social context modelling can be divided into two types: *stance-based* and *propagation-based.*

- *Stance-based:* Users' perspectives from relevant post contents are used in stance-based strategies to infer the validity of original news articles. The task of automatically assessing whether a person is in favour of, neutral toward, or against a specific entity, event, or idea from a post is known as *stance detection* [9].
- *Propagation-based:* Fake news detection methods based on propagation consider the interrelationships of relevant social media posts to forecast news believability. The underlying premise is that the legitimacy of relevant social media posts is closely related to the credibility of a news event.

2.2 The Theory of Evidence

In this section, we briefly recall some basic notions of Dempster-Shafer theory. For this purpose, let $\Omega = \{\omega_1, ..., \omega_k\}$, and let $\wp(\Omega) = \{A_1, ..., A_q\}$ be its power set, with $q = 2^k$. A function m defined from $\wp(\Omega)$ to $[0, 1]$ is called a "basic belief assignment (bba)" or "masse function" if $\sum_{A \in \wp(\Omega)} m(A) = 1$.
The difference with the probabilities is that here the element A may be the union of more than one hypothesis. Thanks to this principle, the theory of evidence makes it possible to model uncertainty.

From the sets of masses obtained on each information source, it is possible to implement a combination rule to provide a combined set of masses. Several modes of combination have been developed within the framework of belief theory, for example:

Dempster's Rule (DR). This rule was initially proposed by *Dempster* [2]. *Dempster*'s combination rule is the normalized conjunctive operation that aims to aggregate evidence from multiple independent sources. This rule is given for any $A \neq \emptyset$ of $\wp(\Omega)$ and for $N \geq 2$ information sources by:

$$m_{DR}(A) = \frac{1}{1-K} m_{Conj}(A) \tag{1}$$

where K and $m_{Conj}(A)$ denote the conflict measure and the unnormalized conjunctive rule respectively:

$$K = \sum_{\substack{B_i \in \wp(\Omega) \\ \cap_{i=1}^{l} B_i = \emptyset}} \prod_{j=1}^{N} m_j(B_i) \tag{2}$$

$$m_{Conj}(A) = \sum_{\substack{B_i \in \wp(\Omega) \\ \cap_{i=1}^{l} B_i = A}} \prod_{j=1}^{N} m_j(B_i) \tag{3}$$

However, scholars suggest that when the conflict between sources is severe, this combination rule behaves abnormally [11]. An alternative is:

Majority Consensus Rule (MCR). Proposed by *Sebbak et al.* [10], the rationale behind this combination rule is that it redistributes global conflict into already involved focal element sets, resulting in a majority and consensus. This rule is given for any $A \neq \emptyset$ of $\wp(\Omega)$ and for $N \geq 2$ information sources by:

$$m_{MCR}(A) = \frac{1}{N+1-K} \left(m_{Maj}(A) + m_{Conj}(A)\right) \tag{4}$$

where $m_{Maj}(A)$ denotes the majority rule, it is given by:

$$m_{Maj}(A) = \sum_{j=1}^{N} m_j(A) \tag{5}$$

3 *ES-VRAI* Architecture and Design

The system extracts the content of the tweet with its comments automatically. This data is then processed at the application server level to perform particular text-prepossessing operations. The result of these operations is directed to the inference server and the database. The inference server contains the two models, and the database stores the results for future use by other features of our system.

3.1 Data Extraction Module

The module retrieves the content of the tweet and comments. It contains an "Extractor" class responsible for extracting data from the social network Twitter. The class succeeded in extracting data from Twitter thanks to the "tweepy" library, which is used to interact with the Twitter database.

3.2 Text Preparation and Preprocessing Module

Verifying the veracity of information requires preprocessing the text containing the information. This module applies natural language processing preprocessing steps using the "nltk" library. The main steps are: convert text to lowercase, remove punctuation; remove stop words; word stemming; lemmatization of words. After receiving the file containing the texts retrieved by the extraction module, the preprocessing results are saved in the same file.

3.3 Style-Based and Stance-Based Detection Modules

The models' architecture uses Long Short-Term Memory (LSTM) networks [6]. The "Embedding" layer uses Word2Vec [8] to calculate the feature vector of each word. The style-based model was trained on the "Fake and real news dataset"[1], where it reached a validation accuracy of 97.75%. The stance-based model was trained on the "Fake News Challenge"[2] stance detection dataset, where it reached a validation accuracy of 96.06%. Figure 1 shows the layers of the two models.

3.4 Data Fusion Module

The system must generate two probability values $P_{t,C}(True)$ and $P_{t,C}(False)$. First, the fusion module obtains the values $P_t(True)$ and $P_t(False)$, which respectively represent the probability that the tweet is true and the probability that it is false according to the Style-based module. Then, it retrieves the values of the position of each comment relative to the content of the same tweet. So for each comment $c_i \in C$, we will have: $P_{c_i}(Agree), P_{c_i}(Disagree), P_{c_i}(Discuss)$ and $P_{c_i}(Unrelated)$.

[1] https://www.kaggle.com/datasets/clmentbisaillon/.

[2] http://www.fakenewschallenge.org/.

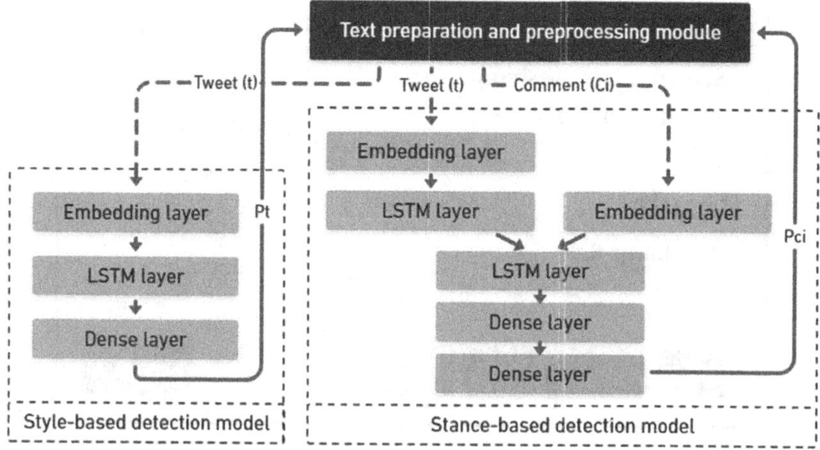

Fig. 1. Style-based and stance-based models.

We must convert the probability functions into mass functions. For the first model the conversion is straightforward, $m_t(True) = P_t(True)$, $m_t(False) = P_t(False)$ and $m_t(\{True, False\}) = 0$. For the second model, we elaborated a new "bba" strategy. It proceeds in two steps:

- *Hypotheses restriction:* in this step we exclude all the comment c_j that are unrelated to the tweet t, i.e., $argmax(P_{c_j}) = Unrelated$.
- *Hypotheses projection:* each person commenting on the tweet implicitly indicates their opinion in relation to this tweet. That is, if the user's opinion agrees with the tweet, so it shows that the tweet is true, then: $m_{c_i}(True) = P_{c_i}(Agree)$. If it disagrees with the tweet so it shows that the tweet is fake then: $m_{c_i}(False) = P_{c_i}(Disagree)$. The rest of the belief will be considered as ignorance: $m_{c_i}(\{True, False\}) = P_{c_i}(Discuss) + P_{c_i}(Unrelated)$.

Once all the "bbas" are constructed, we aggregate them in two steps:

- *Stance bba's fusion:* for the mass functions issued from the *Stance-based* model we will use the "MCR" fusion rule. The final mass function denoted $m_{C'}$ will describe the majority consensus opinion of the crowd.
- *Style and Stance fusion:* once the $m_{C'}$ calculated we will use "DR" to aggregate it with m_t. It will produce a mass of certainty only for the singletons denoted m. This is a probabilistic case and the desired probability will be: $P_{t,C}(True) = m(True)$ and $P_{t,C}(False) = m(False)$.

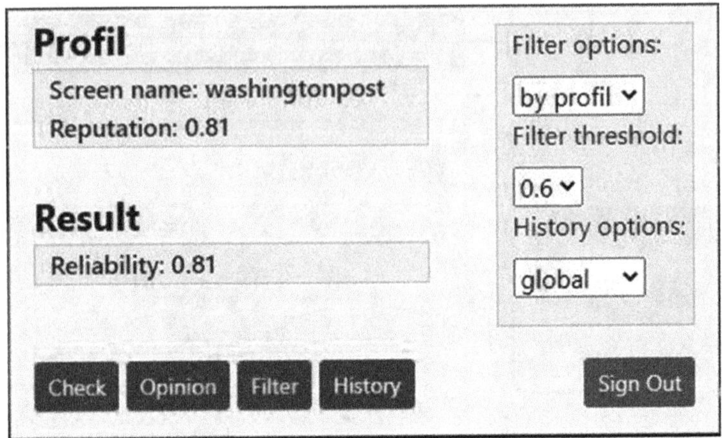

Fig. 2. *ES-VRAI* home page.

3.5 Results Visualization Module

Our system is intended for use in social networks (Twitter in the first place), which are websites. We thought of using an extension to offer our services because it is the most suitable solution. Figure 2 represents the *ES-VRAI* home page.

3.6 Database Management Module

Our system needs a database to store the different data indicated during the information verification phase to be able to satisfy the other functionalities: consultation of the history of tweets already verified, filtering of the news feed by profile or by tweet and the expression of opinion, which allows the users to give their opinion on the information they receive on Twitter.

4 Experimental Results

ES-VRAI is attended to be an extensible system. Its design considers the possibility of expanding to other social media and using other approaches (Knowledge-based and Propagation-based) to give a more reliable result. Nevertheless, its architecture relies on evidential fusion, which can be more or less convenient depending on the number of information sources and their degree of conflict. In this section, we try to assess the efficiency of the evidential fusion in real-time fake news detection on social media by comparing the time complexity and the intuitiveness of the results by giving different scenarios.

Dempster's criterion for integrating pieces of evidence sometimes yields counterintuitive conclusions that do not accurately reflect the distribution of beliefs. In some situations, such as the loss of majority opinion, absolute certainty to the minority opinion, and undue certainty, this latter does not accurately reflect the distribution of opinions. We conducted experiments using certain well-known situations reported in the literature where Dempster's rule (DR) provides counterintuitive outcomes. Table 1 summarizes the combination results and comparison of current combination rules. The table's underlined combination results indicate that the findings are thought to be counterintuitive.

Table 1. Combination results for well-known situations.

Cases	DR	MCR
Certainty convergence		
$m_1(\{a\}) = 0.5$	$m(\{a\}) = 0.667$	$\underline{m(\{a\}) = 0.545}$
$m_1(\{b\}) = 0.5$	$m(\{b\}) = 0.333$	$\underline{m(\{b\}) = 0.273}$
$m_2(\{a\}) = 0.5$		$\underline{m(\{a,b\}) = 0.182}$
$m_2(\{a,b\}) = 0.5$		
Total certainty to minority opinion		
$m_1(\{a\}) = 0.9$	$\underline{m(\{b\}) = 1}$	$m(\{a\}) = 0.448$
$m_1(\{b\}) = 0.1$		$m(\{b\}) = 0.104$
$m_2(\{b\}) = 0.1$		$m(\{c\}) = 0.448$
$m_2(\{c\}) = 0.9$		
Loss of majority opinion		
$m_1(\{a\}) = 0.9$	$\underline{m(\{c\}) = 1}$	$m(\{a\}) = 0.299$
$m_1(\{a,c\}) = 0.1$		$m(\{b\}) = 0.166$
$m_2(\{a,b\}) = 0.8$		$m(\{c\}) = 0.169$
$m_2(\{a,c\}) = 0.2$		$m(\{a,b\}) = 0.266$
$m_3(\{b\}) = 0.5$		$m(\{a,c\}) = 0.100$
$m_3(\{c\}) = 0.5$		
Unearned certainty		
$m_1(\{a\}) = 0.5$	$\underline{m(\{a\}) = 1/3}$	$m(\{a\}) = 0.273$
$m_1(\{b,c\}) = 0.5$	$\underline{m(\{b\}) = 1/3}$	$m(\{b\}) = 0.090$
$m_2(\{c\}) = 0.5$	$\underline{m(\{c\}) = 1/3}$	$m(\{c\}) = 0.278$
$m_2(\{a,b\}) = 0.5$		$m(\{a,b\}) = 0.182$
		$m(\{b,c\}) = 0.182$

For the certainty convergence case, "DR" is well suited for our system, where the final combination rule must produce a mass of certainty, which will be interpreted as a probability. This experiment shows that the use of the "MCR" preserves the majority opinion, does not give an absolute certainty to minority opinion and does not give undue certainty. This is why it should better represent the public's opinion regarding some pieces of information shared on social media where opinion conflict is mainly predominant.

Even if "MCR" accurately represents the opinion in the highly conflicted context of social media, the time it needs to produce its outcome depends on the number of information sources. We conducted experiments involving generating random mass functions with varying degrees of conflict (K). For each number of sources (N), we consider three scenarios where the conflict between the sources varies from low to medium to high. In this experiment, we used the "PyDS"[3] library, which is a Python library for performing calculations in the Dempster-Shafer theory of evidence. We extended it with our implementation of "MCR". The experiment was conducted on an 8^{th}generation *intel core i5* processor laptop using Python version 3.7.9. Table 2 summarizes the results of the experiment.

Table 2. Combination time for different number of sources.

Number of sources (N)	Degree of conflict (K) l: low m: medium h: high	Fusion time (t in ms)	Average time (T in ms)
	$K_l = 0.234$	1	
10	$K_m = 0.535$	1	1
	$K_h = 0.775$	1	
	$K_l = 0.197$	3	
10^2	$K_m = 0.597$	3	3
	$K_h = 0.949$	3	
	$K_l = 0.173$	27	
10^3	$K_m = 0.605$	27	27
	$K_h = 0.995$	27	
	$K_l = 0.160$	282	
10^4	$K_m = 0.603$	272	275
	$K_h = 0.999$	271	
	$K_l = 0.156$	2831	
10^5	$K_m = 0.603$	2887	2813
	$K_h = 1.000$	2722	
	$K_l = 0.155$	27884	
10^6	$K_m = 0.603$	27765	27716
	$K_h = 1.000$	27500	
	$K_l = 0.155$	299993	
10^7	$K_m = 0.603$	290674	291353
	$K_h = 1.000$	283394	

[3] https://github.com/reineking/pyds.

We can observe from Table 2 that the degree of conflict does not affect the fusion time for a specified number of sources $N = n$. Nevertheless, the degree of conflict can significantly increase with more sources. This is relevant in the medium and the high-conflict scenarios. Regarding the average combination time, we observe that for realistic scenarios with $N \leq 10^4$, it is mainly under 1 s. For unrealistic cases with $N \geq 10^5$, we observe a significant combination time that may deteriorate the system's performance.

It is also clear that the average combination time is directly correlated with the number of sources. In Fig. 3, we plotted the average combination time in terms of the number of sources in logarithmic scales. The linearity between the two variables is distinguishable.

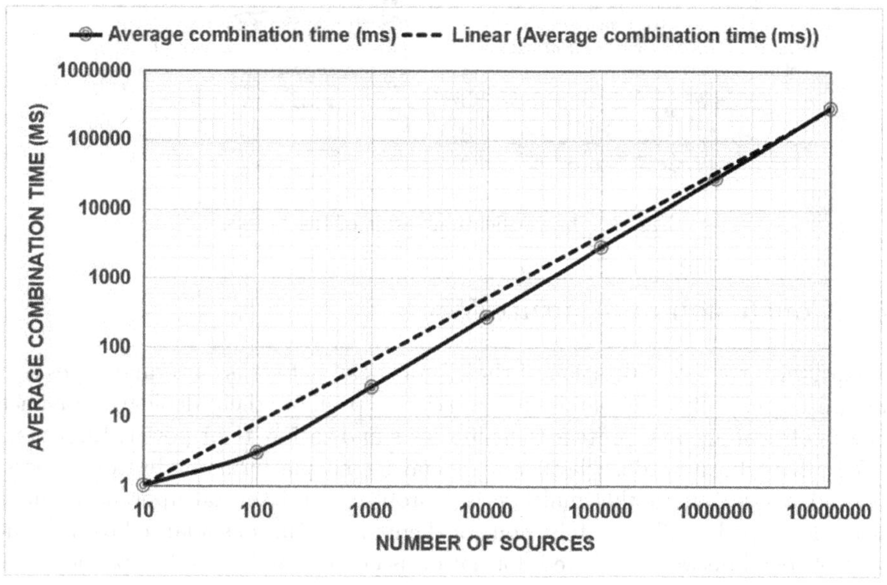

Fig. 3. Average combination time with varying number of sources.

Based on those experiments, we can conclude that the evidential fusion framework offers a comprehensive and flexible way to model and detect in real-time deviant information in the context of social media. Figure 4 shows two cases where the system could distinguish between a real piece of news and a fake one.

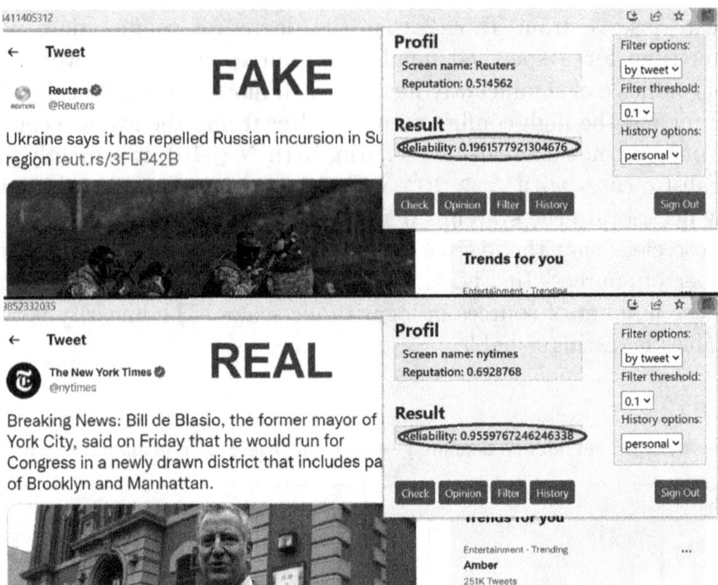

Fig. 4. The verification result of the tweets.

5 Conclusion and Future Work

Today, with the generalization of the use of social networks, several entities and organizations seek to share false information to promote their ideologies, advance their political agenda, protect their interests and satisfy their power. Enormous efforts have been made, whether by social media platforms or by researchers, to find a solution to this multifaceted problem, and several approaches have been developed. Unfortunately, none of them gives solutions adapted to the context of social networks, where information is created and shared at phenomenal speeds. This work presents a coherent system for detecting false information on the Twitter social network. This system responds to two intrinsic limits of the systems currently in use, namely real-time detection by exploiting artificial intelligence and the exposure to fraudulent content by using filtering tools based on the reputation and reliability of sources of information.

In this work, we studied how to classify fraudulent content using evidence theory. In order to reduce data uncertainty in the area of false content categorization, we devised an evidence-based technique. This study developed a method based on the fusion of diverse information sources to discern between typical and abnormal behaviour. The evidential fusion framework provides a thorough and adaptable method to model and identifies in real-time deviant material in the domain of social media, according to experiments.

ES-VRAI is intended to be expandable; as such, its design takes into account the potential for extension to other languages (especially Arabic), other social media and the usage of other methodologies (such as knowledge-based and propagation-based ones) to provide a more trustworthy outcome. One may argue that taking into account unverifiable sources of information can lead to an unfair judgment. Using contextual discounting techniques that are part of the evidential framework may solve this problem.

References

1. Digital 2022: April Global Statshot Report & mdash; DataReportal - Global Digital Insights, 21 April 2022. Accessed 08 June 2022
2. Dempster, A.P.: Upper and lower probabilities induced by a multivalued mapping. Ann. Math. Stat. 325–339 (1967)
3. Gupta, A., Anjum, A., Gupta, S., Katarya, R.: Recent trends of fake news detection: a review. Mach. Learn. Adv. Comput. Renew. Energy Commun. 483–492 (2022)
4. Hamache, A., et al.: Uncertainty-aware Parzen-Rosenblatt classifier for multi-attribute data. In: Destercke, S., Denoeux, T., Cuzzolin, F., Martin, A. (eds.) BELIEF 2018. LNCS (LNAI), vol. 11069, pp. 103–111. Springer, Cham (2018). https://doi.org/10.1007/978-3-319-99383-6_14
5. Hassan, N., et al.: The quest to automate fact-checking. In: Proceedings of the 2015 Computation+ Journalism Symposium (2015)
6. Hochreiter, S., Schmidhuber, J.: Long short-term memory. Neural Comput. **9**(8), 1735–1780 (1997)
7. Lazer, D.M., et al.: The science of fake news. Science **359**(6380), 1094–1096 (2018)
8. Mikolov, T., Sutskever, I., Chen, K., Corrado, G.S., Dean, J.: Distributed representations of words and phrases and their compositionality. In: Advances in Neural Information Processing Systems, vol. 26 (2013)
9. Mohammad, S.M., Sobhani, P., Kiritchenko, S.: Stance and sentiment in tweets. ACM Trans. Internet Technol. (TOIT) **17**(3), 1–23 (2017)
10. Sebbak, F., Benhammadi, F.: Majority-consensus fusion approach for elderly IoT-based healthcare applications. Ann. Telecommun. **72**(3), 157–171 (2017)
11. Sebbak, F., Benhammadi, F., Mataoui, M., Bouznad, S., Amirat, Y.: An alternative combination rule for evidential reasoning. In: 17th International Conference on Information Fusion (FUSION), pp. 1–8. IEEE (2014)
12. Shafer, G.: A Mathematical Theory of Evidence. Princeton University Press, Princeton (1976)
13. Shu, K., Sliva, A., Wang, S., Tang, J., Liu, H.: Fake news detection on social media: a data mining perspective. ACM SIGKDD Explor. Newsl. **19**(1), 22–36 (2017)
14. Xu, P., Deng, Y., Su, X., Mahadevan, S.: A new method to determine basic probability assignment from training data. Knowl.-Based Syst. **46**, 69–80 (2013)
15. Xu, P., Davoine, F., Zha, H., Denoeux, T.: Evidential calibration of binary SVM classifiers. Int. J. Approx. Reason. **72**, 55–70 (2016)

References

Author Index

H. Drias et al. (Eds.): AID 2022, CCIS 1852, pp. 303–304, 2023.
https://doi.org/10.1007/978-981-99-4484-2

Printed in the United States
by Baker & Taylor Publisher Services